POLITICAL MARKETING IN THE UNITED STATES

Political Marketing in the United States explores how politicians and parties utilize marketing concepts and tools, providing an up-to-date and broad overview of how marketing permeates U.S. politics. The volume focuses on current and recent elections and leaders, and covers a range of topics, including market research, marketing parties and volunteers, strategy and branding, communications, delivery, and marketing in government.

The main themes and objectives of the book cover:

- New and emerging trends in political marketing practice
- Analysis of a broad range of political marketing aspects
- Empirical examples as well as useful theoretical frameworks
- Discussion of state/local level as well as presidential politics

This is the first comprehensive treatment of the subject available and captures the field as it is rapidly growing. It is a must-read for students and scholars of political parties, political communication, applied politics, and elections.

Jennifer Lees-Marshment is an international expert in political marketing at the University of Auckland, New Zealand. Her books include *The Routledge Handbook of Political Marketing* (Routledge 2012), *Political Marketing: Principles and Applications* (Routledge 2009), *Global Political Marketing* (Routledge 2010), *The Political Marketing Game* (2011) and *Political Marketing in Canada* (2012). See www.lees-marshment.org for further details.

Brian Conley is Assistant Professor of Government at Suffolk University in Boston, MA. His principal research interests are in the areas of U.S. electoral politics, political parties, and political marketing and branding.

Kenneth Cosgrove is Associate Professor of Government at Suffolk University in Boston, MA. He is the author of *Branded Conservatives: How the Brand Brought the American Right From the Fringes to the Center of American Politics*. His research interests center on political marketing with a focus on branding in North American politics.

POLITICAL MARKETING IN THE UNITED STATES

Edited by
Jennifer Lees-Marshment, Brian M. Conley
and Kenneth Cosgrove

NEW YORK AND LONDON

First published 2014
by Routledge
711 Third Avenue, New York, NY 10017

and by Routledge
2 Park Square, Milton Park, Abingdon, Oxon OX14 4RN

Routledge is an imprint of the Taylor & Francis Group, an informa business

© 2014 Taylor & Francis

The right of the editor to be identified as the author of the editorial material, and of the authors for their individual chapters, has been asserted in accordance with sections 77 and 78 of the Copyright, Designs and Patents Act 1988.

All rights reserved. No part of this book may be reprinted or reproduced or utilised in any form or by any electronic, mechanical, or other means, now known or hereafter invented, including photocopying and recording, or in any information storage or retrieval system, without permission in writing from the publishers.

Trademark notice: Product or corporate names may be trademarks or registered trademarks, and are used only for identification and explanation without intent to infringe.

Library of Congress Cataloging-in-Publication Data

Political marketing in the United States / edited by Jennifer
  Lees-Marshment, Brian Conley and Kenneth Cosgrove.
    pages cm
  1. Marketing—Political aspects—United States. 2. Communication in politics—United States. 3. Public relations and politics. I. Lees-Marshment, Jennifer. II. Conley, Brian. III. Cosgrove, Kenneth.
  JA85.2.U6P64 2014
  324.70973—dc23
  2013045712

ISBN: 978-0-415-63285-0 (hbk)
ISBN: 978-0-415-63286-7 (pbk)
ISBN: 978-0-203-09521-8 (ebk)

Typeset in Bembo
by Apex CoVantage, LLC

Printed and bound in the United States of America by Publishers Graphics, LLC on sustainably sourced paper.

For Paul-John Greenaway, James Lees-Marshment and Hazel Greenaway for supporting the time I spent away on overseas trips without which this book would not have happened.

For Lisa, Lila and Elliot.

For Mary P. Cosgrove (Kineavy). What better tribute to a woman who taught me how to read by using ads and political journalism than a book on political marketing. Deeply loved, missed and appreciated.

CONTENTS

List of Tables		*ix*
List of Figures		*xi*
Acknowledgments		*xiii*
Foreword by Professor Dennis W. Johnson		*xv*

1 Marketing US Politics 1
   Jennifer Lees-Marshment, Brian M. Conley, and Kenneth Cosgrove

2 The Emergence of Voter Targeting: Learning to Send the
   Right Message to the Right Voters 26
   Michael John Burton and Tasha Miracle

3 Database Political Marketing in Campaigning and Government 44
   Lisa Spiller and Jeff Bergner

4 Boutique Populism: The Emergence of the Tea Party Movement
   in the Age of Digital Politics 61
   André Turcotte and Vincent Raynauld

5 Primary Elections and US Political Marketing 85
   Neil Bendle and Mihaela-Alina Nastasoiu

6 Branding the Tea Party: Political Marketing and an
   American Social Movement 112
   William J. Miller

7 Access Hollywood: Celebrity Endorsements in
American Politics 130
Alex Marland and Mireille Lalancette

8 Personal Political Branding at State Level 148
Kenneth Cosgrove

9 Brand Management and Relationship Marketing in Online
Environments 165
Darren G. Lilleker and Nigel Jackson

10 Relationship Marketing in Social Media Practice:
Perspectives, Limitations and Potential 185
Christine B. Williams and Girish J. "Jeff" Gulati

11 Mama Grizzlies: Republican Female Candidates and the
Political Marketing Dilemma 202
Robert Busby

12 The Market Research, Testing and Targeting behind
American Political Advertising 220
Travis N. Ridout

13 Crisis-Management, Marketing, and Money in US Campaigns 236
R. Sam Garrett

14 Communicating Contemporary Leadership in Government:
Barack Obama 253
Edward Elder

15 Does Obama Care? Assessing the Delivery of Health Reform
in the United States 272
Brian M. Conley

16 US Political Marketing Trends and Implications 289
Jennifer Lees-Marshment, Brian M. Conley, and Kenneth Cosgrove

List of Contributors *307*
Index *311*

TABLES

4.1	Weekly Volume of #teaparty Tweets	71
4.2	Weekly Number of Tweeters Contributing at Least Once to the #teaparty Tweeting Dynamic	73
4.3	Number of #teaparty Tweets by Organizations Affiliated with the Tea Party Movement	79
4.4	Number of #teaparty Tweets by Media and Political Personalities Affiliated with the Tea Party Movement	80
4.5	Number of #teaparty Tweets by Senate Contenders Affiliated with the Tea Party Movement	80
5.1	Word Classification	103
5.2	Strategic Advice Summary	107
7.1	Model of Celebrity Public Endorsements	136
7.2	Celebrity Endorsers, 2012 Presidential Campaign	140
7.3	Examples of News Headlines about Presidential Celebrity Endorsements (2012)	142
8.1	10 Principles of Effective Personal Political Branding at State Level	153
9.1	Components for Testing the Concepts of Interactivity	173
9.2	The Hybrid Approach to Political Marketing	179
10.1	Framework for Assessing Practitioners' Perspectives on Relationship Marketing in Social Media	188
10.2	Necessary/Important (Dominant Theme)	190
10.3	Cost Calculus (Infrequent)	191
10.4	Situation Specific (Infrequent)	192

10.5	Opponent's Actions (Rare)	192
10.6	Target: Specifically Identified (Just over Half)	193
10.7	Target: (Cont.)	193
10.8	Target: (Cont.)	194
10.9	Target: (Cont.)	194
10.10	Goals and Plan: Articulated	195
10.11	Goals and Plan: Articulated (Cont.)	196
10.12	Goals and Plan: Articulated (Cont.)	196
10.13	Goals and Plan: Absent (Rare)	197
10.14	Framework for Relationship Marketing in Social Media Practice	199
12.1	Volume of and Spending on Presidential Advertising by Type of Television (January 1, 2012–Election Day)	228
12.2	Obama Campaign Ad Buys by Cable Network	230
13.1	Spending Affecting the 2012 Presidential Campaign	244
13.2	Top Five Television Advertising Spenders in the 2012 Presidential Race April 11–October 29, 2012	245
14.1	Framework for Market-Oriented Governing Leaders' Communication (Summarized)	257
14.2	Barack Obama—Backyard Town Hall—Falls Church, VA—September 22, 2010, Highlights of Media Text	265

FIGURES

1.1	Political Marketing Activity	4
2.1	Transformation of Political Marketplace	31
2.2	Increasing Value of Voter Targeting	32
2.3	Unsupervised Learning	38
2.4	Supervised Learning	38
3.1	A Model of a Market-Oriented Party	49
4.1	Political Marketing Principles for a Populist Movement	67
4.2	Network Analysis of @replies with at Least One #teaparty Hashtag (December 14 to December 20, 2009)	76
4.3	Network Analysis of @replies with at Least One #teaparty Hashtag (November 1 to November 7, 2010)	77
4.4	Network Analysis of @replies with at Least One #teaparty Hashtag (October 25 to October 31, 2010)	78
4.5	Network Analysis of @replies with at Least One #teaparty Hashtag (January 10 to January 16, 2011)	79
4.6	Joe W. Millier's June 15, 2010, Tweet	80
4.7	Sharron Angle's May 10, 2010, Tweet	80
5.1	Voters Ideological Positions and the Impact of Sincere and Strategic Preferences	89
5.2	The Market Problem: Primary and General Election Markets Differ	92
5.3	The Market Problem: Primary Electorate Not a Subset of General Electorate	93
5.4	The Market Problem: Election Type Alters Voter Distribution	93
5.5	The Market Problem: Election Format Changes Market	94

5.6	The Market Problem: Voter Inequality	94
5.7	Percentage of Voters Choosing Electability as More Important Than Policy	98
5.8	Liking for Barack Obama and Hillary Clinton, Early 2008	99
5.9	Liking of Barack Obama Linked to Prediction of His Viability	100
5.10	Bush and McCain Advertising, Policy	101
5.11	Bush and McCain Advertising, Character	102
5.12	Word Use on Facebook	104
5.13	Republican 2012 Candidate Word Clouds	106
6.1	Principles of Effective Political Movement Branding	121
9.1	The Political Loyalty Ladder	170
9.2	Comparing the Candidates' Use of Hypermedia Campaigning in 2008 and 2012	174
9.3	Communication Style within Webspaces: Comparing Average Use of the Internet by Candidates 2008–2012	176
9.4	Mapping Candidates' Online Communication Styles and Marketing Approach within Systemic Contexts	181
11.1	Model of Mama Grizzly as a Political Sub-Brand	210
12.1	Johnson's Framework for Developing and Marketing Political Advertising	225
14.1	The Change in Voter-Leader Communication	256
15.1	Public Opinion on the Cost of Health Reform	283

ACKNOWLEDGMENTS

Groundbreaking, innovative research needs people who support its birth and we appreciate all those who helped along the road to the completion of this book. We would like to thank Suffolk University in Boston whose funding and hosting of a visit by Jennifer Lees-Marshment in 2011 led to the idea for this book, and in particular: Ken Greenberg for supporting the visit through the Distinguished Visiting Scholar program of the College of Arts and Sciences level; Julia Collins-Howington from the John Joseph Moakley Institute for funding and hosting the one-day workshop for practitioners; Rachael Cobb for supporting it from the departmental level; Kelly Pinard and Meri Power for organizational and logistical support; Daniel Mann and other students for their good work on the visit and individuals such as Dave Paleologos for taking part in various events.

Ken and Jennifer would also like to thank APSA, and Christine Williams, one of the editors of the *Journal of Political Marketing*, who helped organized an APSA short course on political marketing in 2010 during which the idea of the Suffolk visit was born.

Jennifer would also like to thank Auckland University for a departmental grant for funding the research assistance to format this manuscript for this book, and Edward Elder for completing that work. And last, but not least, she would also like to thank the Centre for American Studies at Keele University in the UK, especially staff such as Professor Chris Bailey, for fostering her love of American politics—indeed politics itself—as an undergraduate student. It feels good to return "home" and complete a book focused on American politics.

FOREWORD

Political Marketing and American Politics

During this second decade of the twenty-first century, the American people and the United States government have been going through difficult times. Trust in government is at a historic low; many citizens are disillusioned with politics and policymakers; Congress seems to be hopelessly divided, with extreme voices on the right in no mood to compromise and quite willing to hold legislation hostage. Governing and leadership are in short supply. No sooner had President Barack Obama won re-election in early November 2012 than commentators, bloggers, and political odds makers were speculating on who would run in the 2016 presidential election. And opinion polls show that most Americans are willing to kick all the rascals out of Congress and start all over again.

Anger and mistrust are fueled by talk radio, blogging, Twitter messages, social media, and other forms of communication. Elected officials, candidates, and policy makers try to cut through the clutter of old and new media, making their case to audiences (and voters) that matter. The U.S. Supreme Court has unshackled corporations, unions, and wealthy donors, permitting them to spend as much money as they'd like to develop their own Super PACs to carry their messages to voters, office holders, and aspiring politicians.

So much has changed in the way we identify likely voters, reach out to communicate with them, and try to persuade them to vote, that if candidates for office are stuck in twentieth-century campaign mindsets, they will be at a great disadvantage. The last two presidential elections bear this out, as both John McCain, the Republican running in 2008, and Mitt Romney, the Republican running in 2012, were mired in old ways of campaigning and incapable of using the latest techniques. By contrast, Barack Obama's 2008 and 2012 campaigns were the most sophisticated and most technologically proficient campaigns ever seen in America.

In the United States, we are accustomed to frequent elections and we are asked to choose from a wide variety of candidates and issues. In fact, we have more elections, more often, than any other democratic nation. There are approximately 513,200 elected officials and over a million elections held over a four-year cycle in the United States. Most of those elections attract little attention—members of a local mosquito control board, dog catcher, or a ballot issue on whether to increase the local sewage tax by 1 percent. However, many candidates for office or proponents and opponents of ballot issues receive assistance from campaign professionals. Statewide candidates, big city mayors, even local school boards are either managed or assisted by professional consultants. Millions of dollars are spent by gubernatorial candidates, who employ campaign managers, pollsters, online communication experts, and targeting and get-out-the-vote specialists. Not long ago, the average cost of a campaign for winning congressional candidates passed $1 million; 20 years ago, a million-dollar race was a rarity. U.S. Senate races average $10 million, with contests in the largest states of California and New York easily topping $50 million per candidate. An election for Congress once only involved the candidates themselves, but now many of them have become pawns in the national battle for supremacy in Congress. Outside voices, such as ideological interest groups, corporate and union interests, Super PACs with innocent-sounding names, step in to nationalize heretofore local contests.

Elections boil down to three very fundamental things: identifying likely voters, communicating with them, and getting them to the voting booth on election day. And the goal is very clear: in a two-way race, receive a majority of votes plus one; in multiple-candidate races, gain enough votes to defeat the other candidates. But to accomplish these very simple tasks often requires very sophisticated resources and a deep appreciation for and understanding of political marketing theories and concepts. Commercial companies hope to successfully launch new products or increase market share. They employ increasingly sophisticated marketing techniques to reach that goal: messages and communications are carefully tested and refined; audiences are identified and their opinions and preferences recorded; new customers are identified; new trends are monitored; new online ways of communicating are refined; products are rebranded, improved, and refocused. Over the years, many of the practices in the commercial marketplace have been adapted by candidates for office and by elected officials trying to sell their ideas.

This volume on political marketing in the United States is a very welcome addition to the study of campaigns, elections, political communications, and governance. It provides us with solid writing on a variety of topics critical to how candidates and elected officials cope with the enormous task of reaching out and communicating with like-minded individuals. I commend Jennifer Lees-Marshment, Brian

M. Conley, and Kenneth Cosgrove for assembling an experienced and distinguished group of communications and marketing specialists who offer us the latest understanding of the complexities of American politics, including campaigns and elections but also public policy, political leadership, and governance.

Dennis W. Johnson,
George Washington University

1
MARKETING US POLITICS

Jennifer Lees-Marshment, Brian M. Conley, and Kenneth Cosgrove

In modern American politics, much is written and discussed about political brands, selling candidates and issues, what techniques work to get people to turn out, and the latest innovations in organizing and mobilization, but rarely do such comments integrate understanding from academic marketing theory or provide a comprehensive analysis of the different activities involved in the marketing of US politics. We know that marketing is taking place in American politics and in practice the logic, analytical tools, and techniques of marketing have become ubiquitous. Yet, there is little holistic discussion of the marketing of US politics by journalists or academics; what there is tends to be piecemeal, ad hoc, and partial rather than situated in the context of the rich and diverse scholarly field of political marketing. This book aims to change that and begin a broad conversation about the role marketing plays in America's political life. Political marketing techniques and strategies, as well as the popular discussion of them, have become omnipresent in modern American politics. They are used by politicians, parties, groups, movements, and governments to advance a range of political goals. These goals include winning elections, gaining donations, attracting volunteers, managing reputations, and supporting the existence and advancing the agendas of interest groups and think tanks or advancing a particular cause or policy position. Americans are most familiar with the use of political marketing in campaigns, but marketing is employed by a variety of entities to inform every aspect of politics. Government departments, policy groups, and incumbent political leaders utilize concepts and techniques from marketing to advance their agendas through government and build public support for policies. Indeed, as anyone who has ever spent time in the Washington, D.C., area knows, from the moment one lands at the airport to the time one is walking around the city to time spent watching TV in the evening, one is literally in the middle of a giant b-to-b (business-to-business) marketing effort in which political marketers try to explain to those who make and implement policy, especially those in Congress around budget time, why what they support is in the national interest. Political marketing exists at all levels of government: federal, state, county, and local. It is used by presidents, governors, senators, representatives, big city mayors and councilors.

Political marketing has developed as American politics has become more professionalized. In addition to individual candidates and their campaign staffs, there exists an army of political and marketing professionals across the country working on politics and public affairs topics. The epicenter of this professionalized, marketed politics is obviously the nation's capital, but political marketing practitioners can be found in all corners of the country. The political professionals who are involved in political marketing are a diverse lot and serve in a variety of positions inside and outside of government. They include policy staffers, campaign consultants, communications and media officers, public relations officers and strategists, lobbying firms, and those who work in the bureaucracy of government as well as the West Wing of the White House. Politicians and the professionals who serve them value political marketing because it offers modern, applied methods and approaches to help them better identify and understand their stakeholders in order to provide better service, representation, and responsiveness to their needs and desires. Understanding their constituencies are very important to politicians and political professionals. Marketing begins with a study of the audience because doing so helps the political marketer understand the needs extant in their constituency, and then formulate a brand, policies, and strategy to meet such needs. Parties, candidates, and interest groups vie to define the marketplace then win sufficient support for their products. In particular, political marketing offers a way of structuring an organization so as to satisfy internal and external stakeholders, and to communicate in a way that not only persuades and sells the political product but also forges a positive, interactive relationship between elites and their public. In doing so, politics becomes like any other product in society: it is packaged, branded, and marketed to specific audience segments. What limits its ability to serve as a manipulative tool is the existence of organizational rivals attempting to serve the same market with a different product.

From an academic perspective, there is considerable value in studying political marketing as a holistic activity. It is important for scholars to understand the constituent parts of political marketing and the ways in which these parts affect the mechanics of their fields of endeavor, but it is also important to examine the bigger picture. This book is aimed at both the bigger picture and the practical application of political marketing concepts, and is therefore unique in the American academy in that it provides an academically informed understanding of the scope, practice, and impact of the political marketing approach that affects every area of political life from organizing to campaigning to policy making and governing. The book engages in cross-disciplinary research, adapting marketing concepts and theories to the academic analysis of politics in the same way that marketing is adapted by political practitioners in the practice of politics. The research identifies the rationale behind many visible forms of political marketing; shows what goes on behind the scenes in elections but also in government; and critiques the potential and limitations of marketing politics both from a pragmatic and normative perspective.

This chapter will outline the nature of political marketing and discuss political marketing in practice, the field of political marketing research, and gaps in the US political marketing literature. It will also explain the rationale for this book and outline its overall structure and approach. By doing so, it will give the reader a sense of what political marketing is and why it is valued by political practitioners, what constitutes its major techniques and how they work, and how political marketing is done in general, as well as what the rise of marketed politics means for the health of American representative governance. The combination of theory and practice, holistic and specific examination of the phenomenon, and writing from across the academy gives this book significant value as a guide to understanding what's happening in contemporary American political life, and most importantly, why things happen as they do now and how they happen differently from things done in the past.

The Distinctive and Broad Scope of Political Marketing

Political marketing is the application of marketing concepts and tools by political actors and organizations to achieve their goals. Branding, market segmentation, delivery management, internal political marketing, market-oriented strategies, and positioning are just some of the tools marketing offers politics. There are four main areas of political marketing activity, though they interact and overlap with each other: researching, strategizing, organizing, and communicating; see Figure 1.1.

In a political marketing approach researching includes not just polling, which is already studied in scholarship on campaigns, but a whole range of qualitative and quantitative research tools such as focus groups, role play, and co-creation where voters are asked to identify solutions and design the political product instead of just voicing their demands. Understanding the nature of the political market is crucial to strategic decisions. For example, in running for governor of Texas, one would look at the electorate overall as the market, then decide which parts of it would constitute its audience targets, taking into account the candidate's partisan affiliation and party positions, but also identifying ways to attract new forms of support. There is no possibility that a Texas Republican could get elected on a platform of gun control, but a Texas Democrat with the right brand and market might. The market is also the number of potential consumers willing to make the political equivalent of purchasing a product via either voting or mobilizing to advocate for it. Some political products (and these can be policies or politicians) are not saleable because they lack a market.

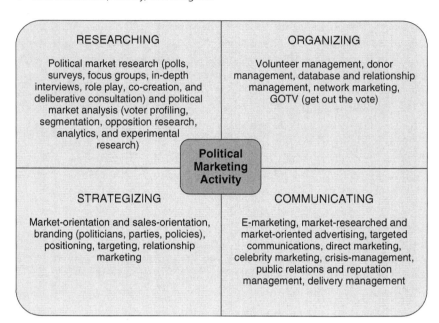

FIGURE 1.1 Political Marketing Activity

This is why successful politicians from one part of the country often have trouble when they try to run for national office and why there is significant variance in the kinds of politicians who make up the national political parties. They represent different marketplaces, and what can work in one can assure failure in the other. Consider the problems that Mitt Romney and Rick Perry had running for the Republican presidential nomination. Both struggled outside of their home markets because they were working to adapt to markets composed of different kinds of voters. In addition, political products can be either mass or niche and can have the same kinds of adoption and life cycles as other products have. A political marketing approach is also suited for use with both quantitative and formal theoretical techniques. Researching also encompasses analysis of the market, especially voters, through tools such as segmentation and voter profiling, which breaks the market down into smaller groups. Information gathered then can be synthesized with data on voters' lifestyles, homes, and family lives, and with political canvassing information to predict their needs and potential reactions and possibly pre-test policies, positions, and political communication through various forms of experimental marketing.

Political marketers then chose a strategy and design a product and brand in relation to the results from their research. As part of building a strategy, political marketers usually have to answer a series of questions. The most important of these is obviously, What's our product? Is it a politician, a series of policies, a party, or something else? Should we try to follow what another politician or party is doing? Are we trying to give people what they think they want or teach them why something else might be better? Who are our strongest supporters within the market, and can we expand their levels of support and turnout within those segments or try to persuade new people to support us? What is our brand visually and emotively, and at which groups of people is it pitched? What position do we want to hold in the market and in the mind of the public (i.e., does my candidate want to be the conservative candidate or someone in favor of strong social programs or some other position)? What kind of market space and space in the mind of our audience targets do we want to occupy? And with which audiences do we want to build a long-term relationship (assuming the candidate wants to do so), and how can we go about doing that? By answering these questions, a political marketer can figure out what the candidate is trying to do, to whom they are trying to sell, and, in part, what their product is exactly. Political marketing is, then, about research, conceptualization, and, as *Saturday Night Live* jokingly put it, referring to the George W. Bush administration, "strategery."

Political strategy includes decisions about how and whether to follow or try to lead what the market wants, as well as consideration of demographics and psychographics. While the emergence of analytic marketing and big data has attracted significant attention, it is not just the data itself, but the strategic decisions made in relation to it. As Issenberg (2012: 12) noted, "[S]ome of the early decisions that shaped how the [2012] presidential race would be run were built on technical innovations invisible to the outside world." One of the ways that political marketing is different from the older forms of political organizing with which political scientists are familiar is that political marketing places a great deal of emphasis on understanding voter demands, building voter databases and archetypes, and then designing political products that respond to and represent the concerns of the audience. In this sense, political marketing is a highly civic activity because it aims to bring the public's opinions, wants, and needs into the design of the political product. There are of course problems in how politicians use research in that too much segmentation can lead to niche marketing that has the ability to build strong bonds within but not across segments (Turow 1997). Some might argue that both Barack Obama and George W. Bush reflected the strengths of marketing in terms of giving people a strong sense of affiliation and involvement with their campaigns and administrations, yet also the limitations of the current age of niche marketing, as neither was ever fully able to persuade the vast majority of the population to support them even while they dominated within their own targeted segments. However, more effective leaders will integrate understanding from research and strategizing into an overall brand vision for society that forges an emotional connection between them and the public, and concepts such as relationship marketing seek to build and maintain positive interactions and relationships between elites and their political market.

Political parties and politicians have found it useful to make pragmatic use of marketing tools and concepts about how to run a party or group; recruit, activate, and retain volunteers and donors; and get out the vote during campaigns and legislation. In organizing, political market research is used again to identify the needs, wants, and behavior of volunteers and donors, and segment them into smaller groups just like voters. They are also further subdivided into smaller groups just like any sales-oriented organization does with its customers. Donors often receive different access in exchange for contributions based on the amount they've given, the number of years they've given, and the frequency of the donations that they've made. For example, US ambassadorships in desirable locales often go to persons who have been large donors themselves or fundraisers. Volunteers are similarly accorded different levels of access based on their levels and length of involvement, just as is the case with any selling business.

Once these questions are answered, political marketers then have to figure out what needs to be done to sell the product. Having the product, the money, the volunteers, and the understanding aren't enough unless the political marketer can explain what he or she is offering to the public. Political marketing communication is both narrow and broad, general and highly targeted, and takes place across a number of different platforms, but is most of all based on research about the market, the message, and the medium in question. It includes advertising informed by research and market-oriented strategies, targeted communications in response to market segmentation, and direct marketing in mail, DVD, email, and Internet forms as well as celebrity marketing. Political marketers understand and take advantage of the power of celebrity to sell to the general public, but also to reach specific demographic and psychographic segments with a message from someone with whom the audience feels comfortable and to whom they ascribe a high degree of credibility.

Political marketing communication is relevant to government as well as elections and includes the use of delivery management once in power to convey progress in delivering the political product and, when necessary, to deal with shorter-term crisis-management, especially when handling difficult and unpredictable issues. It also encompasses more interactive e-marketing, which is used to win an election or a legislative lobbying battle, but also to build the kind of long-term relationship that can facilitate a conversation between a candidate and their supporters that lasts for years. Public relations and reputation management offer additional tools to maintain positive relationships between elites and their stakeholders, particularly once politicians are in power or when organizations are hoping to build support for particular policies.

As Savigny and Temple (2010: 1049) note, "[C]ontemporary politics has become dominated by the use of marketing strategies, techniques and principles . . . [and] political marketing has become an important sub-field in the discipline of politics." Political marketing literature "provides political science with the vocabulary through which to analyse this" (Savigny and Temple 2010: 1052). This wide range of concepts and tools offers political elites new ways to attract and increase support from their stakeholders for their product. Political marketing is not confined to elections or campaigns and goes beyond existing political science theories of political communication. It does so by applying concepts from business marketing to those areas traditionally studied by political scientists, including parties, elections, policy making, legislating, governing, and leading. As Butler and Harris (2009: 151) observed, "[T]he broader conceptualization of political marketing goes far beyond election campaigns. Placing the formal campaign as the central issue is akin to focusing only on the sale negotiation as the core of marketing [and] . . . diminishes the opportunities of theorizing in the field." Instead, political marketing operates continuously throughout every aspect of politics. As Newman (1999a: 47) observes, "[P]olitical candidates will continue to win elections and succeed in office because they reposition their policies and images in response to the changing needs and wants of voters following the same marketing formula that works for companies."

Different political marketing activities interact with each other, with research being used to inform decisions on strategy, organization, and communication for the purposes of maximizing their potential effectiveness. Political marketing is a complex interactive area of behavior among political figures and organizations and their stakeholders. It is not just about specific techniques such as experimental market research or direct email, but a way of thinking, doing, and being—a philosophy. As in the commercial sector, where the mantra of "the customer is king" dominates, political marketing also offers strategies to guide how elites should respond to their markets—which include not just voters, but party members, volunteers, donors, the media, and other political organizations and practitioners. Strategies include using political marketing to sell the political product, but also to design that same product and brand, creating in the process something the public will want to vote for. As Newman (1999a: 39) notes, "[M]arketing research is used by political leaders to shape policy. Presidents . . . have relied extensively on opinion polls to help determine the direction of their presidencies" for decades.

However as practice develops, political elites are also finding ways to use political marketing in more relational forms to blend public demands with leadership vision more effectively so that elites and the public work in more of a partnership to achieve their shared goals. The *Routledge Handbook of Political Marketing*, published in 2012, argued that there has been a movement from researching voter demands to co-creating the political product; from neglecting members to seeing internal stakeholders as integral to successful political marketing; from short-term sales to long-term, mutual, and interactive communication; and from campaigning to governing necessitating greater integration of political marketing into leadership (Lees-Marshment 2012: 368–73). Political market research tools are used for different purposes—not just to identify existing demands, but to involve the political consumer in creating the solution for how to meet those demands. Organizational political marketing seeks to design internal structures and cultures that will allow party members, activists, and volunteers to become involved in the way that suits them, building positive and mutually beneficial relationships. At the same time, communication is becoming more relationship focused, enabling interaction and connectivity so that political elites can choose to use "more dialogical and transformational approaches to achieve and maintain relationships with political consumers over the long term," which provides greater room for leadership and effective governing.

Political Marketing Practice: The Growing Importance of Marketing Politics in the United States

Political marketing—or at least elements of it—has been utilized in US politics for decades if not centuries. In 1956, Leonard Hall, a Republican national chairman, claimed that "you sell your candidates and your programs the way a business sells its products" (Busby 2009: 14).[1] It could be argued that President Franklin D. Roosevelt understood the need to be market oriented, seeking to convey a responsive image to the public through his fireside chats delivered by radio. What makes the modern era unique is that we have entered an era of integrated product marketing that is routinized and professionalized. It has its own industry, centered in Washington, D.C., in the same way that New York is the center of the financial sector, Los Angeles the center of the entertainment industry, Nashville the center of the country music business, or the San Francisco Bay area the center of the computer industry.

Furthermore, political marketing now integrates a range of concepts rather than a single technique, is informed by a variety of market research tools at every step, and impacts political behavior and decisions rather than just communication. It also permeates governing, not just campaigning, and all levels of government, not just the presidency, as well as all political organizations, not just campaign offices or party headquarters. Public opinion and presidential research already identifies how political leaders have used polling (see Cohen 1997; Jacobs and Shapiro 2000; Canes-Wrone 2006; and Kernell 2006, for example). The field of political marketing adds an understanding of the broader context and thinking that leads to elite decisions and behavior. It analyzes strategic decisions made about policy, positioning, targeting, communication, and delivery management that are made in response to that polling (and indeed a whole range of market research tools) to create an effective political product and brand. It seeks to explore what goes on behind the scenes in political offices to create the communication or policy decisions that other areas of political science have traditionally analyzed from the outside.

Bill Clinton, for example, relied on market research to forge the New Democrat brand in the 1990s, which targeted middle-income Americans through a focus on the economy and issues like welfare reform and deficit reduction. In particular, Clinton proposed a detailed economic plan and spoke about his background in the "Man from Hope" video in response to focus group research that showed voters felt as though they did not know enough about him and were skeptical about his policy proposals. In his economic plan, Clinton scaled back a number of his earlier spending pledges and promises, including his plans for infrastructure spending, in order to address voter concerns that his ideas were too vague (Ingram and Lees-Marshment 2002; see also Newman 1994). During George Bush senior's 1988 campaign, an independent PAC produced the so-called Willie Horton Ad, which attacked Bush's Democratic opponent, Michael Dukakis's record on crime. The content and tone of the controversial ad was based on focus group research which showed that the story of the criminal who committed assault, robbery, and rape while on a weekend release program when Dukakis was governor in Massachusetts made voters concerned about Dukakis's crime policy. Indeed, Ronald Reagan was one of the earliest presidents to use political marketing, creating a moderate conservative brand in the 1980s in response to market research. A study of the Reagan presidency argued that survey data were used to identify "political opportunities where it could accomplish some of its ideological goals and satisfy some of its partisan constituents, while staying within broad constraints established by majority opinion" (Murray 2006: 495). The Republicans used political branding to build a distinct and unique vision around their candidates, movement, and issues to help them win and also implement policies once in power over several decades, starting with Reagan's creation of a brand heritage that subsequent candidates all played on (Cosgrove 2007a).

Targeting and segmenting the market is a significant part of US political marketing and, as some of the authors in this book explain, dates back to the 1930s. Newman (1999a: 263) observed how Bill Clinton's presidential re-election bid in 1996 succeeded by creating a message that appealed to the desire for an American dream across four segments of voters:

- rational voters, driven by their American dream expectations;
- emotional voters, driven by the feelings aroused by their desire to achieve the American dream;
- social voters, driven by the association of different groups of people and their ability to achieve the American dream; and
- situational voters, driven by situations that might influence their decision to switch to another candidate.

The US presidential campaign of George W. Bush in 2000 reached out to new target markets including middle-class and Hispanic voters with policies on health care and childhood education, nontraditional Republican issues. In the 2004 US presidential election, Republicans divided Michigan voters into 31 political categories, noting numbers and likelihood of voting Republican in each one, such as religious conservative Republicans; tax-cut conservative Republicans and flag and family Republicans; anti-pork, anti-terrorism Republicans; and harder-to-reach groups such as wageable weak Democrats (Johnson 2007). In the 2012 US presidential election both Obama and Romney targeted single women voters in the styling and message of their advertisements,[2] and Michelle Obama encouraged the public to join "Women for Obama" to help the campaign. It also occurs at a much more detailed level, with Davidson and Binstock (2012: 25) noting how parties and candidates break down the senior market into more diverse categories. US politicians have targeted seniors since John F. Kennedy's campaign for president in 1960 with campaign events held in places such as nursing homes, senior centers, congregate meal sites, and retirement and assisted living communities. Strategists also take into account those states that have a higher proportion of seniors and are also swing states with a large number of electoral votes. But market research is also used to identify diverging policy needs within the senior target, which inform both policy development and communication.

Not all US political marketing is so publicly visible, but it can still be as influential in helping build effective political organizations. Internal political marketing was behind the organizational changes made by Republicans under George W. Bush and then followed by the Democrats after their loss in 2004. The US Republicans managed and trained volunteers to get the vote and message out using network marketing, which, as Ubertaccio (2009: 514) observes, "merges old-fashioned grassroots methods with sophisticated modern messages." The success of the 2008 Obama campaign using online forms of communication was due to the way it stimulated face-to-face participation and responded to market-oriented principles of creating a structure that enabled voters to get involved in the way that suited them, not the party or campaign, and built on effective internal political marketing structures already put in place by the DNC under the chairmanship of Howard Dean. Lees-Marshment and Pettit (2014) noted how the Democrats created "volunteer-centered structures. Instead of asking people to get involved where the campaign needed them, they used online methods to enable volunteers to help out in the way that suited them." They cite DNC staffer Parag Mehta, for instance, who explained how volunteers could go to Obama's website, my.barackobama.com, and type in their home address, and using Google mapping technology find their home and 25 targeted voters closest to their house. In this way and others, the campaign sought to make it as easy as possible for people to volunteer.

The United States is often seen as the world leader in political marketing, particularly with regard to innovations in the use of technology, like online social networking in the 2008 presidential election. However, political marketing strategy has also been copied by other countries. Similarities have been noted between Ronald Reagan's moderate conservative brand developed in response to market research, for example, and how Margaret Thatcher attracted the skilled working classes to the Conservatives to become the first female UK prime minister in the 1970s (see Cooper 2013, for example). Bill Clinton's New Democrat appeal to middle America, which blended traditional Democratic themes with economic responsibility in response to market research, was adapted by leaders in many other countries, from UK Prime Minister Tony Blair's New Labour brand in 1997 to Australian Prime Minister Kevin Rudd's "economic conservative" Labor in 2007. Political marketing strategy travels back and forth between countries, including developing democracies, as political consultants increasingly work internationally and adapt ideas to suit whichever campaign they are advising at the time (Lees-Marshment and Lilleker 2012).

US political marketing is also commonly featured in media commentary and popular culture. Recent movies and documentaries that cover or touch upon elements of political marketing strategy include *Game Change*, *The Iron Lady*, *The Ides of March*, and *No*. Journalist Sasha Issenberg's book *The Victory Lab*,[3] which explores analytical and experimental marketing that uses research to predict voter reaction and make advertising more persuasive, is a bestseller. Obama's brand was much discussed in 2008, including in an article in *USA Today* (Goldberg 2009); and searches for "Obama" and "brand" in 2013 identified a wide range of media outlets discussing political branding. In the 2012 US presidential election, issues of branding were broadly discussed.

CNN's Adam Hanft (2012), for example, ran a feature called "Why GOP Branding Isn't Working" that explored how political parties are "essentially brands" and how difficult it had become for the Republicans to convey one clear brand vision. Hanft explained, "[P]arties out of office, by definition, find it harder to create and project a unified, focused brand identity. The lack of a leader, an ability to hand out plum jobs, bitter infighting and posturing for the next election, are all brand-destructive."' A story on the use of psychographic marketing in the US 2012 election appeared on MSNBC (Watkins 2012) commenting on how "political candidates use many psychological and marketing tactics to increase their likelihood of victory on election day . . . as more political candidates are running their campaigns like corporate brands doing whatever it takes to increase market share instead of promoting their actual beliefs and values." Delivery marketing by Obama during his first and second terms has also been discussed by *The Washington Post*, which explored the use of research to inform communication about and increase support for health care both before and after the law passed. Shear (2009) noted that in 2009, when creating speeches on health care, "Obama and his team carefully calibrate[d] his language with intensive polling, surveys and focus-group data" because "the president's team believes in the use of sophisticated data to make sure his rhetoric does not strike a dissonant tone with the majority of the listening public" and the need to connect with the public's fears and emotions. It was for this reason that Obama discussed his own story, such as how he watched his mother worry about whether her insurer would claim her cancer was a pre-existing condition so it could get out of providing coverage. In 2013, Klein and Kliff (2013) explored how the White House was using research to create targeted communications to sell Obamacare to segments such as young voters to ensure they buy the new health insurance. Moreover, get-out-the-vote initiatives and the problematic use of marketing segmentation and voter profiling software have attracted debate (Gallagher 2012; Farfer 2012). US political marketing is ubiquitous and impacts every area of politics: party building, candidate emergence, policy decisions and positioning, electoral campaigns and organization, selling policy, and governing. What this book will do is build on such commentary to provide a scholarly analysis informed by academic theory and in-depth empirical analysis.

Political Marketing Research: A New but Thriving Field in Global Political Science

Political marketing is now an established area of research in both marketing and political science As Butler and Harris (2009: 149) commented, "[P]olitical marketing research has made significant progress in recent years as evidenced by its own dedicated journal, special issues of international marketing journals, handbooks and edited volumes, special research interest groups of the academy, dedicated academic and practitioner conferences and articles in leading field journals." Its first handbook was published by Sage in 1999 (Newman 1999a); the *Journal of Political Marketing* was created in 2002; and a textbook and second handbook were commissioned by Routledge in 2009 and 2012 (Lees-Marshment 2009, 2012), as well as a collection of articles (Baines 2011). Books on political marketing have been published since 1989 (O'Shaughnessy 1990). The largest hive of activity has been the UK, with early works exploring the use of market research to inform persuasive communication (Kavanagh 1995; Scammell 1995), while later work looked at how it was also informing the design of the political product (Lees-Marshment 2001a; Wring 2005; Barber 2005; Lilleker et al. 2005). The UK also gave birth to the Political Marketing Group, under the auspices of the Political Studies Association, which now has an international membership.[4] UBC Press published *Political Marketing in Canada* in 2012 (Marland et al. 2012) and there have been books on political marketing in a range of other countries including India (Kumar 2009), Denmark (Nielsen 2011), and Nigeria (Worlu 2011), as well as comparative analysis (Bowler and Farrell 1992; Lees-Marshment and Lilleker 2005; Lees-Marshment et al. 2010).

Other books have explored a range of aspects, including the theoretical foundations of the field and democratic implications (e.g., Savigny 2008; Gouliamos et al. 2013; Newman and Williams 2012; Johansen 2012; Ormrod et al. 2013), its relationship to lobbying (Harris 2009), political marketing and populism (Busby 2009), political PR (Kiousis and Strömbäck 2011), PR and international relations (McKie and Toledano 2013; Potter 2009), the perspectives of practitioners who carry out political marketing (Lees-Marshment 2011), get out the vote (Green and Gerber 2008), and political branding (Cosgrove 2007a; Spiller and Bergner 2011). Such scholarship, by adapting marketing techniques and concepts from business analysis, moves way beyond what some scholars might see as the origins of political marketing in terms of the rational-choice or economic approaches to politics pioneered by Hotelling (1929) and Downs (1957). The resource site www.political-marketing.org lists the wealth of literature—and other resources for teaching—in political marketing.

Until the turn of the century, political marketing was generally misunderstood. It was commonly thought that political marketing was equivalent to spin-doctoring, advertising, or campaigns. This hindered development of scholarship and teaching in the field, as it failed to use marketing concepts and tools and limited analysis to communication and campaigning, and thus failed to observe and critique a major area of political behavior that occurs continuously in politics, not just campaigns, and influences all aspects of politics including policy, organization, and leadership in government.

However, research has since diversified beyond communication and been applied to a wider range of marketing concepts. It is now broadly accepted that high-quality political marketing research needs to be comprehensive and apply marketing to the whole behavior of a political organization, not just its communication or campaign activities. It must use marketing concepts, not just techniques, and adapt marketing theory to suit the distinct nature of politics (Lees-Marshment 2003). In addition to the aforementioned books, Butler and Collins (1996) pioneered one of the first strategic concepts with a model of how parties might position themselves against each other in the political marketplace with a leader, follower, challenger, and niche categorization; Lloyd (2005) developed a concept of the political product, and there have been studies of internal marketing (Lebel 1999; Dean and Croft 2001; Bannon 2005; Granik 2005; Pettitt 2012; Marland 2012; Van Aelst, van Holsteyn, and Koole 2012), local political marketing (Lilleker and Negrine 2003), and stakeholders (Hughes and Dann 2006a, 2006b), along with studies examining the branding of candidates, parties, and policy (Needham 2005; Reeves et al. 2006; Smith 2009; Smith and French 2009; French and Smith 2010; Marsh and Fawcett 2012; Busby 2012), e-marketing (Jackson 2005), the market-orientation of political advertisements (Robinson 2007, 2010), and delivery (Esslement 2012a, 2012b).

Political marketing is now taught and studied all around the world in political science, marketing, and communication departments, and applied politics or political management programs in the United States and Canada. A political marketing group was founded within the UK Political Studies Association in 2005, which has an international membership and coordinators; a Canadian version was created in 2012–2013. However, there is one big, glaring—and surprising—gap in political marketing scholarship and awareness, and that is in research related to US politics.

US Political Marketing Research, the Gaps, and the Rationale for This Book

Given that there is so much world attention on US politics, along with considerable international influence of US consultants, you would expect political marketing scholarship to be greatest in the United States. But this is not the case. Those who do not understand what political marketing is may object to this claim, seeing the plentiful, excellent, and significant US political science literature that exists on campaigns and political advertising as proof that the United States leads the world in this area. But as explained in the first section of this chapter, political marketing is not the same as campaigns and advertising. To be sure, there are campaign studies that analyze marketing elements such as polling; the growing role of consultants, including market researchers; and overall campaign strategy. But they do so without a broader examination of political marketing research, which encompasses a whole range of market research tools (focus groups, role play, co-creation) carried out on a permanent basis not just during campaigns, and concepts like segmentation, positioning, and branding. There is also a substantial literature analyzing US political advertising, but without exploring advertising in relation to marketing tools and concepts. There is also work on political positioning, but again, it lacks reference to market positioning theory or consideration of market-orientation. Political marketing research covers how marketing permeates a wide range of aspects of political behavior, from campaigning through to governing, analyzes how the different parts of political marketing interact with each other, and most importantly, integrates understanding from the source—the substantial and significant literature on *business* marketing—which can and should be adapted to understand *political* marketing. Compared to the UK and Canada, very little informed scholarship on political marketing is coming out of the United States, whether focused on US politics or written by US academics.

On one hand, some of the earliest work on political marketing focused on US politics. US scholar Bruce Newman's 1994 book *The Marketing of the President: Political Marketing as Campaign Strategy* (Sage) was one of the first books to be published on political marketing and explored how Bill Clinton utilized a range of political marketing tools, using a model that argued candidate positioning involves the 4 Ps: product (campaign platform); push marketing (grass roots efforts); pull marketing (mass media); and polling (research). In a second book, Newman examined how Clinton succeeded in 1992 by building a market-oriented campaign "built around voters' concerns and desires rather than his own" positions, which maximized message effectiveness, noting that Clinton's campaign was informed by regular market intelligence to help frame political communication (Newman 1999a: 77–85). Newman (1999a: 90–1) also pointed out that in the 1992 US presidential campaign Bill Clinton used targeting to focus on three groups of states, categorized by criteria such as economic performance, presidential historical preferences, Democratic performance, the Southern factor, and constant polling. His typology included (1) top-end states: possible to win with limited resources, such as Arkansas, Illinois, and California; (2) play hard states: possible to win with extensive resources; and (3) big challenge states: not very likely to win. Energy and resources were focused on the last two, which included Maryland, Missouri, Pennsylvania, Iowa, Ohio, Louisiana, Michigan, and New Jersey. The Democrats competed with the Republicans for these states. Thirty-two states were targeted and 19 left out; of the 32, Clinton won 31. Newman, however, is a marketing scholar, not a political scientist. Newman also discussed the limits of Clinton's delivery marketing once in power, noting that while the opponents of health reform clearly articulated their argument against the legislation, using the "Harry and Louise" ads, for example, to give a face to their campaign, this was something the Clinton administration never did. The White House did respond by attempting to simplify its core message in order to target those people who would most benefit from health reform, namely the uninsured, but their targeting nonetheless continued to be "out of touch with market changes taking place as it was being developed, and was too complex" in contrast to effective opposition campaigning (Newman 1999a: 101). One of the earliest pieces on political marketing focused on direct mail and telemarketing by US presidential candidates, but the authors, O'Shaughnessy and Peele (1985), were UK, not US, scholars.

Smaller pieces on US political marketing written in the 1990s and early 2000s have included Steger (1999: 668–9), who noted how elected officials in Congress engage in delivery marketing (our term, not his) by claiming credit for a number of activities in their states such as fixing funding formulas to the benefit of their key market segments, opposing potentially damaging regulatory legislation, fighting for benefits and grants, and helping the public with problems with government agencies. At the same time, Lebel (1999: 141) set out principles for effective volunteer management so that volunteers need to feel wanted and valued. "Internal communication is extremely important to help them feel recognized and part of the overall campaign," he explained. Sherman (1999), on the other hand, explored the use of direct mail in fundraising by presidents including Bill Clinton, and Paleologos (1997) explored the problems with the overuse of polling. Knuckey and Lees-Marshment (2005) explored how George W. Bush utilized elements of a market-oriented approach in 2000, balancing the need to appeal to internal and external markets by emphasizing his conservative credentials during the primaries by temporarily replacing his "compassionate conservative" slogan with "a reformer with results," but then moving back toward the center after winning the nomination. There was also the Ingram and Lees-Marshment (2002) work discussing how Bill Clinton followed a market-oriented strategy in 1992 that included changes to the product, but again they were UK scholars.

More recently, research in US political marketing has seen a certain growth and diversification. The first work on political branding in the United States was completed by Cosgrove (2007a, 2007b), and explored Republican branding; it was followed by Spiller and Bergner's (2011) exploration of how the 2008 Obama campaign used research-informed targeting to reach different segments and fundraise to develop a unique brand. Parker (2012) explored registered voters' perceptions of multidimensional brand equity for the four candidates for the presidential nomination and election (Hillary Clinton, Barack Obama, John McCain, and Mike Huckabee). Green and Gerber (2008) have studied methods to get out the vote

(GOTV); Burton and Shea (2003, 2010) discuss the use of strategy and targeting in their books on campaign management; and Johnson's (2007) work on consultants has included discussion of their advice and activity in relation to political marketing research. Ridout et al. (2012), who are specialists in political advertising, noted how ads have been targeted in presidential elections, while Hersh and Scaffner (2013) questioned the effectiveness of highly targeted ads using "big data" or hyper-segmentation, especially if it is built on assumptions which end up incorrect, thus resulting in mis-targeting. Barreto et al. (2011: 304–5) discuss how in the 2000 US presidential election both Democrats and Republicans adopted an integrated marketing communications approach, combining targeting to market segments and direct and indirect marketing to mobilize. Their research suggested that while generic political advertisements help with GOTV, messages that are direct and targeted to particular groups are more effective.

Arterton (2007) analyzed strategy in the US government, noting how it was underdeveloped and hindered by the machinery of the federal government itself. And there were a number of chapters in the 2012 *Routledge Handbook of Political Marketing* that focused on the United States and were written by US scholars, such as Ubertaccio's (2012) work, which investigated the use of direct marketing by the Republican Party during the George W. Bush presidency to support the creation of networks to attract, retain, and activate volunteers, and Conley (2012), who explored the challenge of branding US political parties as opposed to individual leaders, particularly within the Democratic Party after Obama's 2008 election. Cosgrove (2012) also provided an analysis of political branding by candidate and then President Obama, Nancy Pelosi and the New Democratic Congress, as well as the Republicans' Bundled Policy Initiatives, concluding that branding works best when the brand is clearly and consistently positioned, when it is supported by strong messaging, and when it moves up the benefits ladder from specific attributes to high level values. Burton (2012) discussed how targeting is used to help politicians identify and select which voter groups to focus on to help find the most cost-effective means of accumulating enough votes to win the election, and Davidson and Binstock (2012) analyzed how segmentation is being used to better understand the aging population when developing policy as well as campaigning, so politicians are aware of the potential reaction of seniors to a wide range of policy issues, not just those relating to Medicare, Social Security, or health care. Cogburn and Espinoza-Vasquez (2011) explored how Obama's use of social media succeeded because it also used marketing concepts such as direct marketing and was volunteer-friendly, which also stimulated donations.

However, there still is no book focused on US political marketing. Some of the work that calls itself political marketing or is published in the *Journal of Political Marketing* fails to follow the principle of utilizing marketing theory to provide an analysis distinct from existing a political science analysis of elections and campaigns. There are, as a result, fewer scholars in the United States who would identify themselves as political marketers. Indeed, until now the more influential theoretical and empirical work in the political marketing field has come out of Europe and Canada. We can only speculate as to why. Perhaps it is because elements that supported the growth of political marketing in the UK and Canada have not been present in the United States. Or it could be that the prevalence of quantitative methodology in US political science has encouraged a more narrow focus that lacks the necessary analytical space for new thinking about how a market-orientation is changing politics in the United States. The work by US historians working on politics such as David Greenberg *Nixon's Shadow: The History of an Image* is more typical of the analysis conducted by political marketing scholars. There is no book dedicated to US political marketing; there is no organizational network on political marketing within US political science or marketing; and nurturing political marketing scholars who engage in the informal work of encouraging new scholars interested in the field have not emerged in the United States. Political marketing is a distinctive area of political science research (see Scammell 1999; Lees-Marshment 2001b) that incorporates marketing concepts and theories into the analysis of a substantial and significant area of political behavior that is now influenced by marketing.

This is, therefore, the rationale for this book. Political marketing is ubiquitous in politics: politicians, governments, campaigns, consultants, and interest groups are all borrowing tools and concepts from business marketing to achieve their goals in the political marketplace. Political marketing impacts all areas of politics at all times, yet there is a gap in scholarship on US political marketing that this book seeks to fill.

Political science scholars in areas such as campaigning, public opinion, voting behavior, and parties, as well as marketing scholars, should read this book on political marketing for the following reasons:

1. Political marketing helps us understand what is happening in contemporary politics—decisions on policy, organization, and communication are informed by research into stakeholder views, and without understanding such research and branding concepts we cannot understand those decisions.
2. Understanding political marketing thus helps academics provide a more informed commentary on changes in the way government and elections operate.
3. Political marketing is not just about campaigning or voting behavior. It is about all aspects of political behavior and how they are informed by marketing tools and concepts, and how they intersect with each other. Political marketing therefore offers a holistic approach to political behavior by considering what happens after the election in government and behind the scenes within party organizations as well as campaigns and elections of interest to various sub-fields in political science.
4. Political marketing has application to real world problems, and including it in the research and teaching of the academy helps promote debate on topical issues among scholars, students, and practitioners.

5. Teaching political marketing increases the employability of students. There are a range of jobs that utilize political marketing, and thus teaching both political science and marketing students about political marketing offers them training in something they can go and do after graduation. It is also useful to those who are not political science majors to understand the way the political world actually works, which will help them should they end up in other occupational spheres such as journalism.
6. Teaching political marketing also is teaching effective citizenship. A focus on the prevalence of the marketing orientation and its tools in teaching is in fact teaching students to understand the political world as it is, rather than as academics would like it to be.

Thus, this book is of relevance to a variety of different disciplines, as is the field itself, and the market for it should also include communication and marketing scholars.

The book project emerged from a short course we organized at the 2010 APSA (American Political Science Association) conference held in Washington, D.C. This workshop was inspired by the Canadian counterpart organized by Alex Marland and colleagues in Ottawa in 2009, which also led to the Canadian book *Political Marketing in Canada*. Two of the coeditors of this book (Jennifer Lees-Marshment and Ken Cosgrove) attended the Canadian workshop and one was involved in editing the book. Ken and Jennifer then came up with the idea of doing an event in the United States and worked with Christine Williams, who is one of the editors of the *Journal of Political Marketing*, to run the APSA workshop. The workshop attracted a great range of papers and speakers, including advisors to presidential candidates and presidents, like Anita Dunn, who served on Obama's communication staff during the campaign and in the first years in the White House. Ken then arranged for Jennifer to visit Suffolk University in Boston in 2011 and it was during that visit that we all came up with the idea for a book on political marketing in the United States. We would like to acknowledge those who gave support to these initiatives that have led to this book—APSA for accepting the short course proposal; George Washington University, which provided the room and refreshments; and staff at Suffolk University, who sponsored Jennifer's trip in 2011 and who are detailed in our acknowledgments.

The Approach and Structure of This Book

This book will explore a wide range of political marketing aspects, with chapters written by leading and emerging scholars in political marketing from around the globe. Subjects include targeting, utilizing research databases, the Tea Party, social media and populism, marketing in primary elections, marketing policy by influencing candidates, celebrity marketing, personal political branding at the state level, online brand management and relationship marketing, marketing and gender, research-led and targeted political advertising, crisis-management in campaigns, communicating leadership in government, and delivery marketing.

All chapters review the previous literature, set out a theoretical framework, and provide an empirical illustration such as a case study. Empirical analysis is obviously crucial to a book focused on political marketing in one country. But theory is also crucial, because it helps to explain the concepts informing the work, and thus provides a framework that can be applied by other scholars in future research. Chapters were selected through a rigorous and extensive review process: first, potential authors were invited to submit an outline of their proposed chapter, which was reviewed; second, those selected submitted a first draft of the chapter, which was double reviewed by the lead editor and at least one coeditor, and detailed recommendations were made to both improve the quality and coherence of the chapters as part of the overall book; and third, the lead editor reviewed the final second draft, with the coeditors involved in any chapters where there was debate.

The chapters utilize a range of methodologies, including analysis of qualitative and quantitative primary and secondary data. Qualitative methodology has dominated previous political marketing research, seeking to create conceptual and theoretical frameworks to understand and reflect on the complex interaction of different areas of political behavior influenced by marketing tools and approaches. The standard "effects" approach adopted in some areas in political science is felt to be less appropriate for an area that seeks to provide a more theoretical as well as practical account of a broad of range of political behavior rather than a narrower focus on a few isolated variables. Nonetheless the book exhibits methodologies such as a quantitative assessment of tweets using the open-source data collection and archiving website Twapper Keeper; a qualitative data analysis (QDA) computer program to code and test Obama's media texts including speeches, interviews, video blogs, and town hall meetings against a grounded theory framework; a content analysis of the online presence of presidential candidates in 2008 and 2012 to test the presence or absence of 59 features using a coding sheet assessing vertical information flows, horizontal information flows, and interactive information flows; and survey and TV advertising data. Other chapters utilize interviews with candidates, synthesis of academic literature, theory construction, analysis of media sources, and candidate, party, and government documents, media appearances, and behavior usually found in internationally peer-reviewed political marketing publications. Authors are drawn from the United States itself and around the globe. This provided us with a multiplicity of perspectives and methodologies. Given the United States' position on the world stage, many academics are avid scholars of American politics and possess the same skills and familiarity to write cogently about it as those geographically based in the United States.

This book is driven by a vision and a desire. We see the day when American scholars are as aware of political marketing as are their practitioner counterparts and strongly believe that this book, which is an exercise in explaining and showing this audience what the nature and value of political marketing is, will be the catalyst for considerable growth in the field in the United States. *Political Marketing in the United States* showcases research on US political marketing, but also seeks to stimulate further scholarship in the field, including events and publications. Furthermore, drawing on existing literature in the field, utilizing the best and dedicated authors, and subjecting the chapters to a rigorous review process has produced work that will also advance global research and teaching in political marketing. For example, unlike the majority of previous research, many chapters explore more than one aspect of political marketing, demonstrating the interrelatedness of different areas of political marketing, specifically how they impinge on, constrain, and relate to each other. For example, the chapters show how personal branding can be constrained by party branding; the communication of market-oriented leadership in government is affected by delivery marketing; and marketing by groups such as the Tea Party makes clear that different elements of political marketing (e.g., segmentation, targeting, internal marketing, e-marketing) can be combined to create powerful volunteer support building mechanisms on key political issues. But it is also important to note that marketed movements can have an impact on major parties; that online political marketing communication can be used to stimulate internal participation by volunteers; and that advertising is made more effective when it is combined with market research and segmentation. Chapters also explore branding and e-marketing by individual politicians for Congress rather than just political/party leaders, and by movements and groups instead of just parties; celebrity political marketing; gender and political marketing; political marketing's impact on political advertising; crisis-management; and political marketing in primary elections—aspects that have not been covered much or at all in previous political marketing research. The book covers recent events, with many examples from the 2012 election, but it is not just about 2012. Furthermore it explores how new trends in political marketing—toward more relational forms of interaction between political elites and the public—could impact the nature of politics itself, such as how the rise of voter targeting is helping to empower individuals and take power from traditional party organizations. After the 14 chapters, the final chapter will summarize the overall findings of the book and discuss such broader themes.

Notes

1 Busby reproduced this quote, originally cited in Richard W. Waterman, Robert Wright, and Gilbert St. Clair, *The Image-Is-Everything Presidency* (Boulder, CO: Westview Press: 1999), 74.
2 See, for example, a collation of political ads for women run in October 2012 on www.youtube.com/watch?v=qUmh4KCzrjc.
3 www.thevictorylab.com/
4 The Political Marketing Group website is at https://sites.google.com/site/psapmg/home. Anyone can join and receive regular free newsletters and notifications about political marketing–related events. There is also a Facebook page. See www-political-marketing. org for a resource list.

References

Arterton, C.F. (2007). Strategy and politics: The example of the United States of America. In T. Fischer, G. P. Schmitz, & M. Seberich (Eds.), *The strategy of politics: Results of a comparative study* (pp. 133–172). Gütersloh, DE: Bertelsmann Stiftung.

Baines, P. (2011). *Political marketing.* London, UK: Sage.

Bannon, D. (2005). Relationship marketing and the political process. *Journal of Political Marketing, 4*(2/3), 73–90.

Barber, S. (2005). *Political strategy: Modern politics in contemporary Britain,* Liverpool, UK: Liverpool Academic Press.

Barreto, M.A., Merolla, J., & Soto, V.D. (2011). Multiple dimensions of mobilization: The effect of direct contact and political ads on Latino turnout in the 2000 presidential election. *Journal of Political Marketing, 10*(4), 303–327.

Bowler, S., & Farrell, D.M. (Eds.). (1992). *Electoral strategies and political marketing.* Houndmills, Basingstoke, UK: PalgraveMacmillan Press.

Burton, M.J. (2012). Strategic voter selection. In J. Lees-Marshment (Ed.), *The Routledge handbook of political marketing* (pp. 34–47). London, UK: Routledge.

Burton, M.J., & Shea, D.M. (2003). *Campaign mode: Strategic vision in congressional elections.* Lanham, MD: Rowman & Littlefield.

Burton, M.J., & Shea, D.M. (2010). *Campaign craft: The strategies, tactics, and art of political campaign management* (4th ed.). Santa Barbara, CA: Praeger.

Busby, R.D. (2009). *Marketing the populist politician.* Basingstoke, UK: Palgrave Macmillan.

Busby, R.D. (2012). Selling Sarah Palin: Political marketing and the "Wal-Mart Mom." In J. Lees-Marshment (Ed.), *The Routledge handbook of political marketing* (pp. 218–229). London, UK: Routledge.

Butler, D., & Collins, N. (1996). Strategic analysis of political markets. *European Journal of Marketing, 30*(10/11), 25–36.

Butler, P., & Harris, P. (2009). Considerations on the evolution of political marketing theory. *Marketing Theory, 9*(2), 149–164.

Canes-Wrone, B. (2006). *Who leads whom? Presidents, policy, and the public.* Chicago, IL: University of Chicago Press.

Cogburn, D.L., & Espinoza-Vasquez, F.K. (2011). From networked nominee to networked nation: Examining the impact of Web 2.0 and social media on political participation and civic engagement in the 2008 Obama campaign. *Journal of Political Marketing, 10*(1/2), 189–213.

Cohen, J. (1997). *Presidential responsiveness and public policy-making.* Ann Arbor, MI: University of Michigan Press.

Conley, B.M. (2012). The politics of hope: The Democratic Party and the institutionalization of the Obama brand in the 2010 mid-term elections. In J. Lees-Marshment (Ed.), *The Routledge handbook of political marketing* (pp. 124–134). London, UK: Routledge.

Cooper, J. (2013). "Superior to anything I had seen in the States": The "Thatcherism" of the Republican strategy in 1980 and 1984. *Journal of Transatlantic Studies, 11*(1), 1–2.

Cosgrove, K.M. (2007a). *Branded conservatives: How the brand brought the right from the fringes to the center of American politics.* New York, NY: Peter Lang.

Cosgrove, K.M. (2007b). Midterm marketing: An examination of marketing strategies in the 2006, 2002, 1998, and 1994 elections. Paper presented at the annual meeting of the American Political Science Association, Hyatt Regency Chicago and the Sheraton Chicago Hotel and Towers, Chicago, IL, August 30, 2007. http://citation.allacademic.com/meta/p209749_index.html

Cosgrove, K.M. (2012). Political branding in the modern age—Effective strategies, tools & techniques. In J. Lees-Marshment (Ed.), *The Routledge handbook of political marketing* (pp. 107–123). London, UK: Routledge.

Davidson, S., & Binstock, R.H. (2012). Political marketing and segmentation in aging democracies. In J. Lees-Marshment (Ed.), *The Routledge handbook of political marketing* (pp. 20–33). London, UK: Routledge.

Dean, D., & Croft, R. (2001). Friends and relations: Long-term approaches to political campaigning. *European Journal of Marketing, 35*(11/12), 1197–1216.

Downs, A. (1957). *An economic theory of democracy*. New York, NY: Harper.

Esselment, A. (2012a). Delivering in government and getting results in minorities and coalitions. In J. Lees-Marshment (Ed.), *The Routledge handbook of political marketing* (pp. 303–315). London, UK: Routledge.

Esselment, A. (2012b). Market orientation in a minority government: The challenges of product delivery. In A. Marland, T. Giasson, & J. Lees-Marshment (Eds.), (2011) *Political marketing in Canada* (pp. 123–138). Vancouver, BC: UBC Press.

Farfer, D. (2012, November 9). Why Romney's orca killer app beached on election day. *CNET*. http://news.cnet.com/8301-13578_3-57547183-38/why-romneys-orca-killer-app-beached-on-election-day/

French, A., & Smith, G. (2010). Measuring political brand equity: A consumer oriented approach. *European Journal of Marketing, 44*(3–4), 460–477.

Gallagher, S. (2012, November 10). Inside team Romney's whale of an IT meltdown: Orca, the Romney campaign's "killer" app, skips beta and pays the price. *Arts Technica*. http://arstechnica.com/information-technology/2012/11/inside-team-romneys-whale-of-an-it-meltdown/

Goldberg, J. (2009, January 6). Obama and the Democratic brand. *USA Today*, p. 9A.

Gouliamos, K., et al. (2013). *Political marketing: Strategic "campaign culture."* London, UK: Routledge.

Granik, S. (2005). Membership benefits, membership action: Why incentives for activism are what members want. In W. Wymer & J. Lees-Marshment (Eds.), *Current issues in political marketing* (pp. 65–90). Binghamton, NY: Haworth Press.

Green, D.P., & Gerber, A.S. (2008). *Get out the vote: How to increase voter turnout* (2nd ed.). Washington, DC: Brookings Institution Press.

Hanft, A. (2012, August 30). Why GOP branding isn't working. *Special to CNN*. http://edition.cnn.com/2012/08/29/opinion/hanft-gop-messaging/

Harris, P. (2009). *Lobbying and public affairs in the UK: The relationship to political marketing*. (Unpublished doctoral dissertation). University of Otago, Dunedin, New Zealand.

Hersh, E.D., & Schaffner, B.F. (2013). Targeted campaign appeals and the value of ambiguity. *Journal of Politics, 75*(2), 520–534.

Hotelling, H. (1929). Stability in competition. *Economic Journal, 39*, 41–57.

Hughes, A., & Dann, S. (2006a). Political marketing and stakeholders. Australia and New Zealand Marketing Academy Conference. Queensland University of Technology, Brisbane, Queensland, December 4–6, 2006.

Hughes, A., & Dann, S. (2006b). Political marketing 2006: Direct benefit, value, and managing the voter relationship. Australia and New Zealand Marketing Academy Conference. Queensland University of Technology, Brisbane, Queensland, December 30, 2006.

Ingram, P., & Lees-Marshment, J. (2002). The Anglicisation of political marketing: How Blair "out-marketed" Clinton. *Journal of Public Affairs, 2*(2), 44–57.

Issenberg, S. (2012). *The victory lab: The secret science of winning campaigns*. New York, NY: Crown.

Jackson, N. (2005). Party e-newsletters in the UK: A return to direct political communication. *Journal of E-Government, 1*(4), 39–43.
Jacobs, L.R., & Shapiro, R.Y. (2000). Polling and pandering. *Society, 37*(6), 11–13.
Johansen, H.P.M. (2012). *Relational political marketing in party-centred democracies: Because we deserve it.* Burlington, VT: Ashgate.
Johnson, D. (2007). *No place for amateurs* (2nd ed.). New York, NY: Routledge.
Kavanagh, D. (1995). *Election campaigning: The new marketing of politics.* Oxford, UK: Blackwell.
Kernell, S. (2006). *Going public: New strategies of presidential leadership* (4th ed.). Washington, DC: Congressional Quarterly Press.
Kiousis, S., & Strömbäck, J. (2011) *Political public relations: Principles and applications.* New York, NY: Routledge.
Klein, E., & Kliff, S. (2013, July 17). Obama's last campaign: Inside the White House plan to sell Obamacare. *The Washington Post.* www.washingtonpost.com/blogs/wonkblog/wp/2013/07/17/obamas-last-campaign-inside-the-white-house-plan-to-sell-obamacare/
Knuckey, J. & Lees-Marshment, J. (2005). American political marketing: George W. Bush and the Republican Party. In J. Lees-Marshment & D.G. Lilleker (Eds.), *Political marketing: A comparative perspective* (pp. 39–58). Manchester, UK: Manchester University Press.
Kumar, A. (2009). *Political marketing in India.* New Delhi, IN: Regal Publications.
Lebel, G. (1999). Managing volunteers: Time has changed—or have they? In B. Newman (Ed.), *Handbook of political marketing* (pp. 129–142). Thousand Oaks, CA: Sage.
Lees-Marshment, J. (2001a). *Political marketing and British political parties.* Manchester, UK: Manchester University Press.
Lees-Marshment, J. (2001b). The marriage of politics and marketing. *Political Studies, 49*(4), 692–713.
Lees-Marshment, J. (2003). Political marketing: How to reach that pot of gold. *Journal of Political Marketing, 2*(1), 1–32.
Lee-Marshment, J. (2009). *Political marketing: Principles and applications.* London, UK: Routledge.
Lees-Marshment, J. (2011). *The political marketing game.* Hampshire, UK: Palgrave Macmillan.
Lees-Marshment, J. (Ed.). (2012). *The Routledge handbook of political marketing.* London, UK: Routledge.
Lees-Marshment, J., & Lilleker, D. (2012). Knowledge sharing and lesson learning: Consultants' perspectives on the international sharing of political marketing strategy. *Contemporary Politics, 18*(3), 343–354.
Lees-Marshment, J., & Lilleker, D.G. (Eds.). (2005). *Political marketing: A comparative perspective.* Manchester, UK: Manchester University Press.
Lees-Marshment, J., & Pettitt, R. (2014). Mobilising volunteer activists in political parties: The view from central office. *Contemporary Politics* .
Lees-Marshment, J., Stromback, J., & Rudd, C. (Eds.). (2010). *Global political marketing.* London, UK: Routledge.
Lilleker, D., Jackson, N., & Scullion, R. (Eds.). (2005). *The marketing of political parties: Political marketing at the 2005 British general election.* Manchester, UK: Manchester University Press.
Lilleker, D., & Negrine, R. (2003). Not big brand names but corner shops: Marketing politics to a disengaged electorate. *Journal of Political Marketing, 2*(1), 55–76.
Lloyd, J. (2005). Square peg, round hole? Can marketing-based concepts such as the "product" and the "marketing mix" have a useful role in the political arena? In W. Wymer &

J. Lees-Marshment (Eds.), *Current issues in political marketing* (pp. 27–46). Binghamton, NY: Haworth Press.

Marland, A. (2012).Yes we can (fundraise):The ethics of marketing in political fundraising. In J. Lees-Marshment (Ed.), *The Routledge handbook of political marketing* (pp. 164–176). London, UK: Routledge.

Marland, A., Giasson,T., & Lees-Marshment, J. (Eds.). (2012). *Political marketing in Canada.* Vancouver, BC: UBC Press.

Marsh, D., & Fawcett, P. (2012). Branding public policy. In J. Lees-Marshment (Ed.), *The Routledge handbook of political marketing* (pp. 329–341). London, UK: Routledge.

McKie, D., & Toledano, M. (2013). *Public relations and nation building: Influencing Israel.* London, UK: Routledge.

Murray, S.K. (2006). Private polls and presidential policymaking: Reagan as a facilitator of change. *Public Opinion Quarterly, 70*(4), 477–498.

Needham, C. (2005). Brand leaders: Clinton, Blair, and the limitations of the permanent campaign. *Political Studies, 53,* 343–361.

Newman, B.I. (1994). *The marketing of the president: Political marketing as campaign strategy.* Thousand Oaks, CA: Sage.

Newman, B.I. (1999a). *The mass marketing of politics: Democracy in an age of manufactured images.* Thousand Oaks, CA: Sage.

Newman, B.I. (1999b). *Handbook of political marketing.* Thousand Oaks, CA: Sage.

Newman, B.I., & Williams, C.B. (Eds.). (2012). *Political marketing in retrospective and prospective.* London, UK: Routledge.

Nielsen, W. (2011) *Political marketing—Persons, parties and praxis.* Copenhagen, DK: Karnov Group.

Ormrod, R.P., et al. (2013). *Political marketing:Theory and concepts.* London, UK: Sage.

O'Shaughnessy, N.J. (1990). *The phenomenon of political marketing.* Hampshire, UK: Macmillan.

O'Shaughnessy, N. J., & Peele, G. (1985). Money, mail and markets: Reflections on direct mail in American politics. *Electoral Studies, 4*(2), 115–124.

Paleologos, D.A. (1997).A pollster on polling. *American Behavioral Scientist, 40*(8), 1183–1189.

Parker, B.T. (2012). Candidate brand equity valuation: a comparison of U.S. presidential candidates during the 2008 primary election campaign. *Journal of Political Marketing, 11*(3), 208–230.

Pettitt, R. (2012). Exploring variations in intra-party democracy: A comparative study of the British Labour Party and the Danish centre-left. *The British Journal of Politics and International Relations, 14*(4), 630–650.

Potter, E.H. (2009). *Branding Canada: Projecting Canada's soft power through public diplomacy.* Montreal, QC: McGill-Queen's University Press.

Reeves, P., de Chernatony, L., & Carrigan, M. (2006). Building a political brand: Ideology or voter-driven strategy. *Brand Management, 13*(6), 418–428.

Ridout,T.N., Franz, M.M., Goldstein, K.M., & Feltus,W.J. (2012). Separation by television program: Understanding the targeting of political advertising in presidential elections. *Political Communication, 29*(1), 1–23.

Robinson, C. (2007). Images of the 2005 campaign. In S. Levin & N.S. Roberts (Eds.), *The baubles of office: The New Zealand general election of 2005* (pp. 180–196). Wellington, NZ: Victoria University Press.

Robinson, C. (2010). Political advertising and the demonstration of market orientation. *European Journal of Marketing, 44*(3/4), 451–459.

Savigny, H. (2008). *The problem of political marketing.* London, UK: Continuum.

Savigny, H., & Temple, M. (2010). Political marketing models: The curious incident of the dog that doesn't bark. *Political Studies, 58*(5), 1049–1064.

Scammell, M. (1995). *Designer politics: How elections are won.* New York, NY: St Martin's.

Scammell, M. (1999). Political marketing: Lessons for political science. *Political Studies, 47*(4), 718–739.

Shear, M. (2009, July 30). Polling helps Obama frame message in health care debate. *The Washington Post.* www.washingtonpost.com/wp-dyn/content/article/2009/07/30/AR2009073001547_2.htm

Sherman, E. (1999). Direct marketing: How does it work for political campaigns? In B.I. Newman (Ed.), *Handbook of political marketing* (pp. 265–388). London, UK: Sage.

Smith, G. (2009). Conceptualizing and testing brand personality in British politics. *Journal of Political Marketing, 8*(3), 209–232.

Smith, G., & French, A. (2009). The political brand: A consumer perspective. *Marketing Theory, 9*(2), 209–226.

Spiller, L., & Bergner, J. (2011). *Branding the candidate: Marketing strategies to win your vote.* Santa Barbara, CA: Praeger.

Steger, W.P. (1999). The permanent campaign: Marketing as a governing tool. In B.I. Newman, (Ed.), *Handbook of political marketing* (pp. 661–684). Thousand Oaks, CA: Sage.

Turow, J. (1997). *Breaking up America.* Chicago, IL: University of Chicago Press.

Ubertaccio, P. (2009). Network marketing and American political parties. In D.W. Johnson (Ed.), *The Routledge handbook of political management* (pp. 509–523). New York, NY: Routledge.

Ubertaccio, P.N. (2012). Political parties and direct marketing: Connecting voters and candidates more effectively. In J. Lees-Marshment (Ed.), *The Routledge handbook of political marketing* (pp. 177–189). London, UK: Routledge.

Van Aelst, P., van Holsteyn, J., & Koole, R. (2012). Party members as part-time marketers: Using relationship marketing to demonstrate the importance of rank-and-file party members in election campaigns. In J. Lees-Marshment (Ed.), *The Routledge handbook of political marketing* (pp. 151–163). London, UK: Routledge.

Watkins, L.M. (2012, October 26). Big Bird, binders, and bayonets: Psychographic marketing and the 2012 presidential election. *The Grio, MSNBC.* http://thegrio.com/2012/10/26/big-bird-binders-and-bayonets-psychographic-marketing-and-the-2012-presidential-election/

Worlu, R.E. (2011). *Marketing strategies of Nigerian political parties: A comparative analysis.* Berlin, DE: LAP LAMBERT Academic Publishing.

Wring, D. (2005). *The politics of marketing of the Labour Party.* Hampshire, UK: Palgrave Macmillan.

2

THE EMERGENCE OF VOTERS TARGETING

Learning to Send the Right Message to the Right Voters

Michael John Burton and Tasha Miracle

Overview of the Topic

A dozen or more campaign manuals offer to guide strategists through the process of sending the right message to the right voter. To learn about targeting neighborhoods, mailboxes, or individual voters, strategists might read Catherine Shaw's *The Campaign Manager* (2014) or John Klemanski and David Dulio's *The Mechanics of State Legislative Campaigns* (2005), both of which offer step-by-step instructions. Alternatively, the work can be outsourced to a professional. Consultants with a knack for targeting often specialize in survey research, direct mail, or statistical modeling. Old-style party bosses would not recognize a political marketplace filled with independent professionals and trained amateurs. Voter targeting is still learnable at party headquarters by working with a field coordinator—but in a time when campaigns are run by consultants and when candidates hire their own teams, burgeoning experts need not apprentice themselves to party officials.

Voter targeting is the process of subsetting an electorate according to politically salient characteristics and reaching out to groups that comprise high concentrations of receptive voters. If many voters on one side of town tend to be more persuadable than their neighbors down the road, a campaign will have little reason to spend time and money reaching out to everyone. Resources are better spent contacting only those voters who are open to the campaign's message. By ignoring less persuadable neighborhoods, a political analyst hopes to increase the efficiency of campaign outreach and decrease the cost of gaining new votes.

Targeting therefore involves two major components: finding voters amenable to the campaign's message and selectively reaching out to those voters. The basic arithmetic is straightforward. Given some collection of constraints, a campaign should maximize the number of votes gained per unit of expenditure (see Burton 2012; Green & Gerber 2008). A subsetting scheme must be developed—precinct lines are commonly used—and for each subset (e.g., each precinct) and outreach program (e.g., direct mailing), a strategist might estimate the possible effect (perhaps from some combination of survey research, precinct analysis, and gut instinct, or in recent years, complex data modeling). Subsets can then be ranked according to the expected cost of gaining votes in each one, with the subsets offering the least expensive votes given highest priority. The strategist would use the priority listing as the basis for outreach. Ideally, the message would be matched to the subsets.

There is virtually no difference between an abstract scholarly account written by an econometrician in the mid 1960s and a comprehensive treatment from a political practitioner more than 40 years later (compare Kramer 1966; Malchow 2008). What *has* changed is the sophistication of targeting models and the application of those models. Political-economic theories of "rent" help illustrate these changes.

Rent is unwarranted privilege. In politics, it can be seen in quasi-monopolistic control over resources like campaign contributions, access to loyal supporters and activists, and strategic know-how. So long as practical knowledge about targeted voter outreach is retained within political organizations, party officials can enjoy unwarranted privilege in the electoral system. But if strategic knowledge finds its way to the public domain, privilege dissipates—as indeed party officials lost power when they were forced to rely on volunteers and outside consultants. While the "trade secrets" of targeting were never fully hidden, the past half-century has seen a diffusion of strategic know-how that diminished much of the parties' influence.

Until the 1950s, the two major American parties could exercise market privilege by restricting access to political resources—a manageable task at a time when electoral politics was largely constituted by personal relationships. But as old political ties frayed and a more depersonalized politics emerged, the parties were forced to rely on outsiders, both professionals and amateurs. This phenomenon will be illustrated by the parties' publication of their own targeting advice, the efforts of ambitious women to accelerate dispersion of that information, and the rise of political "microtargeting" as a distinct category of political marketing.

The role of voter targeting in American politics is important to a full understanding of contemporary political marketing. Without a political marketplace that is roughly accessible to the general citizenry, there is no political marketing—at least, not in the way current scholars use the term, with political actors functioning like businesses (Lees-Marshment 2009: 28)—so research into the way voter targeting helped undermine the monopoly position of American party organizations can perhaps offer scholars a deeper view into the development of political markets in other democratic societies.

Review of Previous Literature

Building a literature on targeting is important because strategic voter selection and outreach targeting are central to modern electioneering. In a typical electorate, only a fraction of prospective voters are open to a campaign's message. Most people are set in their ways. They are going to vote or not; they are going to be supportive or not. If, say, only 5 percent of voters are ready to listen, then contacting everyone means 95 percent waste. Finding the right voters but sending the wrong message can be equally wasteful. For practitioners, not knowing how to target voters risks crippling inefficiency. For scholars, not knowing how targeting expertise has evolved can result in a merely partial understanding of a changing political marketplace, whereas research into this key element of political marketing can show how targeting helped to erode the privileged position of political parties in the American system.

The transformation of major political party organizations is well studied (see Mayhew 1986; Cohen et al. 2001). While the parties have always lacked cohesion (see Key 1942), in the 1970s scholars began to argue that the loose hierarchies were loosening further. Morris Fiorina later summarized the main thrust of the "decline of parties" literature: the party structures were "deteriorating, decomposing, and disappearing" (Fiorina 2002: 94). Change has been attributed to the end of spoils politics, the introduction of the Australian ballot, and the selection of candidates through primaries and caucuses. Shifting partisan alignments led to a decreased role for partisan cues and the increased impact of political messages. Each of these changes undermined the privileged position of party officials who once managed organizations largely constituted by personal relationships, not so dependent upon message-based targeting.

In the 1990s, scholars saw the parties changing yet again, and as years passed they saw renewed party strength and indeed renewed partisanship (Rae 2007). Party organizations had begun to recruit candidates, provide training and "ongoing consultation," liaise with political action committees, give technical assistance, and extend "general political advice and intelligence" (Menefee-Libey 2000: 94–5)—a reorganization prompted by the "new style" of political campaigning (Agranoff 1972). Journalist Sidney Blumenthal depicted a "permanent campaign" structure rooted in the growing network of political consultancies (1980). Larry Sabato was among the first scholars to document this trend (1981); in the 2000s, abundant scholarly research concluded that parties were operating as service organizations reliant upon outside professionals (Thurber & Nelson 2000; Johnson 2013; Dulio 2004; Burton & Shea 2010). Voter targeting was not only necessary to this novel mode of electioneering; the practice was emerging as a distinct business and an essential part of the changing relationship between campaign strategists and party officials.

Most of the work on voter targeting comes in the form of instructional materials (e.g., Shaw 2014), but a growing body of research looks at the concepts behind and implications of voter targeting. Journalist Sasha Issenberg's *The Victory Lab* (2012) shows how social science research is deployed by targeting professionals, while political analyst Nate Silver's *The Signal and the Noise* (2012) demystifies predictive analytics. A number of scholarly works straddle the divide between operations and academics (Kramer 1966; Burton 2012; Burton & Shea 2010; Klemanski & Dulio 2005; Strachan 2003). The most comprehensive version of this approach is from Kosuke Imai and Aaron Strauss (2011), who illustrate how a practitioner might build a targeting model that incorporates randomized, controlled experimentation (see also Green and Gerber 2008). Paul Baines has shown how voter targeting results from a process that combines information like historical data, internal records, and demographics to identify voting groups of interest to the campaign (1999). In *The Problem of Political Marketing*, Heather Savigny (2008) expressed a concern shared by many observers that narrow targeting leaves untargeted voters out of the political discussion.

The present research attempts to fill gaps in the literature on voter targeting and political marketing by placing the activity into an established theory of markets—"rent-seeking" and "rent-dissipation." It explores the role of outside professionals and trained amateurs as well as the growing availability of open-source guidance that helped undermine traditional party monopolies.

Theoretical Framework

Social scientists are familiar with political-economic theories of "rent-seeking": If one group restricts access to a valued resource, the price of the resource will be heightened and profits will redound to the resource-holder even when no new value is produced (Tullock 1967; Krueger 1974). The resource in question might be land—hence the reference to "rent"—or it could be regulatory favor, accreditation, or practical expertise. In the age of trade guilds, novices endured painstaking apprenticeships in order to join an exclusive class of artisans, but once accepted into the fold they could reap the rewards of membership. Unevenly distributed resources distort the market. If the marketplace is political and the resource is strategic know-how, then market distortions can amount to anti-democratic practices: gated pockets of society retaining both political power and the means of acquiring it.

Theories of rent-seeking behavior have been used to explain economic stagnation (Posner 1975) and social inequality (Stiglitz 2012). In politics, the theory has been widely employed to explain relationships among office-holders, lobbyists, voters, and commercial industries (see McChesney 1987). Rent-seeking also illuminates the marketing of candidates and policies. Kai Konrad has examined rent-based campaign promises (2004), while Roger Congleton, who notes that "[p]olitical contests have all the usual characteristics of rent-seeking games" (1986: 249), has applied the framework to elections. Building on Gerald Kramer's (1966) decision-theoretic approach to voter targeting, Congleton showed how competitive political advertising can sum to zero effect, with ads from Candidate A canceling out ads from Candidate B and vice versa. The more efficient the targeting, Congleton argues, the more true is this principle of mutual cancellation (261).

While "rent" theory is burdened by an antiquated lexicon—"privilege" might be the better term—the conceptual framework, which goes to possession of a valuable resource, is instructive: for campaign professionals, practical know-how is a resource worth guarding. In a matter of months, a campaign organization will be established, reach full capacity over a wide range of functions, complete its mission, and then close its books shortly after Election Day. There is little opportunity to learn from mistakes. A skilled commercial marketing professional can be flummoxed by the tight budgets and quick deadlines of a political campaign, the need to gain a majority market share, constant threats of blowback, unique legal and normative rules, and "consumer" demands unlike those in the commercial sphere. So long as party organizations retain targeting knowledge within their ranks, the political marketplace will be distorted and party regulars will hold privileged positions in it.

The bosses might have preferred to keep targeting wisdom behind the doors of party headquarters, but competitive barriers are contingent upon conditions, and conditions change.

Old-style targeting was transaction based. It took the form of personal contact and material benefit, and political privilege was maintained by protecting trade secrets and keeping the gates of electoral politics. The shift toward message-based voter targeting came with the rise of electronic communications, computational power, and political diversity. In the 1950s, television demanded advertising professionals who knew their own craft; women, minorities, and young people were joining political campaigns; and, as computers progressed and data accumulated, strategists could "slice and dice" ever narrower groups of voters, though few party officials would have possessed the expertise required to run digital systems. The parties were compelled to cede a measure of authority to professionals and amateurs, and once this had happened, the outsiders started running campaigns based on targeted messaging, which further undermined party advantage.

From a macro-level view, a gradual dispersion of political power can be seen in three events that helped dissipate the parties' ability to monopolize campaign know-how and to control entry into the system: (1) the publication of campaign advice, which reflected the loosening of party ties; (2) the involvement of women in electoral politics, an example of halting democratization; and (3) the rise of voter targeting, including microtargeting, as a new category in the business of political marketing (see Figure 2.1). Loosened social and party ties meant that campaigns needed to rely on outsiders for partisan activities, and the resulting publication of targeting advice moved this skill into the public domain. Later, pressure to diversify political power combined with the proliferation of targeting guidance and the consequent widespread availability of targeting expertise meant that women, for example, could learn the campaign craft. Finally, new computational resources—in terms of data and the processing of data, along with narrow-gauge outreach channels (like automated phone calls, emails, and person-to-person contacts)—gave rise to a new class of microtargeting professionals. Traditional party privilege was crowded out by new ways of doing business.

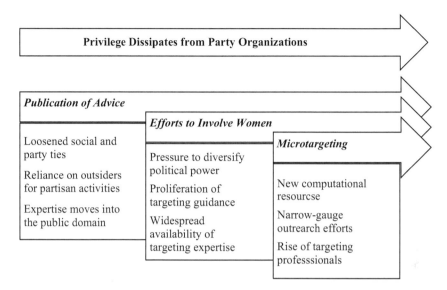

FIGURE 2.1 Transformation of Political Marketplace

From a micro-level viewpoint, the calculation that drove the big-picture shift is clear-cut business economics. Individual strategists need not look at the grand scheme, just the costs and benefits applicable to their own campaigns. When the cost of targeting was high (as it was when data, computing, and targeted messaging were expensive) but the benefit of message delivery was low (as it was when personal relationships, not campaign messages, were the key to victory), there was little point to undertaking a comprehensive voter-targeting program. But as the costs of data and computing fell and as voters became more amenable to political messaging, targeting became an increasingly viable option (see Figure 2.2).

Hence, macro- and micro-level forces worked side by side to simultaneously increase the value of voter targeting and dissipate old party privileges—not by grand design, but as an unintended consequence of countless individual efforts to maximize the value of voter outreach.

Empirical Illustrations

If outsiders can learn about voter targeting from a book, a party boss is going to lose a degree of authority; if new players—women, for example—are brought into the targeting game, the old-boy network will lose more ground; and if the process of targeting becomes so technical that it requires an advanced degree in statistics, mathematics, or a related field (as new forms of targeting often do), then these talents generate a workable business proposition outside direct party control.

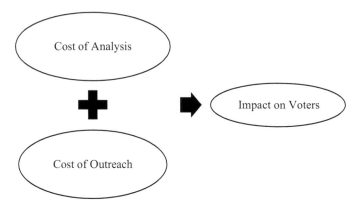

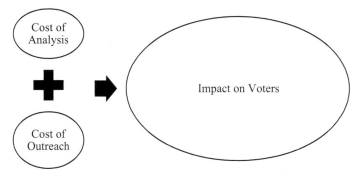

FIGURE 2.2 Increasing Value of Voter Targeting

Loosening of Party Ties: Publication of Campaign Advice

Post-war America saw fundamental social changes that would enhance the need for calculated messaging strategies. As the country became more mobile and old ties began to unwind, television picked up some of the slack. Dwight D. Eisenhower, himself an outsider to the party system, employed advertising executive Rosser Reeves to produce the first television commercial run in a presidential campaign. The sheer cost of television advertising made efficient targeting essential. Of course, party regulars were familiar neither with media production nor with buying the time slots that would maximize the effectiveness of commercials. Moreover, old strategies seemed to be losing relevance as scholars were reporting social fragmentation and as critics were bemoaning increased depersonalization and a concomitant reliance on mass communications. Changing conditions demanded new approaches and new players—some of them skilled professionals in other industries, like Rosser Reeves, and others of them rank amateurs who would need to learn the political craft from start to finish.

John F. Kennedy responded to the challenge by developing a novel approach to voter targeting. Instead of consulting old-timers and making the right connections, the Kennedy operation mapped concentrations of persuadable voters. Legendary Boston pol Tip O'Neill later wrote, "I had never seen anybody studying the voting patterns of ethnic and religious groups in a systematic way before" (O'Neill & Novak 1987: 86). In 1958, only a dozen years after the advent of programmable electronic computers, Kennedy's operation was churning out poll-driven simulations in an effort to find useful subsetting schemes (Issenberg 2012). Kennedy's approach lacked the personal touch that Bostonians knew so well, but the process that would later be called "analytics" was well suited to media-driven politics and it would set the tone for the future of political marketing.

Not only was Kennedy developing new computational tactics, he was assimilating amateurs into his campaign by reducing folkways to writing. Many of Kennedy's loyalists were trained by veteran Democrat Larry O'Brien, who assembled campaign procedures into "several mimeographed sheets stapled together" (O'Brien 1986: 22). The "O'Brien Manual" would become the standard guidebook for campaign training when it was published under the title *The Democratic Campaign Manual, 1964* (Democratic National Committee 1964). By 1972, O'Brien had become chairman of the DNC, and the new version of his manual was far more detailed than its predecessors, with a strong focus on voter targeting (Democratic National Committee 1972). In addition to instruction on the use of computers (which tracked voters on punch cards), the 1972 *Manual* detailed the use of precinct-level vote calculations, survey research, and demographic analysis.

Worksheets and sample maps explained the procedures. The book's discussion of "Past Vote Information" came closest to contemporary microtargeting techniques. Aggregate registration and vote counts were used to reveal hidden, but calculable, information about subsets of the electorate. A precinct or county, it was assumed, would likely vote in the next election in numbers roughly equal to past elections. It will also have something like the same number of voters casting ballots for Democrats and for Republicans. Some parts of an electorate, however, may be less predictable—not solidly Republican or Democratic. A candidate, the *Manual* advises, "should have his staff prepare a detailed study of the demographic characteristics of the marginal and weak-Democratic, weak-Republican regions" (41). (The same may be said for areas where a strong candidate occasionally gains votes from members of the other party.) Outreach follows: "He will want to allot more of his media money and staff resources . . . to these decisive centers. In the high Democratic areas, the candidate will want to develop a strong organization to get out the vote on election day" (ibid.).

O'Brien's guidebook was written for outsiders. As O'Brien later recalled, "[O]f all of these people who were volunteering to help Jack Kennedy there wasn't one, probably, in fifty who had ever been active in politics. What do you do with these people?" (O'Brien 1986: 22). Written guidance was part of the answer for Democrats. Likewise, the Republican National Committee produced "Campaign Seminars" made up of "ten self-contained pamphlets" on each of several campaign functions (Bosley 2000: 60). State parties were replicating this effort (60–2).

The *Manual* was widely published in the United States and abroad, but one downside of publishing strategic and tactical advice is that adversaries also gain access to the information. O'Brien would later report that GOP senator Barry Goldwater, by his own account, "had followed the Kennedy campaign procedure throughout[;] he and his people had carefully reviewed the so-called O'Brien manual and had implemented it in all respects" during Goldwater's 1964 bid for the presidency (O'Brien 1986: 2).

Variants on O'Brien's targeting procedure became a regular feature of campaign manuals. In the 1980s, a growing line of works such as Ann Beaudry and Bob Schaeffer's *Winning Local and State Elections* (1986) outlined targeting methods similar to those found in the 1972 *Manual*, as did other practitioner-oriented publications. *Campaigns & Elections*, a magazine established in 1980 to serve the growing community of political marketers, edited a guide to electioneering that featured comprehensive instructions on targeting (Fishel 1998a, 1998b). Knowledge of how to target voters was working its way into the public domain.

Halting Democratization: Involving Women

At the end of the 1960s, many politically involved women were helping men get elected rather than spending time getting *themselves* elected. The bulk of campaign know-how was still held within old-boy networks, and while publications like the 1964 O'Brien *Manual* offered advice, unless this sort of guidance was actually in the hands of women it would not be terribly useful. Additionally, learning the craft of electioneering might require more than generic manuals; without mentors and trainers, book knowledge about voter targeting may prove incomplete.

Moreover, women seemed to face unique challenges, many of which persist to the present day. Scholarly research has shown that women are typically responsible for family caregiving, tend to worry about the kinds of media coverage that follow women candidates, and believe they are less likely to raise sufficient funds and less likely to win election (see Lawless & Fox 2010). Women who embark on campaigns tend to be older than their male counterparts and they can expect to have their attire, hairstyle, make-up, and jewelry scrutinized. Kelly Dittmar has argued that "gender is not only embedded in expectations for and behavior of candidates, but also influences the psyche and strategic considerations of all those involved" (2012: 1). (Even today, the proportion of women in elective office remains well below their share of the American electorate [Current Numbers of Women Officeholders 2012].)

One of the most important efforts to expand awareness of voter targeting among women came in a series of tightly scripted "institutes" run by the bipartisan National Women's Education Fund (NWEF) in the mid to late 1970s. From an internal report on a pair of multi-day training sessions: "In March, eighty upper Midwestern women participated in a Milwaukee Institute, and in July, 120 Southeastern women came to the Atlanta Institute. These women are in turn expected to reach hundreds more through dissemination of workshop concepts and techniques in their local associations" (National Women's Education Fund 1974: 1). NWEF training was a routinized, nationwide effort to find, educate, and elect women of both major parties, and some of the most technical elements of the training went to procedures that reiterate the same targeting principles expounded by other campaign manuals.

In 1978, the NWEF published its *Campaign Workbook*. The *Workbook* argued that voter targeting is the "most important research tool that the campaign will develop" (National Women's Education Fund 1978: 2-1). Other campaign manuals written by and for women followed. Cathy Allen's *Political Campaigning* (1990) is typical in its dedication "[t]o the Women Who Run[,] and the Women and Men Who Support Them." Christine Pelosi wrote her *Campaign Boot Camp* (2007) for anyone who wanted to become a leader, even "a young mom leafleting your neighborhood" (6). These manuals tend to have a more personal flare than guidebooks written by men, often punctuating advice with personal anecdotes. (One woman-authored book devoted a chapter to "Dealing with Emotions" [Guber 1997: 149–52].)

Among the most comprehensive manuals published by any expert, man or woman, is Catherine Shaw's *The Campaign Manager* (2014). Shaw's book is filled with technical detail aimed at solving problems that might challenge candidates who have not grown up in a political culture. *The Campaign Manager* includes step-by-step instructions on creating spreadsheets and provides user-friendly formulas to calculate voter propensities. Shaw's description of professional microtargeting carries an air of suspicion: a candidate looking to target voters will find in *The Campaign Manager* a do-it-yourself system that, Shaw suggests, may yield votes more cost effectively than a system purchased from a high-cost consultancy (5–6).

Cathy Allen's *Taking Back Politics* (1996) was written for a general audience, but her earlier work, *Political Campaigning* (1990), published by the National Women's Political Caucus, was directed to women. Allen discussed the "gender gap" and furnished advice on how women should reach out to demographically distinct groups of voters (including women voters). Allen gave blunt counsel: Rather than dwelling on political obstacles and worrying about sexism, women should "identify votes they can WIN, and then go out and positively and aggressively court them" (220). Cleverness counts. Some of the men who might otherwise be put off by a woman's strong ideals will not even notice woman-centered messages if voters are targeted by direct mail, and indeed, "Like many conversations among ourselves, 'women's issues' often go unheard by, or remain invisible to, most men" (221).

One side of targeting strategy is finding the right voters; the other is sending the right message. Pelosi has made clear that a candidate's sartorial fashion should be chosen according to the venue in which it is to be worn (2007: 118). Former state legislator Susan Guber's *How to Win Your 1st Election* emphasized the importance of dressing appropriately, noting the colors and types of dresses and skirts that she herself wore on the campaign trail (1997: 95–7). Shaw, another elected official turned advisor, warned that women with young children are often viewed differently than their male counterparts; a female candidate with children by her side is much more likely to be frowned upon than a male candidate with kids (Shaw 2014: 256).

Because women candidates have to manage expectations in order to avoid unnecessary roadblocks, Jewel Lansing writes:

> Male political consultants say a candidate has only two roles during a campaign—raising money and meeting voters. A woman candidate has a third role, though: preparing herself to be an authority, an expert, on major issues which arise during the campaign as well as two or three issues she can claim for her own. (1991: 96)

The reason, according to Lansing, goes partly to experience (or lack of it). "To gain needed self-confidence, women need to feel qualified," Lansing says, "to be an expert, an authority" (97).

The spirit of mass publication expanded beyond books like Lansing's *101 Campaign Tips for Women Candidates and Their Staffs* (1991) and into graduate programs, one-off workshops, and seminars that explained the art and science of electioneering to future strategists, male and female. Clearly, when the basic formulas, and the practical application of those formulas, are made available to anyone willing to learn, then whatever secrecy might once have accompanied the art of voter targeting has disappeared. But even if the parties lost their privileged position and the political marketplace has been flattening, the value of an efficient, proprietary approach to targeting has not disappeared. There is always demand for new and better ways to target voters. This evolving need would be filled by the new business of microtargeting.

Vendable Expertise: The Rise of a Business Category

The arithmetic presented in most campaign manuals requires little more than high school math, and sometimes it suffered from vagueness. In many early works on electoral campaigns, targeting procedures would need to be teased out of the text if they were to be operationalized. Where they were specific, they were simplified. Durable precinct lines made for stable models and the complications entailed by combinatorial subsetting and comparative costing were not always considered. By keeping the number of variables low and the subset boundaries fixed, the thumbnail models sketched in published guidebooks have been able to streamline the potentially byzantine calculus of voter targeting.

The core problem of advanced voter targeting is the so-called "curse of dimensionality": A handful of variables easily renders millions of targeting options. The challenge is not so much that of sorting through all possible combinations as it is finding clever ways to build models that maximize (or at least optimize) the number of votes gained for a given investment. Ideally, such a task draws on statisticians, mathematicians, experts in machine learning, and data engineers. These are skills not typically developed within the confines of party organizations.

Credit for developing microtargeted outreach is often given to the 2004 presidential campaign of George W. Bush (Sosnik et al. 2007). In the 2010s, partisans on the right side of the aisle could avail themselves of services rendered by TargetPoint, a business formed by veteran GOP operative Alexander Gage, while politically progressive campaigns could work with Catalist, which offered, among other services, an "Analytics Export of over 700 fields of commercial, census, and synthetic data, so that clients (and their consultants) may build their own custom models" (Catalist n.d.). Both companies (and their competitors) have developed proprietary procedures meant to increase target efficiency.

In addition to firms that specialize in generating models are those that sell richly augmented electoral databases and the tools needed to manage them. A campaign interested in sending narrowly tailored messages can select from among hundreds of variables to extract a small set of voters who might be ready to hear its message. And the "Big Data" approach, when applied to phone calls and fieldwork, can function both ways: data can inform the voter contact process, and the data gained from the act of contacting voters can then be added to the database in an ongoing data cycle. While the idea of a continuous loop often works best as an abstract notion—the reality of merging, purging, and updating campaign datasets can be daunting—progress in data hygiene and integration, as well as model optimization, seems to be lifting campaign strategists closer to the ideal.

Of course, campaigns have used demographics, survey research, and vote histories for decades—in this sense, microtargeting is a mere refinement of past tactics, even as microtargeting professionals are now adding consumer-preference data from third-party vendors to the mix. A key difference between the old and new ways is that contemporary microtargeters generate computational models by compounding otherwise discrete data points. The transition from survey samples and aggregated data to individualized voter scores is intended to help campaigns send more and more precisely tuned messages to smaller and smaller subsets of the electorate.

Statistical and computer sciences offer a variety of procedures for subsetting an electorate, including supervised and unsupervised algorithms. Unsupervised algorithms look for common characteristics among members of a population. For example, if voters are arrayed over a two-dimensional ideological space representing views on the economy and social issues, an unsupervised algorithm might work up from the data points to discover clusters and then carve the space accordingly (see Figure 2.3). Supervised algorithms, by contrast, start with a variable of interest such as voter partisanship and then segment the electorate according to values associated with the variable. For example, with a decision-tree algorithm, the whole population might be split according to household income. Low-income voters, in turn, might be split by population density, with urban low-income voters siding with the Democratic Party and rural low-income voters allied with the Republicans. High-income voters might split between social conservatives who go with the GOP and social liberals who are more undecided (see Figure 2.4).

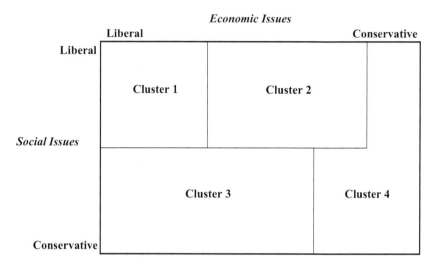

FIGURE 2.3 Unsupervised Learning

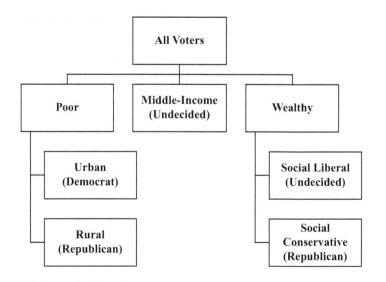

FIGURE 2.4 Supervised Learning

In the 1980s and 1990s, computer scientists were hacking at algorithms that could subset data in meaningful ways, few of which were computationally feasible when Kennedy's team was running electoral simulations. By the 2010s, a strategist on a statewide political campaign may or may not know the difference between supervised and unsupervised algorithms or how to interpret a metric called a "Receiver Operating Characteristic Curve"—but this lack of expertise is inconsequential because the job of choosing between, say, a random forest algorithm and a support vector machine can be relegated to outside professionals.

Conclusions for Research and Practice

The latest advances in voter targeting come from the 2012 presidential campaign of Barack Obama. While Obama's effort in 2008 was acclaimed for its innovative use of social media, microtargeting, and continually updated databases, his 2012 campaign would, in many ways, reinvent the data-informed approach to electioneering. In the summer of 2011, the Obama team was advertising on technology blogs to find savvy data personnel who might help it marry technical and political expertise. The result was a massive strategic operation housed in an office dubbed "The Cave"—a $25 million investment that pumped data through a continuous feedback loop of inputs and outputs geared to maximize the efficiency of campaign expenditures (Alter 2013: 100). Political commentator Jonathan Alter has remarked, "Obama's reelection campaign was like running for Chicago alderman over and over with the help of nerdy kids who spoke a math language no one else understood" (2013: 98).

While Obama's "cave-dwellers" were at the forefront of voter targeting in 2012, their core principles have a long history, even if campaign guidebooks were once concerned with the major parties. In 1934, Michael H. Judge published a thin pamphlet called *Election Day Strategy*. Part of his book offered chestnuts of advice; the rest gave reasons for backing the Democratic Party. In 1946, John L. East published a *Republican Precinct Worker's Handbook*, which, like Judge's work, took an activist's partisanship for granted. Readers of the 1964 version of the *Democratic Campaign Manual* found stirring words from the president of the United States and the chairman of the Democratic National Committee, along with an admonition that "co-operating with existing Democratic Party leadership is mandatory" (front matter).

Strategic voter selection also has historical roots, and the task has often been handed to outsiders. William McKinley's key strategist, Mark Hanna, used his business experience to reach distinct sectors of the electorate with custom messages. Richard Nixon's core team included H. R. Haldeman, who, like Rosser Reeves, entered politics from the advertising industry. In the run-up to the 1960 presidential campaign, Haldeman wanted to recruit a group of young ("approximately 30–40"), dedicated, geographically diverse men to be trained in workshops (Haldeman 1959b) and given an instructional manual (Haldeman 1959a).

"Political experience," Haldeman wrote, was "helpful but not necessary" (ibid.). A 1967 manual from Haldeman included an "Advance Man Check List" that commanded operatives to make sure pre-event publicity would include stories of interest to "workers" as well as a "women's angle" (Haldeman n.d.: 53–7).

In 1969, the Research Division of the Republican National Committee produced a technical manual on voter targeting that linked demographic and electoral analysis to voter outreach (Republican National Committee 1969). In *Vote History and Demographic Analysis* (a publication that "corresponds to Electronic Data Processing Technical Manual No. 4" [cover page]) operatives learned that "[t]he campaign manager must have a basic formula established by previous vote statistics to effectively guide his candidate into the most productive areas" (42). Computers were important to the process: "This is especially true ... when making multivariate priority listings (i.e., obtaining the right combination of factors, performing various rankings in descending order, etc.)" (36). Demographic factors to be gleaned from census data included "median education, median family income, median male and female ages, owner occupancy of the dwelling unit, and ethnic origin" (47). The authors of the 1969 Republican manual seemed to glimpse the future of data modeling.

Mapping electoral landscapes and reaching out to subsets of the electorate led to an expanded circle of campaign professionals. Proliferating campaign manuals, many of them written by women, dissipated some of the parties' old privilege. Outsiders who have developed contemporary voter targeting systems and businesses built on analytic operations each have an incentive to work closely with, but maintain distance from, party organizations. Overall, recognizing the importance of targeting know-how in a time of depersonalized politics has resulted in a slow, incomplete opening of the political marketplace.

For practitioners, the value of published advice is obvious. Conservative Peter J. Fusco, in *Running: How to Design and Execute a Winning Political Campaign*, frankly admits, "I robbed as much material as I could from successful Democratic strategists" (2010: iv). The availability of campaign advice lets partisans of any stripe adopt knowledge generated by competitors. Hal Malchow, who has worked with Democrats, shared targeting formulas in *The New Political Targeting* and on a CD-ROM that accompanied his book (2008). Operatives can map their own data on Malchow's spreadsheets. The idea that candidates should do the math of their districts has long occupied campaign manuals, but an entire book on the topic, complete with user-friendly software, shows the deepening technical detail available to up-and-coming professionals or to citizens who want to learn voter targeting.

For scholars, the history of targeting casts new light on the development of a political marketplace. While women and minorities still face unfair challenges and still run for office in disproportionately low numbers, strategic literacy has been gradually undermining old-boy networks, including those entrenched in political party organizations. Further, the rise of targeting allowed professional strategists to build operations that are (1) critical to campaigns, and (2) largely outside the party organizations. Because marketing requires an open market, the dissipation of political privilege by releasing practical knowledge on political targeting to amateurs and professionals in the United States may well illuminate the manner in which political markets can emerge elsewhere.

Whatever the context, virtually all published campaign guidebooks agree on basic principles: The electorate should be broken down into groups and prioritized by levels of support, persuadability, likelihood of mobilization, and even cost of outreach; volunteers are critical to this effort; voters need to be contacted with messages they will actually hear. Campaigns should target swing voters for persuasion and base voters for mobilization. That is to say, the basic arithmetic of voter targeting is trivial and has not changed over time. Nothing in the introduction of high-performance computing has altered the fundamental algorithm.

References

Agranoff, R. (1972). *The new style in election campaigns.* Boston, MA: Holbrook Press.
Allen, C. (1990). *Political campaigning: A new decade.* Seattle, WA: National Women's Political Caucus.
Allen, C. (1996). *Taking back politics: An insider's guide to winning.* Seattle, WA: Jalapeno Press.
Alter, J. (2013). *The center holds: Obama and his enemies.* New York, NY: Simon & Schuster.
Baines, P. (1999). Voter segmentation and candidate positioning. In B.I. Newman (Ed.), *Handbook of political marketing* (pp. 403–420). Thousand Oaks, CA: Sage Publications.
Beaudry, A., & Schaeffer, B. (1986). *Winning local and state elections.* New York, NY: Free Press.
Blumenthal, S. (1980). *The permanent campaign.* New York, NY: Simon and Schuster.
Bosley, G. O. (2000). *Campaigning to win: A manual for conservatives.* San Leandro, CA: Smart Local Politics Publications.
Burton, M.J. (2012). Strategic voter selection. In J. Lees-Marshment (Ed.), *Routledge handbook of political marketing* (pp. 34–47). London, UK: Routledge.
Burton, M.J. & Shea, D. M. (2010). *Campaign craft: The strategies, tactics, and art of political campaign management.* Santa Barbara, CA: Praeger/ABC-CLIO.
Catalist. (n. d.). www.catalist.us/product
Cohen, J. E., Fleisher, R., & Kantor, P. (2001). *American political parties: Decline or resurgence?* Washington, DC: CQ Press.
Congleton, R. (1986). Rent-seeking aspects of political advertising. *Public Choice, 49*(3), 249–263.
Current Numbers of Women Officeholders (2012). Available from www.cawp.rutgers.edu/fast_facts/levels_of_office/Current_Numbers.php
Democratic National Committee. (1964). *Democratic Campaign Manual, 1964.* Washington, DC: Author.
Democratic National Committee. (1972). *Democratic Campaign Manual, 1972.* Washington, DC: Author.
Dittmar, K. E. (2012). *Campaigns as gendered institutions: Stereotypes and strategy in statewide races.* (Unpublished doctoral dissertation). Rutgers University, New Brunswick, NJ.

Dulio, D. A. (2004). *For better or worse?: How political consultants are changing elections in the United States.* Albany, NY: State University of New York Press.
East, J. L. (1946). *Republican precinct worker's handbook.* Washington, DC: National Precinct Workers.
Fiorina, M. P. (2002). Parties and partisanship: A 40-year retrospective. *Political Behavior, 24*(2), 93–115.
Fishel, M. (1998a). Electoral targeting, part I: Do-it-yourself. In R. Faucheux (Ed.), *The road to victory: The complete guide to winning political campaigns—Local, state and federal* (pp. 171–180). Dubuque, IA: Kendall Hunt Publishing Company.
Fishel, M. (1998b). Electoral targeting, part II: Analyzing the data. In R. Faucheux (Ed.), *The road to victory: The complete guide to winning political campaigns—Local, state and federal* (pp. 181–203). Dubuque, IA: Kendall Hunt Publishing Company.
Fusco, P. J. (2010). *Running: How to design and execute a winning political campaign.* Schenectady, NY: CreateSpace.
Green, D. P., & Gerber, A. S. (2008). *Get out the vote: How to increase voter turnout.* Washington, DC: Brookings Institution Press.
Guber, S. (1997). *How to win your 1st election.* Boca Raton, FL: St. Lucie Press.
Haldeman, H. R. (1959a). Letter from H. R. Haldeman to Robert Finch. November 18, 1959, Haldeman Personal, Box 1:6, HRH Series: I, Campaigns, Richard M. Nixon Library.
Haldeman, H. R. (1959b). Political Advance Man Organization: 1960 recommendations. November 18, 1959, Haldeman Personal, Box 1:6, HRH Series: I Campaigns, Richard M. Nixon Library.
Haldeman, H. R. (N. d.) The Advance Man's manual. Advance Man Material, Box 2:12, HRH Series: I Campaign, Richard M. Nixon Library.
Imai, K., & Strauss, A. (2011). Estimation of heterogeneous treatment effects from randomized experiments, with application to the optimal planning of the get-out-the-vote campaign. *Political Analysis, 19*(1), 1–19.
Issenberg, S. (2012). *The victory lab: The secret science of winning campaigns.* New York, NY: Crown Publishing Group.
Johnson, D. W. (2013). *No place for amateurs: How political consultants are reshaping American democracy.* New York, NY: Taylor & Francis.
Judge, M. H. (1934). *Election day strategy.* Mishawaka, IN: M.B. Tarman.
Key, V. O. (1942). *Politics, parties, and pressure groups.* New York, NY: Crowell.
Klemanski, J. S., & Dulio, D. A. (2005). *The mechanics of state legislative campaigns.* Belmont, CA: Thomson Wadsworth.
Konrad, K. (2004). Inverse campaigning. *Economic Journal, 114*(492), 69–82.
Kramer, G. (1966). A decision-theoretic analysis of a problem in political campaigning, *Mathematical applications in political science II.* Dallas, TX: Southern Methodist University Press.
Krueger, A. (1974). The political economy of the rent-seeking society. *American Economic Review, 64*(3), 291–303.
Lansing, J. B. (1991). *101 campaign tips for women candidates and their staffs.* Saratoga, CA: R & E Publishers.
Lawless, J., & Fox, R. (2010). *It still takes a candidate: Why women don't run for office.* Cambridge, UK: Cambridge University Press.
Lees-Marshment, J. (2009). *Political marketing: Principles and applications.* New York, NY: Routledge.
Malchow, H. (2008). *The new political targeting.* Washington, DC: Predicted Lists.

Mayhew, D. R. (1986). *Placing parties in American politics: Organization, electoral settings, and government activity in the twentieth century.* Princeton, NJ: Princeton University Press.

McChesney, F. (1987). Rent extraction and rent creation in the economic theory of regulation. *Journal of Legal Studies, 16*(1), 101–118.

Menefee-Libey, D. (2000). *The triumph of campaign-centered politics.* New York, NY: Chatham House Publishers.

National Women's Education Fund. (1974). Report: Campaign Techniques Institutes. NWEF Archives, Rutgers University Library.

National Women's Education Fund. (1978). *Campaign workbook.* Washington, DC: The Fund.

O'Brien, L. (1986, April 9). Transcript, Larry O'Brien oral history interview XI, by Michael L. Gillette. Available from www.lbjlib.utexas.edu/johnson/archives.hom/oralhistory.hom/obrienl/OBRIEN09.PDF

O'Neill, T., & Novak, W. (1987). *Man of the House: The life and political memoirs of Speaker Tip O'Neill.* New York, NY: Random House.

Pelosi, C. (2007). *Campaign boot camp: Basic training for future leaders.* San Francisco, CA: Berrett-Koehler Publishers.

Posner, R. A. (1975). The social costs of monopoly and regulation. *Journal of Political Economy, 83*(4), 807–827.

Rae, N. (2007). Be careful what you wish for: The rise of responsible parties in American national politics. *Annual Review of Political Science, 10*, 169–191.

Republican National Committee. (1969). *Vote history and demographic analysis: A manual for utilizing election statistics.* Washington, DC: Author.

Sabato, L. (1981). *The rise of political consultants: new ways of winning elections.* New York, NY: Basic Books.

Savigny, H. (2008). *The problem of political marketing.* New York, NY: Continuum.

Shaw, C. (2014). *The campaign manager: Running and winning local elections* (5th ed.). Boulder, CO: Westview Press.

Silver, N. (2012). *The signal and the noise: Why so many predictions fail—but some don't.* New York, NY: Penguin Press.

Sosnik, D. B., Fournier, R., & Dowd, M. J. (2007). *Applebee's America: How successful political, business, and religious leaders connect with the new American community.* New York, NY: Simon & Schuster.

Stiglitz, J. (2012). *The price of inequality.* New York, NY: Penguin Books Limited.

Strachan, J. C. (2003). *High-tech grass roots: The professionalization of local elections.* Lanham, MD: Rowman & Littlefield.

Thurber, J. A., & Nelson, C. J. (2000). *Campaign warriors: The role of political consultants in elections.* Washington, DC: Brookings Institution Press.

Tullock, G. (1967). The welfare costs of tariffs, monopolies, and theft. *Western Economic Journal, 5*(3), 224–232.

3

DATABASE POLITICAL MARKETING IN CAMPAIGNING AND GOVERNMENT

Lisa Spiller and Jeff Bergner

Overview of the Topic

Technology has long played a role in political campaigning. It has also played a role, though a lesser one, in governing. Consider this: in 1896, U.S. presidential candidate William Jennings Bryan crisscrossed America by rail, making more than 600 campaign speeches. Never before had this degree of direct outreach to voters occurred. Even still, if we make the generous assumption that each of his speeches was heard by 1,000 people, only 600,000 Americans—or 1% of the population—ever directly saw the face or heard the voice of Bryan.

The advent of radio changed all that. Radio brought the voice of the candidate directly to the people. By 1928, Republicans devoted the majority of their party's campaign publicity budget to radio (Jamieson 1992: 19–20). The full possibilities of radio were demonstrated by President Franklin Roosevelt, whose "fireside chats" brought the president directly into the living room of every American family with a radio.

But it was television that brought a new, lasting, and far deeper connection between both candidates and officials on the one hand and publics on the other. Television campaign ads aired in American presidential campaigns in 1948, 1952, and 1956. But the Nixon-Kennedy debate in 1960 displayed television's full power to create a bond between a candidate and the voters: those watching the debate on television believed overwhelmingly that Kennedy had won, whereas those listening on radio gave the nod to Nixon. Presidents regularly have utilized the power of televised Oval Office addresses to the nation ever since.

We are now in the midst of another technological revolution: the use of the Internet to forge powerful and personally targeted communications between candidates and voters. Key to this technology is the creation of extensive customer or citizen databases that permit direct marketing to occur in ever more precise and targeted ways. These databases have demonstrated their utility in many areas of political marketing, especially in campaign message delivery, fundraising, supporter mobilization, and get-out-the-vote activities. Their use in governing is a relatively new and developing field.

The importance of a customer database for marketing was recognized long ago. "As the concept of marketing has matured and as its technology has become increasingly powerful, and as marketing has become directed or targeted, databases have emerged as a characteristic and a requirement of direct marketing" (Stone 1994: 37). In fact, before the term *database marketing* was even coined its value was predicted and discussed. In the late 1980s, with more advanced database management systems came the advent of data mining where customer data could be used for estimation and prediction as well as for clarification and segmentation. Marketing databases are essential to twenty-first-century marketing and the terms *direct* and *database marketing* are often used synonymously (Stone and Jacobs 2008: 44).

The expansion of the Internet has contributed to database marketing applications becoming part of mainstream marketing applications for many political marketers—including political parties, pressure groups, and individual politicians. Many political campaigns are now integrating database marketing with web-based tools and techniques that enable these organizations to implement greater interactivity and personalization in their marketing activities.

In this chapter we will explore the uses—and some of the limitations to date—of sophisticated databases in campaigning and governing. We will do so by looking at the state-of-the-art use of campaign databases by the Obama presidential campaigns of 2008 and, to a lesser extent, 2012. We will also look at the Obama administration's use of databases in governing during its first term. We will offer conclusions and suggestions for further research.

Review of Previous Literature

The database and its many applications have become a critical asset to the decision-making of entire organizations, and its use is on the rise in political marketing (Dean and Croft 2001; McClymont and Jocumsen 2003; Granik 2005; Jackson 2005; Stanton 2006; Henneberg and O'Shaughnessy 2009; Ubertaccio 2012). Any political organization that is able effectively to create, analyze, and use its database will have a competitive advantage over those that cannot (Davenport, et al. 2010). Indeed, database marketing has altered the political marketing landscape in America over the past decade, and its strategic use is becoming a necessary component to win campaigns and to govern effectively (Sherman and Schiffman 2002; Jackson 2005; Lees-Marshment 2009).

More than two decades ago Webster (1992) proposed that the relationship marketing paradigm would redefine marketing practice and the role of marketing in the entire organization. Previous researchers have declared database marketing as an *instrument* to the conduct of relationship marketing (Das 2009; Lindgreen

2001; Dean and Croft 2001; McClymont and Jocumsen 2003; Ubertaccio 2012). Relationship marketing entails a mutual exchange and fulfillment of promises whereby relationships are established, maintained, and enhanced so that the objectives of the parties involved are met (Gronroos 1994, 1996; Harker 1999; Das 2009; Gummersson 2002). Gummersson (2002) described relationship marketing as relationships, networks, and interaction whereby the history of contact between producers and consumers is acted upon by marketers. Among the reasons why marketers place great emphasis on relationship marketing is to gain greater customer loyalty; fewer resources are needed to retain customers than are required to acquire new ones, and loyal customers tend to spread positive word-of-mouth communications (Baier, Ruf, and Chakraborty 2002; Stone and Jacobs 2008; Spiller and Baier 2012). The key technological tool that enables marketers to build and maintain long-term or lifetime customer relationships is the database (O'Malley and Mitussis 2002; Henneberg and O'Shaughnessy 2009).

The concept of building lifetime relationships with individual voters that goes beyond the basic marketing concepts of targeting groups or market segments has been gaining popularity over the years (Bruce 1992; Kavanagh 1995; Norris and Gavin 1999; Dean and Croft 2001; Gibson and Rommele 2006). However, Henneberg and O'Shaughnessy (2009: 22) claim that political relationship marketing has been neglected by theoreticians despite a 20-year publication history in this field in marketing theory. They explain that political relationship marketing must now be treated seriously because we are moving more toward value-based politics and that relational concepts are more effective to produce sustained relationships than are appeals to economic self-interest (Henneberg and O'Shaughnessy 2009: 23). In essence, political marketers are more likely to attract loyal customers or supporters if they use a need-satisfying approach as opposed to a sales approach (Morgan and Hunt 1994; Lees-Marshment 2006).

Many claim that relationship marketing in politics should not be limited to the voter or supporter, but should focus on building and maintaining relationships more broadly via a robust database (Christopher, Payne, and Ballantyne 1991; Dean and Croft, 2001; Jackson 2005). Long ago Sheth and Parvatiyar (1995) suggested that family and social norms, peer group pressures, government mandates, religious tenets, employer influences, and marketer policies are key influences on consumers to consider in relationship marketing. Empirical research results also point to the role of internal influences, such as values functional motivations, socialization, and job satisfaction, on citizens' relationship with political parties and their level of activism (Granik 2005). The Six Markets Model created by Christopher et al. (1991) overviews the role of some of the traditional stakeholders involved in the political marketing relationship—including internal markets such as influencers, potential employees, suppliers, and referral markets.

Some researchers have called for relationship marketing theories that cover all aspects of political marketing, including both campaigning and governing (Dean and Croft 2001; Lees-Marshment 2009). Indeed, academic research into political marketing has addressed both campaigning and governing for years (Butler and Collins 1994; Culver and Howe 2004; Lees-Marshment 2001; Lees-Marshment 2006; Ormrod 2006; Coleman 2007). However, until recently, most of the political relationship marketing emphasis has been on campaigning (Henneberg and O'Shaughnessy 2009).

Dean and Croft (2001) argue that relationship marketing approaches should be used both to maximize electoral participation and to legitimize the entire democratic process. Lees-Marshment (2009: 207–8) offers a step-by-step process by which political parties can use interactive marketing with constituencies to go beyond mere communication to influence product or service design. Parties that follow this process are referred to as "market-oriented parties"; these parties design their service delivery in response to voter input and aim to meet voter needs and wants when possible. Parties that typically sell what they believe to be best for their constituents without input from the citizens they are representing are labeled "sales-oriented parties." She notes that "most of the conditions in government work against fostering a market orientation and the reflection and responsiveness it requires" (Lees-Marshment 2009: 209). Long ago Newman (1999: 110) pointed out that "governing is different from being in opposition" and that a candidate's political marketing must adapt "from the campaign marketplace to the governing marketplace." Culver and Howe (2004: 52) claim that "one way some governments have responded to the heightened democratic discontent of recent years is to seek greater input from citizens in the policy-making process in large-scale public consultations."

Although there are numerous studies of the evolution of campaign and governance strategies in the United States (Jamieson 1992; Quelch and Jocz 2007; Kenski, Hardy, and Jamieson 2010), there is very little material, other than anecdotal work, that explores in depth the Obama campaign's or administration's creation and use of databases for relationship marketing. Plouffe (2009) provides the best overall account of the Obama 2008 campaign's strategies and tactics, while Harfoush (2009) overviews the use of databases and social media. The creators of the database have, for understandable reasons, not spoken publicly about their enterprise.

Theoretical Framework

Scholars have developed several models by which to understand the use of marketing in political campaigns and governing, such as the Multiple Markets Model (Dean and Croft 2001); the Market-Oriented Party (MOP) Model (Lees-Marshment 2001); the Political Market Orientation Model (Ormrod 2005); the Political Marketing Process Model (Spiller and Bergner 2011: 169); the Multiple Market Model for Political Parties (Pettit 2012: 139); and the previously discussed Six Markets Model (Christopher et al. 1991).

Dean and Croft's Multiple Markets Model demonstrates the significant impact that multiple groups, beyond the voter, have on political decision-making processes.

Their model examines the interrelationship among these different groups, along with the ability of the candidate or party to control the political marketing message (Dean and Croft 2001: 1207). Ormrod's Political Market Orientation Model proposes four attitudinal constructs and four behavioral constructs. The attitudinal constructs include voter orientation, competitor orientation, internal orientation, and external orientation. The behavioral constructs include information generation, information dissemination, member participation, and consistent external communication. Ormrod contends that there is a natural progression between each of the four behavioral constructs—in that information has to be generated before it can be disseminated, disseminated before it can be made sense of by members participating in strategy formulation, and so on (Ormrod 2005: 60). Each of the attitudinal constructs may affect each of the behavioral constructs, so that the proposed model accounts for the idiosyncrasies of political markets and political party structures that may exist.

Pettit's Multiple Market Model helps us to better understand the multiple stakeholders associated with a political party. His model argues that a party has eight markets, three internal and five external. The internal markets include the party in central office, party in elected office, and the party on the ground, while the external markets include campaigning professionals, media, voters, associational interest groups, and institutional interest groups (Pettit 2012: 139).

Both the Market-Oriented Party (MOP) Model of Lees-Marshment (2001) and the Political Marketing Process Model of Spiller and Bergner (2011) address the use of political marketing for both campaigning and governing activities. Spiller and Bergner's Political Marketing Process Model details how political marketing is interactive and multidimensional. The process has a front-end or campaigning element, along with a back-end or governing dimension. Candidates and political parties may use database political marketing for both campaigning and governing. However, political campaigning is the prevalent use for most candidates and parties. The Market-Oriented Party (MOP) Model of Lees-Marshment describes how the political marketing process requires a candidate or party to identify voters' needs and wants *before* the candidate or party determines how to behave and what political message to convey to the voters. According to Lees-Marshment (2009: 207), "A Market-Oriented Party uses party views and political judgment to design its behaviour to respond to and satisfy voter demands in a way that meets their needs and wants, is supported and implemented by the internal organisation, and is deliverable in government." The Lees-Marshment MOP Model outlines a process by which political candidates and parties design their products to create voter satisfaction. This model suggests that a market orientation should be capable of delivering a party's product and message while simultaneously implementing a responsive attitude to voters' preferences. In reality, the MOP Model should be a platform for candidates and parties to use to both win elections and effectively govern.

The model we utilize in this chapter is that of Jennifer Lees-Marshment, shown in Figure 3.1. It is our contention that the Obama campaign of 2008 was an

STAGE ONE: MARKET INTELLIGENCE

The party aims to understand and ascertain market demands. Informally it "keeps an ear to the ground," talks to party members, creates policy groups, and meets with the public. Formally it uses methods such as polls, focus groups, and segmentation to understand the views and behavior of its market, including the general public, key opinion-influencers, MPs, and members. It uses market intelligence continually and considers short- and long-term demands.

STAGE TWO: PRODUCT DESIGN

The party then designs "product" according to the findings from its market intelligence, before adjusting it to suit several factors explored in Stage 3.

STAGE THREE: PRODUCT ADJUSTMENT

The party then develops the product to consider:
Achievability: Ensures promises can be delivered in government.
Internal reaction: Ensures changes will attract adequate support from MPs and members to ensure implementation, taking into account a party's ideology and history, retaining certain policies to suit the traditional supporter market where necessary.
Competition: Identifies the opposition's weaknesses and highlights own corresponding strengths, ensuring a degree of distinctiveness.
Support: Segments the market to identify untapped voters necessary to achieve goals, and then develop targeted aspects of the product to suit them.

STAGE FOUR: IMPLEMENTATION

Changes are implemented throughout the party, needing careful party management and leadership over an appropriate timeframe to obtain adequate acceptance, to create party unity and enthusiasm for the new party design.

STAGE FIVE: COMMUNICATION

Communication is carefully organized to convey the new product, so that voters are clear before the campaign begins. Not just the leader, but all MPs and members, send a message to the electorate. It involves media management but is not just about spin-doctoring; it should be informative rather than manipulative, and built on a clear internal communication structure.

STAGE SIX: CAMPAIGN

The party repeats its communication in the official campaign, reminding voters of the key aspects and advantages of its product.

STAGE SEVEN: ELECTION

The party should not just win votes but attract positive perception from voters on all aspects of behavior including policies, leaders, party unity, and capability, as well as increased quality of its membership.

STAGE EIGHT: DELIVERY

The party then needs to deliver its product in government..

FIGURE 3.1 A Model of a Market-Oriented Party
Source: Adapted with permission from Jennifer Lees-Marshment

excellent example of consumer-centric marketing. The campaign moved beyond the traditional sales or product-centric approach and became fully market oriented, with strong channels of communication back and forth between the campaign and potential voters. The campaign was characterized by a full use of all of Lees-Marshment's market-oriented features.

However, we demonstrate that the first term of the Obama administration was not successful in creating a market-oriented form of governance. In part, this was the result of intrinsic differences between campaigning and governing, and in part because the Obama administration's governance style reverted to a more traditional "sales" or product-centric approach. In fact, no more than two of Lees-Marshment's six market-oriented governance activities (Lees-Marshment 2009: 211) characterized the Obama administration's style of governance. Neither the usefulness nor the limits of a market-orientation in governing have yet been determined in practice.

Empirical Illustration: The 2008 Obama Campaign and Obama's First Presidential Term

The Obama Campaign of 2008

There is no question that a clear and attractive brand, delivered consistently across many types of media, is indispensable to a well-run campaign. But equally important is the creation and management of a comprehensive database. Researchers proclaim that effective political marketing requires parties and candidates to develop fast-feedback facilities, two-way direct communications, and the means to process, assess, and respond to feedback (Gibson and Rommele 2006; Henneberg and O'Shaughnessy 2009). In 2008, the Obama presidential campaign did just that in its efforts to connect with voters, grow its support base, and mobilize the electorate.

The process of conducting database marketing is relatively simple in theory, yet it is challenging in practice. The process entails obtaining basic data about voters, converting those data into relevant information and using that information to create knowledge about voters and their preferences, developing strategy to effectively communicate with voters on a personal level, and finally, interacting with voters to strengthen this relationship and gain even more data (Spiller and Baier 2012: 32).

Obama began building his supporter database before he became a presidential candidate. Early in 2006, Obama reached out to political consultant Anita Dunn to help revamp Hopefund, Obama's political action committee (PAC), which consisted of a small email list of donors (Heilemann and Halperin 2010: 32). Every time Obama spoke at a campaign event for a fellow Democratic candidate, Hopefund would require the candidate to submit the attendees' email addresses to the PAC (Heilemann and Halperin 2010: 32). The Obama database quickly grew and reflected the diversity of America—including teachers, retirees, small-business owners, farmers, and students (Plouffe 2009: 261). In addition, the Obama campaign team used campaign rallies and SMS text messages to target its database by geographic region and grow its database. Voters were offered incentives such as free campaign gear including buttons and bumper stickers for signing up to the campaign's text messaging list (Harfoush 2009: 116–17). The Obama campaign ended up in November 2008 with a massive database of more than 13 million supporters.

The Obama team used its database to communicate effectively with these 13 million supporters on a personalized, one-to-one basis via email and text messages. Tailoring campaign messages to the unique tastes of individual voters on a high-volume scale is referred to as *mass customization* (Kerin, Hartley, and Rudelius 2011: 224) and the Obama campaign implemented mass customization via its email database to motivate campaign supporters and grow its volunteer base. The database was a crucial factor in Obama's ability to connect with American voters. Sophisticated databases are used for a variety of campaign activities, as follows.

Creating Grassroots Support Networks and Mobilizing Voters

The Obama campaign created and trained grassroots networks of volunteers via the Obama Fellowship Program. Fellows committed to a six-week unpaid intensified volunteer training and recruitment program and were deployed to key battleground states. These fellows wrote letters to the editor, walked in parades, put up yard signs, represented the campaign at community gatherings, and helped with get-out-the-vote (GOTV) initiatives and various administrative tasks. This program was highly effective, with more than 3,600 Obama fellows dispatched into 17 states to recruit and train new volunteers during the summer of 2008 (Harfoush 2009: 41).

Launching a Loyalty Rewards Program to Motivate Campaign Volunteers

To keep volunteers motivated, the Obama campaign implemented a type of database loyalty program designed to track and monitor each user's *recent* volunteer activity via its website, my.barackobama.com, often called "MyBO." Site members accrued points for campaign activities, such as hosting or attending political campaign events, making campaign donations, knocking on neighbor's doors, and posting blogs (Harfoush 2009: 79). Members were ranked against each other and a spirit of friendly competition ignited to see which members were making the greatest difference for Obama's campaign. This type of traceable point-oriented loyalty program created a sense of community among site members, solidified the personal connection between members and the candidate, and maximized campaign support for Obama. The results were equally impressive with 70,000 MyBO personal fundraising pages, which generated more than $35 million for the Obama campaign (Harfoush 2009: 78).

Implementing a Telemarketing Campaign to Raise Funds

Obama's telemarketing campaign, called *Neighbor to Neighbor*, was an online phonebanking tool that allowed supporters to make calls on behalf of the campaign from the comfort of their own homes. Supporters were trained and given lists of independent voters in their ZIP code area and neighborhood to target. The lists came with printable maps with directions that showed volunteers exactly where to go for follow-up visits, scripts for making the right campaign pitch, and a record sheet to keep track of results (Harfoush 2009: 90).

Conducting Stealth Marketing Communications

Stealth communications is interacting with voters or voter groups without other voters or groups knowing about it. This type of communication is more than targeted—it is under the radar, highly personalized, and extremely effective. For example, discreet and highly customized emails from Barack Obama were drafted and sent by Obama's director of email and online fundraising, Stephen Geer, and his team (Harfoush 2009: 100). By the end of the campaign, the Obama campaign had sent more than one billion emails (Vargas 2008). Personally addressed daily emails were used to communicate regularly with Obama campaign supporters to inform and motivate supporters to help by volunteering, working the polls, donating and fundraising, referring and contacting friends, making telephone calls, attending political rallies and events, watching debates and television appearances, writing blogs, and much more. Some of these emails were used to provide supporters with information to fight the negative attacks or "smears" that campaign opponents were using. Obama supporters were invited to subscribe to the "Obama Supporter Rapid Response team"—a list that could be mobilized via email to take action against any campaign attack by writing letters to newspapers or television stations. Once a supporter was on the Obama email list, he or she was asked over and over again for continued support of Obama's candidacy.

> Text messaging was also used to conduct stealth communications and build the Obama campaign database via an Obama advertisement that targeted young voters. The ad asked people to text "hope" to 62262 (Obama) and those who responded were quickly added to Obama's MyBO site and email distribution list—and enlisted as campaign volunteers who would receive regular pleas for additional campaign assistance. By the end of the campaign, one million voters registered as part of the Obama campaign's texting program. (Vargas 2008)

In summary, the Obama team's campaign strategy was constantly and consistently centered on building and using its database to create and cultivate relationships with potential voters and voter groups. This consumer-centered campaign was market oriented and produced an impact that was historic in the political marketing arena.

Market-Oriented Governing in the First Obama Presidential Term

Governing in the United States has long been product or sales oriented. Presidents have maintained at least since the 1960s, and even before, an extensive media operation in the White House. They hold regular press briefings and reach out to various constituent groups who will be affected by, or who might help advance, White House policies or legislative agendas. Members of Congress have used many of these tools as well. For decades members of Congress have maintained mailing lists of constituent groups that are especially concerned about one or another policy area; lists include, for example, constituents concerned about agriculture, veterans' benefits, the state of Israel, and many other issue sets.

Presidents and members of Congress have also utilized polling information in governing since the 1960s. Polling helps these officials to know the "mind" of their constituents on important legislative and policy questions. For example, it would be surprising if any single member of Congress did not know where his or her constituents stood on an issue like the Iraq War. In using regular polling, presidents and members of Congress discover what will be the reaction of their constituents, even if this information does not change their own positions.

However, there is an anecdotal character to much of this outreach. It certainly falls far short of what might be called genuinely interactive outreach to constituents, or a genuinely market-oriented approach to governing. The Obama administration aimed to move beyond these historical limits and become the first "digital administration." It believed that its database of more than 13 million email addresses could offer a powerful new tool with which to govern. Let's evaluate Obama's database initiative, using Lees-Marshment's model of market-oriented governing (Lees-Marshment 2009). This model is a subset of her larger model and outlines six aspects of market-oriented governance: delivery management; continual market consultation; responsive product redevelopment; product refinement; maintenance of a market-oriented attitude; and engagement in market-oriented communication. How does Obama's first-term "digital administration" fare when put against this model?

Email addresses were transferred from my.barackobama.com to a new website called Organizing for America (OFA). This site was located at the Democratic National Committee, under the control of Obama loyalists, in order to assure its security and to avoid government requirements relating to archiving and problems with Freedom of Information requests. The purpose of the database was twofold. First, it would continue to provide to Obama supporters regular "unfiltered" (by the media) information, would keep the database updated, and would raise funds in order to maintain its infrastructure.

But the real value of OFA was thought to lie elsewhere. OFA would provide an army of loyalists who would advocate for the administration's initiatives and help the president achieve his policy agenda. Just as the campaign had emailed its list to gain votes, volunteers, and funds, so OFA would email its list to develop support for his policies. OFA would serve as the Obama "channel," galvanizing supporters to reach out across the nation and develop grassroots support for the president's policy initiatives. OFA would be a national-level community organizing tool; as one campaign worker said, "Obama hopes to turn the MyBO community into a powerful grassroots base that can help him promote his legislative agenda" (Harfoush 2009: 176). The Obama administration would aim to use OFA to develop support for the economic stimulus bill, the health care reform bill, the cap and trade bill, and other significant legislative initiatives.

The Obama administration had a particular, and narrow, understanding of how it would use its extensive database to govern. Outreach to the 13 million members of its database would certainly accomplish the first of Lees-Marshment's six market-oriented governance tasks: it would offer a new means of delivery management and communication. Outreach was less frequent than during the frenetic days of the campaign; instead of daily (or even hourly) communications, communication from OFA occurred once or twice a week in the early days of the administration (interview with former Obama campaign official, October 28, 2010). This outreach offered a way to let Obama's political base know that it still cared about them and to share its policy priorities. In this way, regular contacts from OFA also fulfilled the sixth of Lees-Marshment's market-oriented governance tasks: ongoing engagement.

But OFA was never intended seriously to consult the views of its database, much less to refine or redevelop its legislative products in the light of these views. The work of OFA was never intended to be a genuinely market-oriented form of governing, but rather to be a product, or at best a sales-oriented approach to governing. OFA would offer one more—and hopefully a new and powerful—sales tool. OFA's database was to be used to sell the legislative and policy products of the Obama administration, not to create a format for feedback about what those products should be.

Let's look at the case study of health care reform, arguably the Obama administration's most important initiative, and one in which OFA was employed to help sell it to the American people. President Obama originally called upon Congress to complete work on health care reform prior to the August 2009 recess. When Congress missed that deadline, members returned to their districts to encounter significant grassroots opposition to the legislation that was pending. In an attempt to regain momentum for the legislation, senior White House advisor David Axelrod sent a lengthy mass email to the entire OFA database. In both the subject line entitled "Something worth forwarding" and the text of the email, Axelrod urged supporters to forward his email to anyone who had questions about health care reform. Here is an excerpt from that email:

> Dear Friend,
>
> This is probably one of the longest emails I've ever sent, but it could be the most important. Across the country we are seeing vigorous debate about health insurance reforms. Unfortunately, some of the old tactics we know so well are back—even the viral emails that fly unchecked and under

the radar, spreading all sorts of lies and distortions. . . . At the end of my email, you'll find a lot of information about health insurance reform. . . . Right now, someone you know probably has a question about reform that could be answered by what's below. So what are you waiting for? Forward this email.
Thanks

David
David Axelrod
Senior Advisor to the President

(Axelrod 2009)

Here was an acid test of the OFA database's value in governing. Unfortunately, many Obama supporters took Axelrod's advice and shared his email widely, including to both supporters and die-hard opponents of health care reform. The effect was generally negative. One advertising expert wrote that within weeks the Obama team had gone from "a digital-marketing case study to being regarded as a lowly spammer" (Bush 2009). Another marketing expert noted an "arrogance" and a "fundamental shift happening in their approach" (Bush 2009).

After initially blaming "outside groups" for sharing the email with opponents of the legislation, the White House issued a statement expressing regret at any inconvenience that might have been caused by receiving an unwanted email. Unfortunately, the problem was compounded by the almost simultaneous creation of two new websites. One offered a video of an administration official addressing criticisms of the health care reform legislation. The other, and more problematic, website featured White House communications official Linda Douglass asking supporters to email any "fishy" information about heath care reform to the new website flag@whitehouse.gov. Republicans and opponents of health care reform predictably attacked the website as "Orwellian," but the American Civil Liberties Union also said that the website was "a bad idea that could send a troublesome message" (FoxNews.com). The website was taken down.

The Obama administration was no more successful in utilizing its database to sell other initiatives, including economic stimulus legislation, financial services reform, and energy legislation. The 2009 economic stimulus legislation, for example, was a thousand-page compendium of provisions and projects, including many long-standing items from the Democratic legislative wish list. Outreach to supporters of President Obama was insufficient to overcome concerns of the opposition political party about both the particulars of the legislation and its overall cost. Moreover, the Obama administration made no effort to shape the stimulus legislation according to the wishes of OFA's email list, but simply to seek support for an overall bill whose provisions were largely written by Democratic legislators.

Why didn't the Obama administration succeed in these political sales tasks, leaving aside the more ambitious goal of genuinely market-oriented governance?

There are intrinsic differences between campaign communications and policy communications. Political campaigns are finite, intense, and winner take all. The sides are drawn and the goal is clear: to win. Government policy initiatives are far different. They are often complex, they change frequently as they wend their way through the legislative process, and there is often no fixed date by which they must be completed. Moreover, the ultimate product is likely to be some kind of compromise rather than a clear-cut victory or loss.

A political campaign is focused on one point—the candidate. It is far more difficult to generate the enthusiasm of the campaign for a complex policy initiative like health care reform or financial services reform. One could easily imagine Obama supporters reaching out to friends and neighbors urging them to vote for Barack Obama. It is far harder to imagine them reaching out to friends and neighbors to explain the virtues of a 2,000-page financial services reform bill.

The Obama administration did not understand the differences between campaign communications and communications relating to governance. One lesson is clear. Governments that seek to sell their policy products to constituents must choose their targets carefully. The general rule is the simpler the better; the more the essence of an issue can be boiled down to one or two strong, even moral, points relating to justice or fairness, the easier it will be to sell government policy products. Communicating arcane health policy arguments and counter-arguments—as David Axelrod did in his email to the OFA database—does not recapture the enthusiasm of campaign communications and is not a formula for creating a powerful grassroots base of advocates.

In conclusion, the Obama administration was not successful in transferring market-oriented techniques to governing. This was true in the first instance because it inadequately understood the differences between campaigning and governing. Its effort to use the database to "sell" its policies was inadequately thought through, and the hopes of a new and revolutionary "digital administration" did not come to pass. Secondly, however, it is perhaps fair to say that the Obama administration failed to create a market-oriented form of governance because it did not try to do so. It aimed to sell its vision to the country and not to shape and reshape its vision according to what it learned from ongoing communication with either its own database or the larger electorate. To a certain extent one could say that one major promise of candidate Obama, who was poll driven and market oriented throughout his campaign, was realized: he would not govern according to the polls.

Conclusions for Research and Practice

Databases in Campaigning

The campaign database enabled targeted, tailored, and perfectly timed communication with voters to support a candidate that was created and shaped based on expressed desires from the electorate. Hence, Barack Obama has been hailed as "Campaigner in Chief," and his campaign team has raised the bar for successful political campaign strategies. The database was highly effective in encouraging voter mobilization on a state-by-state basis.

According to Lees-Marshment (2009: 207), "[W]ith the market-oriented party, identifying voters' needs and wants comes before a party determines how to behave." That precisely sums up the Obama campaign strategy. The database marketing process was truly interactive; the Obama campaign used its interactive communications with voters to shape its campaign messages to deliver promises to the voters that corresponded directly to what they said they wanted. However, it is well established that candidates can promise whatever they please when campaigning, and if they fail to live up to their campaign promises, there is no immediate recourse for voters (Spiller and Bergner 2011: 28). Due to this reality, the political campaign process may deviate from stage three of Lees-Marshment's Market-Oriented Party (MOP) model, whereby the party adjusts its model product design to ensure promises can be delivered in government.

Databases in Governing

We have considered several obstacles to the successful use of databases in governing and in creating a true market orientation. First, governing is a more diffuse and ongoing project than the limited, highly focused political campaign. It is more difficult to engage constituents on complex and rapidly changing policy initiatives than to support a candidate.

Second, product delivery is slow in governance. Unexpected events arise that require reactive responses and that divert administrations from their initial goals. There is no better example than the attacks of 9/11 in the first year of the Bush administration; executing a "war on terror," which became the signature activity of George Bush's two terms, was nowhere on the horizon in the planning of the early Bush administration in 2001. Moreover, product delivery is a special challenge in the United States, whose Constitution was designed to impede rapid product delivery. It will always be harder under the American separation of powers to deliver legislative products than it is in a parliamentary system or, for that matter, in any system where power is concentrated in one or a few individuals.

Third, there remain questions related to the proper ends of governing. No one expects that governing should consist exclusively in following the day-to-day wants of majorities. Leadership is required. As Philip Gould, an advisor to Tony Blair, has well said, "If you become too much of a listening party you just get nowhere. If you become too much of a leadership government, then you start to disconnect your voters, which is bad also" (Lees-Marshment 2009: 210).

These problems are intrinsic to governmental communications; other problems are self-inflicted, such as remaining in the "bubble" that surrounds high-level officials. Leonard Marsh, a founder of the beverage company Snapple, has said, "We never thought of ourselves as any better than our customers" (Khermouch 1993). The Obama campaign lived that message. It reached out to its supporters and empowered them; they were part of the team. The Obama administration has not acted in this manner, and has allowed a degree of aloofness and arrogance to creep into its operations. This was—and still is—a fixable error.

What are the prospects for genuinely market-oriented governance? What if a government should undertake steps two through five of Lees-Marshment's governance model seriously and attempt to reach out to constituents and incorporate their feedback into ongoing policy formulation? What would this look like in the American case? The Obama administration has attempted one version of such outreach in a program called "We the People." This program, which is loosely modeled on a British government program, guarantees an administration response to any online petition that receives at least 25,000 signatures. This is admittedly an imperfect solution to market-oriented governing, as it does not seek and utilize feedback for the administration's own policy proposals; but it is outreach to constituents that constitutes more than an effort to sell the administration's own proposals. To date, the administration has issued 82 responses to more than 94,000 petitions. The value of this is mixed at best. Many of the petitions—and the most popular ones at that—call for nationalizing the Twinkie industry, creation of a Death Star, or secession from the union. It seems that here too a serious outreach/feedback/refinement/outreach process has been elusive.

The current Obama database is now considerably larger than the 13 million names it held in 2008. The Obama organization has decided to transfer its database from Organizing for America to a new entity called Organizing for Action (OFA). The new OFA has a reputed database of nearly 29 million names, and it is OFA's expressed intent to use this email list to develop support for second-term policy initiatives. But a subtle change is under way. The Obama administration seems to have made a calculation that its policy agenda will be better advanced by gaining a Democratic majority in the next House of Representatives than in using its email list for direct policy support. OFA is in the process of becoming an organization whose email list will be employed in the 2014 midterm elections. It is raising corporate and other large donor contributions and is looking less like a policy promotion organization than an independent expenditure campaign organization. As a 501(c)4 organization, OFA can engage in electoral politics, so long as that is not its "primary" purpose.

There is clearly much theoretical and practical work to be done in determining the value of extensive databases for governance. This work includes new and more effective ways to deploy the database to advance policy objectives; new ways to create a better feedback loop to incorporate popular views without undermining the critical role of leadership; and the maintenance and transferability of databases for other candidates and causes.

References

Axelrod, D. (2009, August 13). Email. info@messages.white house.gov
Baier, M., Ruf, K., & Chakraborty, G. (2002). *Contemporary database marketing.* Chicago, IL: Racom Communications.
Bruce, B. (1992). *Images of power: How the images makers shape our leaders.* London, UK: Kogan Page.
Bush, M. (2009, August 24). Hail to the spammer in chief: Where Obama went wrong. *Advertising Age, 80*(28), 3–17. http://connection.ebscohost.com/c/articles/43987332/hail-spammer-chief-where-obama-went-wrong
Butler, P., & Collins, N. (1994). Political marketing: Structure and process. *European Journal of Marketing, 28*(1), 19–34.
Christopher, M., Payne, A., & Ballantyne, D. (1991). *Relationship marketing.* Oxford, UK: Butterworth Heinemann.
Coleman, S. (2007). Review of *Political marketing in comparative perspective* edited by Darren Lilleker and Jennifer Lees-Marshment. *Parliamentary Affairs, 60*(1), 180–186.
Culver, K., & Howe, P. (2004). Calling all citizens: The challenges of public consultation. *Canadian Public Administration, 47*(1), 52–75.
Das, K. (2009). Relationship marketing research (1994–2006): An academic literature review and classification. *Marketing Intelligence & Planning, 27*(3), 326–363.
Davenport, T. C., Gerber, A. S., Green, D. P., Larimer, C. W., Mann, C. B., & Panagopoulos, C. (2010). The enduring effects of social pressure: Tracking campaign experiments over a series of elections. *Political Behavior 32*(3), 423–430.
Dean, D., & Croft, R. (2001). Friends and relations: Long-term approaches to political campaigning. *European Journal of Marketing, 35*(11/12), 1197–1216.
Gibson, R., & Rommele, A. (2006). Down periscope: The search for high-tech campaigning at the local level in the 2002 German federal election. *Journal of E-Government, 2*(3), 85–111.
Granik, S. (2005). Membership benefits, membership action: Why incentives for activism are what members want. *Journal of Nonprofit & Public Sector Marketing, 14*(1/2), 65–89.
Gronroos, C. (1994). Quo vadis marketing? Toward a relationship marketing paradigm. *Journal of Marketing Management, 10*(5), 347–60.
Gronroos, C. (1996). Relationship marketing strategic and tactical implications. *Management Decision, 43*(4), 5–14.
Gummersson, E. (2002). Relationship marketing and a new economy: It's time for deprogramming. *The Journal of Services Marketing, 16*(7), 585–589.
Harfoush, R. (2009). *Yes we did: An inside look at how social media built the Obama brand.* Berkeley, CA: New Riders.
Harker, M. (1999). Relationship marketing defined? An examination of current relationship marketing definitions. *Marketing Intelligence and Planning, 17*(1), 13–20.
Heilemann, J., & Halperin, M. (2010). *Game change.* New York, NY: Harper Collins.
Henneberg, S., & O'Shaughnessy, N. (2009). Political relationship marketing: Some macro/micro thoughts. *Journal of Marketing Management, 25*(1/2), 5–29.
Jackson, N. (2005). Vote winner or a nuisance: Email and elected politicians' relationship with their constituents. *Journal of Nonprofit & Public Sector Marketing, 14*(1/2), 91–108.
Jamieson, K. H. (1992). *Packaging the presidency: A history and criticism of presidential campaign advertising.* New York, NY: Oxford University Press.
Kavanagh, D. (1995). *Election campaigning: The new marketing of politics.* Oxford, UK: Blackwell.
Kenski, K., Hardy, B., & Jamieson, K. H. (2010). *The Obama victory: How media, money, and message shaped the 2008 election.* New York, NY: Oxford University Press.
Kerin, R., Hartley, S., & Rudelius, W. (2011). *Marketing* (10th ed.). New York, NY: McGraw-Hill/Irwin.

Khermouch, G. (1993, May 17). All Snapple needs is love—and a dash of cleverness. *Brandweek*, 44–46.

Lees-Marshment, J. (2001). *Political marketing and British political parties.* Manchester, UK: Manchester University Press.

Lees-Marshment, J. (2006). Political marketing theory and practice: A reply to Ormrod's critique of the Lees-Marshment Market-Oriented Party Model. *Politics, 26*(2), 119–125.

Lees-Marshment, J. (2009). Marketing after the election: The potential and limitations of maintaining a market-orientation in government. *The Canadian Journal of Communication, 34*, 205–227.

Lindgreen, A. (2001). A framework for studying relationship marketing dyads. *Qualitative Marketing Research: An International Journal, 4*(2), 75–88.

McClymont, H., & Jocumsen, G. (2003). How to implement marketing strategies using database approaches. *Database Marketing & Customer Strategy Management, 17*(2), 135–148.

Morgan, R., & Hunt, S. (1994). The commitment-trust theory of relationship marketing. *Journal of Marketing, 58*(3), 20–38.

Newman, B. (1999). *The mass marketing of politics: Democracy in an age of manufactured images.* Thousand Oaks, CA: Sage Publications.

Norris, P., & Gavin, N. (Eds.). (1999). *Britain votes 1997.* Oxford, UK: Oxford University Press.

O'Malley, L., & Mitussis, D. (2002). Relationships and technology: Strategic implications. *Journal of Strategic Marketing, 10*, 225–238.

Ormrod, R. (2005). A conceptual model of political market orientation. *Journal of Nonprofit and Public Sector Marketing, 14*, 47–64.

Ormrod, R. (2006). A critique of the Lees-Marshment Market-Oriented Party Model. *Politics, 26*(2), 110–118.

Pettitt, R. T. (2012). Internal party political relationship marketing: Encouraging activism amongst local party members. In Jennifer Lees-Marshment (Ed.), *Routledge handbook of political marketing* (pp. 137–150). New York, NY: Routledge.

Plouffe, D. (2009). *The audacity to win.* New York, NY: Viking.

Quelch, J. A., & Jocz, K. C. (2007). *Greater good: How good marketing makes for better democracy.* Boston, MA: Harvard Business Press.

Sherman, E., & Schiffman, L. (2002). Trends and issues in political marketing strategies. *Journal of Political Marketing, 1*(1), 231–233.

Sheth, J., & Parvatiyar, A. (1995). Relationship marketing in consumer markets: Antecedents and consequences. *Journal of the Academy of Marketing Science, 23*(4), 255–271.

Spiller, L., & Baier, M. (2012). *Contemporary direct & interactive marketing* (3rd ed.). Chicago, IL: Racom Communications.

Spiller, L., & Bergner, J. (2011). *Branding the candidate: Marketing strategies to win your vote.* Santa Barbara, CA: Praeger.

Stanton, A. D. (2006). Bridging the academic/practitioner divide in marketing: An undergraduate course in data mining. *Marketing Intelligence & Planning, 24*(3), 233–244.

Stone, B. (1994). *Successful direct marketing methods* (5th ed.). Chicago, IL: NTC Books.

Stone, B., & Jacobs, R. (2008). *Successful direct marketing methods* (8th ed.). New York, NY: McGraw-Hill.

Ubertaccio, P. N. (2012). Political parties and direct marketing: Connecting voters and candidates more effectively. In J. Lees-Marshment (Ed.), *Routledge handbook of political marketing* (pp. 177–188). New York, NY: Routledge.

Vargas, J. A. (2008, November 20). Obama raised half a billion online. *The Washington Post.* http://voices.washingtonpost.com/44/2008/11/obama-raised-half-a-billion-on.html

Webster, F., Jr. (1992). The changing role of marketing in the corporation. *Journal of Marketing, 56*(October), 1–17.

4

BOUTIQUE POPULISM

The Emergence of the Tea Party Movement in the Age of Digital Politics

André Turcotte and Vincent Raynauld

Overview of the Topic

At 11:18 pm EST on November 8, 2012, CNN projected that Barack Hussein Obama would win re-election. While not totally unexpected, this announcement infuriated many Republicans who had grown obsessed with defeating the forty-fourth president of the United States. There were many losers that night but the defeat was particularly bitter for adherents of the Tea Party Movement (TPM). They, more than anyone else, had become fixated on removing Barack Obama from the Oval Office. As noted by Skocpol and Williamson, "[N]owhere are Tea Party fears more potently symbolized than in the presidency of Barack Hussein Obama. The policies and person of the forty-fourth President were the subject of immense suspicion at every Tea Party event or interview we attended. It is no coincidence that Tea Party activism began within weeks of President Obama's inauguration" (2012: 77).

The common wisdom that emerged after the Obama landslide in 2008 was that the Republican Party was facing a long period of internal dissensions and political marginalization in Washington. After all, the new president was young, energetic, popular, and even perhaps transformative. Moreover, the Democratic Party controlled both the House of Representatives and the Senate for the first time since 1995. But within a few months after his inauguration, President Obama would be facing an unexpected challenge from an unlikely opponent.

The ascendency of the Tea Party has been nothing short of astonishing. But perhaps even more intriguing was the way the Tea Party accomplished its meteoric rise. This chapter suggests that it introduced a new form of political marketing competition whereby marketing by social and political movements challenges established market-oriented parties, political institutions, and other formal political organizations in ways that have not been previously witnessed nor researched.

The rancor and activism of early Tea Party supporters were the latest incarnation of an old American phenomenon, namely old-fashioned American conservative populism. Populist appeals have played a prominent role in Western-style democracies for decades. Such appeals typically come and wane but never totally disappear from the political landscape. Over the last 20 years, several populist movements have captured voters' imagination. From Preston Manning in Canada to Ron Paul, Howard Dean, and Jesse Ventura in the United States, as well as Austria's Jörg Haider, Italy's Silvio Berlusconi, and France's Jean-Marie Le Pen, we have seen the numerous faces of populism. Not surprisingly, populism has been extensively scrutinized by academics, but it is only in recent years that it has become the object of analysis from a political marketing perspective. In this study, we examine the Tea Party movement in order to strengthen our understanding of populism as a political marketing technique. We suggest that because the emergence of the Tea Party movement coincided with the maturation of social media, there was something fundamentally different, and to some extent transformative, about this new permutation of populism.

Specifically, we build on previous works by Lederer, Plasser, et al. (2005), Busby (2009), and Winder and Tenscher (2012), who have examined populism not from a political or social movement perspective but as a marketing technique. Also of interest to this study is Kenneth Cosgrove's *Branded Conservatives* (2007), which showed the extent to which "populism is a key aspect of the Conservative brand story" (40). We argue that the grassroots-intensive communication, mobilization, and marketing practices associated with the Tea Party movement are of particular interest to the political marketing literature because they modify the impact of market intelligence on party strategy; have an effect on the product design and the development of a party's communication and organizing plan; and redefine the relationship between party elite, their members, and the public in general. The new practices also pose significant strategic challenges to the implementation of coherent electioneering approaches. The chapter concludes with a general discussion about the implications of such changes and the extent to which the emergence of the Tea Party movement and its manifestation in the Web 2.0 mediascape may represent a glimpse of not only what will be the next generation of populism, but of "permanent campaigning" (Blumenthal 1980) in and out of traditional electoral politics and party politics, as well as legislative and governing processes.

Review of Previous Literature

There are three key streams of literature relevant to this chapter: populism, online communication, and political marketing work related to populism. Populism has typically been studied by political scientists (Ionescu and Geller 1969; Kuzminski 2008) or from the broader perspective of social movements and democratic theory (Goodwin 1978; Kazin 1998; Panizza 2005). While this chapter addresses some of those previous theoretical perspectives, its main focus is on analyzing the rise of the Tea Party movement within the political marketing literature and more specifically the more recent work on "populism as a political marketing technique" (Winder and Tenscher 2012) and how it is impacted by social media.

Populism has been defined in many ways, oftentimes with negative connotations. The term "populism" originated during "postbellum nineteenth-century American politics" (Kuzminski 2008: 3), but its intellectual legacy goes back to Ancient Greece. The concept can be used to refer to "political phenomena ranging from the Russian *narodnichestvo* of the nineteenth century to William Jennings Bryan and smaller farmer movements in the 1930s, and Latin American populism of the 1940s and 1950s" (Arditi 2005: 73). Populism is anchored around an ideological core that perceives society "separated into two homogeneous and antagonistic groups, the 'pure people' versus 'the corrupt elite'" (Winder and Tenscher 2012: 231). It has also been associated with the fanatical side of politics or what Hofstadter referred to as the "paranoid style in American politics" (1952: 3–41). For the purpose of this analysis, we divert our attention away from the academic discussion related to the nature of populism. We adopt Winder and Tenscher's perspective, which defines populism as "a political communication style that is strategically deployed by political actors in order to mobilize potential voters and to establish stable relationships with specific target groups" (2012: 230). Before discussing the political marketing literature on populism, we turn our attention to the other theoretical dimension guiding our analysis, which relates to the impact of social media on cyber politicking.

While traditional political players have been the main drivers behind web politics in the United States since its mainstream emergence in 1996, the last four years have been marked by the hyper decentralization of e-politicking. It is worth noting that U.S. midterm and presidential election cycles between 2004 and 2008 have been marked by the development of cyber campaigning tactics that have affected the structure of the digital political mediascape. Kreiss (2011: 380) believes that the innovative use of online media tools by the Dean for America campaign in 2004 "reshaped the cultural grounds of Internet politics." More recently, Gibson (2012: 79) argues that the Obama campaign's heavy reliance on social networking services for voter outreach in 2008 had "reprogramming" effects on the overall dynamics of e-electioneering. While these campaigns have contributed in their own way to the reengagement of some segments of the public in the electoral process, they have still followed an essentially top-down, centralized politicking model as they were driven by an influential political figure and their focus was limited to a relatively small number of broad-based issues.

The hyper decentralization phenomenon can be defined as the diffusion of the initiative, the execution, and the control of digital political communication, mobilization, and organizing from political elites to a growing number of individuals and organizations with wide-ranging preferences, interests, and objectives. Because of this inherent impetus toward decentralization, it is not surprising that it would be a populist movement like the Tea Party that would capitalize on Web 2.0 media tools' distinct capabilities to promote and market itself and establish its political influence.

Specifically, the rise and rapid popularization of social media and the adoption by an increasing number of U.S. Internet users of postmodern political dispositions in recent years have contributed to the hyper decentralization phenomenon in three distinct ways. First, they have led to the mobilization of previously peripheral, and in many cases resource-poor, political players by encouraging them to be actively involved in the political process. The distinct structural and technical properties of Web 2.0 media tools have significantly lowered the threshold to political participation (e.g., financial resources, technical knowledge and expertise, time constraints, etc.), while the political dispositions of a growing proportion of Internet users, which are anchored in personal values such as freedom, creativity, assertiveness, self-mastery, and personal empowerment, have encouraged them to engage in highly personalized digital participatory patterns (Gil de Zúñiga, Jung, et al. 2012; Bennett, Wells, et al. 2011), more broadly known as "micro-activism" (Christensen 2011).

Second, the distinct interactive capabilities of social media platforms have given politically savvy Internet users more opportunities to interact with each other and, to some extent, develop and maintain relationships that can generate political dividends. Conversely, they have contributed to traditional political players' steady loss of control on public political information flows and social relations (Gil de Zúñiga, Jung, et al. 2012; Himelboim, Lariscy, et al. 2012; Gibson 2012). This is one of the emerging developments leading us to label the new type of populism as *boutique* in nature. The analogy points to a contrast between a more centralized or *big-store* relationship where a few elite political actors could offer a vast choice of policy options in order to mobilize a large group of supporters. As will be demonstrated when we examine the presence of the Tea Party in the Twittosphere, Web 2.0 media channels have been used by Tea Partiers to offer very specialized messages aimed at developing a relatively small but devout following outside of the realm of political elites.

Third, while political parties with mass appeal and other social and political institutions were central components of the U.S. political landscape before the early 1960s, they have gradually lost their relevance, credibility, and influence among the electorate during subsequent decades. Many citizens prefer to be part of informal groups or be involved in ad hoc mobilization initiatives giving them more political engagement latitude (Gunther and Diamond 2003; Bennett, Wells, et al. 2011). This situation has enabled informal political players to emerge and play a bigger role in the political arena. Specifically, they have progressively abandoned the highly centralized "command and control" approach to politics privileged by political elites (Wring and Ward 2010: 813) and turned to strategies tailored to the political mindset of a growing portion of the electorate and the structural and technical properties of social media. In other words, new media tools have favored horizontal political organizing by enabling Internet users to bypass traditional political and media structures and independently launch and manage political mobilization initiatives. Many Tea Party supporters grabbed onto the opportunities this new technological environment had to offer.

A more recent approach to examine populism was inspired by the growing field of political marketing. Two studies in particular set the tone for future analysis. In "The Rise and Fall of Populism in Austria," Lederer, Plasser, et al. (2005) studied the transformation of Austria's Freedom Party (FPÖ) between 1986 and 2002 (132). The authors used the framework developed by Lees-Marshment (2001) to show how the FPÖ evolved away from being a classic product-oriented party (POP) and how this transformation proved limiting. In an attempt to become more market-oriented, Haider and the FPÖ conducted haphazard market intelligence that led to a focus on populist strategies with limited popular appeal. The party was also unable to shed its leader-centric appeal, typical of populist parties but oftentimes an obstacle to electoral victory in a parliamentary system. Of particular interest to our study is the authors' conclusion that the constraints of populism made it difficult for Jörg Haider's FPÖ to develop a coherent market strategy and therefore "to design, implement and communicate a cohesive product" (144).

A follow-up effort by Georg Winder and Jens Tenscher (2012) provided the necessary theoretical framework to analyze populism from a political marketing perspective. They expand on previous attempts to define populism from a communicative dimension. As noted above, they argue that "populism is a political communication style that is strategically deployed by political actors in order to mobilize potential voters and to establish stable relationships with specific target groups" (2012: 231). They also suggest that populism as a communication strategy can be linked with political marketing concepts and market orientation as first defined by Lees-Marshment (2001). In specific terms, Winder and Tenscher argue that the successful use of populism as a communication strategy depends on a series of intervening factors. First, populism is likely to be more successful in candidate-centered democracies with a party system featuring high levels of polarization and weak fragmentation (235). Populism is also more likely to thrive in "societies with a dominating focus on achievements and performances of the political elite" (ibid.) and within "liberal, highly competitive media systems" (ibid.). The electoral objectives of populist appeals—beyond the obvious vote-seeking imperative—tend to be short term and neglect the development of long-term relationships with voters. More directly related to our analysis, Winder and Tenscher state that "political parties with a top-down structure and a leader-focused hierarchy are privileged to turn to populism" (ibid.). Their assertions worked efficiently in explaining the relative success and shortcomings of three recent populist phenomena. The 1992 Ross Perot campaign featured many of the characteristics of a successful populism-based marketing campaign (236–7). Winder and Tenscher can also explain Hugo

Chavez's mercurial rise in Venezuela (237–8) and support Lederer, Plasser, et al.'s conclusions about the populist appeal of Jörg Haider in Austria (238–9).

Two other works also influenced the theoretical framework used for our analysis. Cosgrove made two specific observations in his book *Branded Conservatives* (2007). He noted the extent to which U.S. conservatives capitalized on technological changes to disseminate their branded political products (50), and how this allowed them to target specific lifestyle niches. Cosgrove's analysis preceded the emergence of the Tea Party movement but his descriptions sound almost prophetic. The author also suggested that the branding efforts done by the conservatives were fundamentally driven by elites (37). While this was undeniably true for the period he studied, we will suggest that social media may have changed this dynamic. In *Marketing the Populist Politician* (2009), Robert Busby explored how populism has been used as "a manufactured political identity" (7) in recent years and how leaders have chosen the appeal of ordinariness to win popular support. We will contend that the hyper decentralizing effects of social media render non-genuine populist appeals harder to sustain as a communication strategy because the dissemination of messages and mobilization efforts are removed from party elites.

Theoretical Framework

From the review of the previous literature on populism, online communication, and political marketing, and from our own analysis, we propose several key principles for how a populist political movement can apply a marketing approach to online communication to build support and challenge mainstream market-oriented parties. In broad terms, the key principles can be organized into three complementary groupings: organization, mobilization, and messaging (see Figure 4.1).

Organization

Social media technology has empowered populist movements to set up a structure that can operate effectively outside of the scope of traditional political parties and political institutions. In the past, populist movements have arisen to challenge what they perceived as abuse of power from the elites but remained dependent on existing political and media structures to grow and disseminate their message of reform. As the case of Austria's Freedom Party demonstrated, the internal conflicts between simultaneously maintaining a market-oriented party structure and fueling populism fervor are untenable. The simplicity, rapidity, and low-cost nature of Web 2.0 tools allow political actors to sidestep established structures.

This has clear consequences. First, through the use of new online communication tools, it is possible to set up a structure capable of launching and managing independent mobilization efforts. Second, it significantly diminishes the control of the party elites over the product design phase of a campaign since populist

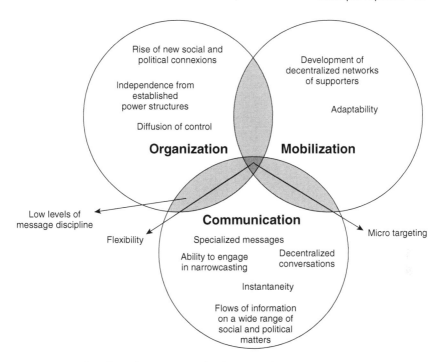

FIGURE 4.1 Political Marketing Principles for a Populist Movement

movements can develop messages that are "boutique" in nature, i.e., highly specialized messages designed to build support among a small but devout following operating outside mainstream party channels.

Mobilization

The mobilization benefits of the new dynamic relationship between populist movements and online communication are manifold. First, it allows for the targeting of communication messages to specific segments of the population who might support the populist challenge to mainstream parties. Second, the quasi-instantaneous content production and distribution as well as social interaction capabilities of Web 2.0 media platforms enable populist movements to engage in repeated communication that can create long-term relationships among the targeted groups. Third, social media allows for supporters to stay connected and organized outside the control of the party structure.

Under such circumstances, it becomes almost impossible for a market-oriented party to develop a coherent campaign strategy that would appeal to a broad pool of voters. Market intelligence would be inefficient in helping to develop a campaign strategy since different segments would potentially have divergent strategic objectives. It would also be near impossible to impose message discipline.

Communication

Communication-related principles to some extent permeate organizational and mobilization principles. However, we can add two specific principles from a direct communication perspective. New online communication forms allow populist movements to focus messaging on salient or populist issues where mainstream elites are weak (such as immigration, health care, gun rights, and fiscal responsibility in the United States). The new tools permit the use of communication channels such as Twitter to foster decentralized conversations and connections among followers and enable them to express emotion and views. The following analysis aims to expand on this framework by looking at the Tea Party movement.

Empirical Illustration

The Tea Party movement emerged as a powerful force in the U.S. political landscape in a fairly low-key and innocuous manner. In early 2009, Seattle-based conservative political activist and blogger Keli Carender, also known as "Liberty Belle," organized a series of "porkulus" demonstrations in opposition to the American Recovery and Reinvestment Act (ARRA), which she described as "the most frightening bill on Earth" in a blog post on February 10, 2009[1] (Disch 2011: 125; Berg 2011). On February 19, 2009, CNBC's Rick Santelli fumed against the decision of the Obama administration to provide foreclosure relief through different policy initiatives such as the Homeowners Affordability and Stability Plan (HASP). In Santelli's words, "The government is rewarding bad behavior! [...It plans] to subsidize the losers' mortgages" (Sckocpol and Williams 2012: 7). Santelli invited all American capitalists to mobilize and attend a Chicago Tea Party to denounce this situation (Sckocpol and Williams 2012; Disch 2011).

We suggest that the Tea Party movement can be defined as one of the first large-scale manifestations of *online politicking 3.0* in the United States. While some scholars have labeled this movement a "genetically modified grassroots organization (GMGO)" (Bratich 2011: 342), or as an Astroturf political phenomenon (Langman 2012; Skocpol and Williamson 2012), it is in fact a hyper decentralized and fragmented movement fueled by a diverse range of formal and informal political players with often narrow preferences, interests, and objectives. It focuses on a large number of social, political, and economic issues such as immigration, health care, gun rights, and fiscal responsibility (Bailey, Mummolo, et al. 2012; Skocpol and Williamson 2012). Its impact was felt quite rapidly. The Tea Party movement is credited with shaping the course of several local and regional electoral races across the United States during the 2010 midterm elections (Karpowitz, Monson, et al. 2011; Disch 2011). In the words of Perrin, Tepper, et al. (2011: 74), it was the main "story of the 2010 midterm elections."

In order to determine the extent to which the fusing of populist fervor and Web 2.0 media channels has opened up new ways for political actors to reach their audience and market themselves, we turn our attention to a quantitative assessment of the manifestation of the Tea Party movement in the Twitterverse. Specifically, this chapter features an analysis of all the tweets with at least one #teaparty hashtag that were posted on Twitter's public timeline between December 9, 2009, at 10h41 pm +0000 and March 19, 2011, at 3h40 pm +0000, a time period roughly coinciding with the 2010 midterm U.S. election cycle (including other important political moments such as the January 2010 special senatorial contest in Massachusetts and the health care reform debate during the summer months of 2010).

Hashtags, which are not native to Twitter but have become associated with this micro-communication platform, can be defined as a "community-driven convention" that have gained traction among tweeters since the San Diego area forest fires in 2007 (Small 2011: 873–4). They generally consist of a single word or a textual or numerical expression immediately preceded by the pound sign (#). Due to the fact that a hashtag is "hyperlinked in the Twitter interface" (Teevan, Ramage, et al. 2011: 39), it enables users who click on it to automatically launch a search for all tweets with the same hashtag. It can serve different purposes: classifying tweets by linking them to broad or narrow topics of interest, helping to establish and coordinate quasi-synchronous or asynchronous decentralized conversations between tweeters who might or might not be formally following each other or share social connections, and enabling users to express themselves by issuing comments, feelings, or opinions (Small 2011; Larsson and Moe 2012).

The open-source data collection and archiving website Twapper Keeper was used to gather information on different aspects of #teaparty tweets, such as their content, the time of their publication, and details about their author. There are no ways to verify independently whether all #teaparty tweets shared on Twitter's public timeline between early December 2009 and mid-March 2011 were archived by the platform Twapper Keeper. In the words of Wilson and Dunn (2011: 1251), "[T]here is no definitive method for determining if the tweet set is complete." However, we are confident based on the large size of the #teaparty dataset that even if some tweets were missed during the archiving process, it would have minimal to no effects on the validity and the explanatory value of this investigation's conclusions.

This analysis looks at 1,688,681 tweets comprising at least one #teaparty hashtag posted by 79,564 unique tweeters during the 67-week period considered in this study. Many recent investigations have examined the involvement of Internet users in Twitter-based politicking phenomena in different national contexts (e.g., Burgess and Bruns 2012; Mascaro and Goggins 2012). However, they have taken into account relatively short periods of time and often a small number of micro-blog entries. While their findings provide some insights on Twitter-based politics, they fail to deliver a detailed characterization of tweeters' involvement in online politicking activities. We believe the "big data" nature of this study is critical to better understand the different facets of the manifestation of the Tea Party movement in the Twittosphere.

In order to provide a detailed assessment of the #teaparty tweeting activity, an analysis of the weekly breakdown (from Monday to Sunday) of the publication of #teaparty tweets was conducted (see Table 4.1). Due to the constraints associated with the time period selected for this investigation, the first week only features five days (from December 9, 2009, at 10h41 pm +0000 to December 13, 2009, 11h59 pm +0000),[2] while the last week contains six days (Monday, March 14, 2011, at 12h00 pm +0000 to March 19, 2011, at 3h40 pm +0000).

As shown in Table 4.1, the rapid intensification of #teaparty tweeting in late April 2010 and early May 2010 can be attributed to several contextual factors, such as the heated Republican primary races in several states involving candidates sympathizing with Tea Party ideals and objectives, different community-based and national Tea Party mobilization initiatives, and the growing attention that this movement received from the U.S. mainstream press (Boykoff and Laschever 2011: 356; Burghart and Zeskind 2010). The final days of April 2010 and the first weeks of May 2010 were also marked by the adoption of laws and other regulations in several states addressing some of the social and economic concerns of Tea Partiers. For example, Arizona governor Jan Brewer signed into law SB 1070 on April 23, 2010, and HB 2281 on May 10, 2010, which sought "to streamline undocumented migration and . . . [to essentially erase] La Raza and Mexican-American Studies at the Tucson Unified School District" respectively (Torres 2012: 231).

#teaparty tweeting reached peak levels during the two-week period immediately preceding the elections on November 2, 2010, and the whole week of the elections. Specifically, 65,609 #teaparty tweets were posted between October 18 and October 24, 2010 (3.89 percent of the dataset), 72,088 tweets were published between October 25 and October 31, 2010 (4.27 percent of the dataset), and 75,409 posts were shared between November 1 and November 7, 2010 (4.47 percent of the dataset). On Election Day alone (November 2, 2010), #teaparty tweeters shared 16,613 micro-blog entries, a number far surpassing the tweeting volume observed during 30 weeks considered for this study.

A weekly breakdown of the number of tweeters who took part in #teaparty information flows and social relations in the Twitterverse was also conducted (see Table 4.2). It revealed that the number of unique #teaparty contributors reached its highest levels during the two-week window leading up to the U.S. midterm contest and the week of the elections. Interestingly, 4,188 Internet users participated in the #teaparty tweeting dynamic on November 2, 2010, alone. More #teaparty tweeters were active on that day than during 35 of the 67 weeks (52.2 percent) that were covered in this study. In fact, no less than 4,400 individuals posted at least one #teaparty tweet between the week of April 26 to May 2, 2010, and the week of November 29 to December 5, 2010.

It can be inferred from these results that the #teaparty politicking dynamic was highly heterogeneous and, by extension, not necessarily driven by a small number of influential "A-list" tweeters. In other words, a large number of individuals and

TABLE 4.1 Weekly Volume of #teaparty Tweets

#	Weekly Breakdown	Number of Tweets	Percentage	#	Weekly Breakdown	Number of Tweets	Percentage
1	09-dec-09 to 13-dec-09	9,495	0.56	21	26-apr-10 to 02-may-10	18,709	1.11
2	14-dec-09 to 20-dec-09	16,984	1.01	22	03-may-10 to 09-may-10	35,136	2.08
3	21-dec-09 to 27-dec-09	14,364	0.85	23	10-may-10 to 16-may-10	34,006	2.01
4	28-dec-09 to 03-jan-10	17,560	1.04	24	17-may-10 to 23-may-10	39,426	2.33
5	04-jan-10 to 10-jan-10	15,883	0.94	25	24-may-10 to 30-may-10	35,274	2.09
6	11-jan-10 to 17-jan-10	15,039	0.89	26	31-may-10 to 6-jun-10	22,336	1.32
7	18-jan-10 to 24-jan-10	12,206	0.72	27	07-jun-10 to 13-jun-10	20,293	1.20
8	25-jan-10 to 31-jan-10	17,870	1.06	28	14-jun-10 to 20-jun-10	37,973	2.25
9	01-feb-10 to 07-feb-10	14,333	0.85	29	21-jun-10 to 27-jun-10	37,599	2.23
10	08-feb-10 to 14-feb-10	11,607	0.69	30	28-jun-20 to 04-jul-10	37,708	2.23
11	15-feb-10 to 21-feb-10	15,643	0.93	31	05-jul-10 to 11-jul-10	42,352	2.51
12	22-feb-10 to 28-feb-10	18,822	1.11	32	12-jul-10 to 18-jul-10	48,197	2.85
13	01-mar-10 to 07-mar-10	17,576	1.04	33	19-jul-10 to 25-jul-10	29,793	1.76
14	08-mar-10 to 14-mar-10	10,332	0.61	34	26-jul-10 to 01-aug-10	36,078	2.14
15	15-mar-10 to 21-mar-10	6,849	0.41	35	02-aug-10 to 08-aug-10	45,947	2.72
16	22-mar-10 to 28-mar-10	9,558	0.57	36	09-aug-10 to 15-aug-10	42,111	2.49
17	29-mar-10 to 04-apr-10	9,439	0.56	37	16-aug-10 to 22-aug-10	43,538	2.58
18	05-apr-10 to 11-apr-10	15,538	0.92	38	23-aug-10 to 29-aug-10	29,944	1.77
19	12-apr-10 to 18-apr-10	11,315	0.67	39	30-aug-10 to 05-sep-10	51,555	3.05
20	19-apr-10 to 25-apr-10	8,261	0.49	40	06-sep-10 to 12-sep-10	51,888	3.07

(Continued)

TABLE 4.1 (Continued)

#	Weekly Breakdown	Number of Tweets	Percentage	#	Weekly Breakdown	Number of Tweets	Percentage
41	13-sep-10 to 19-sep-10	24,318	1.44	55	20-dec-10 to 26-dec-10	9,728	0.58
42	20-sep-10 to 26-sep-10	64,310	3.81	56	27-dec-10 to 02-jan-11	5,184	0.31
43	27-sep-10 to 03-oct-10	47,710	2.83	57	03-jan-11 to 09-jan-11	10,731	0.64
44	04-oct-10 to 10-oct-10	58,459	3.46	58	10-jan-11 to 16-jan-11	10,813	0.64
45	11-oct-10 to 17-oct-10	58,493	3.46	59	17-jan-11 to 23-jan-11	4,237	0.25
46	18-oct-10 to 24-oct-10	65,609	3.89	60	24-jan-11 to 30-jan-11	6,740	0.40
47	25-oct-10 to 31-oct-10	72,088	4.27	61	31-jan-11 to 06-feb-11	1,489	0.09
48	01-nov-10 to 07-nov-10	75,409	4.47	62	07-feb-11 to 13-feb-11	2	0.00
49	08-nov-10 to 14-nov-10	43,319	2.57	63	14-feb-11 to 20-feb-11	94	0.01
50	15-nov-10 to 21-nov-10	36,458	2.16	64	21-feb-11 to 27-feb-11	1,472	0.09
51	22-nov-10 to 28-nov-10	31,827	1.88	65	28-feb-11 to 06-mar-11	2,535	0.15
52	29-nov-10 to 05-dec-10	34,846	2.06	66	07-mar-11 to 13-mar-11	1,599	0.09
53	06-dec-10 to 12-dec-10	5,361	0.32	67	14-mar-11 to 19-mar-11	7,313	0.43
54	13-dec-10 to 19-dec-10	0	0.00		Total	1,688,681	100.00

TABLE 4.2 Weekly Number of Tweeters Contributing at Least Once to the #teaparty Tweeting Dynamic

#	Weekly Breakdown	Number of Unique Tweeters	#	Weekly Breakdown	Number of Unique Tweeters
1	09-dec-09 to 13-dec-09	1,572	21	26-apr-10 to 02-may-10	4,416
2	14-dec-09 to 20-dec-09	2,513	22	03-may-10 to 09-may-10	6,083
3	21-dec-09 to 27-dec-09	2,268	23	10-may-10 to 16-may-10	5,405
4	28-dec-09 to 03-jan-10	2,369	24	17-may-10 to 23-may-10	7,059
5	04-jan-10 to 10-jan-10	2,592	25	24-may-10 to 30-may-10	5,957
6	11-jan-10 to 17-jan-10	2,388	26	31-may-10 to 06-jun-10	4,632
7	18-jan-10 to 24-jan-10	2,499	27	07-jun-10 to 13-jun-10	4,714
8	25-jan-10 to 31-jan-10	2,951	28	14-jun-10 to 20-jun-10	5,387
9	01-feb-10 to 07-feb-10	3,235	29	21-jun-10 to 27-jun-10	4,669
10	08-feb-10 to 14-feb-10	2,719	30	28-jun-20 to 04-jul-10	5,903
11	15-feb-10 to 21-feb-10	3,150	31	05-jul-10 to 11-jul-10	5,676
12	22-feb-10 to 28-feb-10	3,635	32	12-jul-10 to 18-jul-10	6,920
13	01-mar-10 to 07-mar-10	3,300	33	19-jul-10 to 25-jul-10	5,873
14	08-mar-10 to 14-mar-10	2,321	34	26-jul-10 to 01-aug-10	5,451
15	15-mar-10 to 21-mar-10	2,243	35	02-aug-10 to 08-aug-10	5,522
16	22-mar-10 to 28-mar-10	3,003	36	09-aug-10 to 15-aug-10	5,131
17	29-mar-10 to 04-apr-10	2,632	37	16-aug-10 to 22-aug-10	5,542
18	05-apr-10 to 11-apr-10	3,143	38	23-aug-10 to 29-aug-10	5,256
19	12-apr-10 to 18-apr-10	3,295	39	30-aug-10 to 05-sep-10	6,916
20	19-apr-10 to 25-apr-10	2,715	40	06-sep-10 to 12-sep-10	6,697

(Continued)

TABLE 4.2 *(Continued)*

#	Weekly Breakdown	Number of Unique Tweeters	#	Weekly Breakdown	Number of Unique Tweeters
41	13-sep-10 to 19-sep-10	5,595	55	20-dec-10 to 26-dec-10	2,152
42	20-sep-10 to 26-sep-10	7,520	56	27-dec-10 to 02-jan-11	1,537
43	27-sep-10 to 03-oct-10	5,615	57	03-jan-11 to 09-jan-11	3,968
44	04-oct-10 to 10-oct-10	6,452	58	10-jan-11 to 16-jan-11	3,604
45	11-oct-10 to 17-oct-10	7,084	59	17-jan-11 to 23-jan-11	1,463
46	18-oct-10 to 24-oct-10	8,487	60	24-jan-11 to 30-jan-11	2,171
47	25-oct-10 to 31-oct-10	9,823	61	31-jan-11 to 06-feb-11	621
48	01-nov-10 to 07-nov-10	12,602	62	07-feb-11 to 13-feb-11	2
49	08-nov-10 to 14-nov-10	6,323	63	14-feb-11 to 20-feb-11	91
50	15-nov-10 to 21-nov-10	5,978	64	21-feb-11 to 27-feb-11	899
51	22-nov-10 to 28-nov-10	4,980	65	28-feb-11 to 06-mar-11	1,094
52	29-nov-10 to 05-dec-10	4,995	66	07-mar-11 to 13-mar-11	784
53	06-dec-10 to 12-dec-10	1,484	67	14-mar-11 to 19-mar-11	2,703
54	13-dec-10 to 19-dec-10	0			

organizations used Twitter to post content and engage in social interactions with other Internet users.

An analysis of direct social interactions between #teaparty tweeters was also conducted through the consideration of tweets serving a @reply function (tweets starting with the "@" sign immediately followed by the username of a tweeter and the text of the interaction (@username ABC) with a #teaparty hashtag. It indicated that only 85,629 tweets with the @reply mechanism (approximately 4 percent of all #teaparty tweets) were posted by 11,296 unique tweeters (close to 14.20 percent of all #teaparty tweeters). In order to understand the structure of the #teaparty conversation, a network analysis of direct social contacts was conducted with the help of the data visualization platform Gephi (version 0.8.1 beta). Only @replies posted during four specific weeks (Monday through Sunday) were taken into account in the network analysis:

- Week in 2009 with the highest volume of #teaparty publications;
- Two weeks in 2010 with the highest volume of #teaparty tweets;
- Week in 2011 with the highest volume of #teaparty posts.

Unlike 2009 and 2011, where only one week's worth of tweets was considered in the analysis, two weeks were considered in 2010 because more tweets were posted per week during that year than during the two other years. Moreover, the entire year of 2010 was considered in this investigation, while only a partial month was studied in 2009 and approximately two-and-a-half months were taken into account in 2011.

Four graphs (one per week) were produced with the help of Fruchterman and Reingold's "force-based" algorithm (1991) (see Figures 4.1, 4.2, 4.3, and 4.4). It determined the layout of the nodes, which represent tweeters who were involved in #teaparty social interactions (both senders and receivers), and edges, which can be defined as social interaction links. According to this algorithm, nodes sharing links tend to be attracted by each other while non-linked nodes tend to repulse each other much like electric forces of different charges.

The graphs show that while some tweeters were part of more social interactions than others and could be therefore defined as conversation catalysts (see Figure 4.4), the #teaparty conversation was for the most part highly decentralized. This dynamic fell far outside the traditional "command and control" nature of campaign communication. In such a situation, it is near impossible for a market-oriented party to impose message discipline and to follow a structured campaign script. The repercussions of this new dynamic were evident during the 2010 midterm election when Joe Miller (Alaska), Christine O'Donnell (Delaware), and Sharron Angle (Nevada) derailed the Republicans' attempt to take control of the Senate.

In order to demonstrate the *boutique* nature of the Tea Party brand of populism, we examined the involvement of political elites in the #teaparty tweeting dynamic.

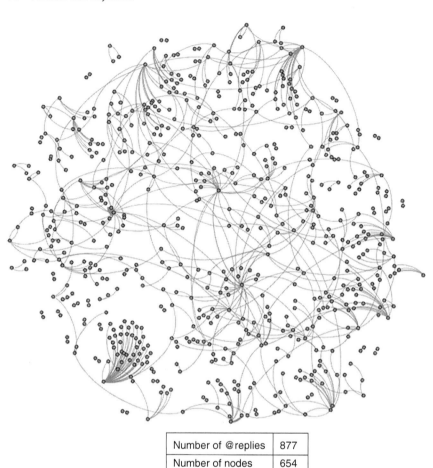

Number of @replies	877
Number of nodes	654
Number of edges	648

FIGURE 4.2 Network Analysis of @replies with at Least One #teaparty Hashtag (December 14 to December 20, 2009)

While some formal and informal political players (e.g., elected and nonelected politicians, interest groups, media personalities, etc.) considered as leading voices of the Tea Party movement in the U.S. political landscape engaged with varying intensity in #teaparty tweeting, many others played a more peripheral and, in some cases, quasi-nonexistent role.

As shown in Table 4.3, national organizations Tea Party Patriots and Tea Party Nation were actively involved in #teaparty tweeting. Comparatively, FreedomWorks only shared 5 #teaparty micro-blog entries, while other national groups affiliated with the Tea Party movement, such as Tea Party Express or ResistNet, did not even participate in the #teaparty tweeting dynamic. In fact,

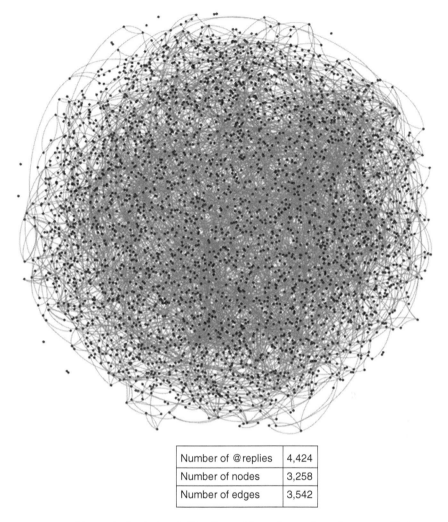

FIGURE 4.3 Network Analysis of @replies with at Least One #teaparty Hashtag (November 1 to November 7, 2010)

a large number of small and midsize regional and national Tea Party groups did not post #teaparty tweets during the time period considered in this study. Many of them, such as the Tea Party Federation, Nationwide Tea Party Coalition, and TeaParty365, were not even present in the Twitterverse during the 16-month period covered by this study, despite the fact that they were present on other Web 1.0 and Web 2.0 media platforms.

While many of the public figures and organizations listed in the previous tables did not partake in the #teaparty tweeting dynamic, most of them did publish at least one tweet during the time period considered for the quantitative content

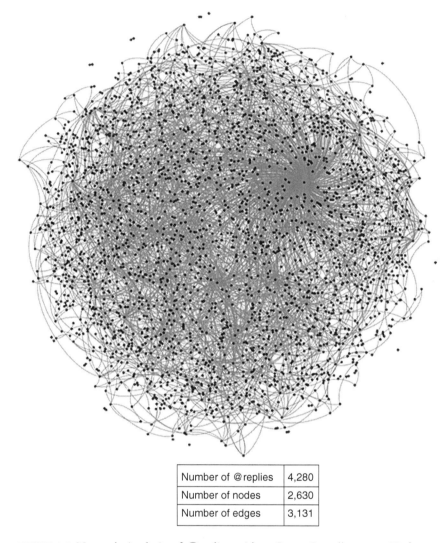

FIGURE 4.4 Network Analysis of @replies with at Least One #teaparty Hashtag (October 25 to October 31, 2010)

analysis (see Tables 4.4 and 4.5). In fact, the overwhelming majority of those who were active in the Twitterverse discussed in a mostly unidirectional manner a wide range of issues that could be of interest to Tea Partiers. They also engaged in mostly top-down political mobilization operations by inciting their followers to donate money to their campaign or by taking part in different online or real-world mobilization efforts. For instance, senatorial hopeful Joe W. Miller in Alaska tweeted the information shown in Figure 4.6 on June 15, 2010, at 16:39 +0000.

Also, Nevada Senate candidate Sharron Angle posted the tweet shown in Figure 4.7 on May 10, 2010, at 20:00 +0000.

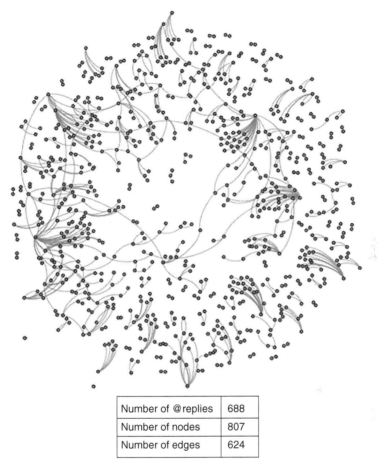

Number of @replies	688
Number of nodes	807
Number of edges	624

FIGURE 4.5 Network Analysis of @replies with at Least One #teaparty Hashtag (January 10 to January 16, 2011)

TABLE 4.3 Number of #teaparty Tweets by Organizations Affiliated with the Tea Party Movement

Organization	Number of Tea Party Tweets
Tea Party Patriots	2,553
Tea Party Nation	105
FreedomWorks	5
Tea Party Express	0
ResistNet	0

TABLE 4.4 Number of #teaparty Tweets by Media and Political Personalities Affiliated with the Tea Party Movement

Political or Media Personality	Number of Tea Party Tweets
Andrew P. Napolitano	35
Glenn Beck	12
Rush Limbaugh	5
Dick Armey	0
Sarah Palin	0

TABLE 4.5 Number of #teaparty Tweets by Senate Contenders Affiliated with the Tea Party Movement

Senate Contenders	Number of #teaparty Tweets
Joe W. Miller (Alaska)	921
Christine O'Donnell (Delaware)	168
Sharron Angle (Nevada)	102
Pat Toomey (Pennsylvania).	2
Jim DeMint (North Carolina)	1
Rand Paul (Kentucky)	0
Ken Buck (Colorado)	0
Marco Rubio (Florida)	0

Today's Meet 'n Greet, 5-7 PM, #Alaska Cab, K-Beach, between Murwood & Trinity Greenhouse, #Kenai #teaparty Looking forward to meeting you.

FIGURE 4.6 Joe W. Millier's June 15, 2010, Tweet

Have you watched my latest YouTube videos? Hear my radio ads, how I can win & much more: www.youtube.com/sharronangle #tcot #teaparty

FIGURE 4.7 Sharron Angle's May 10, 2010, Tweet

Our analysis points to one specific conclusion: the #teaparty conversation in the Twittosphere was mostly fueled by ordinary Internet users during the 2010 U.S. midterm election cycle. They were able to develop and sustain a political discourse largely outside the control of mainstream political actors. In other words, it was not driven by elected or nonelected politicians, conventional media organizations and personalities, or elite-led political groups, which have traditionally been the primary drivers of campaign discourse. We conclude with a broad discussion about the potential repercussions of our findings.

Conclusions for Research and Practice

Previous research has shown that populism can be used efficiently as a political marketing technique. When developed in that manner, populism helps a leader-focused party mobilize supporters for short-term political gains through the dissemination of a central party message. The Tea Party experience shows that the maturation of social media has accentuated the pressure on the sustainability of the inherent contradiction of populism, which is used to mobilize and energize a large group of devoted people while relying on an elitist directional communication flow too often based on a charismatic leader emboldened by his or her ability to energize "the people" and speak on their behalf. We believe that in many ways, the Tea Party political communication, mobilization, and marketing model proves to be the opposite, with a declining leadership influence and the emergence of a hyper decentralized network of individuals and organizations sharing a large number of preferences, interests, and goals. In fact, it points toward the bottom-up democratization of populism, or the true rise of "people-powered politics" (Nielsen 2009: 271), which is likely to affect not only traditional electoral politics, but all aspects of party politics as well as legislative and governing processes in many national contexts over the upcoming decades. In other words, we believe that the Tea Party movement constitutes the materialization of an insurgent political marketing technique that has the potential to redefine the structure of political mobilization, engagement, and organizing in the near future.

Our analysis expressly highlights the challenge posed by the Tea Party experiment for the Republican Party. As mentioned previously, the Republican Party relied on populism in its efforts to appeal to American conservatives and promote its branded political products (Cosgrove 2007). This situation benefited the Republican leadership as long as it retained control of the development and implementation of the strategy and was able to placate the diverse elements of its coalition. Our findings indicate that this control may be slipping away, and it will be increasingly difficult to keep both populist fervor and moderate market-oriented aspirations under the Republican tent.

Finally, our analysis shows that the way the Tea Party movement capitalized on the possibilities of social media will impact how political parties organize, mobilize, and communicate. Social media services have enabled populist movements to set up a structure that can operate outside the scope of traditional political parties and political institutions. The Tea Party experience demonstrated that online communication can be used to enable political movements to promote marketed messages that challenges mainstream parties. With the inevitable proliferation of social media, market-oriented parties will find it increasingly impossible to develop and implement broad-based and coherent campaign strategies that would appeal to a large pool of voters. It will also be more and more difficult to impose message discipline. Market-oriented parties will have to accept the decentralized and disorganized aspect of politicking in the new social media environment or witness a further erosion of their legitimacy.

The communication, organizing, and marketing impact of the Tea Party is likely to be felt in the future. In fact, several social and political movements mimicking the Tea Party blueprint in its entirety, or with some modifications, have gained varying levels of traction in different national contexts since 2009. For instance, the U.S.-based Coffee Party movement, the transnational #Occupy movement, the student protest in reaction to university tuition hikes in the Canadian province of Quebec, and the #idlenomore movement in Canada (Mascaro, Novak, et al. 2012; Gaby and Caren 2012; Sawchuk 2012) have all shown how the Tea Party template can be used to promote specific public policy causes and organize effective protest. Future citizen-driven political mobilization initiatives are likely to improve on the Tea Party mobilization experience, and its legacy will transcend the realm of electoral politics.

Notes

1 www.redistributingknowledge.blogspot.ca/2009/02/seattleites-out-there.html#links
2 There were abnormally low tweeting levels during 3 of the 67 weeks considered in this study (December 13 to December 19, 2010; February 7 to February 13, 2010; and February 14 to February 20, 2011). This situation is caused by a minor technical issue linked to the archiving of the date and time of publication of 58,625 #teaparty microblog entries.

References

Arditi, B. (2005). Populism as an internal periphery of democratic politics. In F. Panizza (Ed.), *Populism and the mirror of democracy* (pp. 72–98). London, UK: Verso.
Bailey, M. A, Mummolo, J., & Hans, N. (2012). Tea Party influence: A story of activists and elites. *American Politics Research, 40*(5), 769–804.
Bennett, W. L., Wells, C., & Freelon, D.G. (2011). Communicating civic engagement: Contrasting models of citizenship in the youth Web sphere. *Journal of Communication, 61*(5), 835–856.
Berg, J. (2011). Why the Tea Party? The challenge of progressive politics in the US. American Political Science Conference, Seattle, WA, September 1–4.
Blumenthal, S. (1980). *The permanent campaign: Inside the world of elite political operatives.* Boston, MA: Beacon Press.
Boykoff, J., & Laschever, E. (2011). The Tea Party movement, framing, and the US media. *Social Movement Studies, 10*(4), 341–366.
Bratich, J. Z. (2011). Pox populi network populism, network sovereigns, and experiments in people-powers. *Cultural Studies <=> Critical Methodologies, 11*(4), 341–345.
Burgess, J., & Bruns, A. (2012). (Not) the Twitter election: The dynamics of the #ausvotes conversation in relation to the Australian media ecology. *Journalism Practice, 6*(3), 384–402.
Burghart, D., & Zeskind, L. (2010, Fall). Tea Party nationalism: A critical examination of the Tea Party movement and the size, scope, and focus of its national factions. Special report from the Institute for Research & Education on Human Rights, Kansas City, MO, 1–94.

Busby, R. (2009). *Marketing the populist politician: The demotic Democrat.* London, UK: Palgrave Macmillan.
Christensen, H. S. (2011). Political activities on the Internet: Slacktivism or political participation by other means. *First Monday, 16*(2).
Cosgrove, K. M. (2007). *Branded conservatives: How the brand brought the right from the fringes to the center of American politics.* New York, NY: Peter Lang Publishing Inc.
Disch, L. (2011). Tea Party movement: The American "precariat"? *Representation, 47*(2), 123–135.
Fruchterman, T.M.J, & Reingold, E. M. (1991). Graph drawing by force-directed placement. *Software—Practice and Experience, 21*(11), 1129–1164.
Gaby, S., & Caren, N. (2012). Occupy online: How cute old men and Malcolm X recruited 400,000 US users to OWS on Facebook. *Social Movement Studies: Journal of Social, Cultural and Political Protest, 11*(3–4), 367–374.
Gibson, R. K. (2012). From brochureware to "MyBo": An overview of online elections and campaigning. *Politics, 32*(2), 77–84.
Gil de Zúñiga, H., Jung, N., & Valenzuela, S. (2012). Social media use for news and individuals' social capital, civic engagement and political participation. *Journal of Computer-Mediated Communication, 17*(3), 319–336.
Goodwin, L. (1978). *The populist moment.* New York, NY: Oxford University Press.
Gunther, R., & Diamond, L. (2003). Species of political parties. *Party Politics, 9*(2), 167–199.
Himelboim, I., Lariscy, R. W., Tinkham, S. F., & Sweetser, K.D. (2012). Social media and online political communication: The role of interpersonal informational trust and openness. *Journal of Broadcasting & Electronic Media, 56*(1), 92–115.
Hofstadter, R. (1952). *The paranoid style in American politics.* New York, NY: Alfred A. Knopf.
Ionescu, G., & Geller, E. (1969). *Populism.* London, UK: MacMillan and Co.
Karpowitz, C. F., Monson, J. Q., Patterson, K. D., & Pope, J. C. (2011). Tea time in America? The impact of the Tea Party movement on the 2010 midterm congressional elections. *PS: Political Science and Politics, 44*(2), 303–309.
Kazin, M. (1998). *The populist persuasion.* Ithaca, NY: Cornell University Press.
Kreiss, D. (2011). Open source as practice and ideology: The origin of Howard Dean's innovations in electoral politics. *Journal of Information Technology & Politics, 8*(3), 367–382.
Kuzminski, A. (2008). *Fixing the system.* New York, NY: The Continuum International Publishing Group Inc.
Langman, L. (2012). Cycles of contention: The rise and fall of the Tea Party. *Critical Sociology, 38*(4), 469–494.
Larsson, A. O., & Moe, H. (2012). Studying political micro-blogging: Twitter users in the 2010 Swedish election campaign. *New Media & Society, 14*(5), 729–747.
Lederer, A., Plasser, F., & Scheuder, C. (2005). The rise and fall of populism in Austria: A political marketing perspective. In D. G. Lilleker & J. Lees-Marshment (Eds.), *Political marketing: A comparative perspective.* Manchester, UK: Manchester University Press.
Lees-Marshment, J. (2001). *Political marketing and British political parties.* Manchester, UK: Manchester University Press.
Mascaro, C. M., & Goggins, S. P. (2012). Twitter as virtual town square: Citizen engagement during a nationally televised Republican Primary debate. American Political Science Conference. New Orleans, LA, August 30–September 2.
Mascaro, C. M., Novak, A., & Goggins, S. P. (2012). The daily brew: The structural evolution of the Coffee Party on Facebook during the 2010 United States midterm election season. *Journal of Information Technology & Politics, 9*(3), 234–253.

Nielsen, R. K. (2009). The labors of Internet-assisted activism: Overcommunication, miscommunication, and communicative overload. *Journal of Information Technology & Politics, 6*(3–4), 267–280.

Panizza, F. (2005). Introduction. In F. Panizza (Ed.), *Populism and the mirror of democracy* (pp. 1–31). London, UK: Verso.

Perrin, A. J, Tepper, S.J., Caren, N., & Morris, S. (2011). Cultures of the Tea Party. *Contexts, 10*(2), 74–75.

Sawchuk, K. (2012). La grève est étudiant/e, la lutte est populaire: The Québec student strike. *Canadian Journal of Communication, 37*(3), 499–504.

Skocpol, T., & Williamson, V. (2012). *The Tea Party and the remaking of Republican conservatism*. New York, NY: Oxford University Press.

Small, T. A. (2011). What the hashtag? *Information, Communication & Society, 14*(6), 872–895.

Teevan, J., Ramage, D., & Morris, M.R. (2011, February 9–12). #Twittersearch: A comparison of microblog search and web search. Proceedings of the Fourth ACM International Conference on Web Search and Data Mining in Kowloon, Hong Kong (pp. 35–44). New York: Association for Computing Machinery.

Torres, R.S. (2012). Border challenges and ethnic struggles for social justice in Arizona: Hispanic communities under siege. In M. Lusk, K. Staudt, & E. Moya (Eds.), *Social justice in the US-Mexico border region* (pp. 231–246). New York, NY: Springer.

Wilson, C., & Dunn, A. (2011). Digital media in the Egyptian revolution: Descriptive analysis from the Tahrir data sets. *International Journal of Communication, 5*, 1248–1272.

Winder, G., & Tenscher, J. (2012). Populism as political marketing technique. In J. Lees-Marshment (Ed.), *Routledge handbook of political marketing* (pp. 230–242). London, UK: Routledge.

Wring, D., & Ward, S. (2010). The media and the 2010 campaign: The television election? *Parliamentary Affairs, 63*(4), 802–817.

5
PRIMARY ELECTIONS AND US POLITICAL MARKETING

Neil Bendle and Mihaela-Alina Nastasoiu

Overview of the Topic

In the 2012 Republican presidential primary Jon Huntsman, Jr., was feared by the Democrats (Gibson 2012). Sadly for the former Utah governor, he may have appealed to the Republicans' pragmatic desire to win, but he failed to ignite their passion and floundered. Political marketing research usually focuses on serving the general electorate, but in the United States candidates first must win a primary, meaning candidates face at least two markets. Thus here we discuss and test: (1) What does a voter's preference in a primary mean? and (2) What market do candidates focus on?

Presidential primary rules are complex. Reports suggested that Hillary Clinton's experienced 2008 team misunderstood the process (Tumulty 2008). These reports' plausibility illustrates primaries' confusing nature. The generic term, primaries, covers caucuses, community meetings that can involve a considerable commitment of time and effort, and primaries that have more modest demands, e.g., merely ticking a ballot. Caucuses favor candidates with a fervent but not necessarily extensive following. Primaries favor candidates with wide, but not necessarily deep, support (Redlawsk, Tolbert, and Donovan 2011). As primaries are administered at the state level, rules differ. Open primaries allow all electors to participate, whereas closed primaries are restricted to registered party supporters. An open primary theoretically selects candidates nearer the general public's preferences, favoring electable candidates (Kaufman, Gimpel, and Hoffman 2003) but risking sabotage (Fact Check 2008). (In 2008 conservative provocateur Rush Limbaugh urged Republicans to support Hillary Clinton to prolong her battle with Barack Obama.) As formats vary, recommended strategies may differ. For example, the 2008 Texas Democratic primary had a dual primary/caucus structure. Should candidates serve the primary voters, or more involved caucus goers? Furthermore, political entities whose members cannot vote in the presidential election, e.g., Puerto Rico, vote in primaries. Primary voters are thus not simply a subset of the general electorate.

Candidates must garner support from a majority of delegates (awarded by representation in Congress and population) attending the party conference held later in the election year. The delegate allocation rules are Byzantine and differ between parties. The Democrats, embracing irony, appoint around one-fifth of the delegates. These superdelegates—party elders—may support any candidate.

As later states seem merely to rubber-stamp decisions, going early is desirable. In 2008 Michigan and Florida scheduled primaries ahead of their party assigned dates and were punished with a reduced convention delegation (Parnes and Zenilman 2008). Iowa (the first caucus) and New Hampshire (the first primary) are currently followed by the more ethnically diverse South Carolina and Nevada. After that states often cluster together. The day with the largest number of delegates awarded is called "Super Tuesday" but there is no guarantee this ends the campaign. (In the 2008 Democratic primaries, February 5 saw 25 contests that ultimately changed little.) The sequential process allows marketers and voters to learn from electoral feedback. Losing momentum (Kenney and Rice 1994) dooms campaigns. For example, in 2008 Rudy Giuliani's poor showing in states he deliberately ignored generated a perception that he was a loser before he vigorously contested an election (MacAskill 2008). Serving all voters equally may be less electorally successful than only serving early states. This may explain the resilience of certain policies, e.g., ethanol subsidies thought to favor Iowa (*Economist* 2011).

All these issues—formats changing voter average involvement and ideological position, differing electorates, and voters having unequal influence—challenge the marketing concept. Even ignoring complexities, such as markets for donations and press coverage, it is exceptionally difficult to achieve a clear market orientation when the market is so amorphous.

Applying the marketing concept to politics requires that voters have clear preferences. In primaries, however, voters are often thinking beyond their own preferences. Normative decision-making advice suggests considering (a) the predicted preferences of general election voters, a candidate's electability, and (b) viability: Can the candidate win the nomination? Given this advice, should candidates serve the voters' sincere or strategic preferences?

Primaries create secondary challenges. The temporal gap between elections fuels the cliché that candidates become more extreme in the primaries and moderate for the general election. This resetting post primary, an "Etch-a-Sketch" approach, was imprudently outlined by the Romney campaign's Eric Fehrnstrom. The logic of repositioning between elections is impeccable but implementation difficult (Knuckey and Lees-Marshment 2005). Finally, given that the US system is candidate-centric, parties' and primary candidates' interests all matter and may not align. We consider the impact of any misalignment.

In the rest of the chapter we review relevant prior literature. We examine how candidates might follow the marketing concept when voter preferences are complex, and the market targeted is ambiguous. We use data to better understand voter preferences and candidate strategies, and conclude by calling for more research on primaries.

Review of Previous Literature

Primary elections have unique implications for political marketing theory and practice, but the limited political marketing research on primaries has largely used them to examine general questions. Our research rectifies this by stressing primaries' uniqueness.

In commercial marketing, other consumers' preferences may matter to a consumer. Network goods give increasing utility as more use them, e.g., telephones, software, and fashion (Amaldoss and Jain 2005). In political science Abramowitz and his colleagues studied strategic voting (Abramowitz, McGlennon, and Rapoport 1981; Abramowitz and Stone 1984; Abramowitz 1989; see also Abramson et al. 1992). Strategic voting, considering what is achievable given other voters' preferences, is not exclusive to primaries, e.g., tactical voting first-past-the-post parliamentary elections. Strategic voting occurs when voters consider *electability*, the collective preferences of general election voters, and/or *viability*, the collective preferences of primary voters (Abramowitz 1989). Research suggests that electability and/or viability can matter. As considering other voters' preferences increases the possibility of error, Redlawsk, Tolbert, and Donovan (2011) argue a benefit of the Democrats' Iowa caucus is that it encourages sincere preference expression on the first round by allowing later support switching. The marketing concept suggests serving voter preferences, but strategic and sincere preferences may differ. Sincere preferences are the default assumption in political marketing, but how should strategic voters be served?

Momentum research in political science generates theories relevant to primaries. Kenney and Rice (1994) study secondary data, so cannot delve deeply into individual thought processes, but suggest five distinct ways momentum might matter.

1. Contagion (enthusiastic herding toward winners).
2. Supporting the Winner (less enthusiastic herding).
3. Strategic Voter (use early primary wins as electability signal).
4. Cue-taking (follow others' judgment).
5. Inevitability (vote for non-favored candidate who will win anyhow).

In political marketing Newman and Sheth (1985) examined how voters make primary decisions. Johnson's (2006) review highlighted the difference between competitive and noncompetitive primaries. Recently Parker (2012) examined politicians' brands, and Hassell (2011) money in the 2008 primaries. Ormrod and his colleagues' (2007) work focusing on a UK party leadership campaign has interesting parallels with US primaries. These scholars suggest that individual candidates have distinct market orientations. We use this idea to consider how primary candidates behave, a logical extension given US politics' candidate centricity. Other US political marketing research, not explicitly primary focused, employs primaries as its backdrop. For example, Knuckey and Lees-Marshment (2005) discuss how the primaries impacted George W. Bush's positioning.

Bannon's (2005) concept of internal management is important given that primaries highlight intra-party tensions. Politicians upsetting party supporters, focusing exclusively on the general electorate, may be "primaried," i.e., challenged in the primary. While the evidence of the impact of being primaried is mixed (Boatright 2009), in the Tea Party era it worries incumbents. With high congressional reelection rates (Friedman and Holden 2009), general elections are often relatively uncompetitive and a primary is many politicians' most challenging election. The advice to a candidate focused only on winning becomes to pay more attention to internal than external marketing. Should candidates really focus on their supporters and not the wider electorate? Concentrating power in the hands of party voters at the expense of the public undermines the democratic accountability argument for political marketing (Lees-Marshment 2009). This is less of a concern in presidential than congressional campaigns, however, as rarely does nomination effectively guarantee the presidency; presidential candidates must always appeal beyond their party bases.

Not only do primaries pose fascinating challenges, but Bowler, Donovan, and Fernandez (1996) suggest that reforms such as California's reduced party control over nominations, i.e., more important primaries, since the 1970s drove industry growth.

In summary, the literature suggests that primaries raise theoretical challenges around the nature of voter preferences and market focus. Furthermore, primaries create strategic challenges and employment opportunities for political marketers. Primaries matter.

Theoretical Framework

What Preferences to Serve?

In many ways the primary process is a wonderful expression of democracy. Party grandees cannot anoint the nominee in smoke-filled rooms. Primaries expand democracy, extending voter input from choosing between candidates to selecting the competing candidates. Primaries also bring challenges for political marketing theory.

US political parties have a loose structure (Knuckey 2010). Ordinary voters, rather than paid-up party members, identify as Republican or Democrat and choose candidates. A large number of loosely associated voters give primaries surface commonalities with presidential elections, i.e., mass enfranchisement of the relatively uninvolved. One critical difference from a general election is the complexity of the voter's decision. Primary elections select candidates for a future election; voters are therefore advised to consider the future electorate's anticipated preference. This predicted appeal to the wider electorate is a candidate's electability. Candidates must not only appeal to primary voters but also must reassure the primary voters that they can appeal to general election voters. Similarly, in primaries with three or more candidates, voters should consider whether a candidate is viable, i.e., can win the nomination. Most primaries feature numerous candidates, at least initially, so viability matters. Consider a Democrat in 2004 who preferred Joe Lieberman, or a Republican who favored Jon Huntsman in 2012. A voter might conclude that these candidates were not viable and so support his or her second-favored candidate. Voters strategically prefer a viable second-best candidate over their ideal candidate whom few others favor.

The marketing concept is threatened by confusion over a voter's preference: sincere or strategic (see Figure 5.1).

Market orientation in politics (Lees-Marshment 2001; Marland, Giasson, and Lees-Marshment 2012) is about serving voters within ideological constraints. The party's challenge mirrors the voter's compromise between sincere and strategic voting. Any party unwilling to compromise unpopular beliefs may never achieve power. Too much compromise, however, and the party abandons all to gain power. Analogously, a primary voter wanting his or her party to gain power needs an electable candidate nominated, but some candidates might represent an

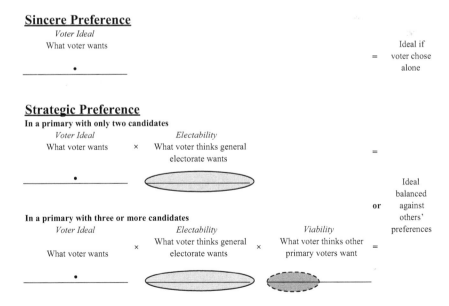

FIGURE 5.1 Voters' Ideological Positions and the Impact of Sincere and Strategic Preferences

intolerable compromise. Balancing the ideal and achievable can be challenging. Our self-knowledge is imperfect but we have some idea what we like. Unfortunately we aren't good at predicting the preferences of large numbers of others (Fields and Schuman 1976). If we poorly predict the future preferences of the entire US voting population, how should we adjust our trade-off to reflect the estimate's imprecision? Even political junkies may doubt their assessments, allowing the media to influence electability perceptions as the voter casts around for advice.

Where voters trade off electability against their ideal, candidates may be able to influence voter choice through their communications. Practitioners will enjoy the opportunity to persuade, but if voters' decisions change with the message, this raises the theoretical problem of preference endogeneity—there is no fixed preference to serve. Labile voter preferences mean a sales orientation, persuading voters to choose an already adopted product, rather than a market orientation, serving exogenous voter preferences, may be relatively more effective as voters don't really know what they want. The influence of election type, primary versus general election, on any orientation's effectiveness deserves empirical testing. Our tentative advice is that primary, compared to presidential, candidates should place relatively greater emphasis on selling existing positions, rather than adapting to the voters' uncertain tastes.

Although the consensus may arise from untested media pronouncement, voters often seem to agree on the electability of candidates. More electable candidates usually win primaries, having done so for at least four of the last six contested presidential primaries: Gore 2000, Kerry 2004, McCain 2008, and Romney 2012. (The 2000 Republican and 2008 Democratic primaries are harder to judge in terms of the competing candidates' electability.) Candidates are thus advised to highlight claims to electability. Candidates embracing policies favored by the general public, if seen as "genuine," should theoretically increase their electability. Though the relationship is complex, increasing electability, all else constant, should increase viability, given that electability influences some primary voters. Less electable candidates must therefore highlight their unique positions, while combating any appearance of unelectablity. Such candidates may hope to persuade primary voters that the country actually supports their ideas. Furthermore, they should emphasize personal qualities that appeal irrespective of policy; for example, Mike Huckabee's humor in 2008. We suggest focusing on "product attributes" all customers like, rather than on elements with niche appeal. A personal narrative that works with the candidate's own party and general electorate is ideal. Opponents know this, however, so candidates using personal narratives must expect pushback. John Kerry's war record was neutralized by "Swiftboating," while John McCain's war record fed the opposition narrative that he was overly hawkish. Barack Obama's appeal in healing the racial divide was deliberately undermined using the provocative words of his former pastor, Reverend Jeremiah Wright.

Primaries, compared to smoke-filled rooms, reduce coercion of party supporters into backing establishment candidates, yet establishment candidates tend to win.

With difficult choices, voters may allow themselves to be persuaded that an establishment candidate is the right pick. John Kerry excited Democrats less than Howard Dean in the 2004 primary, but Iowa voters chose Kerry. Electability may generate self-coercion—voters pick electable, but unexciting, choices. The rebel message may be easier to deploy—e.g., Pat Buchanan in 1996, Newt Gingrich in 2012, John McCain in 2000—but rebels usually end badly. Establishment support helps.

Electability matters when the aim is winning. Though often critical, winning is but one political objective (Butler and Collins 1996). Some campaign to raise issues (Tom Tancredo in 2008), or to gain personal notoriety (Donald Trump and Herman Cain in 2012). Losing primary campaigns air minority views without general election damage. Compare Ron Paul's impact in the 2008 and 2012 Republican primaries (Kleefeld 2012) with Ralph Nader's, a third-party candidate in the 2000 general election who may have sunk Al Gore's campaign (Hedgcock, Rao, and Chen 2009).

What Markets to Serve?

Market orientation usually concerns parties, but our research suggests that both the entity taking the orientation, and the market being oriented toward, need be explicitly defined. This reinforces research noting the complexity of political markets (Lees-Marshment 2001; Ormrod 2005). Ormrod et al. (2007) highlighted in a "UK primary" that candidates have orientations and may focus on several markets, e.g., endorsers, donors, and voters. Orientating against multiple markets causes problems optimizing strategy. The problem of balancing different voters' preferences, already well known, is exacerbated by multiple markets. It is mathematically impossible to optimize against two different goals, serving two different markets, without a clear weighting between them, and weightings are judgment calls. This is a problem in all political marketing but is especially challenging in primaries given market definition issues.

Primary candidates may face an electorate quite different from that in the general election. Knuckey (2010) argues that John Kerry's antiwar position wasn't market oriented in the 2004 presidential election, implicitly assuming the general electorate as the market. Howard Dean's antiwar position, however, may have been primary-market oriented, given Democratic doubts about the Iraq war. Dean may have forced John Kerry to become more antiwar to win the primary. Kerry then faced the problem Knuckey describes. Kerry found it impossible to fully serve the differing preferences of the Democrats and the general public.

A focus on a candidate's own party, internal marketing (Bannon 2005), can backfire. Internal euphoria may describe the 1964 Republican primary. The winner, Barry Goldwater, trenchantly proclaimed his libertarian views to acclaim from the Republican base. Goldwater's Democratic opponent, President Johnson, deployed the famous "Daisy" advertisement. The subtext wasn't subtle—"The

Republicans nominated an extremist, don't give him nuclear weapons." Internal euphoria may also describe recent Republican congressional primaries. The battles of Michael Castle in Delaware in 2010 and Dick Lugar in Indiana in 2012 saw electable candidates defeated by rivals appealing to the party's base. The ideologically pure primary winners, Christine O'Donnell and Richard Mourdock, lost their senatorial elections. The possibility of defeating establishment candidates is a design feature of primaries: forcing candidates to listen to party members. Problems occur, however, when party members' preferences diverge from those of the wider electorate. Would General Mills choose a test market because of the consumers' exceptional involvement and unrepresentative opinions? Parties may maintain a "big tent," a broad base of views to ensure they are representative, at the expense of party distinctiveness and cohesion.

Figure 5.2 illustrates the market problem. Should the primary or general election voters be served? A general election focus is risky. Huntsman, arguably the most electable, wasn't nominated. Such advice raises other concerns: Should candidates ignore US territory voters who can't vote in the general election (Figure 5.3)? Election formats also change the market. The aggregated preferences in Figure 5.4 and the markets in Figure 5.5 differ only through the election rules. Rules change the market without any obvious philosophical justification. Although the general election is, generally, the ultimate aim, we advise practitioners to study primary formats. Delegate allocation systems should drive resource allocation (Ridout, Rottinghaus, and Hosey 2009). For instance, Obama's 2008 campaign focused on the caucus states where motivated support garnered large delegate gains from modest investments.

A final philosophical problem is that some voters are more equal than others. Following the market, therefore, may produce antidemocratic outcomes. The precise impact depends upon the given election, but there exists a perception of declining influence per voter over time in primaries. Should a candidate weight the preferences of voters in early states higher? Even more troubling is the presence of superdelegates. In the 2008 Democratic primary each party elder had around ten thousand times more influence than each common voter (Figure 5.6).

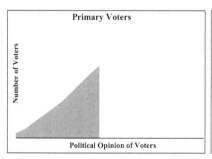 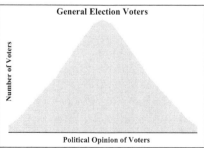

FIGURE 5.2 The Market Problem: Primary and General Election Markets Differ

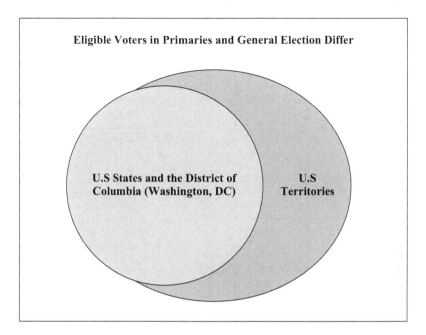

FIGURE 5.3 The Market Problem: Primary Electorate Not a Subset of General Electorate

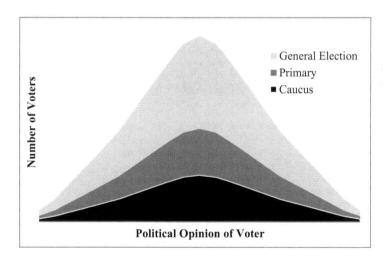

FIGURE 5.4 The Market Problem: Election Type Alters Voter Distribution

If responding to the market is representing superdelegates ten thousand times more actively than common voters, this undermines the idea that political marketing promotes democracy (Lees Marshment 2009). We suggest superdelegates are antithetical to the marketing concept.

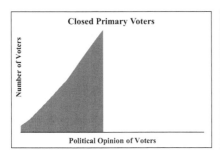 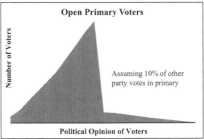

FIGURE 5.5 The Market Problem: Election Format Changes Market

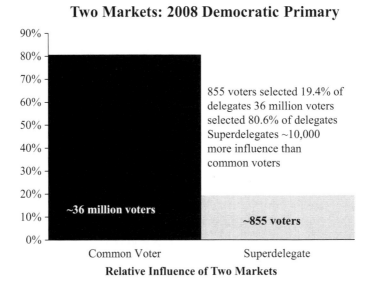

FIGURE 5.6 The Market Problem: Voter Inequality

Strategic Issues

Repositioning toward the political center between the primary and general election should theoretically attract moderate general election voters, but may appear phony, or alienate supporters recruited in the primary. The Republican nominees in 2008 and 2012 seemed unable to effectively moderate post primary. Indeed, pressure from diehard supporters may explain their choice of ideologically pure running mates: Sarah Palin for John McCain in 2008, and Paul Ryan for Mitt Romney in 2012. It is an empirical question whether repositioning without alienating supporters, or appearing phony, is getting easier. Earlier scheduling of primaries creates greater temporal barriers, generating repositioning opportunities, but inconsistency is becoming more easily searchable. The practical advice is that repositioning is tough. As most people tend to excessively discount the future, i.e., ignore problems farther on the horizon, we suggest that candidates take extra care considering the potential general election fallout from primary actions. A candidate such as Mitt Romney in 2012, likely to win the primary, should resist concessions to primary voters that will prove unpopular in the general election. Gaining the nomination by taking positions that spell doom in the general election is counterproductive. Romney's hard line on immigration probably undermined his general election performance, given his appalling support, 26% (RNC 2013), from Hispanic voters. There is an understandable temptation to try to make the primary safer but, deliberately overstating for impact, we suggest a candidate who wins the primary with 50% plus two votes, rather than 50% plus one vote, has conceded too much. Winning today's nomination means little if you lose tomorrow's general election. President Clinton's campaign song, by sheer coincidence, gave the perfect advice to primary candidates. "Don't stop thinking about tomorrow."

Candidate centricity (Ubertaccio 2006; Knuckey 2010) generates highly visible conflicts between candidate and party interests. Parties are relatively weak partly because the primary system limits party leverage. As the candidates have a direct relationship with the voters it is difficult for parties to maintain coherent orientations or brand identities. This has benefits: responding to the United States' diverse nature, Republicans field quite different candidates in the Northeast than the South, but many commercial marketers would flee the challenge of managing a political brand.

Primaries expose fault lines within parties. The party is like a couple who every four years argue viciously before swiftly reconciling to berate the neighbors. The predictable fights, e.g., libertarians versus the Republican mainstream, excite journalists, but the regularity in both parties with which rifts emerge and fade suggests that they are rarely fatal for unity. In 2008, journalists wrongly suggested Clinton's female supporters wouldn't unite behind Obama after the divisive primary. The Republicans put a woman on their ticket, yet Obama still won 56% of women's votes (CAWP 2008). In 2004, Howard Dean quickly endorsed John Kerry after defeat. On the Republican side, despite reported animosity, Mitt Romney endorsed John McCain in 2008, while Newt Gingrich and Rick Santorum endorsed Mitt Romney in 2012. Perhaps the most significant unity challenge of recent times came in 2000. The Bush campaign in South Carolina, a state struggling with a history of racism, was accused of insinuating that John McCain had fathered an African American child outside marriage. Despite this, the party unified when McCain endorsed Bush. The narrative's sheer predictability—irreconcilable primary differences followed swiftly by reconciliation—suggests that voters, the media, even the candidates themselves may, in the heat of the struggle, underestimate the chance of unifying for the general election.

As the media ignore long-shot candidates, all claim they "expect to win" but strategic choices may reveal otherwise. A frugal strategy, maximizing survival time, is often advisable when campaigning to raise issues. Viable candidates, in contrast, generally gamble resources early to generate momentum. Such strategic analysis will be compromised if candidates aren't realistic—a plausible conjecture given politicians are optimistic souls. Indeed, even the most improbable may gain comfort from rollercoaster primary polling. The 2012 Republican primary polls gave almost all candidates (especially Bachmann, Perry, Romney, Gingrich, Cain, and Santorum) cause for optimism at some point.

In sequential elections candidates drop out as they reconcile to inevitable failure, but should a candidate struggle until mathematical defeat or bow out gracefully earlier? Party and candidate interests may diverge. Nominees can be hurt by a lengthy primary struggle (Kenney and Rice 1987). A floor fight at the 1980 Democratic convention between incumbent President Carter and Ted Kennedy damaged the already vulnerable Carter. The party might therefore want to unite, but a trailing candidate, with a non-trivial chance of an upset, may want to soldier on. This candidate's dilemma is analogous to a prisoner's dilemma. Each candidate has an incentive to keep fighting but the optimal group outcome comes from the candidate conceding. Several reasons, however, suggest primary struggles may damage less than is feared. First, losing candidates' ongoing careers may dampen aggressiveness; Mitt Romney conceded relatively early in 2008, eyeing 2012. Second, long primaries can strengthen the winner. Barack Obama faced numerous attacks from Hillary Clinton; the same attacks later failed to resonate for John McCain in the general election. Obama may have developed a defense, or voters may have become inoculated. Third, though primary campaigns' "waste" party supporters' donations on infighting, funding concerns may limit the attacks. Donors loyal to the party may not fund excessively fratricidal assaults. Funding concerns, central to primaries (Hassell 2011), may solve the candidates' dilemma by moving power from candidates to donors. Candidates have to concede though they personally want to limp on, hoping for a miracle. Finally, we may simply overestimate the damage primaries cause. The last two presidents faced tougher primaries than their rivals. George W. Bush lost six primaries and Al Gore none, while serious opposition to Barack Obama lasted till June, and John McCain's last serious rival folded on March 4. Tough primaries cause problems but are hardly kryptonite. Candidates will, of course, still urge their rivals to quit for the sake of party unity, but they shouldn't be petrified of a primary struggle.

Empirical Illustration

We examine two areas:

1. Understanding voter preferences. What is the impact of electability and viability on voter preferences?
2. Understanding candidate strategies toward markets. Which market (the primaries or general election) are candidates focused upon? Does this vary by candidate?

Using survey data from the 2004 and 2008 Democratic primaries, three questions uncover voter preferences. First, do voters consider electability, and if so, when? Second, does within-party liking mirror the general public's liking? Third, are voters' assessments of other voters' opinions subjectively determined? Turning to candidate strategy, we consider if strategy is influenced by the candidate's electability and viability, and whether candidates were focused more on the primary or general election. To consider this, we look at the strategies of Bush and McCain in 2000 using TV advertising data. We also look at the 2012 Republican primaries using Facebook postings.

Understanding Voter Preferences

We investigated how voters integrated electability into their preferences. If voters don't care about electability, then some of the theoretical concerns above can be ignored. We relied on self-reports from Pew Research (2003, 2007) surveys taken several months before the 2004 and 2008 primaries. Respondents were asked if they thought it was most important to:

> Pick a candidate who comes closest to your positions on the issues {POLICY}
> [or]
> Pick a candidate who has the best chance of defeating the [other party's] nominee in next year's election {ELECTABILITY}.

Given the normative advice suggests a tradeoff, this is difficult to answer. We consider evidence of strategic preferences when a large fraction of respondents say electability is the most important factor. A quarter or more of respondents (Figure 5.7) say electability is more important than a candidate's policies. In line with prior research (Abramowitz, McGlennon, and Rapoport 1981; Abramson et al. 1992) we find electability matters. Primaries candidates must serve voters with strategic preferences.

Next we consider if electability's impact varies between elections. Figure 5.7 shows the proportion considering electability more important, excluding don't knows/others. A probit model showed the responses from the 2007 surveys significantly differed from those in 2003 (−.26, $p<.01$). The importance voters assign to electability seems to change with the specific contest rather than being a stable trait of the voter. Given that we compare different surveys, we can only conjecture about reasons; perhaps greater electability differences prompt attention to electability.

We then considered whether within party affection mirrors liking from the general public. If so, viability is a proxy for electability, and vice versa. Voters can form strategic preferences more easily (see Figure 5.1). We examine the American National Election Studies (ANES 2011)[1] data for the primaries between Barack Obama and Hillary Clinton. Unsurprisingly, both candidates were more popular

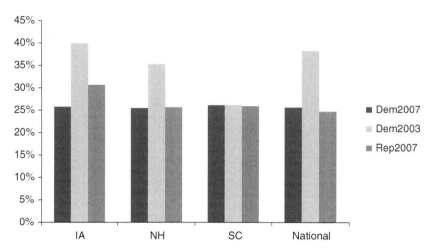

FIGURE 5.7 Percentage of Voters Choosing Electability as More Important Than Policy
Source: Pew Research 2003, 2007

with Democrats than non-Democrats. Early in 2008 those who had voted in the Democratic primaries on average liked Obama and Clinton roughly equally. On a scale anchored by "I like him/her a great deal" (3) and "I dislike him/her a great deal" (-3) (ANES 2011), Obama averaged 1.1 versus Clinton's 1.0. A t-test showed no difference (t(184) = .53, p<.3).

More interestingly, non-Democratic primary voters (n = 1,425) viewed Obama significantly more positively (0.55) than Clinton (–0.27), (t(1424) = 12.67, p<.001). See Figure 5.8. A voter who judged electability by assuming the general public mirrored Democratic primary voters may have overrated Clinton's relative electability. The voter's decision remains complex. Popularity in the party is not strong evidence of wider popularity. Huntsman's fate suggests the opposite may also be true; relatively electable does not automatically imply within-party popularity.

A final illustration of the difficulty of forming a strategic preference concerns the subjective assessment of other voters' preferences. Electability and viability assessments that mirror personal preference aren't independent. They might be biased and thus of less value in forming a strategic preference. To better understand viability predictions we examined primary voters in the ANES survey who, in January/February 2008, thought Barack Obama would lose the nomination. We compared the voters who, when re-interviewed in March/April 2008, had revised their prediction to an Obama win with those whose predictions didn't change. We tested whether those who changed their minds were different in their prior attitudes (i.e., attitudes in January/February) to those whose minds did not change. On average all respondents over the first few months of 2008 moved toward predicting Barack Obama would win the nomination. Rather than examining this logical response to Obama's successful campaign, we tested whether

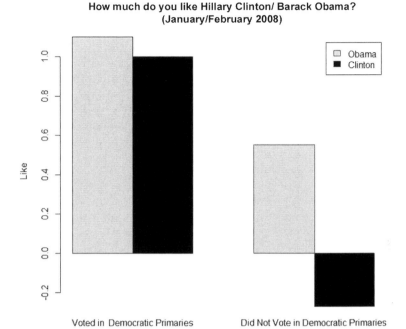

FIGURE 5.8 Liking for Barack Obama and Hillary Clinton, Early 2008
Source: American National Election Studies 2008

those respondents who changed predictions differed from those who didn't change. Assuming all had access to the same information, were those who initially liked Obama more open to accepting he was going to win? If those who liked Obama were more easily persuaded of his viability than those who didn't, this provides evidence of subjectivity.

Those 714 respondents who thought another candidate would be nominated in the first wave on average neither liked nor disliked Barack Obama: 0.16 on a scale from "I like him/her a great deal" (3) to "I dislike him/her a great deal" (–3). Those, however, who changed to predicting an Obama win (n = 398) between wave 1 (January/February) and wave 2 (March/April) initially liked Obama at an average of .45. Those who continued predicting an Obama loss (n = 316) liked him less initially, at −0.21 (see Figure 5.9). A two-sample t-test showed the groups were different in their initial liking for Obama: t(712) = –4.6, p<.01. Respondents showing relative liking for Obama initially were more likely to be persuaded by the mounting evidence that he would become the nominee. We conclude that strategic preferences are subjective and potentially biased.

Complex voter preferences in a primary are hard to serve, challenging the marketing concept. Our advice is to seek to understand voter choice in a specific election. More electable candidates should ensure the media know this. Finally, if

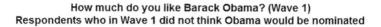
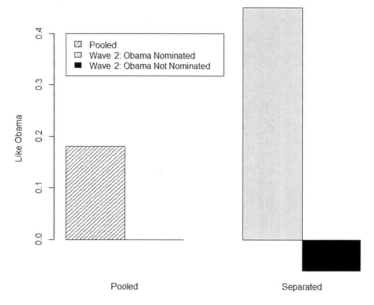

FIGURE 5.9 Liking of Barack Obama Linked to Prediction of His Viability
Source: American National Election Studies 2008

a candidate is likeable this may make it easier to sell the candidate's appeal to other voters. We next turn to how candidates cope with the challenges.

Understanding Candidate Strategies Toward Markets

We infer strategies from two data sets. The Wisconsin Advertising Project (Goldstein, Franz, and Ridout 2002)[2] tracking candidate advertising, and candidates' posts on their Facebook pages.

In the 2000 Republican primary the Wisconsin Advertising Project tracked candidate television advertisements and coded them, e.g., about taxes. This primary focused on the struggle between George W. Bush and John McCain. While both were credible candidates, Bush was widely seen as favorite. McCain's impressive win in the New Hampshire primary on February 1 challenged this ranking, leading to a momentous primary battle in South Carolina. Amid anonymous vicious personal allegations against McCain (Steinhauer 2007), Bush won and went on to a relatively comfortable nomination. Figure 5.10 and Figure 5.11 illustrate the TV advertising strategies of the campaigns. The end-of-day prices for a candidate contract on the Iowa Electronic Market give a market estimate of the candidate's probability of winning the nomination. We plot the daily number of ads focusing only on the most relevant classifications.

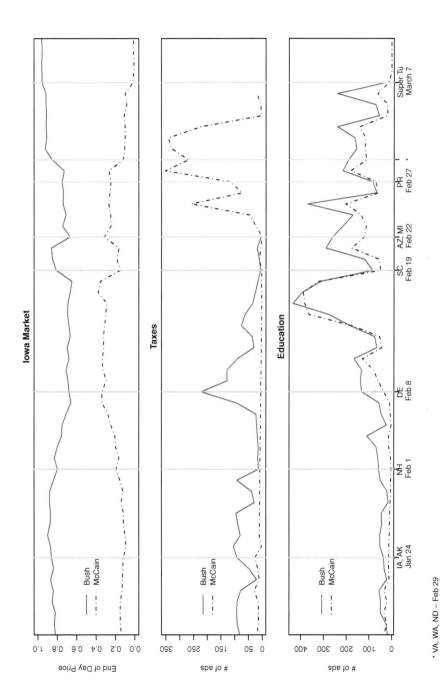

FIGURE 5.10 Bush and McCain Advertising, Policy

Source: Wisconsin Advertising Project 2000 Data and Iowa Electronic Markets (2000) http://tippie.uiowa.edu/iem/

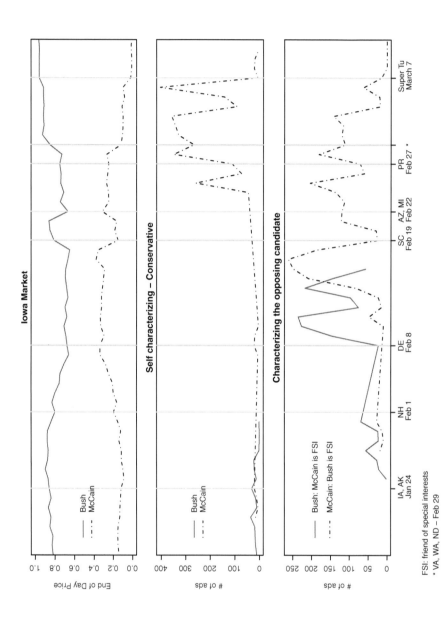

FIGURE 5.11 Bush and McCain Advertising, Character

Source: Wisconsin Advertising Project 2000 Data and Iowa Electronic Markets (2000)

In Figure 5.10 the Iowa prices show Bush as consistent favorite, but McCain's price increases between New Hampshire (NH), February 1, and South Carolina (SC), February 19. After South Carolina, McCain's prices show a downward trend, ameliorated somewhat by the Arizona (AZ) and Michigan (MI) primaries on February 22. The variation allows us to consider how strategy is impacted by the likelihood of success. Tax-focused advertising is considered, as taxes matter strongly to Republican voters. After defeat in South Carolina, McCain, presumably fearing the primary was slipping away from him, started discussing what the voters wanted to hear about: taxes. In contrast, Bush tackled taxes early on in his campaign, building conservative support. Once nominated, Bush strengthened his electability. The number of ads focused on education increased. Education is (unlike taxes) less obviously a "Republican topic," so by focusing on education, Bush seemed able to address his campaign to the general electorate, not only to primary voters.

Figure 5.11 further illustrates this strategy shift. McCain begins to portray himself more conservatively as his chances fade, presumably in the hope of appealing to conservative primary voters. McCain risks damaging his image for the general election, but faced with primary defeat, he probably thinks focusing on today's election is essential. McCain's allegations that Bush is a friend of special interests (FSI), which began before South Carolina, continue despite the more civil tone of the later primaries. Bush's strategy is different. Around the time of South Carolina, he stops FSI attacks on his opponent. Bush seems to begin focusing on the general election. He thinks, or wants voters to think, that the primary is over. His message: Republicans should unite behind Bush, their inevitable nominee. Bush's campaign strategy, facilitated by his success, seems ideal—he focuses on the general election while fighting the primary.

Turning to more recent data, all serious presidential candidates maintain a significant social media presence to communicate with potential voters. We assumed the campaigns control posts, and we can therefore uncover a candidate's focus, primary or general election, by examining posts on their Facebook pages. (We ignore feeds and, as candidates' feed use varies, we therefore cannot discuss total activity.) We infer what market candidates focus on by their use of key words in the early primary season, December 15, 2011, to March 15, 2012. We categorize words as about the primary or general election. For example "Obama" or "nation" show a general election focus and "primary" or "Iowa" a primary focus (see Table 5.1).

TABLE 5.1 Word Classification

Primary Focus	*General Election Focus*
debate, Iowa, Hampshire, Carolina, primary, primaries, caucus, poll, campaign, contribut*, endors*, nomination, delegate	America, Obama, presiden*, country, nation, government, Barack

* All words from stem, i.e., "contribut*" covers "contributor," "contribution," etc.

Figure 5.12 shows the candidates' focus. We aggregated the Facebook data by week and smoothed it out (Loess function, $\alpha = .08$). We took the end-of-day prices from the Iowa electronic market. The Iowa markets did not code Santorum as a candidate. Those betting on Santorum could purchase contracts for "other," which we therefore label as Santorum. The interesting relationship is between the primary and general election focus. Ron Paul has a clear primary focus, using numerous "primary" but few "general election" words. Rick Santorum posts many primary words, but maintains some focus on the general election, consistent with Santorum believing he had a slightly higher chance of nomination. Newt Gingrich's data lack a clear pattern (unfortunately more of his Facebook communications were not posts, and therefore were missing data). Gingrich's focus is somewhat split between the elections. Mitt Romney, the Iowa market's consistently

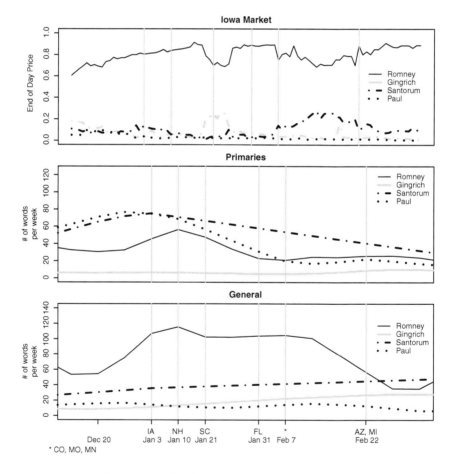

FIGURE 5.12 Word Use on Facebook
Source: Data Collected from Facebook and Iowa Electronic Markets (2012)

heavy favorite, maintains a heavier focus on the general election. This focus is consistent with greater confidence that he will contest that election. Note, however, our earlier contention that Romney may have conceded too much to the primary electorate, especially on immigration. Romney's excessive lead in the Iowa market is also consistent with playing the primary too safe, giving too many policy concessions to conservatives even while attempting to focus communications on the general election.

Another approach to the strategic problem presented by primaries was suggested by Bendle (forthcoming). Using an analytical model based upon Prospect Theory (Kahneman and Tversky 1979), Bendle suggested that electable candidates should attempt to focus primary voters on the other party, describing the disaster that would occur if the other side won. Less electable candidates should attempt to focus primary voters on their own position, emphasizing within-party differences. Bendle discussed how in 2004 Howard Dean (popular in his party but less electable) may have erred by focusing primary voters on defeating President Bush, a task for which John Kerry, perceived as more electable, seemed better suited. Dean lost Iowa, prompting "the scream," maybe partly bemoaning his own faulty strategy. In the 2012 primary, most concluded that Romney was the most electable, followed by Gingrich, with Paul and Santorum relatively unelectable. The model suggests that Romney should attempt to focus voters on the opposition party, increasing electability's weight in strategic preferences. Santorum should be keen to focus voters on the unique benefits he offers his supporters, decreasing electability's weight. Electable Republicans should be self-effacing, asking primary voters to think about the Democrats' flaws. Less electable candidates should seem self-obsessed, stressing what they personally offer. To test this we produced word clouds from the candidates' Facebook postings (Figure 5.13). Word clouds give greater prominence to words said more frequently, e.g., large words are those repeated often. We plotted the candidates arranged by our assessment of electability, moving clockwise from Mitt Romney. The figure suggests the candidates may have learned from Howard Dean's mistakes, as they largely employ the recommended communication strategies. Romney, the most electable, attempts to focus Republican primary voters on President Obama. The subtext: "Nominate me or President Obama will win a second term." Conversely, arguably the least electable candidate, Rick Santorum, asks Republican primary voters to concentrate on him: "Nominate me and get your ideal champion."

We conclude that the market focused on what may, indeed should, be a function of a candidate's electability and viability. Practitioners should assess how much their candidate must focus on the primary. Ideally, a candidate's strong position allows focusing on the general election during the primary, as did Bush's in 2000. This requires courage—few want to emulate Huntsman and position well for the general election while losing the primary. Still, excessive focus on the primary is also fatal. Mitt Romney was always likely to win the 2012 primaries and may have hurt himself with unnecessary concessions to the primary electorate. The ultimate goal is to find a theme that plays well in the primaries and the general election.

FIGURE 5.13 Republican 2012 Candidate Word Clouds
Source: Data from Facebook, word cloud from wordle.net

Sometimes the candidate is successful (or maybe lucky). Obama's message of hope and change worked well for both Democrats and the general public in 2008. His opponent, Clinton, had voted for the Iraq war, so Obama was able to "feel" relatively liberal without making significant policy commitments. Sometimes it is harder to do. In 2004, Kerry had to adopt anti–Iraq war positions to defeat Dean's surprisingly strong primary challenge, positions that may have hindered him later.

The specific issues unique to primaries pose fascinating questions for political marketing theory and practice. The field would benefit greatly from more research in this area and we encourage the study of this fascinating area.

Conclusions for Research and Practice

Strategic Advice

To conclude we consolidate our advice (Table 5.2). The focus and message we recommend depend upon the strength of a candidate's position in any given

TABLE 5.2 Strategic Advice Summary

			General Election (Perceived Electability)		
			Likely to Lose	Toss Up	Likely to Win
Primary (Perceived Viability)	Likely to Lose	*Focus*	Primary	Primary	Primary
		Message	Anything dramatic and game changing.	Depends; Stress candidate's strength	Save country from other party
		Example	Ron Paul (2008 and 2012), e.g., End the Fed	Jon Huntsman, Jr., (2012) stressed electability and duty (served as Obama's ambassador)	Hillary Clinton after Super Tuesday (2008), "only she could win"
	Toss Up	*Focus*	Primary	Primary	Primary
		Message	Raise perception of electability	Raise perception of electability	Save country from other party
		Example	John McCain in early primaries (2008) emphasized leadership	John McCain before South Carolina (2000) highlighted personal story	Barack Obama early in 2008 discussed change
	Likely to Win	*Focus*	General Election	General Election	General Election
		Message	Create appeal to general public	Create appeal to general public	Create appeal to general public
		Example	Bob Dole (1996) emphasized character	George W. Bush (2000) after South Carolina focused on education	Barack Obama after Super Tuesday (2008) discussed racial reconciliation

election. Is the candidate electable and/or viable? We argue that, when focused on the primary, electable candidates should contrast with the opposition, while less electable candidates should focus on what they personally offer. Ideally, however, candidates have such a strong position that they can largely ignore the primary, and position themselves as presidential candidates by discussing issues relevant to the wider electorate.

Summary

Electability and viability involve voters balancing other voters' preferences against their own. The candidate must uncover the voters' preference, sincere or strategic, and decide which to serve. This is a challenge for political marketing theory, but our practical advice is to understand the level of strategic voting. When this is significant, highlight the candidate's characteristics that make him or her popular with the general electorate. A second problem is that it isn't always clear what market the candidate should serve. Most critically, should a candidate focus on the general election or the primary? We demonstrate evidence that candidate strategies differ by their position and success. The general election is the ultimate market; candidates, where possible, focus on this. The ability to do this, however, is a luxury that depends heavily on the strength of a candidate's position. When focused on the primary, we advise relatively electable candidates to communicate more about stopping the other party, while less electable candidates communicate what only they personally can offer. We also noted the considerable challenge of repositioning after a primary and used primaries to consider within-party tensions. Our parting thought: the study of primaries has much more to offer political marketing theory and practice.

Acknowledgment

Thanks to Monica Kozycz for her research support on this chapter.

Notes

1 These materials are based on work supported by the National Science Foundation under grants SES-0535334, SES-0720428, SES-0840550, and SES-0651271, Stanford University, and the University of Michigan. Any opinions, finding and conclusions or recommendations expressed in these materials are those of the author(s) and do not necessarily reflect the views of the funding organizations.
2 The data were obtained from a joint project of the Brennan Center for Justice at New York University School of Law and Professor Kenneth Goldstein of the University of Wisconsin–Madison, and include media tracking data from the Campaign Media Analysis Group in Washington, D.C. The Brennan Center–Wisconsin project was sponsored by a grant from the Pew Charitable Trusts. The opinions expressed in this article are those of the authors and do not necessarily reflect the views of the Brennan Center, Professor Goldstein, or the Pew Charitable Trusts.

References

Abramowitz, A.I. (1989). Viability, electability, and candidate choice in a presidential primary election: A test of competing models. *The Journal of Politics, 51*(4), 977–992.

Abramowitz, A., McGlennon, J., & Rapoport, R. (1981). A note on strategic voting in a primary election. *The Journal of Politics, 43*(3), 899–904.

Abramowitz, A., & Stone, W.J. (1984). *Nomination politics: Party activists and presidential choice.* New York, NY: Praeger.

Abramson, P.R., Aldrich, J.H., Paolino, P., & Rohde, D.W. (1992). "Sophisticated" voting in the 1988 presidential primaries. *The American Political Science Review, 86*(1), 55–69.

Amaldoss, W., & Jain, S. (2005). Pricing of conspicuous goods: A competitive analysis of social effects. *Journal of Marketing Research, 42*(1), 30–42.

The American National Election Studies (ANES) (2011). The ANES 2008 Time Series Study [dataset]. Stanford University and the University of Michigan [producers]. Ann Arbor, MI: Inter-university Consortium for Political and Social Research [distributor]. www.electionstudies.org

Bannon, D.P. (2005). Relationship marketing and the political process. *Journal of Political Marketing, 4*(2–3), 73–90.

Bendle, N. (Forthcoming). Reference Dependence in Political Primaries. *Journal of Political Marketing.*

Boatright, R.G. (2009). Getting primaried: The growth and consequences of ideological primaries. "State of the Parties" Conference. The Ray C. Bliss Center, University of Akron, Akron, OH, October 14–16, 2009.

Bowler, S., Donovan, T., & Fernandez, K. (1996). The growth of the political marketing industry and the California initiative process. *European Journal of Marketing, 30*(10/11), 166–178.

Butler, P., & Collins, N. (1996). Strategic analysis in political markets. *European Journal of Marketing, 30*(10/11), 25–36.

Center for American Women and Politics (CAWP). (2013, December 24). Current numbers of women officeholders. http://www.cawp.rutgers.edu/fast_facts/levels_of_office/Current_Numbers.php

Economist (2011, May 25). Tim Pawlenty's crusade for truth. Available at www.economist.com/blogs/democracyinamerica/2011/05/ethanol_and_iowa

Fact Check. (2008). Republicans Go for Hillary in TX, Ohio Primaries? Available at www.factcheck.org/2008/03/republicans-go-for-hillary-in-tx-ohio-primaries/

Fields, J.M., & Schuman, H. (1976). Public beliefs about the beliefs of the public. *The Public Opinion Quarterly, 40*(4), 427–448.

Friedman, J.N., & Holden, R.T. (2009). The rising incumbent reelection rate: What's gerrymandering got to do with it? *The Journal of Politics, 71*(2), 593–611.

Gibson, G. (2012). *Jim Messina: What I learned in the election.* Available at www.politico.com/news/stories/1112/84103.html

Goldstein, K., Franz, M., & Ridout, T. (2002). Political advertising in 2000. Combined File [dataset]. Final release. Madison, WI: The Department of Political Science at the University of Wisconsin–Madison and the Brennan Center for Justice at New York University.

Hassell, H.J.G. (2011). Looking beyond the voting constituency: A study of campaign donation solicitations in the 2008 presidential primary and general election. *Journal of Political Marketing, 10*(1–2), 27–42.

Hedgcock, W., Rao, A.R., & Chen, H.A. (2009). Could Ralph Nader's entrance and exit have helped Al Gore? The impact of decoy dynamics on consumer choice. *Journal of Marketing Research (JMR), 46*(3), 330–343.

Johnson, D. (2006). First hurdles: The evolution of the pre-primary and primary stages of American presidential elections. In P. Davies and B.I. Newman (Eds.), *Winning elections with political marketing*. New York, NY: The Haworth Press.

Kahneman, D., & Tversky, A. (1979). Prospect theory: An analysis of decision under risk, *Econometrica, 47*(2), 263–292.

Kaufmann, K.M., Gimpel, J.G., & Hoffman, A.H. (2003). A promise fulfilled? Open primaries and representation. *The Journal of Politics, 65*(2), 457–476.

Kenney, P. J., & Rice, T.W. (1987). The relationship between divisive primaries and general election outcomes. *American Journal of Political Science, 31*, 31–44.

Kenney, P. J. & Rice, T. (1994). The psychology of political momentum. *Political Research Quarterly, 47*(4), 923–938.

Kleefeld, E. (2012). *Ron Paul not endorsing Romney: Put me down as undecided*. Available at http://2012.talkingpointsmemo.com/2012/08/ron-paul-not-endorsing-romney-put-me-down-as-undecided.php

Knuckey, J. (2010). Political marketing in the United States. In J. Lees-Marshment, J. Stromback, & C. Rudd (Eds.), *Global political marketing* (pp. 96–112). London, UK: Routledge.

Knuckey, J., & Lees-Marshment, J. (2005). American political marketing: George W. Bush and the Republican Party. In D.G. Lilleker & J. Lees-Marshment (Eds.), *Political marketing: A comparative perspective* (pp. 39–58). Manchester, UK: Manchester University Press.

Lees-Marshment, J. (2001). The marriage of politics and marketing. *Political Studies, 49*(4), 692–713.

Lees-Marshment, J. (2009). *Political marketing: Principles and applications* (1st ed.). Oxford, UK: Routledge.

MacAskill, E. (2008, January 30). Giuliani's disastrous strategy. *The Guardian*. Available at www.theguardian.com/world/2008/jan/30/usa.rudygiuliani

Marland, A., Giasson, T., & Lees-Marshment, J. (2012). *Political marketing in Canada*. Vancouver, BC: UBC Press.

Newman, B.I., & Sheth, J.N. (1985). A model of primary voter behavior. *The Journal of Consumer Research, 12*(2), 178–187.

Ormrod, R.P. (2005). A conceptual model of political market orientation. *Journal of Nonprofit and Public Sector Marketing, 14*(1), 47–64.

Ormrod, R.P., Henneberg, S.C., Forward, N., Miller, J., & Tymms, L. (2007). Political marketing in untraditional campaigns: The case of David Cameron's Conservative Party leadership victory. *Journal of Public Affairs, 7*(3), 235–248.

Parker, B. T. (2012). Candidate brand equity valuation: A comparison of U.S. presidential candidates during the 2008 primary election campaign. *Journal of Political Marketing, 11*(3), 208–230.

Parnes, A., & Zenilman, A. (2008, May 31). DNC panel agrees to seat Mich., Fla. *Politico*. Available at www.politico.com/news/stories/0508/10732.html

Pew Research. (2003, November/December). *Democratic Primary Scene-Setter Survey*. Washington, DC: The Pew Research Center for the People & the Press.

Pew Research. (2007, November). *Primary Scene-Setter Surveys*. Washington, DC: The Pew Research Center for the People & the Press.

Redlawsk, D.P., Tolbert, C., and Donovan, T. (2011). *Why Iowa: How caucuses and sequential elections improve the presidential nominating process.* Chicago, IL: The University of Chicago Press.

Ridout, T. N., Rottinghaus, B., & Hosey, N. (2009). Following the rules? Candidate strategy in presidential primaries, *Social Science Quarterly, 90*(4), 777–795.

Republican National Committee (RNC). (2013). Growth and opportunity project. http://goproject.gop.com/RNC_Growth_Opportunity_Book_2013.pdf

Steinhauer, J. (2007, October 19). Confronting ghosts of 2000 in South Carolina. *New York Times.* Available at www.nytimes.com/2007/10/19/us/politics/19mccain.html?pagewanted=all&_r=0

Tumulty, K. (2008, May 8). The five mistakes Clinton made. *Time Magazine.* Available at http://content.time.com/time/magazine/article/0,9171,1738496,00.html

Ubertaccio, P. N. (2006). Marketing parties in a candidate-centered polity: The Republican Party and George W. Bush. In P. Davies & B.I. Newman (Eds.), *Winning elections with political marketing* (pp. 81–104). New York, NY: The Haworth Press.

6

BRANDING THE TEA PARTY

Political Marketing and an American Social Movement

William J. Miller

Overview of the Topic

When the Tea Party first formulated, pundits, scholars, and Democrats seemingly wrote the movement off as nothing but a collection of crazy extremists. Rather than seeing the beginning of a strong social movement that would have electoral impacts across the country, Tea Party members were instead viewed as being out of touch and unable to articulate their message in a meaningful way. Then the 2010 midterm elections took place. Through the results of the outcome of that election cycle, the Tea Party was able to successfully demonstrate just how seriously its movement deserved to be taken. Now, two years later, the initial excitement (and corresponding media coverage) of the Tea Party has lessened. But the national movement is still having an impact on politics and policy. The Tea Party has used its influence within government (through officials elected in 2010) and within a new wave of candidates to demonstrate that it is more than just a one-hit wonder.

The Tea Party—as it exists today—represents a branded social movement: a loosely coordinated, national movement that bases much of its marketing on social media that conjures up clear images for both supporters and opponents. As a result, this chapter argues that the Tea Party is largely operating in the United States as a brand and marketing itself as such. As part of this brand, the Tea Party is clearly selling a product to voters who are unhappy with the current state of American politics and parties. As Skocpol and Williamson (2012) note, this fact has not been lost on political entrepreneurs such as Dick Armey, who have used current sentiments toward government to attempt to further their individual political aspirations. The product the Tea Party offers American voters is lower taxes, less spending, and more individual autonomy. It is branded as the Tea Party in today's political discourse, and a series of Tea Party movements have taken advantage of the brand to help attempt to create the electoral outcomes they desired. The story has not necessarily changed from that which more conservative Republicans used to overtake the party previously (Cosgrove 2007), but the brand is new. Surveys have clearly shown that the average Tea Party member is a Republican identifier who is no longer supportive of the party. In many ways, this disenchantment traces its roots to unhappiness with the George W. Bush presidency. According to the Tea Party rhetoric, Bush ran for president as a strong conservative and then ran the White House as a liberal. Even before George W. Bush, his father—George H. W. Bush—faced his own problems controlling the conservative base in the aftermath of Ronald Reagan's eight years of strong conservative rule. Ultimately, it cost him much support in his 1992 re-election campaign.

This chapter examines how the Tea Party began and why it has naturally leaned toward becoming a brand. Further, it looks at a set of questions that focus on the strategies undertaken by groups and candidates alike to spread that message in an effort to impact elections and policy in America. With the focus on branding, it is possible to investigate a series of questions and propositions regarding how the Tea Party has come into existence and perhaps more importantly how it can best assure continued momentum while competing against the Republican Party (along with all other forms of political affiliation in the United States). Is the Tea Party original or merely the rebranding of long-held views in American society? How have candidates responded to the brand? Are there different likelihoods for success based on whether a candidate fully accepts the brand or co-opts its rhetoric? And if the Tea Party is a brand, what does it need to do regarding policy to not disappoint those who buy in? Ultimately, the chapter aims to demonstrate—like Keller (2002: 171) concluded—that "as branding is applied in more and more different settings, brand theory and best practice guidelines need to be refined and reflect the unique realities of those settings."

Review of Previous Literature

Political Marketing

For any group or organization, political marketing serves as a potentially powerful tool for distributing messages and ideas to a broader public. As such, techniques can contribute to the establishment of a group's or an advocacy coalition's legitimacy. Yet each group operates differently when it comes to the utilization of political marketing. Lees-Marshment (2001: 1074–6) has helped understand the different types of organizations and their generalized use of marketing techniques. Through her comprehensive political marketing model, we can see the extent to which an organization has included political marketing techniques in its operation. She emphasizes that "marketing concepts as well as techniques can be applied not just to how political organizations communicate with their market, but how they determine their behavior or product."

In her first category of organizations, Lees-Marshment finds groups adopting a product-oriented approach. Groups in this category typically put their cause at the forefront of their decisions and stick to the initial message promoting this cause. Indeed, these groups—which are normally ideological in nature—appear especially reluctant to fit their message to their audience, which could be helpful if they were aiming to increase membership, obtain greater amounts of financial support, or heighten awareness. In fact, one could argue that the groups do not care about developing long-term strategies to ensure larger support. Instead, they argue for what the group stands for and believes in.

In the second category, Lees-Marshment identifies sales-oriented groups that look to stick to messages that promote their cause, regardless of the demands emerging from a political market. Groups found in this classification tend to select the approach in order to cope with highly competitive conditions for either holding the public's attention or raising funds (Lees-Marshment 2004: 99). Given the decreasing nature of social capital (Putnam 2000), there is a tendency to rely on mass communications as an efficient means for reaching supporters in large numbers. In short, these groups are looking to sell arguments to voters.

In the final category from Lees-Marshment, we find market-oriented groups, which try to find "the best means by which to attract and maintain supporters" (Lees-Marshment 2003: 359). By using market intelligence, the groups identify supporter demands, design a product to reflect the results, and communicate progress to maintain (if not grow) support. In nearly all cases, these organizations focus energy on message and regularly undertake market analyses to assure that their chosen message is remaining on point with contributors.

What makes Lees-Marshment's comprehensive political marketing model so effective is that it ties in with the three things organizations or groups do in politics: build awareness, turn on supporters, and sway the undecided (Fine 2008). But how does this relate to social movements? Particularly ones that do not necessarily aim to sway the undecideds? Writing in 1996, Lock and Harris (318) found that political marketing techniques were still being ignored by scholars studying lobbying and interest groups. While progress was being made in understanding how parties and politicians could use marketing techniques to sway voters, lobbyists were not following suit. In recent years, however, studies of political marketing have moved beyond parties and elections, which dominated the research field in the early beginning. Now, interest groups are included—especially when looking at lobbying efforts (Foster, Hudon, and Yates 2012; King 2006; McGrath 2006; Lees-Marshment 2003). For McGrath (2006: 108), this is no surprise, as he had previously noted that the "persuasion function of lobbying can be bound into political marketing theory."

Looking at a study of five interest groups and their marketing strategies, Foster et al. (2012: 328) find that "political marketing approach leads interest groups—and coalitions—to care not only about the needs and interests of their own members, but also to take into account trends in the general public and among other social (and political) actors." But it can be contended that not all groups or movements would agree with such a finding. Newman (1999:78) argues that "marketing has at its root the ability to convince consumers or voters that a product or presidential candidate will help to make their American dream come true." Likewise, Reeves et al. (2006) contend that the product and sales-oriented party categories fall within an ideologically driven political party, while the market orientation is more closely aligned with a voter-driven strategy. In other words, certain elements of Lees-Marshment's model lend themselves toward promoting the cause while others instead aim to win, even if the message gets manipulated or diluted in the process.

If the development of a positive relationship between the voter and the party has been forwarded as the raison d'être of political marketing (Henneberg 2002), what does it mean for social movements and supporters? Interest groups (as organizations), after all, have no ambition to govern. Instead, they are empowered to represent certain interests to persuade elected officials and the public at large that their beliefs are legitimate and acceptable (both politically and socially) (Foster and Hudon 2010). In this way, these organizations are prone to think of their strategies in terms of compromises agreed to in order to prevent being subjected to unilateral solutions imposed by authorities. As such, the legitimacy of groups and coalitions relies on the proceedings allowing internal discussions and expressions of dissent prior to their downstream strategies to influence policy outcomes and on mechanisms and dialogue intended to make arguments or action accepted by the members of a society. With incumbent political parties seeking to secure repeat sales at a time when consumer loyalty is under threat from proliferating choice and social realignment, perhaps social movements are better suited to focus on branding their beliefs and practices in order to assure continued support from their own likely supporters before worrying about influencing policy or electoral outcomes (Needham 2006).

Branding

A brand is defined as "a name, term, sign, symbol, or design, or a combination of them which is intended to identify the goods or services of one seller or a group of sellers and to differentiate them from those of competitors" (AMA 1960). Brands are those associations about a particular object that are held in a person's memory (Keller 2003). In the consumer politics field, brands are made up of a collection of values, ideas, associations, feelings, and emotions that come together to make up a coherent identity or image (Chandler and Owen 2002). The concepts of branding and relationship marketing can be used to highlight the difference between gaining support in the one-off transaction of an election and retaining voter loyalty in a post-purchase setting (Needham 2005). In this way, brands must be simple, unique, reassuring, aspirational, value-based, and credible. Most importantly, the product offered must work as advertised.

"Branding principles have been applied in virtually every setting where consumer choice of some kind is involved, e.g. with physical goods, services, retail stores, people, organizations, places, or ideas" (Keller 2002: 151). As Smith and French (2009: 210) point out, "it is axiomatic that political parties are organizations where politicians seek to exchange ideas and promises for electoral support." As a result, there has been a steady stream of research that has accepted political parties or politicians as brands (Harris and Lock 2001; Kavanagh 1995; Kotler and Kotler 1999; Needham 2006; Reeves et al. 2006; Scammell 2007; Schneider 2004; Smith 2001; White and de Chernatony 2002). Branding does present some concerns, however. When applied in the political marketplace, branding can produce unwanted effects such as narrowing the political agenda, increasing confrontation, demanding conformity of behavior and message, and even increasing political disengagement at the local level (Lilleker and Negrine 2003; Needham 2006; Scammell 1999).

Political branding is the strategic use of consumer branding tactics in the building of a political image. "Brands provide reassurance by promising standardization and replicability, generating trust between producer and consumer, much as parties emphasize unity and coherence in order to build up voter trust" (Needham 2006: 179). In this way, they "are aspirational, evoking a particular vision of the good life or holding out the promise of personal enhancement ... [and] must be perceived as authentic and value-based, necessitating congruence between the internal values of the product or company and its external message" (Needham 2006: 179).

Specifically, political branding refers to the tactics politicians use to gain popularity and election. These political brands serve as heuristics, allowing voters to not necessarily know every detail about every choice but to instead determining support based on what they easily can remember (Smith and French 2009). In this way, "brands simplify choice and reduce dependence on detailed product information, in much the same way as party labels relieve voters of the need to familiarize themselves with all the party's policies" (Needham 2006: 179). Political branding is not just the use of traditional advertising, but is an all-encompassing marketing and image identity campaign (Scammell 2007). The political brand is defined as an associative network of interconnected political information and attitudes, held in memory and accessible when stimulated from the memory of a voter (Smith 2005). Consumers have knowledge structures of political parties in much the same way they have for brands (Schweiger and Adami 1999). In essence, the importance of brands for voting decisions on the part of the consumers derives from their branding functions, such as orientation aid in the form of an "information chunk" or risk-reduction function in the sense of a confidence surrogate (Schneider 2004).

But how does branding work for social movements? To this point, very little research has been conducted. Calfano (2010) has undertaken one of the few interest-based branding studies when he looked at whether a constituency's political brand—defined by him as the reputation that white evangelicals and Catholics have for "pro-life" abortion policy—influences the public abortion position taken by members in six U.S. state Houses of Representatives. Ultimately, he finds the presence of two separate constituencies in the country. Yet even this study does little to explain how branding works for social movements since he utilizes an interest-based angle rather than one based on groups. The lack of current research proves problematic when we consider the similarities and differences in how social movements differ from parties. Political parties have three clearly distinct elements: a trinity with the party as the brand; the politician as its tangible characteristics; and policy as core service offerings (O'Shaughnessy and Henneberg 2007). Social movements, however, have the movements as brand and policy as a service offering, but they lack the same tangible characteristic—especially social movements without national leadership. Needham (2005) reminds us that successful parties develop brand attributes in their leaders to maintain relationships with supporters beyond their initial transaction, although in doing so they create problems for leadership succession. Reeves et al. (2006) argue that there is a tension for political brands in that there is a need for them to be voter driven, while at the same time being responsible for the long term. Hence, they have an objective to drive the market in a way that ensures the future prosperity for the group. Yet again, for social movements this may not be as clearly delineated when considering the purpose of branding.

The Tea Party

As the 2010 election season approached, one of the most prominent questions posed was what the Tea Party actually was. Many believed it had the characteristics of both a political party and a social movement. While it was clear that the idea of direct link to what happened in Boston Harbor in 1773 was marketed by Tea Party members, there were divergent opinions about how to best impact current policies. After all, they were rebelling against their own chosen government instead of an external enemy this time. However, much like in 1773, the wake of Barack Obama's election to the presidency in 2008 ushered America into what Samuel Huntington (1981) calls a creedal-passion period. These periods occur cyclically every few generations and root themselves in the Great Awakening of the 1740s. Characterized by opposition to power, and suspicion of government as the most dangerous embodiment of power, we find these periods arising most frequently in the wake of economic declines, chaotic international conflicts, or the reorganization of societal groups as particular minorities become accepted in the mainstream population. Such an environment led to the creation of the Tea Party. Since early 2007, American citizens experienced an economic recession, increasing gas prices, and new social programs that allow government to play a larger role in citizens' lives. Likewise, the country was active overseas on two military fronts. While there is no minority group making headway as there had been in previous similar periods, rights for homosexuals, ethnic and racial minorities, and even women continue to enter the public sphere of debate.

Less than a month after the first unofficial Tea Party event occurred in Binghamton, New York, the hosts of CNBC's *Squawk Box* referred to Rick Santelli on the floor of the CME Group. In an animated rant, given in the wake of the passage of the American Recovery and Reinvestment Act of 2009, Santelli roared: "We're thinking of having a Chicago Tea Party in July . . . all you capitalists that want to show up to Lake Michigan, I'm going to start organizing it" (Santelli's Tea Party 2009). With that, Santelli reflected to a national audience a sentiment that had been developing on a localized basis.

Organized protest events, most boasting hundreds of attendees, many in the thousands, continued throughout 2009. Although impossible to accurately estimate, as many as 800 events were staged and more than 700,000 people attended Tea Party protests on Tax Day. Protesters shrewdly exploited a preexisting elite network, national and regional talk radio, to foment dissent and publicize protest events. Beyond simply providing a platform for information dissemination, some talk radio personalities openly advocated, promoted, and staged Tea Party activities. Glenn Beck's "9–12 Project" was a sponsor of the September 12 "Taxpayer March on Washington." With the help of talk radio, the Tea Party moved from loosely organized, discrete events to something closer to a cohesive national movement. Skocpol and Williamson (2012) point out that the Tea Party was particularly successful in utilizing social media and new technologies to assure the grassroots nature of their activities.

While citizens continued to try to understand what the Tea Party was, the *Washington Post* set out to study the organizations using the label in October 2010. Its mission was to "understand the network of individuals and organizations at the heart of the nascent political movement" (Tea Party Canvass 2010). It undertook 647 interviews between October 6 and 13 with individuals listed as contacts for Tea Party groups found online and found respondents in all states except for Hawaii. What it found was an interesting descriptive picture of how the organization operated.

For example, a plurality of local organizations was not linked with any of the national organizations. There was little connection between local groups, with each seemingly having its own funding mechanisms and organizational structure. Most groups were extremely small (with a majority identifying fewer than 50 members). Of the members, well over three-quarters were new to politics after years of feeling separated from decision-makers. Of all the groups contacted, the average annual amount of money raised was $800. In short, organizationally, the Tea Party seemed destined to fail.

To a large degree, the emergence of the Tea Party reflects a failure of the modern Republican Party. If the GOP had done its perceived job of curbing wasteful spending and working toward balanced budgets at the federal level, it is quite likely that angry citizens would not have begun claiming to be Taxed Enough Already. Yet the group did emerge and it began firing clear warning shots for center-right Republicans that their days of moderate policy stances and the occasional tax increase would no longer be tolerated by this sect of the party. As a result, it is not necessarily surprising that the canvas found that Tea Party groups were almost as dissatisfied with the mainstream Republican leadership as they were with President Obama. The actions of Bush (both as a campaigner and then as leader) led to many Republican hardliners becoming disenchanted with their party. While this unquestionably contributed to the development of the Tea Party, it was not the sole factor.

Tarrow (1994: 4) defines a movement as "collective challenges by people with common purposes and solidarity in a sustained interaction with elites, opponents and authorities." Stewart, Smith, and Denton identify three types of social movements. The innovative movement "seeks to replace existing norms and values with new ones" (Stewart et al. 2001: 12). A revivalistic movement moves to reinstate values from "a venerable, idealized past" (Stewart et al. 2001: 12). Finally, the objective of a resistance movement is preservation of existing conditions. It seems clear that the Tea Party cannot be classified as an innovative movement. What is less apparent is whether it would be appropriate to characterize the Tea Party as either of the other types. To be sure, the entire notion of the Tea Party is a reference to American lore. Further, appeals to smaller government and drastically reduced spending are occasionally framed with originalist language and reverent references to the Framers. Clearly, the Tea Party exhibits characteristics of a revivalistic movement. However, as the national discourse moved from economic policy to a debate over the nature of health care reform, the Tea Party came to resemble a resistance movement.

It has been suggested that the Tea Party is a hybrid social movement exhibiting characteristics of both revivalistic and resistant social movements (Miller and Walling 2011). However, as the Tea Party became involved in the electoral process, an important question emerged: Is the Tea Party a political party? Epstein (1967: 4) defines a political party as "any group, however loosely organized, seeking to elect government officeholders under a given label." The Tea Party is clearly "loosely organized." However, the critical component of a political party is the objective of electing individuals "under a given label." On the whole, the Tea Party's involvement in elections certainly does not meet this condition. That is not to say that certain candidates, regardless of party affiliation, would not self-identify as supportive of or affiliated with the Tea Party. In short, the Tea Party does not easily fit into the category of an interest group, a social movement, or a political party. Instead, it best appears to be a brand, dating back to the original Tea Party in 1773, and best marketed as such. The goal is clearly to reorient the Republican Party to better align with disenfranchised conservatives who are bitterly disappointed in the moderate performance of its elected leaders, especially George W. Bush (Rodgers 2012). Without running candidates officially under its label, however, it remains a loosely associated group of social movements with an overarching goal that it is successfully branding among a willing audience.

Unlike what we would expect from traditional social movements or interest groups, a plurality of Tea Party organizations said they did not believe a national leader existed from the movement. In recent months, spectators have seen how resistant to leadership the Tea Party is with Dick Armey being removed from his own Tea Party organization, FreedomWorks. Over half of the groups canvassed stated that the purpose of the group was to have a nationwide network of independent organizations. Rather than becoming organized, the groups prefer to maintain their local principles without the potential corrupting influence of becoming a recognized party.

If we instead choose to switch to the individual level of analysis, a 2010 CBS News/*New York Times* poll is useful in painting a picture of all respondents compared to Tea Party supporters.

Compared to the average American, Tea Party supporters lean Republican and are older, whiter, more educated, more likely to be married, more likely to be male, and earning a higher income (Zernike and Thee-Brenan 2010). These demographics fit well to a large extent with the goal of the movement: to raise attention to economic concerns within the United States government. However, they directly refute many of the more popular arguments discussed previously regarding the makeup of the Tea Party movement. One can wonder if deficit reduction would be the hot button issue it is today if not for the Tea Party's efforts to bring it to the forefront of national debate. More than anything else, it is clear that the Tea Party does not represent newly discovered political beliefs or opinions in the United States. Instead, it is working to bring together individuals who share the same sentiments as their forefounders did centuries before.

The seminal academic work on the Tea Party thus far comes from Theda Skocpol and Vanessa Williamson (2012), who utilize a series of grassroots interviews and visits to meetings across the country to reach a series of conclusions regarding who Tea Party supporters are, what they are doing, and why they matter. Their research finds that members are fairly well educated, older, and upper middle class. Perhaps surprisingly given the product the Tea Party sells, supporters appear to favor Social Security, military benefits, and Medicare; they view unnecessary spending as any money headed to freeloaders. Looking at national politics, Skocpol and Williamson (2012) find clear patterns of message co-optation by non–Tea Party leaders. They are simply leveraging new energy created by the group to push their previously existing agendas (especially deregulation and privatization). What

1. Adopt a name or identity that is easily recognizable by prospective members.
2. Ensure that clear values, ideas, and feelings exist that will create a bond between members of the movement.
3. Work to assure distinguishable differences between your movement and other similar organizations or parties.
4. Ensure that no matter how dispersed the movement may be and autonomous local organizations are that the overall brand remains clear, consistent, and standardized.
5. Create as vast a network (using traditional and social media) as possible to convey information about the brand.
6. Regardless of explicit political connections, permit the brand to suggest cues for voters to use when casting ballots.
7. As opposed to broad-based parties, ensure a narrow, focused product that will fit a niche market.
8. Work to be a sales-oriented group by using market analyses to effectively communicate your message. But be prepared to consider becoming market oriented by adjusting the details of the product based on research to permit prolonged impact and relevance.

FIGURE 6.1 Principles of Effective Political Movement Branding

keeps the two groups together is a desire to regain control of the Republican Party and a strong dislike for current president Barack Obama.

Theoretical Framework

Based on the literature discussed, it is possible to create a framework of factors that political movements would be well advised to consider when branding their activities to ensure success. This therefore combines concepts from literature on market and sales-oriented groups, political branding, and studies of the Tea Party. Figure 6.1 lists criteria for effective branding by political movements.

This framework will be used to analyze the Tea Party.

Empirical Illustrations

In early 2012, Republican senator Saxby Chambliss announced that he would not seek to keep his seat in the United States Senate. The year prior, Republican Olympia Snowe did the same. In terms of beliefs and backgrounds, it would be more difficult to find two more different senators: one a moderate female from Maine, the other a staunchly conservative nearly 70-year-old Georgian. The major emphasis of both of their announcements was distaste for the tone and mood of political gridlock in Washington, D.C. Yet pundits continue to point out that both would likely have faced strong primary opposition from more conservative Tea Party politicians had they sought to maintain their position. This is the power and the strength of the movement, which is just four years old. Sitting senators (with impressive records and minimal previous electoral challenges) are stepping away, not because of health or scandal but because of the Tea Party.

With this in mind, we can turn to the previously listed framework for analyzing political movements and assess the state of the Tea Party.

1. Adopt a Name or Identity That Is Easily Recognizable by Prospective Members

The Tea Party has successfully done this—perhaps more so than any previous movement in the history of the United States. When it comes to arguing for less government, the decision to rely on a name that ties a nation back to its initial founding is perhaps the most recognizable connection possible. When people hear the term "tea party" in the U.S., they are immediately drawn to the ideas of protest and less government. Further, it has been consistently utilized across the country.

2. Ensure That Clear Values, Ideas, and Feelings Exist That Will Create a Bond between Members of the Movement

It has become lost on many followers that originally "Tea" stood for Taxed Enough Already. The idea of less spending and taxes has been uniform in the discussions of the various groups. This has allowed for elements of consistency along with providing the ability to reinforce messages easily.

3. Work to Assure Distinguishable Differences between Your Movement and Other Similar Organizations or Parties

For the Tea Party, this was one of the easier aspects of its branding efforts. The movement came into existence largely because of hardline conservative discontent with the Republican Party. As a result, the movement—from its inception—was differentiated from its most similar peers.

4. Ensure That No Matter How Dispersed the Movement May Be and Autonomous Local Organizations Are That the Overall Brand Remains Clear, Consistent, and Standardized

Given that local Tea Party groups were largely left to their own devices, many branding experts would argue that there would not be a clear, consistent, or standardized message. Yet, the opposite occurred. Local groups were successful in taking the overarching messages and themes of the Tea Party and applying them to local conditions and audiences. While many now argue this decentralization contributes to declining favorability of the Tea Party, true followers instead argue that national, outside attempts to co-opt messaging and impacts are causing much internal dissuasion from continuing support.

5. Create as Vast a Network (Using Traditional and Social Media) as possible to Convey Information about the Brand

The Tea Party was highly successful at utilizing both traditional and social media outlets for spreading its message. While the uniqueness and size of the movement in its early stages attracted media attention, social media was the most imperative for the success of the movement. Twitter was particularly important for the Tea Party in the early days. A group of top conservatives using the hashtag #tcot began with only 25 members but quickly rose to well over 1,000. Once membership grew, the hashtag was used to organize town hall meetings, conference calls, and rallies, and to bring together citizens across the country in one place for the world to see. In order to make sure information stayed in one place, organizers eventually switched to utilizing wikis. Through this platform, they were more able to provide advice related to protest strategies and organization techniques.

6. Regardless of Explicit Political Connections, Permit the Brand to Suggest Cues for Voters to Use When Casting Ballots

If we use just the 2010 U.S. Senate races as a microcosm of how politicians have responded to the Tea Party, we see three possible outcomes. Either individuals seeking office have been true Tea Party believers, utilized the rhetoric to increase popularity despite not fully believing, or spoken out against the movement. Looking at the first category, there are observations available that suggest the Tea Party brand leads to victory and similar evidence that the brand can lead to defeat. In terms of those who truly drank the tea, we can look at individuals like Christine O'Donnell, Sharron Angle, and Joe Miller. O'Donnell (running in Delaware) was able to survive allegations of witchcraft and a complete lack of political experience to successfully defeat a moderate Republican challenger in the GOP primary before losing in the general election (highlighting that location and candidate skill matters). She embodied the Tea Party movement: lower taxes and less spending. Likewise, Sharron Angle emerged from nowhere to win the Nevada primary before losing the general election. Joe Miller beat Lisa Murkowski in the Alaskan Republican primary, but Murkowski did not go silently and survived a write-in campaign as an independent, in which she regularly railed on Miller's extreme positions. At the same time, some true Tea Party supporters were quite successful in seeking election. Mike Lee, for example, defeated popular incumbent Robert Bennett in the Republican primary stage in Utah (which also motivated Orrin Hatch to alter his own opinions of the movement). Likewise, Marco Rubio and Rand Paul (both self-declared Tea Party candidates) were cast into the national spotlight due to their consistent, palatable message of reducing the deficit through controlled spending while not raising taxes.

At the same time, there were many Republicans who did not want to run the risk of being Angle or O'Donnell (true Tea Party candidates who succeed in the primaries only to fall flat in the general election). Instead, they spoke the

Tea Party language (allowing Tea Party followers to believe they aligned with the movement) while remaining distant enough as to not become part of the brand. For candidates like Ken Buck, Carly Fiorina, John Raese, and Dino Rossi, their decision did not pan out. But, for Mark Kirk and Ron Johnson, their subtle Tea Party rhetoric coupled with moderate issue stances in other areas (and a moderate demeanor) allowed them to win seats in tightly contested states. Ultimately, it seemed Tea Party candidates are likely to succeed at winning general elections when they use the rhetoric without appearing as true Tea Party politicians. The right candidate, running in the right geographic area and running to win more than just a primary election, is the recipe for Tea Party success in the political realm of the United States today.

This shows two keys for the Tea Party brand: the market matters, as does the candidate. In terms of market, it is no surprise that candidates who fared well were those running in the relatively more homogenous states. But more importantly, differences in candidate skill made a vast difference. Of those hopeful senators who co-opted the Tea Party rhetoric, we see a series of what Herrnson would refer to as political professionals or hopeful candidates. They possessed skills and stood legitimate chances of winning election regardless of Tea Party support. Of the true Tea Party candidates, however, we witnessed a series of political professionals (Rubio, Paul, and Lee) prove successful while a number of amateurs (Angle, O'Donnell, and Miller) were utter failures once the market they were forced to sell their brand to expanded to include less like-minded voters. Thus, successful Tea Party candidates likely would have won without the Tea Party due to their own qualifications and where they were running, while Tea Party losers would have fared ever worse. Regardless, it is clear that the Tea Party brand suggested cues for voters to use when casting ballots.

7. As Opposed to Broad-based Parties, Ensure a Narrow, Focused Product That Will Fit a Niche Market

For the Tea Party, there was a clear niche market present. As results have shown, these candidates are not able to appeal to moderate or opposition voters. Instead, they rely on a strong brand to help assure that supporters work to assure election.

8. Work to Be a Sales-Oriented Group by Using Market Analyses to Effectively Communicate Your Message. But Be Prepared to Consider Becoming Market Oriented by Adjusting the Details of the Product Based on Research to Permit Prolonged Impact and Relevance

From a political marketing perspective, the loosely aligned local groups were left to their own devices to determine how best to spread their message. But, if we look to the Lees-Marshment (2001) categorization, it is debatable as to where to best place the Tea Party (as a unified movement). It clearly has opted to not function as a political party. As a result, there is no recognized national leader to follow the lead of, nor candidates to endorse and rally behind in the same way a political party would. But, at the same time, Tea Party members demonstrated recognition that their only chance to impact policy outcomes was to support candidates who were ideologically similar to their beliefs. The Tea Party could be labeled as taking a product-oriented approach. It promotes a cause and is consistent in its message. It is reluctant to waver in its stated beliefs and seems to only be interested in accomplishing its clearly delineated goals. At the same time, however, there is a sales-oriented element to its decision-making. The American public has a short attention span and as a result, the Tea Party must continue to make strong arguments as to why it should be given citizen attention. In this way, the Tea Party is selling arguments to voters. Further, it has a strong product in a package of lower taxes, less spending, and more individual autonomy. But, alas, the Tea Party could also be just as easily labeled a market-oriented group. The Tea Party has focused heavily on its message from its inception and would be unable to maintain its current activities if not for the fact that citizens appear to find that the message resonates. Further, recent events have shown a willingness by the Tea Party to expand. With the deficit battle having closed, we have seen Tea Party issues related to drone missiles and other constitutional (i.e., noneconomic) debates. This demonstrates an understanding that there will need to be some evolution as it continues to grow (particularly as the economy seems to be turning around).

With it being difficult to accurately place the Tea Party into Lees-Marshment's typology, one can only wonder if a different element of marketing is in play. Instead of focusing on marketing strategies, perhaps the Tea Party is instead focusing on securing a brand image with the American public and then employing it to see potential supporters on the merits of Tea Party beliefs. When the average American thinks about the Tea Party, he or she is likely to draw on one of a few thoughts: taxes, protests, Revolutionary wardrobe, Republican, or less spending. Given the simplicity with which most Americans could make these connections, it appears the Tea Party has become heuristic. Once politicians realized that the Tea Party—no matter where the local affiliate was found—shared similar values, it became another marketing tool through which Republicans could utilize in efforts to win elections (both primary and general). After all, Republicans were well aware (regardless of how conservative they were) that this particular audience of disenchanted party identifiers existed. The Tea Party provided them a brand by which to express their beliefs.

Conclusions for Research and Practice

Since its inception, the Tea Party has largely functioned as a brand. By helping citizens understand the goals and functions of the movement through easy-to-remember beliefs and tactics, the Tea Party has marketed itself by hitting on the beliefs of individual Americans related to spending and taxing (regardless of party identification). But recently it appears that the brand is coming under attack.

Whereas politicians in 2010 were deciding whether to borrow the rhetoric or drink the tea, today there are four groups that seem to be infighting for control of the Tea Party. To some, the Tea Party represents economic populism. Yet given what we know about the demographics of identifiers, it is difficult to believe the movement would seek higher taxes on any given subset of the country. Others see the Tea Party being co-opted by social conservatives who recognize the potential of supporters. After 2010, Republicans realized the Tea Party carried influence and then the right-wing religious base began attempting to insert its messages. Again, however, polling data say the true Tea Party identifier does not worry about social issues. Others claim the Tea Party is being overtaken by an arch-capitalist mentality that pushes capitalism to the brink of harming democracy. And finally, there are signs of a libertarian bend coming across the movement. This conceptualization, however, goes against what Tea Party identifiers and groups tells us they actually care about. If identifiers and groups are not pushing the characterization, it leads us to see that outside forces are trying to use the brand to their political advantage (Salisbury 1969).

But the question still remains: What is the Tea Party? A social movement dispersed into local groups that is attempting to act as a political party for the purposes of pulling the average Republican back toward the conservative base of the party? From a branding perspective, the Tea Party has been quite successful, but the movement had a significant advantage. When the Tea Party formulated after Santelli's rant, there was already a critical mass of niche constituents singing its message and clamoring for its creation. While it never had to worry about providing the broad appeal of a political party, it successfully influenced these constituents. Having a niche market provides the flexibility necessary for higher chances of success. It is difficult to generalize about what the future of social movement branding will look like in American governance. The Tea Party entered the political picture with niche voters unhappy with their own party and the opposition. As a result, after a very successful branding effort, the movement gained in number and momentum quickly. Without that combination, however, the movement could have quickly fizzled out. It will take future studies to examine whether unheard voices get representation more quickly due to good marketing and branding now or if mainstream parties merely become more threatened. For Republicans, there is still no uniform answer on how best to handle the Tea Party. The easiest solution would be to co-opt its message and reabsorb these disenchanted voters into the GOP. Yet given the current electoral trends, pulling national Republicans further to the right could spell doom for the party in future elections.

As the Tea Party continues to work to drop spending and lower taxes, supporters and organizers will need to be careful to protect their brand. Much like political parties, the brand will be judged by successes in implementing change. Electing Tea Party candidates is meaningless if they do not fight for Tea Party issues. In this way, political branding can be extremely problematic. A clothing company can switch from selling to a 40-year-old market to an 18-year-old market overnight and claim the decision was based on market research. If, however, social movements or politicians make such a change for the same reasons, they will be labeled as flip-floppers. With hundreds of small, underfunded groups existing throughout the United States, it will be up to elected officials to help bring about the change the Tea Party movement wants to see. Only by doing so can the Tea Party hope to be remembered as a brand that evokes feelings regarding the betterment of the country and its citizens rather than a collection of bored, out-of-touch Revolutionary War re-enactors.

References

American Marketing Association (AMA). (1960). *Marketing definitions*. Chicago, IL: American Marketing Association.

Calfano, J. R. (2010). The power of brand: Beyond interest group influence in U.S. state abortion politics. *State Politics & Policy Quarterly, 10*(3), 227–247.

Chandler, J., & Owen, M. (2002). *Developing brands with qualitative market research*. Thousand Oaks, CA: Sage.

Cosgrove, K. (2007). *Branded conservatives*. New York, NY: Peter Lang.

Epstein, L. D. (1967). *Political parties in Western democracies*. New York, NY: Praeger.

Fine, J. (2008, December 1). Your brand is not a candidate. *Businessweek*, p. 109.

Foster, E., & Hudon, R. (2010, June 3). The use of political marketing by interest groups. Paper presented at the Annual Meeting of the Canadian Political Science Association. Montreal, Canada.

Foster, E., Hudon, R., & Yates, S. (2012). Advocacy coalition strategies: Tensions about legitimacy in environmental causes. In J. Lees-Marshment (Ed.), *Handbook of political marketing* (pp. 318–330). New York, NY: Routledge.

Harris, P., & Lock, A. (2001). Establishing the Charles Kennedy brand: A strategy for an election the result of which is a foregone conclusion. *Journal of Marketing Management, 17*(9/10), 943–956.

Henneberg, S. C. (2002). Understanding political marketing. In N. O'Shaughnessy & S. C. Henneberg (Eds.), *The idea of political marketing* (pp. 93–171). Westport, CT: Praeger.

Huntington, S. P. (1981). *American politics*. Cambridge, MA: Belknap Press of Harvard University Press.

Kavanagh, D. (1995). *Election campaigning*. Oxford, UK: Blackwell.

Keller, K. L. (2002). Branding and brand equity. In B. A. Weitz & R. Wensley (Eds.), *Handbook of marketing* (pp. 151–178). Thousand Oaks, CA: Sage.

Keller, K. L. (2003). Brand synthesis: The multidimensionality of brand knowledge. *Journal of Consumer Research, 29*(March), 595–600.

King, S. (2006). *Pink ribbons, Inc.* Minneapolis, MN: University of Minnesota Press.

Kotler, P., & Kotler, N. (1999). Generating effective candidates, campaigns, and causes. In B. I. Newman (Ed.), *Handbook of political marketing* (pp. 3–19). Thousand Oaks, CA: Sage.

Lees-Marshment, J. (2001). The product, sales, and market-oriented party. How Labour learnt to market the product, not just the presentation. *European Journal of Marketing, 35*(9/10), 1074–1084.

Lees-Marshment, J. (2003). Marketing good works: New trends in how interest groups recruit supporters. *Journal of Public Affairs, 3*(4), 358–370.

Lees-Marshment, J. (2004). *The political marketing revolution*. Manchester, UK: Manchester University Press.

Lilleker, D., & Negrine, R. (2003). Not big brand names but corner shop: Marketing politics to a disengaged electorate. *American Journal of Political Science, 45*, 951–971.

Lock, A., & Harris, P. (1996). Machiavellian marketing: The development of corporate lobbying in the UK. *Journal of Marketing Management, 12*(4), 313–328.

McGrath, C. (2006). Grassroots lobbying: Marketing politics and policy beyond the beltway. In P. J. Davies & B. I. Newman (Eds.), *Winning elections with political marketing* (pp. 105–130). Binghamton, NY: The Haworth Press.

Miller, W. J., & Walling, J. D. (2011). *Tea Party effects on 2010 U.S. Senate elections*. Lanham, MD: Lexington Books.

Needham, C. (2005). Brand leaders: Clinton, Blair, and the limitations of the permanent campaign. *Political Studies, 53*, 343–361.

Needham, C. (2006). Brands and political loyalty. *Brand Management, 13*(3), 178–187.

Newman, B. I. (1999). A predictive model of voting behavior. In B. I. Newman (Ed.), *Handbook of political marketing* (pp. 259–282). Thousand Oaks, CA: Sage.

O'Shaughnessy, J., & Henneberg, S. C. (2007). The selling of the president 2004: A marketing perspective. *Journal of Public Affairs, 7*, 249–268.

Putnam, R. (2000). *Bowling alone: Civic disengagement in America*. New York, NY: Simon & Schuster.

Reeves, P., de Chernatony, L., & Carigan, M. (2006). Building a political brand: Ideology or voter-driven strategy. *Brand Management, 13*(6), 418–428.

Rodgers, D. T. (2012). *Age of fracture*. Cambridge, MA: Belknap Press.

Salisbury, R. H. (1969). An exchange theory of interest groups. *Midwest Journal of Political Science, 13*(1), 1–32.

Santelli's Tea Party. (2009, February 19). CNBC SqwakBox. http://video.cnbc.com/gallery/?video=1039849853

Scammell, M. (1999). Political marketing: Lessons for political science. *Political Studies, 47*(4), 718–739.

Scammell, M. (2007). Political brands and consumer citizens: The rebranding of Tony Blair. *The ANNALS of the American Academy of Political and Social Science, 611*(1), 176–192.

Schneider, H. (2004). Branding in politics—Manifestations, relevance, and identity-oriented management. *Journal of Political Marketing, 3*(3), 41–67.

Schweiger, G., & Adami, M. (1999). The non-verbal image of politicians and political parties. In B. I. Newman (Ed.), *Handbook of political marketing* (pp. 347–364). Thousand Oaks, CA: Sage.

Skocpol, T., & Williamson, V. (2012). *The Tea Party and the remaking of Republican conservatism*. New York, NY: Oxford University Press.

Smith, G., & French, A. (2009). The political brand: A consumer perspective. *Marketing Theory, 9*(2), 209–226.

Smith, I. G. (2001). The 2001 general election: Factors influencing the brand image of political parties and their leaders. *Journal of Marketing Management, 17*(9/10), 1058–1073.

Smith, I. G. (2005). Politically significant events and their effect on the image of political parties: A conceptual framework. *Journal of Political Marketing, 4*(2/3), 103–126.

Stewart, C. J., Smith, C. A., & Denton, R. E. (2001). *Persuasion and social movements* (4th ed.). Prospect Heights, IL: Waveland Press.

Tarrow, S. (1994). *Power in movement: Social movements, collective action, and politics.* New York, NY: Cambridge University Press.

Tea Party Canvass. (2010). *The Washington Post.* www.washingtonpost.com/wp-srv/special/politics/tea-party-canvass/

White, J., & de Chernatony, L. (2002). New Labour: A study of the creation, development, and demise of a political brand. *Journal of Political Marketing, 1*(2/3), 45–52.

Zernike, K., & Thee-Brenan, M. (2010, April 15). Poll finds Tea Party backers wealthier and more educated. *The New York Times,* p. A1.

7

ACCESS HOLLYWOOD

Celebrity Endorsements in American Politics

Alex Marland and Mireille Lalancette

> "*Even though Americans tend not to trust politicians, they have greater respect for and confidence in celebrities who enter the world of politics.*"
> —West and Orman 2003: 102

Overview of the Topic

Political marketers, fundraisers and campaign managers recognize the positive media that can be generated when a famous person publicly supports and campaigns for a candidate. In theory, the image qualities of the endorser will be transferred to the endorsed politician and the celebrity's followers will be more likely to vote for that candidate. A marketing endorsement makes strategic sense as media becomes fragmented, as popular culture and politics converge, as politicians attempt to control their image and as voters make decisions on the basis of personalities. However, the practice of celebrities endorsing an election candidate has implications for democratic debate, voting behavior and public policy. Little has been written about this from a political marketing perspective.

Celebrities have a long-standing presence in American politics. In 1928, public relations pioneer Edward Bernays sought to soften the public image of President Calvin Coolidge by inviting famous artists for breakfast. Al Jolson, Ed Wynn, the Dolly Sisters, Charlotte Greenwood, Raymond Hitchcock and others complied by munching, posing for photos and singing on the White House lawn, resulting in favorable newspaper headlines (Museum of Public Relations 2013). In *Propaganda*, Bernays (1928) highlighted the importance of the market segment and of selling ideas to the conscience, interest and emotions of specific groups (economic, social, religious, cultural, racial, corporate, regional, etc.). In this sense, his White House breakfast event was not aimed at charming the celebrity crowd, but at leveraging their media status to reach a larger audience of citizen admirers.

The presence of the famous in American politics has persisted. In the 1930s, President Roosevelt used celebrities to sell his New Deal, while in the 1980s President Reagan, himself a movie star, embraced the Hollywood narrative in his political style. Republicans such as Nixon, Reagan and the Bushes and Democrats such as the Kennedys, Clinton and Obama have relied on celebrities in one way or another. In addition to shaping their public image this helps them communicate with groups of the electorate who may otherwise support their opponents. For instance, in 2009 President Barack Obama hosted Sprint Cup champion Jimmie Johnson at the White House. This is believed to be an event designed to reach "NASCAR Dads," a demographic segment mainly consisting of working-class Southern and Midwestern white men aged 25 to 49, many of whom voted Republican in 2008 (Zengerle 2009). Celebrities are therefore attractive to politicians because of their ability to generate publicity and promote a policy or candidate to their fan base.

The fracturing of media platforms combined with citizens' waning interest in politics has further increased the political appeal of celebrities. It is a challenging reality that most Americans do not follow politics and that many get their news from social media. According to the Pew Research Center (2012), 24 percent of Americans paid close attention to Washington politics in 2004; this had declined to 17 percent in 2012. Among youth, only 5 percent follow politics closely, compared with 18 percent who do so with entertainment news. In other words, approximately 4 in 5 Americans and 19 out of 20 young people do not follow political news closely. One reason is that journalists tend to distrust political elites and this contributes to a "spiral of cynicism" of negativity, of reduced public interest in politics and of lower voter turnout (Capella and Jamieson 1997). Moreover, there can be more to gain by making idle chit-chat on daytime TV talk and entertainment shows like *The View* than engaging in a policy debate on *Meet the Press*. It makes strategic sense: the politician is treated like a special guest, is inoculated from difficult policy questions, is seen by undecided voters and becomes more famous. For political marketers, this is an opportunity to communicate with a targeted segment of the electorate and for candidates to show off their personal side. Celebrity politics is thus a means of advancing an agenda and, in an election year, securing votes.

In this fractured media environment, politicians are narrowcasting specific messages to precise audiences instead of broadcasting ideas, and celebrities are drawing attention to political causes (Thrall et al. 2008). The innumerable list of examples includes former vice president Al Gore leveraging entertainers' star power to attract attention to climate change during Live Earth, a 24-hour-long concert; actress Mia Farrow writing to the *Wall Street Journal* about the situation in Darfur; and Bono, lead singer of U2, mobilizing government attention around the AIDS problem in Africa (Cooper 2008). The presence of celebrities in politics reaches different publics, whether policy-makers and/or the public, and sometimes millions of dollars are raised for a political cause.

This brings us to the convergence of politics, popular culture and marketing. On their way to the Oval Office, Bill Clinton famously played the saxophone on *The Arsenio Hall Show*, while Obama showed his dance moves on *The Ellen DeGeneres Show*. Obama has since "slow jammed" the news on *Late Night with Jimmy Fallon*, attracted media attention for calling Kanye West "a jackass," and has impersonated U.S. gymnast McKayla Maroney's "not impressed" look, which became an Internet meme after the 2012 Summer Olympics. These types of performances humanize politicians and give them the opportunity to reach a large public in an age where political disengagement is prominent. For some, the politics of personality is institutionalized and has taken the place of the politics of substance (Gamson 1994). This increases the importance of aesthetics in politics, where image management and style are paramount, and where politicians borrow communication techniques from the entertainment industry (Van Zoonen 2005).

What we are concerned about is the marketing value of candidates receiving a public endorsement from pop culture celebrities. Just as marketers recruit celebrities to recommend products and services, it is also common for political marketers to secure testimonials in favor of their candidate. Given the pervasiveness of fame and celebrity in American culture, there can be countless celebrities to seek endorsements from. Henneberg and Chen (2008: 4) differentiate political and conventional celebrities as "internal" and "external." People in the political game such as former and current senators, members of Congress, governors and mayors have name recognition; however, these internal celebrities tend to endorse along party lines and they matter little to those not paying attention to political news. We are interested in celebrities who are external to politics. This includes athletes, business leaders, religious leaders, military heroes, scientists, inventors, authors, educators, community activists, labor organizers, philanthropists, fashion designers and so on. The largest universe of external celebrities comes from the entertainment industry—musicians, television and movie actors, directors, comedians, media personalities and other types of artists. Securing an endorsement from any of them can lead to specialized media coverage that is ordinarily off limits to politicians and that is prized by political marketers.

Review of Previous Literature

While considerable research exists about the impact of celebrity endorsement on goods and services, few studies exist about the impact of celebrities in politics (Henneberg and Chen 2008; Jackson 2008). It is therefore unclear whether it mattered when Lady Gaga, at the time the world's most followed Twitter user, tweeted after the final 2012 presidential debate that she thought that Obama "was passionate and knowledgable [sic] and modern. Felt almost like he kept poker face last 2 debates and then came like rocky" (Cohn 2012). Conversely, it is difficult to infer what sort of marketing value resulted from the media coverage of Hollywood legend Clint Eastwood speaking to an empty chair at the 2012 Republican National Convention, in a critique of Obama. To provide the groundwork for answers we establish the marketing theory behind celebrity endorsements before proceeding to discuss them in the 2012 presidential campaign.

A celebrity is someone who is well known and who typically connects with audiences on an emotional level. His or her fame is a product of mass media representation, public image, and the cultural industry. For Rojek (2001), there are three forms of celebrity status. *Ascribed* celebrity is predetermined by bloodline and biological descent, such as the children of Hollywood A-list actors. Celebrity can be *achieved* by succeeding in artistic or sports competition, as with Madonna or LeBron James, who are recognized for their talents and skills. Celebrity can also be *attributed* by the concentration of media attention on someone, such as a local weather personality. This latter category includes the growing phenomenon of instant celebrities who gain fleeting fame by virtue of an event, an appearance on reality TV or a video that goes viral. Politicians can themselves achieve celebrity by virtue of holding high office; celebrity can equally be ascribed to politicians' family members, and it can be attributed to those holding lower office if they attract the attention of the broader public. In this context, media representation is the basis of stardom.

Commercial marketers frequently hire celebrities to promote their good or service in the hopes of increasing awareness, trust and liking of what is being endorsed. Roughly a quarter of all television and print advertisements in the United States feature celebrities (Roy 2006); this is also an international phenomenon that can be found in the United Kingdom and Japan (Biswas, Hussain and O'Donnell 2009). Since celebrities are often idolized and considered credible sources of information on some issues (Atkin and Block 1983), it is not surprising to see that the celebrity endorsement of brands has increased over the past 20 years (Madan 2011). In a competitive media market, engaging a celebrity offers differentiation for the brand.

Studies involving experts in marketing and publicity have shown that the product match-up hypothesis plays an important role in the decision to hire a celebrity for endorsing a product. Academic findings have demonstrated that a celebrity is more effective than a non-celebrity endorser with regards to the consumers' attitude toward the brand, buying intentions and actual sales (Erdogan 1999). Experiments have also shown that congruence between the brand and the spokesperson makes the transfer of affect more effective (Misra and Beatty 1990). Finally, investors also believe that celebrity endorsement is a valuable and profitable component of an advertisement strategy. The theory is that a famous person will generate more attention, will improve audience recall of the message and will increase the credibility of the communication.

This said, the involvement of celebrities is a double-edged sword that generates its own set of challenges (Erdogan 1999; Muda, Musa and Putit 2011).

Notwithstanding the fact that hiring celebrities is expensive, and may spark controversy, a famous person can also cast a negative shadow on the brand. First, if the celebrity is powerful and popular, he or she may outshine the product, which can drive consumers to notice the endorser instead of what is being endorsed (Muda, Musa and Putit 2011). Second, should the spokesperson become involved in unrelated controversy, this may bring embarrassment to the company and damage the image of the sponsored brand (Till and Shimp 1998). Companies have dropped their celebrity spokespersons for reasons such as controversial music, domestic assault, marital infidelity and substance abuse. There is much at stake; one study showed a correlation between stock market value and Google search intensity with regards to news related to scandal (Knittel and Stango 2012). The fear of public indignity is sometimes so present that companies prefer to be associated with deceased celebrities since their behavior is no longer unpredictable. There is also a risk of the celebrity severing the relationship, using the opportunity to cause the company embarrassment, as Lady Gaga did in 2011 with Target because the retailer donated to a political action committee that supported an anti-gay candidate. Third, consumers may raise credibility issues when a star is paid to endorse a brand. Fourth, if celebrities praise more than one brand simultaneously, this can blur the message.

The most valuable endorsements come from celebrities with a high Q-score (the industry standard for measuring the popular appeal of celebrities) on the personality attributes that have been deemed likely to resonate among target audiences. The terms of an endorsement agreement vary considerably. Some celebrities donate their time to charitable organizations, whereas others sign lucrative deals to promote a product or service. According to California-based website Look to the Stars (2013), worldwide over 1900 charities have been endorsed by a total of over 3700 celebrities, ranging from Grammy-award nominees donating tickets to charity to former game show host Bob Barker's advocacy for People for the Ethical Treatment of Animals (PETA). By comparison, Nike's army of endorsers has ranged from Michael Jordan to Rory McIlroy, Pepsi signed Beyoncé Knowles, and in infomercials boxer George Foreman has plugged an indoor grill that bore his name. All earned tens of millions of dollars for their efforts.

While many pop culture icons dabble in politics as part of their occupation—such as actors portraying politicians or singers crooning about political issues—some choose to enter the political realm in their spare time. For instance Angelina Jolie, in her role as special envoy for the Office of the UN High Commissioner for Refugees, brings attention to the plight of civilians fleeing political conflict; basketball star Steve Nash wore an antiwar t-shirt to an NBA all-star game; George Clooney was arrested for protesting outside the Sudanese embassy; and actors like Ronald Reagan and Arnold Schwarzenegger have capitalized on their fame to win high office. Politics can also generate media coverage of celebrities whose fame is waning, such as actress Daryl Hannah (best known for the 1984 movie *Splash*), who was arrested in 2012 for protesting the development of an oil pipeline. Celebrities can therefore be motivated not only by an opportunity to attract support for their political beliefs but perhaps by the chance to generate publicity and power for themselves.

The nature of the incentives that are available to entice celebrities to endorse a political candidate is one of the many ways that politics differs from the consumer marketplace. Whereas in the private sector money is used to negotiate and control the terms of the testimonial, in politics the terms are more fluid. Election candidates have long sought public commitments of support from other politicians and newspaper editors, and from non-governmental organizations that are active participants in the public sphere. The endorsee can benefit from increased media visibility, an image of trust and credibility, perceptions of legitimacy of the campaign, the ability to attract resources, campaign momentum and, ultimately, ability to win an election. In return for providing a public "signal regarding that individual's fitness for service," endorsers attempt to obtain support for their own political and/or personal agenda (Vining and Wilhelm 2011: 1075). External celebrities bring something extra. As famous people who are not ordinarily involved in politics they should attract attention from a cynical media and influence their followers to think positively about the political process (Austin et al. 2008). They therefore have the potential to reach out and mobilize an apathetic public. Moreover, they can bring attention to an issue and get hold of the public agenda (Cooper 2008; Thrall et al. 2008).

Henneberg and Chen (2008: 4) define celebrity political endorsement (CPE) as "the use of celebrity endorsement instruments for the purpose of political activities, especially election campaigning." The most famous recent case of American CPE occurred in 2007, when Oprah Winfrey, who at the time was queen of daytime TV, supported Obama's nomination as the Democratic presidential candidate. She interviewed Obama on her talk show, fundraised for him, hosted events and appeared at important campaign rallies. This generated mass media coverage, and although Oprah's endorsement did not change whether Americans liked Obama or not, they did see him as more electable (Pease and Brewer 2008), and one study estimated her endorsement as being responsible for approximately a million votes (Garthwaite and Moore 2012).[1] In this environment, a citizen's vote decision is supposedly influenced by opinion leaders who are not known for their political expertise.

Theoretical Framework

Our review of the literature leads us to distinguish between two types of external celebrity endorsements: celebrity political endorsement (CPE) publicists and fundraisers (see Table 7.1).

We propose that *celebrity political endorsement publicists* are celebrities who by virtue of their position attract media attention for the candidate that they endorse. They benefit from earning news media coverage that influences their own social

TABLE 7.1 Model of Celebrity Public Endorsements

	CPE PUBLICIST	CPE FUNDRAISER
What They Do	Generate media coverage • communicate with fans via social media • issue a statement of endorsement • participate in campaign events	Raise money • appear at fundraising events • host private fundraising functions • issue appeals for donations • make donations
Benefits to Campaign	Positive publicity • emotional connections • heuristic cues for voters • public legitimacy • stronger brand image	More resources • leveraging of celebrity's connections • money to finance other activities • stronger brand image
Benefits to Celebrity	Positive publicity • improved business prospects • increased fame • stronger brand image	Proximity to power • improved business prospects • increased fame and influence • stronger brand image
Risks to Campaign	Negative publicity • campaign goes off-message • mismatch • weakened brand image	Negative publicity • damage control • elitism, ethical questions • weakened brand image
Risks to Celebrity	Negative publicity • fan backlash • harm to business interests • weakened brand image	Negative publicity • fan backlash • harm to business interests • weakened brand image
Post-Campaign Relationship	Endorsement may fade away or be reversed; or, a CPE publicist may become a CPE fundraiser	Politicians pressured to advance a policy agenda and give celebrity special access

status and their relationship with followers who share the same value system. They provide the media with something positive to report on and they keep attendees entertained at campaign rallies. They may increase the attention paid to election ads, whether produced by other celebrities (Will.i.am's 2008 "Yes We Can" video comes to mind) or by political action committees (such as Scarlett Johansson, Eva Longoria and Kerry Washington appearing in a MoveOn.org 2012 spot). The candidate benefits from the ability of the celebrity to attract the attention of a niche audience including through non-political media. In a fractured media environment, one that often includes celebrities communicating directly to fans through social media, the value of CPE publicists seems likely to increase. These endorsements could be rooted in the cultural public sphere dimension of our model. Here the processes of identification are based on emotional and affective choices, not only on rational ones, and plays a role in the mobilization process (Van Zoonen 2005) as well as in audience identification (Thrall et al. 2008). In particular, celebrity appeals could encourage certain electors to turn out to vote on Election Day, given that young and apathetic voters are more difficult to reach and since people paying attention to celebrity culture are less likely to be politically engaged (Couldry and Markham 2007).

Celebrity political endorsement fundraisers tend to belong to a more exclusive club of A-list celebrities. CPE fundraisers take on a significant commitment by leveraging their fame to attract donations to a campaign. These range from celebrities who show up to fundraising events to the powerbrokers who have direct access to the candidate and to policy-makers.[2] For instance, Cher, Ellen DeGeneres and Lady Gaga are among the stars who have attended pricey Obama fundraisers in support of favorable LGBT policies, but there is no evidence of them having special influence with the president. Conversely, Oprah Winfrey—of whom Obama remarked, "just like books, skin cream, when Oprah decides she likes you, then other people like you, too" (Dwyer 2012)—actively campaigned for him in 2008, but in 2012 she chose instead to donate the maximum allowable amount and to participate in intimate fundraising events. One apparent reason is because upon actively endorsing Obama in 2008 her personal Q-score metrics weakened (Klein 2012).

Whether for publicity or fundraising, there are a variety of reasons why convincing a celebrity to publicly endorse a political candidate is, in theory, a sensible political marketing tactic. As Biswas, Hussain and O'Donnell (2009) point out, there are many theoretical models for understanding celebrity endorsement. First, it capitalizes on trends in voter behavior. There is growing recognition that electors consider heuristic cues when deciding how to vote. Many Americans prioritize valence issues like a politician's image or personality, and there is evidence that celebrity endorsements can influence the vote intentions of those who are not normally politically engaged (Veer, Becirovic and Martin 2010). One study showed that governors' endorsements of candidates for the state Supreme Court elections had an effect on the electoral outcome and that this sent a message to activists that the candidate deserves their support (Vining and Wilhelm 2011). The impacts could be more significant on younger Americans as they are more likely to agree with a position when a pop culture celebrity endorses it (Jackson 2008). This is a central reason why recent get-out-the-vote campaigns targeting young people have caused many young Americans to be less apathetic.

Second, celebrity endorsements have relevance through a cultural public sphere lens. This theory points to the need for more affective/emotional communication, one that connects with audiences' emotional state, such as how a smile can convey feelings of happiness (e.g., Geltner 2013). Studies show that consumers hold favorable attitudes toward celebrity endorsements and see the phenomenon as great way of generating attention (Biswas, Hussain and O'Donnell 2009). In addition, not only do electors identify with certain prominent people, but they often assume the characteristics of their role models (Kelman 1961).

Third, there is a social psychology relevance. Social cognitive theory contends that people rely on others to act on their behalf and that they change their behavior in response to cues taken from influential individuals (Bandura 1986). McGuire's (1985) source attractiveness model presumes that perceptions will be positive when assessments of an endorser's expertise and trustworthiness are high. In the source credibility model (Hovland and Weiss 1951), it is the likability, familiarity and similarity of the brand and the celebrity that explains the success of the endorsement. In the meaning transfer model, the better the match between the symbolic properties of the product and celebrity, the higher the likelihood that consumer will choose that product (McCracken 1986). For McCracken (1989), the theory of the celebrity endorsement power is based on source attractiveness and credibility, and on how the meanings of this person could be transferred to the product. In addition, the model of presumed influence (Gunther and Storey 2003) can help us think about the impacts of celebrity endorsement, as electors could perceive some effects of celebrity support on other electors and react to that perception. A celebrity endorsement might be seen as a way to increase the likeability of the candidate and, at the same time, to increase the propensity that people will vote for that candidate.

Fourth, there is a marketing value. When celebrities are involved in campaigns, this can generate more press coverage, awareness, interest and sales. Celebrities are seen as dynamic and attractive with likable qualities (Erdogan 1999). By bringing these outsiders into politics, marketers hope that the star's qualities will be transferred to the politician, and make him or her more attractive (McCracken 1989). During tests, advertisements featuring a famous person have been shown to have a deeper impact, especially among young people, and to improve the image of the brand (Atkin and Block 1983). From a marketing point of view, politicians and celebrities can be seen as brands, and the political endorsement of a celebrity can therefore be envisioned as political co-branding (Seno and Lukas 2007). The co-branding perspective gives an active role to the party who is no longer just receiving support, but is rather part of an exchange with the star, an exchange where both parties bring together their qualities. Celebrities are also useful to reach new markets, like youth, or larger audiences. Finally, since there is a history of stars embracing causes (e.g., AIDS, poverty, environment), politics may well take advantage of this type of activism to persuade people close to such causes to support a similar political agenda.

However, marketing literature also points to limitations of celebrity endorsements. While audiences' attitude toward the brand can improve, this does not necessarily translate into changes in brand recall or purchase intent (Till and Busler 2000). The brand match-up hypothesis stipulates that there must be some consistency between the image attributes of the endorser and the endorsee. This can lead to a mismatch among actors in particular because they are different people off-screen than they are on-screen, which gives rise to the notion that audiences can better relate to irrelevant celebrities who they perceive to be more "normal" (Speck, Schumann and Thompson 1988). The marketing credibility of the endorser in relation to the product matters, and in some circumstances, the endorsement of an unknown expert can be preferable over a pop culture star, especially if the subject matter is complex (Biswas, Biswas and Das 2006). Public perceptions of the credibility of what is being endorsed supersede that of the endorser and the ability of a celebrity to change perceptions of a corporate image or influence consumer attitudes is limited (Goldsmith, Lafferty and Newell 2000). In addition, just as commercial brands risk being associated with a celebrity who is embroiled in scandal, even more caution exists in politics. Thus while celebrities can generate media attention for a candidate among targeted segments of the electorate, there can be a source credibility problem that limits their influence, especially among older voters.

The adaptation of celebrity marketing literature to politics points to a number of ways that political marketing plans can use celebrity endorsements to achieve success. Celebrity endorsements can be used to provide voters with a heuristic cue for when they decide how to vote; to create an emotional connection with voters and gain their attention; to enhance public perception of the candidate by transferring positive symbolism from the celebrity to the politician; and to improve the image of the candidate's political brand. However, this is not without risks. The literature warns that the celebrity must match the candidate's brand and/or policy objectives. This entails a careful analysis of emotional branding and values, of the targeted elector segments and the risks to both the endorser and the endorsee. Even when it is determined that there is a good match the effects of celebrity endorsement should not be overstated, especially among older audiences.

Empirical Illustration

CPE publicists and CPE fundraisers have had a presence in American politics for quite some time (e.g., Critchlow and Raymond 2009) and their influence extends into the international political arena (Cooper 2008). We are concerned with the hundreds of celebrities who endorsed Barack Obama and Mitt Romney during the 2012 presidential campaign (Table 7.2). Actors, musicians, media personalities, writers, comedians and members of the fashion industry were more likely to publicly align with Obama than with Romney. Conversely, some niche markets like NASCAR drivers and religious clergy that we would associate with conservatism were more likely to endorse the Republican candidate.

Most Americans would not be familiar with the 600+ external celebrities who supported Obama or the 200+ who endorsed Romney, most of whom were CPE publicists. But fans of Miley Cyrus and Selena Gomez may have noticed when those celebrities urged a vote for Obama. Their endorsement resonated with a different cohort of electors than those who paid attention when Richard Dean Anderson or Sinbad did the same. Likewise, some voter segments may have responded favorably to YouTube videos endorsing Obama that were posted by the National Jewish Democratic Council, featuring a combination of internal and external celebrities including Broadway star Barbara Streisand, former New York mayor Ed Koch and former U.S. Middle East adviser Dennis Ross (Krieger 2012).

TABLE 7.2 Celebrity Endorsers, 2012 Presidential Campaign

	Obama (Democrat)	Romney (Republican)
Internal celebrities (e.g., former and current elected officials, First Ladies, ambassadors, cabinet officials, military officials, sociopolitical activists)	159	573
Daily newspapers	99	105
External celebrities		
actors	241	45
adult entertainers	8	2
autoracing (NASCAR)	0	6
baseball, basketball and football players (MLB, NBA, NFL)	32	17
business people	24	23
chefs	6	0
clergy	0	7
comedians	24	7
directors, screenwriters, and producers	38	12
fashion designers and models	18	3
media personalities	18	18
musicians and bands	126	45
Nobel Prize laureates and astronauts	69	8
other sports (e.g., boxing, golf, soccer, wrestling)	7	6
winter sports (e.g., hockey, skiing, figure skating)	0	15
writers	25	7

Source: Calculated in February 2013 from lists of celebrity and newspaper endorsements maintained on Wikipedia. We are unable to differentiate between CPE publicists and fundraisers. Intended to be illustrative only.

In this sense, the CPE publicists could play a role in appealing to specific audiences and affecting voting behavior. They can also be employed to support policy-related communication themes, such as gay singer Ricky Martin introducing the president at an event just days after Obama announced his support for same-sex marriage (Nakamura 2012). When adopting a social psychology standpoint, Martin's celebrity attractiveness, expertise, familiarity and credibility on a contentious issue could mean that his message was heard and approved by many citizens who supported the Obama campaign's position.

CPE fundraisers were less common but are a greater source of concern. Celebrities who took on roles as fundraiser bundlers include Jay-Z and Beyoncé, who hosted the president at a private Manhattan fundraiser, and Will Smith and Jada Pinkett Smith, who invited the First Lady to a fundraising luncheon at their home. A number of times the Obama campaign leveraged celebrities to fundraise from ordinary Americans with a pitch that donors would enter a drawing for tickets to attend exclusive celebrity events. In one case tens of thousands of Americans donated an average of $23 each to the Democratic Party for a chance to attend a $40,000 per ticket fundraiser at George Clooney's home (Keegan 2012). While the importance of CPE fundraisers to a campaign seem obvious they nevertheless raise questions just as any fundraising activity would, namely: What do donors get in return? As with other donors they have a range of reasons, which may include adding to their own fame, obtaining political access and/or seeking policy influence. President Obama has spent considerable time mingling with celebrities, such as at a May 2012 dinner with 150 guests at Clooney's cottage that raised $15 million, as well as a June trip on Air Force One with Jon Bon Jovi (Nakamura 2012). In 2012 some of his top CPE fundraisers, including Clooney, Winfrey, Jay-Z, Bon Jovi, Sarah Jessica Parker and Morgan Freeman, visited the White House (Flock 2012). Fundraising for presidential candidates is a way for some celebrities to expand their power and influence, which adds to the many concerns about the implications of lax fundraising regulations for American democracy.

There are a number of indications why the political influence of most CPE publicists is limited compared with that of CPE fundraisers. Many celebrities simply affirm the political positions of their followers. This is especially true in the case of media personalities such as liberal blogger Perez Hilton (who endorsed Obama) or conservative commentators Glenn Beck, Rush Limbaugh and Bill O'Reilly (who endorsed Romney). It is unclear what kind of effect such people have on the credibility and likeability of a candidate when their own role in the media involves criticizing public personalities. Pop culture celebrities have a history of supporting Republicans (Critchlow and Raymond 2009: 7), but are currently thought to be more likely to support liberal values, so it is not surprising that a 2007 poll found that when asked if they felt that celebrities should not get involved in politics, 71 percent of Republicans agreed, compared with 43 percent of independents and just 31 percent of Democrats (Thee 2007). In this context Democrats are wary of promoting their ties to Hollywood because it risks alienating some voters. From a marketing perspective, this is one of the limits of celebrity endorsement: How can parties manage public perception in their favor without risking the disaffection of some voters? For example, the narrow segment of electors who follow the fashion industry may have welcomed news that Anna Wintour, the controversial *Vogue* editor, gathered 20 American designers to a New York event called "Runway to Win." However, this is incongruent with the brand match-up hypothesis because being associated with the fashion industry is out of step with mainstream America. Mass media coverage of the event focused on the Stella McCartney dress worn by co-host Scarlett Johansson and mentioned the high cost of the t-shirts, tote bags and other accessories sold to raise money for the Obama campaign (Morris 2012). Doubts about source credibility of the campaign might likewise be raised. In addition, this could convey a negative image on the endorsed candidate, making him or her appear shallow and superficial. Campaigns in 2012 sought to score political points through their opponents' associations with celebrities, with the Obama team demanding that Romney distance himself from some celebrities' political views, and the Republicans countering that the Democrats' economic strategy was to "deploy Hollywood" (Karmi 2012).

In 2012 most CPE publicists appear to have merely generated some fleeting news coverage for the candidate, while some others incurred less-than-favorable coverage (Table 7.3). For instance, Eastwood was widely mocked for his monologue with an empty chair, and Madonna was booed at a New Orleans concert when she urged her fans to vote for Obama. A few Romney celebrity supporters were critiqued by their peers for not endorsing Obama. There are dangers of voters' disaffection when politics becomes too close to entertainment. When headlines proclaim that "Obama has raked it in from his star backers" (Cline 2012) the candidate is at risk of being branded as an out-of-touch elite who is part of the establishment and who is insensitive to the pocketbook concerns of ordinary Americans. Such media coverage can also bring voters to think that politics is foremost about money, as opposed to ideas and policies. Thus cynicism and apathy could grow among the targeted audiences that parties are trying to reach with the endorsements, negating any marketing value for the product because negative perceptions have been attached to the entire product category. This touches on all the dimensions of our model, namely voting behavior, emotional and psychological appeals and marketing value.

At times the brand values of the CPE publicist may be incompatible with the candidate's brand. Politicians are unable to control the hodgepodge of famous people who choose to publicly endorse them. In a handful of cases in 2012 some endorsers had personal brands that were inconsistent with the candidate's, such as adult film star Ron Jeremy and convicted rapist Mike Tyson, who endorsed Obama, or *Celebrity Rehab*'s Gary Busey and media whipping post Lindsay Lohan, who endorsed Romney. Occasionally political marketing strategists may be spurred into damage control from unsolicited endorsements. This might have been the case when former porn star Jenna Jameson revealed her support for Romney in a strip club, proclaiming: "When you're rich, you want a Republican in office" (Hickey 2012). Whereas an organization like Nike carefully selects which

TABLE 7.3 Examples of News Headlines about Presidential Celebrity Endorsements (2012)

- August 30: Clint Eastwood chair speech: Actor unleashes bizarre lecture at RNC, engaging absent Obama in mock debate (*New York Daily News*)
- September 4: Chuck Norris warns of "thousand years of darkness" if Obama re-elected (*The Hollywood Gossip*)
- September 11: Minaj confirms her rap was no Romney endorsement (Associated Press)
- October 6: Obama fundraiser Sunday with Katy Perry, Bon Jovi to snarl traffic (*L.A. Now*)
- October 8: "Clueless" star dodges backlash for Mitt Romney endorsement (MTV)
- October 10: Obama is even losing Hollywood; Enthusiasm for president fades in his most liberal base (*Washington Times*)
- October 10: Lady Gaga under fire for political comment on Facebook: Should celebrities stay out of politics? (*Politics Daily*)
- October 30: Madonna gets booed by her own fans (*KO News*)

athletes it wants to shill its products and controls messaging in advertising, in politics the image of celebrity endorsers is much more diverse, and there is a reliance on earned media. Parties lack control of which celebrities will endorse them and cannot command the content of the star's message or how it will be reported.

Conclusions for Research and Practice

The concept of celebrity endorsement in politics is a recurring subject in the American media but has yet to attract much attention in political marketing literature. This chapter sheds light on some aspects of the phenomenon and raises a number of avenues for further research. First, in a fragmented media environment where narrowcasting is the new norm, and where "charitainment" is fashionable (Thrall et al. 2008), celebrities are seen as good mediums for targeting and attracting audiences. They appeal to niche audiences and could possibly influence specific voters, in particular the young, the disaffected, the apathetic, the activists and the undecideds. This is significant since these audiences are often important battlegrounds that are the difference between winning and losing an election. Moreover, the two forms of celebrity endorsers, CPE publicists and CPE fundraisers, might be seen as part of larger changes in political practices where the cultural public sphere and the boundaries between politics and popular culture grow thinner every year. While political practices melt the symbolic, the aesthetic and the emotional with the rational, scholars will want to rethink democratic representation.

Second, social psychology and political marketing models help us to assess the implications of celebrity endorsement where issues like source credibility, expertise, attractiveness and trustworthiness have important implications for politicians. Strategists must consider these factors, as well as the risk of negative media coverage associated with celebrity endorsements. As much as possible they should be selective about whom their campaigns are aligned with. However, this is difficult because political marketers do not have the same control over the endorsee that their commercial counterparts command (see also Jackson 2008).

Third, celebrity endorsements of politicians are best seen as an act of co-branding, which raises questions for democracy. By associating with one another and transferring qualities the celebrity and the politician are engaged in a brand exchange agreement (Seno and Lukas 2007). All forms of endorsement are, in part, motivated by achieving publicity for the endorser and endorsee. However, while in commerce there is a straightforward financial exchange, in politics the exchange is one of political influence and future transactions that may involve public goods. This raises questions about the implications of celebrity endorsements on American democracy in general. When matters of credibility and trustworthiness are raised in the media, and potentially by voters, this can add to the spiral of cynicism. Moreover, citizens should wonder about the payoff for CPE publicists and especially for CPE fundraisers and their influence on the political agenda. Yet, although celebrities' involvement can increase the treatment of politics as a "popularity contest" and divert attention from other causes, this must be balanced against the fact that their involvement can increase public interest and participation in politics ('t Hart and Tindall 2009: 271).

Fourth, the choice of a celebrity supporter is linked to cultural orientations and society's values (Choi et al. 2005), and the global nature of media means that celebrity politics does not operate in an American vacuum. For example, "Gangnam Style" by South Korean musician Psy and its "horse dance" became a pop culture hit in 2012. Obama told *People* magazine that he danced around the White House to the song; Britain's prime minister and London's mayor danced to it together; and South Korean presidential candidates danced on the campaign trail—although Psy himself refused political parties' requests for rights to "Gangnam Style" and opted not to endorse anyone (Hyo-won 2012). This global reach extends to celebrity endorsements: in August 2012, Clooney held a fundraiser in Geneva that was sponsored by Americans Abroad for Obama, and in January 2013 Chuck Norris appeared in a YouTube ad endorsing Benjamin Netanyahu for Israeli prime minister. Given the global influence of American political culture and the growing role of celebrities in politics, we may anticipate a greater presence of celebrity fundraisers in elections worldwide. As the convergence of politics, marketing and popular culture grows, and as the importance of money in politics persists, greater attention needs to be paid not to celebrities who endorse candidates but rather to the influence of celebrities who host private fundraising events for candidates. For as Critchlow and Raymond (2009: 1) so aptly observed, "Money, power, and celebrity—the stuff of Hollywood is also the substance of politics."

Notes

1 Note that we are not concerned here with measuring the electoral effects of endorsements, which have been found to have mixed influence (Vining and Wilhelm 2011).
2 Note that celebrities can also fund political causes in other ways, such as through a Super PAC.

References

Atkin, C., & Block, M. (1983). Effectiveness of celebrity endorsers. *Journal of Advertising Research, 23*(1), 57–61.
Austin, E.W., Van de Vord, R., Pinkleton, B.E., & Epstein, E. (2008). Celebrity endorsements and their potential to motivate young voters. *Mass Communication and Society, 11*(4), 420–436.
Bandura, A. (1986). *Social foundations of thought and action: A social cognitive theory*. Englewood Cliffs, NJ: Prentice-Hall.
Bernays, E. (1928). *Propaganda*. New York, NY: Liveright.
Biswas, D., Biswas, A., & Das, N. (2006). The differential effects of celebrity and expert endorsements on consumer risk perceptions. *Journal of Advertising, 35*(2), 17–31.
Biswas, S., Hussain, M., & O'Donnell, K. (2009). Celebrity endorsements in advertisements and consumer perceptions: A cross-cultural study. *Journal of Global Marketing, 22*(2), 121–137.

Capella, J.N., & Jamieson, K.H. (1997). *Spiral of cynicism: The press and the public good.* New York, NY: Oxford University Press.

Choi, S.M., Lee, W., & Hee-Jung, K. (2005). Lessons from the rich and famous: A cross-cultural comparison of celebrity endorsement in advertising. *Journal of Advertising, 34*(2), 85–98.

Cline, S. (2012, September 7). 10 celebrities who have made big donations to Obama. *US News.* www.usnews.com/news/articles/2012/09/07/10-celebrities-who-have-made-big-donations-to-obama

Cohn, A.M. (2012, October 23). Lady Gaga: Obama "like Rocky" in debate. *The Hill.* http://thehill.com/blogs/twitter-room/other-news/263503-lady-gaga-says-obama-was-like-rocky-in-debate

Cooper, A.F. (2008). *Celebrity diplomacy.* London, UK: Paradigm Publishing.

Couldry, N., & Markham, T. (2007). Celebrity culture and public connection: Bridge or chasm? *International Journal of Cultural Studies, 10*(4), 403–421.

Critchlow, D.T., & Raymond, E. (2009). *Hollywood and politics: A sourcebook.* New York, NY: Routledge.

Dwyer, D. (2012, March 17). Obama: Oprah helps me "focus on the big picture." *ABC News.* http://abcnews.go.com/blogs/politics/2012/03/obama-oprah-helps-me-focus-on-the-big-picture/

Erdogan, Z.B. (1999). Celebrity endorsement: A literature review. *Journal of Marketing Management, 15*(4), 291–314.

Flock, E. (2012, December 6). Celebrities who hosted Obama fundraisers also got White House tours, meeting with POTUS. *U.S. News & World Report.* www.usnews.com/news/blogs/washington-whispers/2012/12/06/celebrities-who-hosted-obama-fundraisers-also-got-white-house-tours-meetings-with-potus

Gamson, J. (1994). *Claims to fame: Celebrity in contemporary America.* Berkeley, CA: University of California Press.

Garthwaite, C., & Moore, T. (2012). Can celebrity endorsements affect political outcomes? Evidence from the 2008 US Democratic presidential primary. *Journal of Law, Economics and Organization, 29*(2), 355–384.

Geltner, P. (2013). *Emotional communication.* New York, NY: Routledge.

Goldsmith, R.E., Lafferty, B.A., & Newell, S.J. (2000). The impact of corporate credibility on consumer reaction to advertisements and brands. *Journal of Advertising, 29*(3), 43–54.

Gunther, A.C., & Storey, D.J. (2003). The influence of presumed influence. *Journal of Communication, 53*(2), 199–215.

Henneberg, S.C., & Chen, Y. (2008). Celebrity political endorsement: Campaign management for the Tapei City councillor election 2002. *Journal of Political Marketing, 6*(4), 1–31.

Hickey, W. (2012, October 9). Tons of celebrities have come out in support of Mitt Romney. *The Business Insider.* www.businessinsider.com/romney-celebrity-endorsements-2012-10?op=1

Hovland, C.I., & Weiss, W. (1951). The influence of source credibility on communication effectiveness. *Public Opinion Quarterly, 15,* 635–650.

Hyo-won, L. (2012, December 19). South Korea's president-elect gallops into office "Gangnam Style." *The Hollywood Reporter.* www.hollywoodreporter.com/news/south-koreas-president-elect-gallops-405824

Jackson, D.J. (2008). Selling politics: The impact of celebrities' political beliefs on young Americans. *Journal of Political Marketing, 6*(4), 67–83.

Karmi, O. (2012, June 8). Celebrities could prove crucial in race for the White House. *The National.* www.thenational.ae/news/world/americas/celebrities-could-prove-crucial-in-race-for-the-white-house

Keegan, R. (2012, May 10). George Clooney's Obama fundraiser uses star power with a twist." *Los Angeles Times.*
Kelman, H.C. (1961). Processes of opinion change. *The Public Opinion Quarterly, 25*(1), 57–78.
Klein, E. (2012). *The amateur: Barack Obama in the White House.* Washington, DC: Regnery Publishing.
Knittel, C.R., & Stango, V. (2012). Celebrity endorsements, firm value and reputation risk: Evidence from the Tiger Woods scandal. http://faculty.gsm.ucdavis.edu/~vstango/tiger011_web.pdf
Krieger, H.L. (2012, November 3). Jewish Democrats' secret weapon: Barbara Streisand. *Jerusalem Post.*
Look to the Stars. (2013). Celebrity charity news, events, organizations & causes. www.looktothestars.org/
Madan, R. (2011). Celebrity endorsement: A marketing strategy. In R.R. Thakur, S. Thukral, S. Neeta, & V. Gupta (Eds.), *Challenges of globalization strategies for competitiveness* (pp. 106–112). Delhi, IN: Macmillan.
McCracken, G. (1986). Culture and consumption: A theoretical account of the structure and movement of the cultural meaning of consumer goods. *Journal of Consumer Research, 1,* 71–84.
McCracken, G. (1989). Who is the celebrity endorser? Cultural foundations of the celebrity endorsement process. *Journal of Consumer Research, 16*(3), 10–12.
McGuire, W.J. (1985). Attitudes and attitude change. In L. Gardner & E. Aronson (Eds.), *Handbook of social psychology, volume II* (pp. 233–346). New York, NY: Random House.
Misra, S., & Beatty, S.E. (1990). Celebrity spokesperson and brand congruence. *Journal of Business Research, 21,* 159–173.
Morris, B. (2012, February 8). Showing their colors: Anna Wintour's party for an Obama re-election campaign. *The New York Times.*
Muda, M., Musa, R., & Putit, L. (2011). Celebrity endorsement in advertising: A double-edged sword. *Journal of Asian Behavioral Studies, 1*(3), 1–12.
Museum of Public Relations. (2013). 1928: Warming up Calvin Coolidge. www.prmuseum.com/bernays/bernays_1928.html
Nakamura, D. (2012, June 4). GOP attacks celebrity support for Obama. *The Washington Post.*
Pease, A., & Brewer, P.R. (2008). The Oprah factor: The effects of a celebrity endorsement in a presidential primary campaign. *The International Journal of Press/Politics, 13*(4), 386–400.
Pew Research Center. (2012, September 27). Trends in news consumption: 1991–2012. www.people-press.org/files/legacy-pdf/2012%20News%20Consumption%20Report.pdf
Rojek, C. (2001). *Celebrity.* London, UK: Reaktion Books.
Roy, S. (2006). An exploratory study in celebrity endorsements. *Journal of Creative Communications, 1*(2), 139–153.
Seno, D., & Lukas, B.A. (2007). The equity effect of product endorsement by celebrities: A conceptual framework from a co-branding perspective. *European Journal of Marketing, 41*(1/2), 121–134.
Speck, P.S., Schumann, D.W., & Thompson, C. (1988). Celebrity endorsements: Scripts, schema and roles. *Advances in Consumer Research, 15,* 69–76.

't Hart, P., & Tindall, K. (2009). Leadership by the famous: Celebrity as political capital. In Kane, J., Patapan, H., & 't Hart, P. (Eds.), *Dispersed democratic leadership: Origins, dynamics and implications* (pp. 255–278). Oxford, UK: Oxford University Press.

Thee, M. (2007, September 18). Hollywood and politics. *The New York Times*, p. 24.

Thrall, T.A., et al. (2008). Star power: Celebrity advocacy and the evolution of the public sphere. *The International Journal of Press/Politics, 13*(4), 362–385.

Till, B.D., & Busler, M. (2000). The match-up hypothesis: Physical attractiveness, expertise, and the role of fit on brand attitude, purchase intent and brand beliefs. *Journal of Advertising, 29*(3), 1–13.

Till, B.D., & Shimp, T.A. (1998). Endorsers in advertising: The case of negative celebrity information. *Journal of Advertising, 23*(1), 67–82.

West, D., & Orman, J. (2003). *Celebrity politics*. Upper Saddle River, NJ: Prentice Hall.

Van Zoonen, L. (2005). *Entertaining the citizen: Politics in the fan democracy*. Boulder, CO: Rowman and Littlefield.

Veer, E., Becirovic, I., & Martin, B.A.S. (2010). If Kate voted Conservative, would you?: The role of celebrity endorsements in political party advertising. *European Journal of Marketing, 44*(3/4), 436–450.

Vining, R.L., Jr., & Wilhelm, T. (2011). The causes and consequences of gubernatorial endorsements: Evidence from state Supreme Court elections. *American Politics Research, 39*(6), 1072–1096.

Zengerle, P. (2009, August 19). Obama reaches out to NASCAR nation. Reuters blog. http://blogs.reuters.com/talesfromthetrail/2009/08/19/obama-reaches-out-to-nascar-nation/

8
PERSONAL POLITICAL BRANDING AT STATE LEVEL

Kenneth Cosgrove

Overview of the Topic

This chapter looks at the power of personal branding and how it can help politicians win in unfavorable markets, difficult strategic circumstances and/or in cases where their party has limited organizational resources. The personal brand can be of particular value to the minority party because it takes the focus off of partisanship and puts it onto personality. The personal brand is an understudied phenomenon in the political marketing literature, as is sub-national political marketing. This chapter looks at the state and local level specifically as a small step toward filling this void in the literature. Further, the study of sub-national politics in the United States is a type of comparative political analysis because significant variations exist at the sub-national level. Writing about the national level alone, then assuming that political marketing techniques and/or understanding of them will be equally applicable at the sub-national level, is a questionable assumption that fails to capture the diversity in political marketing as a profession or as a field of study in the United States.

There are significant variations in structure and behavior at the state level that are worthy of examination by political marketers and professionals (see Rosenthal 1997, 2000, 2004). Political marketing is conducted in many ways at the sub-national level, some of which resemble what is done on the national level and some of which do not. Academics from a variety of disciplines have written about the significant variations that occur in state political culture, partisan alignments and systemic distributions of power, but little has been written about the impact that these variations have on the way in which political marketing is done at the sub-national level. Political scientists like V.O. Key (1949) examined Southern politics in depth, arguing that there was significant variation between the South and other parts of the United States at the same time that there was significant variation between Southern states. Daniel Elazar (1966) divided the country into three distinct political culture and journalist/futurist Joel Garreau (1981) divided North America into nine distinct nations. The political marketing literature will benefit from having a more fully developed awareness of the variation in the way in which political marketing is conducted sub-nationally within it.

Consistent with Rosenthal's state level variables (1997, 2000, 2004) we can see the significant differences between two New England neighbors and the impact that these have on the ways in which political marketing is conducted: Massachusetts and New Hampshire. New Hampshire's population is small, lives mostly along the Massachusetts border and is housed primarily in small towns and cities. Given that and the state government's small tax base, it is no surprise that the state has an amateur legislature that only sits for part of the year. This legislature lacks the staff, resources and overall institutional capacity to contest for power against and conduct serious oversight of the executive branch. The New Hampshire governor and executive branch hold most of the capacity and power in the system. Massachusetts has a much bigger population and a bigger state-level tax base, and can support a fully professional legislature that has significant staff, investigative and research capacity. Thus, the Massachusetts legislature is equipped to contest for power with the governor. Population size influences the way in which political marketing is conducted. New Hampshire is more about personal contact while Massachusetts is more about media.

The above are but two examples of the variation that takes place throughout the country. Building awareness of the major systemic differences that exist between American states and their impact on political marketing is one of this chapter's key goals. Based on the significant amount of state-level specialization found among practitioners, the pros have a behavioral understanding of the phenomenon. Some practitioners produce different materials for various parts of their constituency that stress relevant local issues or local ties and some only operate in a single state or a very specific set of states. There's more to understanding political marketing in the United States than understanding the national level. The next section will briefly introduce the political branding concept.

Review of Previous Literature

The political marketing literature has little mention of personal branding or its uses at the sub-national level. This study is unique in its focus on personal political branding and on personal political branding at the state level. In short, a brand is a consciously developed identity able to build awareness of a single product, a product line or even a human being. Two non-political examples of how an individual can build a brand around themselves to support a product are ex-NHL great Wayne Gretzky and basketball icon Michael Jordan. Gretzky uses his uniform number, 99, and the image of a hockey player to build an identity for a product line ranging from restaurants to wineries. Jordan did similar things using an image of him dunking a basketball and engaged in a number of successful co-branding relationships with companies like Nike (see Halberstam 2000). While people liked and admired these men because of their athletic accomplishments, personal branding enabled them to transform these emotions into a powerful symbol able to be applied to market a large number of activities. They could do this because the original favorable feelings people held about them were incorporated into the brand and the brand was then deployed to support a large number of entities far afield from their original activities. Politicians can use personal branding to the same good result that Gretzky and Jordan have used it. Only, instead of selling a product line, they can use it to sell themselves in their quest for office. Like personally branded politicians, both of these personally branded athletes were able to build a brand identity unique from the entity that initially made them famous. Part of their brand identity is the sport that they played, yet a bigger part is comprised of their unique personal traits.

Politicians have adopted branding for the same reasons that people like Gretzky and Jordan have adopted it to sell products. No longer do politicians engage in the kinds of presentation of self of which Fenno (2002) wrote; instead they develop a specific identity that includes specific colors, emotional persona, logo, tag line and music. This is significantly different from simply showing up at various community doings and talking about issues of interest with the voters. Such conversations take place through a variety of channels across a variety of platforms. Nobody needs to show up anywhere physically anymore and, given the ubiquity of smart devices and the Internet, it can be said that American political marketing is no longer a seasonal activity. Candidates build brands because doing so allows them to develop a consistent identity across platforms and communicative channels just as it does for commercial producers.

Political branding works because Americans are inundated with messages urging them to do and buy things continuously. There is so much noise in the environment, how is the average person to figure out what to buy, which politicians to support and what issues matter? A well-constructed brand that has a few aspects can be an effective tool to help people answer such questions. The brand is a flexible tool. It can be broadcasted or narrow-casted, targeted or used as part of a broad-based appeal. When combined with other marketing techniques like targeting and segmentation, the brand can help a politician develop a very clear identity with very specific parts of the population. National-level parties engage in brand building and use branding as a normal part of their marketing mix. They brand themselves, their candidates and their policy proposals. Through experience they have learned how to develop fully branded product lines complete with lifecycles that are aimed at specific segments of the electorate and that can be tweaked to encompass the unique aspects of a large number of different types of individual candidates over time (Cosgrove 2007). The amount of media awareness of and discussion about the technique at the national level has increased significantly in recent years. Scholars such as Newman (1999) and Cosgrove (2007) have looked systematically at branding a campaign in the former case and a political movement in the latter case. There has been some writing about the use of branding in American politics in recent years in terms of its use by the Democrats (Needham 2005; Newman 1999; Spiller and Bergner 2011) and the Republicans (Cosgrove 2007). Newman (1999) looked at the way in which branding helped to elect a single candidate, while Cosgrove (2007) looked at the way in which branding was used by a movement to alter its public perception away from extremism toward respectability and a central place in American political life. Political branding is mentioned in passing by the press but hardly at all in the American politics literature, and mentions by both tend to be in passing, superficial and focused solely on brand image among the electorate, not its uses or construction by political producers.

Political brands, like commercial ones, include consistent design, pictures, words, colors and music. Their goal is to build product identity and customer loyalty. Brands both political and commercial work with a specific set of emotions. They can develop enduring value or equity over time and have the potential to support an individual product or an entire product line and either be used for a single campaign or over a long series of campaigns lasting many decades. The brand, political or commercial, is a shortcut intended to teach potential customers about a product's existence, workings, features and benefits. The visual, verbal and emotional aspects of a brand can provide a signal to some consumers that they might be interested in this product while repelling others, meaning that a brand can be a key tool through which a market becomes segmented (Turow 1997). The brand's increasing use in political life is a direct reflection of all the noise in society but also better segmentation tools that allow marketers to understand very specific portions of their audience targets (Turow 1997). The brand has to be concise and some argue that, given the amount of information with which modern citizens are bombarded, it can't be longer than a single word (Saatchi, 2006). Branding can give people a tie to a specific candidate or party that they otherwise would not have and might motivate them to go out and vote when they otherwise would not have done so. In an environment in which people don't feel that tied to parties or politicians or that interested in politics at all, a great brand can make the difference between an easy electoral win and a crushing defeat.

Given the success national parties have had with it, it is not surprising that political branding has come to the state level. The brand can help a party win a competitive race but a great brand can also make a weaker party competitive, especially when it is built around the kind of person whom the voters might like. The brand also can build a clear identity for the state-level candidate and educate the voters quickly about which candidates are running in their area. Some states have high stimulus elections and a lot of media coverage of their politics while others do not. The brand, especially the personal brand, can be an important tool in either circumstance. The fragmented structure of American broadcasting gives the sub-national candidate an additional challenge as voters from one jurisdiction will likely see and hear about many candidates from others for whom they cannot vote. The brand can solve some of this educational problem, as is shown by the number of candidates who put the name of the place in which they are running as a signaling device. In such a fragmented communicative and usually lower stimulus environment, branding is a key tool through which candidates and parties can build clear public personas, awareness of their personas and policies and audience awareness. Branding works at the sub-national level for the same reason it works at the national level and for commercial producers: a good brand creates a specific identity with the potential for long-term emotional attachment that is capable of promoting a whole product line or an individual product. Because there are so many candidates seeking office at the sub-national level, developing a great brand is imperative.

The coalitional, decentralized American party system incentivizes candidates to develop their own brands. The function of the American political party is more to structure electoral competition and organize the government after an election than it is to act as a membership organization (Aldrich 1995). While they share a name and a brand with the national party, American state-level parties run in unique markets, meaning that their level of electoral viability and organizational capacity varies by region. Consider the variations in the Republican Party's fortunes. It is electorally dominant in Texas and Utah yet barely viable in Massachusetts and Vermont. One way a party can deal with being in such a circumstance is to let candidates able to build their own brands run as individuals. While this may not do much for the party brand or build the party as organization or in the electorate, personal branding by entrepreneurial candidates offers an opportunity to take power where one might otherwise not exist. Personal branding can enhance a party's ability to gain control of important institutions like governorships or individual House and Senate seats that can have a big impact on national-level politics.

Nothing limits individual sub-national candidates from developing their own brands that create distance between themselves and the unpopular national party brand if the strategic environment dictates. The personally branded candidate's brand narrative is usually that of someone who is an outsider and is entering a corrupt public arena to clean it up; it offers something new or something less partisan, and can be the embodiment of specific values such as being a lifelong local resident or a self-made entrepreneur. These traits are presented as evidence in support of the proposition that the candidate will perform well in office. The personal brand is a useful tool because it helps a party run candidates in areas in which its own brand is unpopular or in which it is lacking organizational capacity. The use of personal brands is an understudied aspect of the political marketing literature. That sub-national politicians are developing personal brands is consistent with similar developments in the business and entertainment worlds (see, for example, Liar, Sullivan and Cheney 2005, and for a short, easy introduction to the concept see Wikipedia Personal Branding 2013). It is easy to think of a slew of celebrities and CEOs who have branded themselves and have come to be at least as well known as whatever product they are selling (ibid.). A more positive take on the concept was provided by Tom Peters (1997), who argued that branding can do for people what it does for products and that the current environment is one in which significant incentives exist to brand oneself in order to build a unique identity and stand out from the competing crowd. Personal branding can offer a politician a path to victory that relying on a party brand cannot and, as is the case for athletes, entertainers or CEOs, a personal brand can help a politician stand out from both competitors and a damaged or party brand or weak organization. As Liar, Sullivan and Cheney (2005) argue and the cases of Mitt Romney and Bill Weld show, it has downsides such a producing a highly structured, limited version of a person's overall identity. Its other downside is that it tends to make a person into his or her résumé in a limiting way (ibid.).

Theoretical Framework

An understanding of how candidates might use personal political branding at the state level can be gained by synthesizing and adapting the concepts from different fields of research of political branding, personal branding from business and state-level campaigning. Table 8.1 lays out principles for effective personal branding that will be utilized in the empirical discussion.

These principles will be explored next in the empirical illustration section.

TABLE 8.1 10 Principles of Effective Personal Political Branding at State Level

1. Identify candidates own strengths including non-political aspects such as previous non-political careers (whether acting, business, law), financial achievements (coming from nothing to a position of success)
2. Develop these into a political brand for office: e.g., a political leader who will help others achieve their dreams
3. Connect the candidate with other independent politicians with a positive political brand if it will help the campaign
4. Research and segment the market to identify any changes in the population that the candidate might appeal to that the party might not have responded to yet
5. Identify potential market segments that fit with the candidate's existing brand, especially if they differentiate them from the party brand
6. Be prepared to shift position in relation to the dominant trends in the local market, even if it is against the party line
7. Create a policy product that has components appealing to non-traditional voter segment and core voters, to obtain support from both party identifiers and new potential switchers
8. Make any family and personal ties to the state clear, as they will help give a sense of history not coming from the party brand
9. Identify any emerging salient issues locally and feature this in the campaign, making sure the candidate connects with these in terms of policy but also emotively
10. Reassure voters it is safe to change to the new brand of governor on offer, as it won't change the partisanship of the entire state

Empirical Illustration: How the GOP Beat the Blues with Personal Branding

This section will look at the way personal branding was used in Massachusetts, one of the least favorable markets for Republicans in the country, and in two somewhat better markets, New Jersey and California, to win a series of elections. The Northeastern United States and California do not appear to be growth areas for the Republican Party. Its policy positions are geared toward other sections, making them a difficult sell; the regional demography is unfavorable and the party's infrastructure is at varying levels of development. The Republican Party sometimes wins elections in these places by running candidates who develop a personal brand that clearly differentiates them from the national party brand. Personal branding is a very effective tool because it allows the minority party candidate to stress his or her unique selling proposition and frame the electoral choice as being between individuals with distinct characteristics rather than political parties. The power of the personal pitch has gained steam because the number of independent voters has increased, meaning the number of customers for such a pitch has grown. Personal branding's success is influenced by extant market conditions. The Republicans who have used it effectively have stressed their own traits over partisanship, tapped into popular dissatisfaction with the status quo, added in a few populist issue positions that stimulate their audience targets (education and crime are almost always in the package) and stress pro-growth economic policies. Personal branding can bring about electoral success and allow individual candidates to claim they are like other popular candidates who have run under the party's standard, but it doesn't do much for the party brand.

The first state examined is Massachusetts, in which personally branded Republicans won the governorship three times in a row. These candidates won despite a weak state party and unpopular national brand because each built a clear personal brand that built a tie between themselves and the voters. That these results were the product of personal branding is clear from the record of Republican candidates in recent Massachusetts history, which could kindly be termed abysmal, and the same is true at the legislative level. Ronald Reagan carried the state in 1984 but this wasn't the start of a trend. Personal branding has become the normal strategy for Massachusetts Republicans seeking state or federal office.

The personal brands that Massachusetts Republicans must attract include independents, almost all Republicans and a good number of conservative Democrats in order to win. Even in the de-aligned environment, the Democrats still hold a 25.2% registration advantage (Ring 2011). The Republican successes in Massachusetts show how personal branding can help win elections. In each case, the candidates stressed their unique personal traits, fear of unified Democratic governance and its likely result of shifting policy in a much more leftward direction and a specific set of populist policy proposals aimed at their target audiences: mostly working to middle-class whites having religious affiliations, spouses and kids, who paid a lot of taxes but were not regularly the focus of government largess. What they did not do was present themselves as Republicans or conservatives. They built their own brands and ran on them. In all three cases, these candidates had an extant public profile. Weld had been the U.S. attorney for the region prior to entering electoral politics, Cellucci had been Weld's lieutenant governor and Romney had previously mounted an unsuccessful U.S. Senate campaign. These candidates ran as individuals. The latter two built some fellowship with Weld when possible. None ran as adherents of the national Republican brand. Personal branding may be a tool with which state and local elections can be won, but the process of doing so might limit whatever national-level future a candidate might have unless his or her personal brand is more in harmony with the national party brand than those built by Weld and Romney in the state where they are more akin to Canadian Red Tories than to American conservatives.

Bill Weld

William "Bill" Weld pioneered the personal branding strategy's use in the state. He won in 1990 by stressing his personal traits, the general failure of the outgoing administration and the weakness of the economy. That Weld was able to win at all in a state in which Democrats had a four to one numerical advantage over Republicans and to get 71% of the vote cast in his re-election campaign (Butterfield 1990; *Economist* Staff 1997) is a testimony to the power of personal branding. His brand was comprised of his experience as U.S. attorney and his pleasant personality especially in contrast to that of his first opponent (John Silber) (Butterfield 1990). Weld embraced and made fun of his Yankee background (ibid.). He did not shrink from his origins in an elite part of Cambridge and sold himself as the scion of a family that had been in Massachusetts since the beginning of European settlement (ibid.). He did not hide from his background as the product of elite institutions. Nor did he deny that he had considerable erudition and wealth, but he had a common touch and also raised humorous questions about his own motivation and ambition (Johnson 1997). The combination created a favorable contrast with his opponent, whom the public perceived as being very conservative, personally less pleasant and out of the mainstream on social issues (Butterfield 1990). Weld's personal brand and the state's economic conditions kept the focus on Massachusetts, not national issues. He was able to build an enduring relationship with the electorate that overcame the weaknesses of the GOP brand in the state. His policy platform rooted in small government ideology argued that government had become detached from the fiscal realities of the economy and taxpayers' ability to pay more. Instead he sold a tax cut, a billion-dollar reduction in the state government and a reduction in the number of state workers, and played up his prosecutorial experience with an anti-crime plan (Jacoby 1996). Other Republicans have tried and failed to win with this issue platform but none of them stressed personal traits to the extent Mr. Weld did. In addition, he kept liberals happy and removed the emotive issues that would have allowed Democrats to nationalize the race by advocating strong environmental and pro-gay and abortion rights planks (*National Journal* Staff 1998). Thus he was able to turn the election into a personality contest that he was well positioned to win. The worst his internal opponents could say was that he wasn't conservative enough, hardly a problem in Massachusetts, and his general election opponents were left questioning his level of interest in the job (ibid.). The citizens of Massachusetts liked Bill Weld because they liked his personal brand. They elected him to office twice. He remained popular because he continually stressed his personal traits and because he kept his promises. The state ended up on a firmer fiscal footing, 19 tax cuts were passed, major education reform was launched and welfare reform initiated (Johnson 1997). The Weld brand worked because it was authentic and fit the market in which he found himself. It shows that a favorable personal brand can be the thing that gives a politician an initial edge and, when combined with effective performance in office (which the public felt Weld had, given that he had a 70% approval rating around the time he left office) (Johnson 1997) can be something that others from the same party can build on. This happened twice in Massachusetts, with Mitt Romney and Paul Cellucci both claiming that they had a similar approach to governing as did Weld.

Paul Cellucci

The personal brand is flexible. When Weld departed, he was replaced by Lieutenant Governor Argeo Paul Cellucci, who built a personal brand that differed from Weld's, yet he was able to build fellowship with the administration's accomplishments because he was a member of it. Personal brands have to authentically fit the person using them. This personal brand reflected the different audience targets that he was chasing: working-class whites who regularly voted for the Democrats (*National Journal* Staff 2000). His brand focused on his background in a small town in central Massachusetts, his ethnic heritage and his family's history of work in sales (Harden 1998). His personal brand differed in content from Weld's but not in authenticity and, even though he was more conservative on social issues than Weld had been, he was not tied to the national party because he stressed his personality and ties to the area, not issues. Fellowship was built by Weld saying, "Weld and Cellucci are the same thing" (*Economist* Staff 1997). Indeed, during his administration and by resigning when he did, Weld gave Celucci an opportunity to demonstrate the validity of the claim (*National Journal* Staff 2000). And it wasn't just him saying it; the media also made the point by explaining, "Weld and Cellucci had worked as near co-equals—with Weld as the onstage charmer and Cellucci as the backroom detail guy" (Harden 1998). Even though these two couldn't run on a party brand, the fellowship was incorporated into Cellucci's personal brand.

Cellucci won the 1998 Republican primary by beating an opponent who attacked him on the basis of personality, ethics and ideology (*National Journal* Staff 2000). Cellucci's response was to flip the ethics charges back at his opponent by arguing that his motivation for seeking office was to get his hands on the state budget (Walker 1998). His sales pitch focused on his personal traits and a defense of the administration's record. In responding to attacks from his own party, he was heard to say that given the market in the state, it was a good thing he wasn't conservative (Jacoby 1998). He won the primary with 58% of the vote (Finucane 1998). In the general election, he faced a divided Democratic Party and argued that a vote for Democrats was a vote to bring back the bad times of Dukakis (*National Journal* Staff 2000). Cellucci combined his own personal brand with the same policy positions that sold for Weld (ibid.). While his personal traits differed from what Weld ran on (ibid.), they were equally authentic. He was also running in a favorable market environment, given the impressive performance of the Massachusetts economy during the Weld administration (Harden 1998). He won with a roughly 2% majority over the sitting attorney general, Scott Harshbarger (Niebuhr 1998). Cellucci received an ambassadorial appointment but this time his successor chose not to run, opening the door for Mitt Romney to seek office.

Mitt Romney

While Romney didn't hold the governor's office when he sought it, his party did, and its incumbent, Jane Swift, was heavily criticized. Through the use of personal branding, Romney was able to distance himself from a sitting administration of his own party as well as from the Democrats. Add in the lessons of the earlier unsuccessful Senate race, and it is clear that Romney had significant incentives to stress personal traits over conservative policy. After the Senate campaign, he noted that when he made mistakes during it, voters would not give him the benefit of the doubt because he had failed to build a lasting image with them (Stolberg 2012). He clearly learned from the experience based on the extent to which his campaign for the corner office became about personality and populist policy, not ideology.

Romney's personal brand stressed his experience as a successful entrepreneur and as the savior of the Salt Lake City Olympics. He presented himself as "being a moderate Republican, socially liberal and fiscally conservative. He tried to create fellowship between himself and Weld and was described by observers at the time as being the "anti-Kennedy" (Rimer 1994). By building fellowship with Weld and stressing his own personal story and traits, Romney developed a strong unique personal brand. The use of this strategy meant that his Massachusetts campaigns were accurate predictors of his presidential run against Barack Obama because he sold his managerial skills and his opponents focused on some of the negative consequences of his activities (Rimer 1994), but neither he nor they stressed ideology or party brands. His offering was a personal brand at the state and the national levels.

He had the focus on cleaning up failure and corruption in his brand that his predecessors had. Romney promised to change the culture on Beacon Hill and reduce the importance of connections in its hiring and operation (Ball 2012). Uniquely for a personally branded candidate, Romney tried to increase the Republican Party's representation in the legislature and recruited 131 candidates to run for legislative seats (Pierce 2012) but, despite his own favorable personal brand, success did not come for his recruits.

Personal branding allowed Romney to contrast himself with both the Democrats and his own party. In addition to his personal traits, and consistent with the way the personal strategy is used, Romney's brand presented him as being the fed-up outsider in search of reform and wary of the return of unified Democratic governance. His populist platform focused on education, especially on English-only instruction, economic growth, health care reform and infrastructure improvement. He questioned his opponent's ethics and judgment, raised fears about unified Democratic governance and tried to link her to perceived corruption on Beacon Hill via an ad entitled the "Gang of Three." The gang consisted of his opponent in the role of governor and the Democratic leaders of both houses of the state legislature. Life under "The Gang's" reign would strongly resemble life under the Dukakis regime. Conversely, a vote for Romney was presented as being a vote for progress. Romney launched this brand aspect in response to opponents raising questions about his involvement with his company, Bain Capital, and because the above-the-fray approach he had taken initially was not successful (Viser 2012). Romney's campaign engaged in a series of work days around the state (ibid.). The work days effort has been used in a variety of races across the United States and is usually an effort to show that a candidate understands the lives of everyday citizens. This was a clear attack point against Romney in Massachusetts and in 2012. Romney was successful in his quest for the governorship because he built a strong, authentic brand, something that the structure of the presidential nomination process later limited his ability to do.

Massachusetts Republicans have subsequently had mixed success using the personal branding strategy. In 2006, incumbent lieutenant governor Kerry Healy lacked the prior visibility to use it and did not get to be the sitting governor as Cellucci had because Romney served out his term. In 2010 a Weld administration alumnus who seemed to have the resume of Mitt Romney, Charlie Baker, was defeated. As a first-time candidate, lacking the public profile or common touch his predecessors had, Baker had difficulty using personal branding. His prior positions had been as Weld's chief of staff, an important but low-public-profile job, and as the CEO of a health insurance company. The national GOP brand is not popular in the state, and the Democrats have tried to counteract Republicans' building personal brands by working to tie them to the national party and make the issues on which the election is contested more of a national than a local mix. Examples are provided by the way in which Scott Brown won a U.S. Senate seat in 2010 with a populist, everyman brand combined with complaints about the

Democratic insiders manipulating the process, then was defeated in 2012 by a challenger using more nationalized appeals. Something similar happened in 2013, when the personally branded Gabriel Gomez was defeated by Democrat Ed Markey's nationalization strategy.

Personal branding can work nationwide at the sub-national level. New Jersey and California provide two excellent non-Massachusetts examples of states in which it has worked. These states are excellent comparative cases because they have professional governmental systems and somewhat similar political cultures, yet both have Republican parties that are more viable organizationally and electorally than is the Massachusetts GOP. New Jersey's and California's media environments differ from that found in Massachusetts. New Jersey is one of the country's most densely populated places, yet most of its media comes from either New York City or Philadelphia, both of which have their own big-city and state politics to occupy much of the news coverage. California has multiple major media markets and a number of smaller ones, each of which is concerned with its own affairs, requiring state-level candidates to build strong brands to attract attention. In the Massachusetts case, candidates have to build a personal brand that succeeds in the dominant Boston media market, plus a few smaller ones, while in New Jersey, a candidate needs to develop a personal brand that can precisely reach New Jersey voters in a situation in which a lot of the information they will receive about politics comes from out-of-state sources. In California, a candidate must be able to build a brand that resonates in a wide variety of media markets and within a most diverse political marketplace. Personal branding can help deal with both challenges.

New Jersey governor Chris Christie's experiences are similar to those of the Massachusetts Republicans. He had been in the public eye as U.S. attorney and ran on an issue platform similar to that on which the Massachusetts candidates ran: corruption, government efficiency and education (Halbfinger 2009). The state is commonly thought to have a problem with political corruption and, although the data doesn't support the perception (Sauter and Stockdale 2012), Christie's résumé and platform suited him to use this issue in his campaign. His other populist issues included increasing mammogram access, coming out against an increase in New Jersey's very high property taxes and against increase tolls on the Garden State Parkway and New Jersey Turnpike (Campaign Grid 2012). These are the same kinds of issues that were used in Massachusetts. The big difference was Christie's personality: he was far more polarizing and far more emotive in presentation than were any of the Massachusetts candidates. The solution was to present him as a typical Jersey guy: at times blunt or brusque and at other times warm hearted and caring. He also talked extensively about his great love of New Jersey native Bruce Springsteen's music. Doing this gave his Jersey guy persona authenticity and showed that Christie was an average guy from New Jersey. His opponents derided this as inauthentic, called him a bully and complained about his weight; some suggested that he had engaged in unethical behavior as the U.S.

attorney and others tried to tie him to organized crime (Edge 2009). Christie branded himself but also defined his opponent by pointing out his Illinois background, and used his mistake of calling the Garden State Expressway the Garden State Parkway during the campaign to highlight their different backgrounds (ibid.). Christie also benefitted from his opponent's unpopularity and ran as an agent of change (Hetchkopf 2009). Because he was facing an incumbent, his messaging was intended to tell voters that it was OK to change governors even if they couldn't change the entire system. Christie benefitted from an electorate that was much more favorable in composition to a Republican than what had been in place in the 2008 presidential election in his state (ibid.). The net result was to build a winning personal brand.

California has a decentralized governmental structure, requires a legislative supermajority to pass a budget and has very friendly ballot access rules for initiative petitions. The result of this has been the creation of a system in which elected officials have a difficult time agreeing on a budget because they are not in control of all of the decisions about how much will be spent on what, nor are they easily able to pass tax increases to pay for the new spending that voters often approve through ballot initiatives. In an environment such as this, personal branding can help an elected official build an identity that differentiates him or her from the problems besetting state government and allow him or her to propose reforms independent of partisan attachment. The California case shows how personal branding can allow a party to move away from its record while still attacking that of its opponent. The Republican Party held the governorship for all but 8 of the 33 years between 1967 and 2000, meaning that the party had obviously played some role in creating most of the problems facing the state. The GOP still has a good-sized electoral base but is significantly outnumbered by Democrats, and the fastest-growing voter category is independents (Baldassare, Bonner, Petek and Shrestha 2012). This is a similar combination of environmental conditions that encouraged the GOP to use personal branding in Massachusetts. Further, the national GOP brand is not popular due to some of its issue positions. California differs from the two cases above because it is a magnet for migrants domestic and international, meaning it has a hybrid of the country's political cultures. California offered the Republicans a unique opportunity to run a personal branding campaign because it allows recalls. In addition to convincing the people to vote out a sitting Democratic governor, Grey Davis, the party had to find a candidate who could replace him.

The GOP came up with a candidate who could speak to the state's diverse population yet not be doomed by the state and national party's brand: Arnold Schwarzenegger. In running him, the GOP effectively engaged in the same kind of co-branding that Nike had engaged in with Michael Jordan. Arnold Schwarzenegger later admitted that he ran on an impulse when he announced his intentions on the *Tonight Show* with Jay Leno (Lewis 2011). He fit the pattern of how Republicans use personal branding: reluctant outsider with an extant public profile entering a corrupt political world to clean it up and implement populist policy proposals. His personal traits fit the marketplace because he had a personal story of immigrant success that better positioned him to make appeals that would resonate with most of the electorate on topics of economics, citizenship and immigration and the need for reform than are most California Republicans. He used a movement-based slogan, "Join Arnold," and was a one-word personal brand: Arnold. Once in office he tried repeatedly to keep his promises and, consistent with his brand of being an individual, not a partisan, did so in a variety of ways, using people and ideas from both parties (Lewis 2011). That he left office with a low approval rating can be put down to another economic downturn and the quirks of the California political system (see Lewis 2011) as much as it can be to him personally. A well-constructed personal brand can work in many settings in the United States. Personal branding can work anywhere in the United States, not just in one state or one region, or at one electoral level.

Conclusions for Research and Practice

Candidates can win election by building brands out of their unique traits, populist issues and a sense of outrage at current corruption, underperformance or dysfunction. It is also possible that multiple candidates from the same party can be elected by the same party if they are willing to tweak the brand aspects as the new candidate emerges. In each of the cases that we have looked at, the Republicans were saddled with unpopular products or an unfavorable market, or a relative lack of institutional capacity. Personal branding works because it takes the focus off the party's problems and puts it squarely on the person running. Personal branding works initially as it allows the candidate to sell him- or herself to the voters instead of trying to sell a party. It will also avoid a long discussion of policy and is therefore a tool with which low-information voters can be pitched most effectively. With the entire electorate, pointing out instances of corruption and policy failure by the incumbent party can be a complementary strategy to the personal brand because it allows the personally branded candidate to say these very negative things about his or her opponents while still appearing to be a decent person. In order to build on the initial success of a personal brand, the candidate has to perform in office both well and as advertised. As the Massachusetts case shows, because Bill Weld kept his promises and was perceived as performing well in office (at least at first) he was able to win re-election, then try to build support for his successor when the time came. On the other hand, as Paul Cellucci's administration and that of his successor show, personally branded candidates can survive the policy foibles and scandals of their fellow partisans by focusing on their own unique brand aspects. At least in the short term, personal branding can be a very effective strategy for an individual candidate but also for the party with which they are affiliated because it is a way to get into power and, at a minimum, block one's opponents from implementing their agenda.

The counter to it as done in Massachusetts is to try to link the opponent back to the unpopular national party brand using a personalization strategy. Further, the strategy involves significant risk to a politicians' ability to move up in their own party, as the cases of Bill Weld and Mitt Romney show. The national Republican Party owned conservatism as a brand aspect and core product, yet Romney and Weld both had been elected to the governorship of a very liberal state, meaning their brand heritage was not appropriate for the national-level party and their brand heritage was not that of conservatism. Weld was involved with a difficult Senate confirmation process in which he unsuccessfully battled with conservative Republican senator Jesse Helms, and Romney experienced considerable difficulty in locking up the Republican nomination for president in 2012. In Massachusetts, Romney logically called himself a nonpartisan Republican with progressive views (Lewison 2011). Such a description was the worst way to win the presidency from a party dominated by conservatives and it made Romney's road difficult, so much so that he eventually had to describe himself as being "severely conservative," thus undermining his authenticity and credibility with the general electorate in the process (see Martin 2012). Thus, the personal brands that made these men successful at the state level gave them serious problems with their own party when they tried to move up to national-level politics.

Personal branding can be a powerful tool and, as the case of Paul Cellucci shows, doesn't necessarily limit a candidate's ability to move up just by its use. What can limit a candidate's ability to move from the sub-national to the national level is what they opt to emphasize in their personal brand. Both Weld and Romney stressed things in their brands that were out of sync with the more conservative national Republican brand. Personal branding's impact, like the impact of most marketing tools, depends on the market conditions and the strategic situation in which a campaign finds itself and the way in which a campaign uses it.

References

Aldrich, J. (1995). *Why parties?: The origins and transformations of parties in America*. Chicago, IL: University of Chicago Press.

Baldassare, M., Bonner, D., Petek, S., & Shrestha, J. (2012, August). Just the facts: California voter and party profiles. Public Policy Institute of California. www.ppic.org/main/publication_show.asp?i=526

Ball, M. (2012, May 31). Was Mitt Romney a good governor? *The Atlantic*. www.theatlantic.com/politics/archive/2012/05/was-mitt-romney-a-good-governor/257942/

Butterfield, F. (1990, November 4). The 1990 campaign; Weld hopes personality (his opponent's) will help him in Massachusetts. *The New York Times*. www.nytimes.com/1990/11/04/us/1990-campaign-weld-hopes-personality-his-opponent-s-will-help-him-massachusetts.html?src=pm

Campaign Grid Case Study. (2012). 'New media campaign helps Chris Christie win NJ governors' race. http://campaigngrid.com/_blog/Case_Studies/post/CampaignGrid%E2%80%99s_New_Media_Campaign_helps_Chris_Christie_win_NJ_Governor%E2%80%99s_Race/

Commonwealth of Massachusetts Website. www.mass.gov
Cosgrove, K.M. (2007). *Branded conservatives: How the brand brought the American right from the periphery to the center of American politics.* New York, NY: Peter Lang.
Economist Staff. (1997, May 1). Massachusetts: Weldless. *The Economist.* www.economist.com/node/148186
Edge, W. (2009, October 21). Todd Christie: Christie Foundation gave $1.75 million to charity over four years. *PolitickerNJ.* www.politickernj.com/tags/todd-christie
Elazar, D.J. (1966). *American federalism: The view from the states.* New York, NY: Thomas Y. Crowell Company.
Fenno, R. (2002). *Homestyle: House members in their districts.* New York, NY: Pearson.
Finucane, M. (1998, September 9). The Finalists: It's Cellucci vs. Harshbarger. *Cape Cod Times* www.capecodonline.com/apps/pbcs.dll/article?AID=/19980909/NEWS01/309099774&template=printart
Garreau, J. (1981). *The nine nations of North America.* Boston, MA: Houghton-Mifflin.
Halberstam, D. (2000). *Playing for keeps: Michael Jordan and the world he made.* New York, NY: Three Rivers Press.
Halbfinger, D.M. (2009, June 18). Christie aims at Democrats unhappy with poor schools. *The New York Times.* www.nytimes.com/2009/06/19/nyregion/19choice.html?_r=0
Harden, B. (1998, September 11). With gloves off, GOP hopefuls for Mass. governor point fingers. *The Washington Post.* http://en.wikipedia.org/wiki/Personal_branding
Hetchkopf, K. (2009, November 3). Chris Christie wins New Jersey governors race. www.cbsnews.com. www.cbsnews.com/8301-503544_162-5517051-503544.html
Jacoby, J. (1996). Bill Weld's revolution that wasn't. *City Journal.* Winter. www.city-journal.org/html/6_1_bill_welds.html
Jacoby, J. (1998, August 1). Cellucci, Malone, and the Republican future. *Commonwealth Magazine,* Summer. www.commonwealthmagazine.org/News-and-Features/Features/1998/Summer/Cellucci-Malone-and-the-Republican-Future.aspx
Johnson, G. (1997, August 4). Bill Weld infuses accomplishment with a shot of fun. *The Seattle Times.* http://community.seattletimes.nwsource.com/archive/?date=19970804&slug=2553038
Key, V. O. (1949). *Southern politics in state and nation.* New York, NY: Knopf.
Lewis, M. (2011). California and bust. *Vanity Fair,* November. www.vanityfair.com/business/features/2011/11/michael-lewis-201111
Lewison, J. (2011, December 13). Mitt Romney, 2002: "I'm not a partisan Republican, my views are Progressive." *Daily Kos.* www.dailykos.com/story/2011/12/13/1044868/-Mitt-Romney-2002-I-m-not-a-partisan-Republican-my-views-are-progressive
Liar, D.J., Sullivan, K., & Cheney, G. (2005). Marketization and the recasting of the professional self: The rhetoric and ethics of personal branding. *Management Communication Quarterly, 18,* 307.
Martin, J. (2012, February 12). CPAC "severely" conflicted over Mitt Romney. *Politico.* www.politico.com/news/stories/0212/72749.html
National Journal Staff, (1998, December 1). Massachusetts: Governor Paul Cellucci. *The Almanac of American Politics, 1998.* www.nationaljournal.com/pubs/almanac/1998/magv.htm
National Journal Staff. (2000, January 19). Massachusetts: Governor Paul Cellucci. *The Almanac of American Politics, 2000.* www.nationaljournal.com/pubs/almanac/2000/people/ma/magv.htm
Needham, C. (2005). Brand leaders: Clinton, Blair and the limitations of the permanent campaign. *Political Studies, 53*(2), 343–361.

Newman, B.I. (1999). *The mass marketing of politics: Democracy in an age of manufactured images.* Thousand Oaks, CA: Sage.

Niebuhr, G. (1998, November 4). The 1998 elections: State by state—Northeast; Massachusetts. *The New York Times.* www.nytimes.com/1998/11/04/us/the-1998-elections-state-by-state-northeast massachusetts.html?n=Top%2fReference%2fTimes%20Topics%2fPeople%2fC%2fCellucci%2c%20Argeo%20Paul

Peters, T. (1997). The brand called you. *Fast Company,* August/September. www.fastcompany.com/28905/brand-called-you

Pierce, C. (2012, February 23). Me, me, me: The tale of Mitt Romney in Massachusetts. The Politics Blog, *Esquire Magazine.* www.esquire.com/blogs/politics/mitt-romney-massachusetts-record-6838981

Rimer, S. (1994, October 25). The 1994 campaign: Massachusetts; "Perfect anti-Kennedy opposes the senator." *The New York Times.* www.nytimes.com/1994/10/25/us/the-1994-campaign-massachusetts-perfect-anti-kennedy-opposes-the-senator.html

Ring, D. (2011, March 6). Percent of registered Democrats, Republicans fall from 1982–2010; "unenrolled/other" voters now in the majority. *The Springfield Republican.* www.masslive.com/news/index.ssf/2011/03/percent_of_registered_democrat.html

Rosenthal, A.J. (1997). *The decline of representative democracy: Process, power and participation in state legislatures.* Washington, DC: CQ Press.

Rosenthal, A.J. (2000). *The third house: Lobbyists and lobbying in the states* (2nd ed.). Washington, DC: CQ Press.

Rosenthal, A.J. (2004). *Heavy lifting: The job of the American legislature.* Washington, DC: CQ Press.

Saatchi, M. (2006, June 22). The strange death of modern advertising. *Financial Times.* www.ft.com/intl/cms/s/0/abd93fe6-018a-11db-af16-0000779e2340.html#axzz2qtlRhfjn

Sauter, M.B., & Stockdale, C.B. (2012, March 22). America's most corrupt states. *Foxbusiness.* www.foxbusiness.com/investing/2012/03/22/americas-most-corrupt-states/

Spiller, L., & Bergner, J. (2011). *Branding the candidate: Marketing strategies to win your vote.* Santa Barbara, CA: Praeger Publishers.

State of New Hampshire website. www.nh.gov

Stolberg, S.G. (2012, March 24). Kennedy helped shape Romney's career, and still haunts it. *The New York Times.* www.nytimes.com/2012/03/25/us/politics/ted-kennedy-helped-shape-mitt-romneys-career-and-still-haunts-it.html?pagewanted=all&_r=0

Turow, J. (1997). *Breaking up America.* Chicago, IL: University of Chicago Press.

Viser, M. (2012, October 1). Romney overcame similar deficit in '02 race. Former Mass governor capitalized on debates. *The Boston Globe.* www.boston.com/news/politics/2012/10/01/romney-overcame-similar-deficit-race/eJh9cl9c8tUlYj8FfpR0YP/story.htm

Walker, A. (1998, September 9). Adwatch. *The Boston Globe.*

9
BRAND MANAGEMENT AND RELATIONSHIP MARKETING IN ONLINE ENVIRONMENTS

Darren G. Lilleker and Nigel Jackson

Overview of the Topic

The Obama 2008 campaign saw the Internet placed center stage in election campaigning; it was argued to be a game changer. Developing his techniques as a community organizer, his website provided numerous means for supporters to contribute to the campaign and become closer to the brand, part of a loose milieu around the campaign. Obama's online campaign moved away from the purely transactional approach to campaigning, creating a desire for the product and encouraging the investment of hope (Dermody and Scullion 2001), to a more relational approach designed to involve supporters and build long-term loyalty (Jackson et al. 2012). The unique qualities of the Obama brand in 2008 facilitated building awareness, interest and enthusiasm around the campaign. However, the pressures of incumbency and disorganization at the center of the Democratic Party organization made victory in 2012 less than certain (Bai 2007). It was therefore necessary to re-engage with the online community, in particular the decentralized grassroots progressive movement. Only a relationship marketing approach would be able to connect together these groups and convert them into activists that could be harnessed to the campaign. This chapter analyzes this process, exploring the value of a relationship marketing strategy during election campaigns within candidate-centered systems.

Obama built upon innovations in attracting supporters, raising donations and developing a campaign community introduced by Howard Dean in 2004 and embedded within Democratic Party thinking while Dean was chairman of the Democratic National Committee 2005–9. While Dean in 2004 and Obama in 2008 ran outsider campaigns, Obama demonstrated that the Internet offered huge benefits in terms of generating campaign resources that could catapult an outsider to victory. The Obama campaign social network became a resource generation tool as well as an interactive forum for public political discussion. The creation of Obama as an interactive brand through the website MyBO (www.mybarackobama.com) linked well with his outsider status and change message and proved a highly successful tactic (Jackson et al. 2012).

There has been much comment on Obama's strategy and tactics being replicated globally (Lilleker and Jackson 2011). However, it remains to be seen whether the use of interactive platforms are moving election campaigning towards a new paradigm. Our focus is on what those with casual interest in the Obama brand would see: the brand image, the message, the participatory opportunities and the levels of participation taking place, rather than the hidden tools used by campaigners such as data analytics and cookies. We explore whether the Obama 2008 campaign was a one-off; test the extent to which his innovations were evidenced in 2012 and whether his relationship marketing approach was in any way adopted by his Republican opponent in order to detect whether there is a more relational paradigm of political marketing emerging.

Review of Previous Literature

Applying the Relationship Marketing Paradigm to Online Political Marketing

Theoretically there are two overarching marketing paradigms or philosophies: transactional and relationship. Transactional marketing focuses on the immediate sale, utilizing the traditional 4Ps (product, price, promotion and placement) approach (McCarthy 1960); it involves one-way, persuasive communication from brand to consumer using mass media channels (O'Malley et al. 1999). The only purpose of interaction with the customer is to gain an immediate sale; thus the transactional marketer needs to attract new customers. Transactional marketing seeks to persuade in order to make a sale. Transactional marketing offered the traditional view of how politics could be explained from a marketing perspective (Mauser 1983; Lees-Marshment 2001; Wring 2001). The message focuses on the political product, such as policies, leaders and activities. Moreover, as Johanson (2005) notes, this approach inherently encourages central control of political campaigns. If transactional marketing is present in candidates' campaigns, we would expect primarily top-down, one-way information provision online.

With relationship marketing, the focus is on building longer-term relationships. It is argued that many of the major brands are moving towards the relationship marketing paradigm, developing conversations with their consumers and involving them in the product and service development processes (Duncan and Moriarty 1997). Interactive tools complement persuasive communication to encourage longer-term customer loyalty as well as to create awareness and make the sale (Zineldin and Philipson 2007). The relational paradigm has been advocated by many academics over the last three decades as the solution for brands competing for consumers in a crowded marketplace and fragmented media environment (Gronroos 1994). Morgan and Hunt (1994) suggested long-term profitability can result from a move from sales exchanges to relational exchanges, so that the value of a customer's lifelong association with a brand increases. A key means of achieving this added value is suggested by Reichheld and Sasser's (1990) research, which stressed retention, rather than the transactional marketing focus on recruitment. The association of relationship marketing with the 7Ps (adding in people, process and physical environment) of marketing (Booms and Bitner 1982), and the emphasis on people and their experiences, inherently encourages interactivity between the sender and receiver of a message. This interactivity chimes well with placing the consumer at the heart of the brand, or indeed the supporter at the heart of a political organization (Johansen 2012).

The process of relationship marketing involves moving consumers closer to the organization. A useful metaphor here is the concept of the loyalty ladder, developed first in 1991 and since updated (Christopher et al. 2002). Contacts come in at one level, and then the organization tries to use a relationship marketing strategy over a period of time to move them up the rungs of the ladder. A mixed communication model, involving both persuasive and relational tools, is used to convert prospects, individuals who are identified by demographic and attitudinal characteristics, into consumers or supporters. At the bottom end of the ladder, consumers' interactions with the organization are based on a view of what is in it for them, but at the top rungs consumers become champions who promote the organization to others. While it is recognized that not every prospect will eventually be converted into a partner, the intention of a relationship marketing strategy is to get prospects onto the ladder and then to move up to the optimum level that satisfies the needs of the brand and the consumer.

Though Henneberg (2002) suggests that politicians would not conceptualize what they do in transactional terms, most research has suggested that transactional marketing applies to the political sphere. Yet Dean and Croft (2001) argue that the transactional approach is unsuitable because parties do not concentrate on the sale of a vote at each election. They suggest that relationship marketing provides mutual benefits, the political product can be tailored to meet citizens' wants and needs, interested citizens can find out whether they like political parties, personalities and policies and the party can educate the electorate. Equally, from a branding perspective, if the political organization can build relationships with prospective supporters, and convert them into activists, there are two potential new routes to increasing partisan attachments: a direct route through interaction with the organization as well as an indirect route with activists recruiting further supporters through their social networks, which in theory can be either face to face (Jackson and Lilleker 2007) or purely in digital environments (Norris and Curtice 2008).

There is evidence that relationship marketing has been applied to politics (Bannon 2005). Bannon assumes that politics and vote winning during elections are akin to services marketing, and that personal relationships are an asset for parties (Johansen 2012). This idea of the benefits of relationship management is further developed by Henneberg and O'Shaughnessy (2010) when they suggest that they apply at both a micro level for parties and candidates, and a macro level for the wider political system. They suggest relationship marketing can help parties and candidates win seats, but also potentially encourage re-enfranchisement with the body politic. We argue that interactive tools offered by digital technologies can connect potential supporters to a political organization. Political campaigns may secure loyalty and trust by engaging citizen-voters in conversation over a period of time, with digital technologies facilitating access to a broader range of individuals than traditional communication mechanisms.

No research has yet applied the transactional or relationship approaches to US presidential elections, although there is some evidence that political actors elsewhere have applied a relationship approach online. Looking at how parties used their websites, Bowers-Brown (2003) identified the emergence of a relationship marketing paradigm. Jackson (2005, 2006a) found that parties used email and e-newsletters as part of a relationship marketing approach in the run up to, and during, the UK 2005 General Election (Jackson 2006b). The data on the impact of a relationship marketing strategy primarily support evidence not so much of overt vote winning, or vote switching through online relationship marketing, but generating money and encouraging party membership, though one small study (Jackson 2008) suggests that long-term and effective use of e-newsletters by pioneers did have a small effect on the vote MPs received. More broadly, there is evidence that a relationship marketing paradigm applies best to party systems (Johansen 2012) and to online political marketing in party-dominated systems, but there is no evidence that this is also the case in candidate-centered systems such as the United States. Our case study will explore the extent that relationship marketing offers an insight into the potential offered by digital technologies within the context of candidate-centered elections. Prior to this we relate theoretical perspectives of the use of the Internet for political communication directly to the relationship marketing paradigm.

Interactivity and Hypermedia Campaigning

At the core of debate around the role of the Internet in political communication and campaigning is the extent to which both are developing an interactive dimension (Lilleker and Vedel 2013). There is discussion surrounding the term interactivity, given the various ways in which a visitor can interact with elements of a website (McMillan 2002; Stromer-Galley 2004; Lilleker and Jackson 2011). We define interactivity as any form of communication that replicates face-to-face conversation, "an expression of the extent that in a given series of communication exchanges, any third (or later) transmission (or message) is related to the degree to which previous exchanges referred to even earlier transmissions" (Rafaeli 1988: 111).

Interactivity can involve multiple users and take multiple forms, from true conversations to single interjections (Jackson and Lilleker 2009).

Due to the social adaptation to platforms such as Facebook and Twitter, users of the platforms are able to befriend, like or follow parties and candidates and then have input into campaign communication. Campaigns are becoming co-created, and official communication can sit alongside interjections from a variety of users of digital environments, journalists, academics, activists, satirists and voters who offer their own voice to the conversation. The plethora of opportunities to contribute to this conversation has led to the boundaries between producer and consumer of communication blurring, leading to what James (1991) referred to as "produsers." This has helped create the conditions where the online environment can be viewed as a communication ecosystem: interdependent, with information free-flowing across platforms and websites.

The view of everyone as communicator leads to questions regarding how any organization is able to market itself, and how organizations harness their activists and turn them into advocates. Political campaigns have been slow to adapt to using interactive tools such as weblogs or social networking tools, showing particular caution in allowing visitors to post directly to their own websites (Jackson and Lilleker 2009; Lilleker et al. 2011). Evidence suggests that campaigns largely attempt to earn free labor from their online supporters, but avoid becoming embroiled in lengthy political discussions (Lilleker 2013) due to the controlling logic that dominates political communication (Stromer-Galley 2004). Yet, it is argued that conversational communication may be more appropriate for creating loyalty and building relationships with their online community of supporters (Sweetser 2011). We propose that this can be understood using an adapted version of the loyalty ladder concept (Figure 9.1). The value of this approach is to pave both direct and indirect routes into the organization for potential supporters.

The strategy underpinning online political communications is currently viewed purely from the perspective of meeting general campaign objectives. However, Howard (2006) argues that campaigning has moved into a hypermedia era, where the logic of the campaign is adapting, but also adapting to, the potential and threat from the online communication ecosystem. Hypermedia campaigning builds upon the notion of the postmodern campaign (Norris 2003), embracing the potential of digital technologies. Howard (2006) defines hypermedia campaigning as having a number of strategic functions that fit well with both transactional and relationship marketing paradigms. The balance between components, in terms of how their functionality maps to marketing paradigms, can betray the overall marketing paradigm employed by the campaign strategist.

First, he notes the online environment facilitates the instant transmission of persuasive information. The transmission function fits well with either a transactional or mixed marketing paradigm. Second, electronic communication facilitates tailoring content for multiple forms of consumption and dissemination, meeting the needs of journalists, supporters, activists and web browsers alike. Targeting

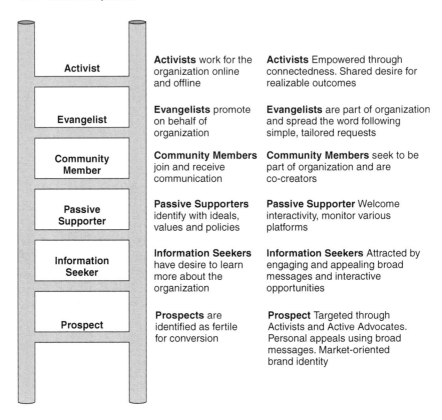

FIGURE 9.1 The Political Loyalty Ladder
Source: Adapted from Christopher et al. (2002) to suit the political environment

involves designing messages for both media and audiences, meeting the requirements of the communicator, medium and receiver. Targeting is key to engaging information seekers and building a desire to learn more and to be involved due to the relevance of messages and shared desires over outcomes. Third, data can be harvested from online environments through the use of visitor counts, tracking tools, the collection of email addresses, and the rich data within the profiles of subscribing social media users. The uses of data, and the means for collection, are beyond the remit of this paper because they refer more to what the campaigner is doing than what the web visitor experiences; however, data harvesting supports a relationship management strategy. Such data feed into direct mail and doorstep campaigns by facilitating further tailoring of messages to the user, thereby developing relationships through message relevance and encouraging information seeking. Data gathered online were also used in the last cycle to build customer profiles of each visitor to websites and then using tracking cookies to target advertisements, thus also supporting a transactional or mixed marketing approach (Madrigal 2012).

Finally, as there will already be online conversations about the party, candidate and contest, the campaign must be part of that conversation and link into the online communication ecosystem. In order to employ and empower community members, developing their roles as evangelists and activists, items created by the campaign must allow sharing and commenting (Boynton 2009), and the campaign needs to expect adaptation through an iterative "decomposition and re-composition of messages" (Howard 2006: 2). This permits co-ownership of communication and the campaign and creates the circumstances within which activists work as brand advocates.

Hypermedia campaigning dovetails with the notion of i-branding, which describes the way a brand creates value by providing a compelling experience for website visitors (Hankinson and Cowking 1993; Ibeh et al. 2005). Brand perceptions online are created through the provision of a range of one-way and two-way communication tools in order that the brand be perceived as relevant and adhering to the "rules" of online environments (Davis 2010: 313). I-branding argues that a brand's online presence should deliver a mixed marketing model, combining persuasive information consistent with a transactional approach and relational tools that permit interactions with the brand, its personnel and input into communication and product development. Consistent with the functions of hypermedia campaigning, Simmons (2007) proposes four pillars of i-branding. Brands must capture data in order to understand visitors (harvesting); develop personalized marketing communication tools (targeting); interact asymmetrically and symmetrically (interacting); and provide unique, compelling and shareable content (transmitting). Of these, interaction is argued to be crucial as this facilitates the building of trust and mutuality (Simmons 2008), the foundations for relationship building, which are required for a shift towards a relationship marketing paradigm. Our analysis focuses on the extent to which we can identify a relationship marketing paradigm emerging within the context of an election through the detection of i-branding, designed to convert visitors into supporters, community members, evangelists or even activists.

Theoretical Framework

Our operationalization first involves a content analysis of the online presences of the post-primary candidates standing for the Democratic and Republican parties in 2008 and 2012. In both contests the Democratic candidate was Barack Obama, standing as challenger in 2008 and incumbent in 2012; a Republican president was the incumbent in 2008 but John McCain was not president so technically also a challenger; in 2012 the Republican candidate was Mitt Romney. The content analysis uses an adapted version of the Gibson and Ward (2000) schematic and seeks the presence or absence of 59 features. The coding sheet sought to differentiate the candidates' online activity by looking at vertical information flows (both downward from the campaign and upward from visitors to the campaign); horizontal information flows (hyperlinks); and interactive information flows (synchronous and asynchronous). The analysis was conducted in the final week of the campaign, the first week of November, during both election cycles.

The features were then categorized as adhering to the functions of the hypermedia campaign: informing, targeting, harvesting data or interactive. The process for categorization follows that of previous work (Jackson and Lilleker 2009; Lilleker and Jackson 2011; Lilleker and Koc-Michalska 2013). For every single category we developed an average online performance score (AOP) for each candidate at the election, an average based on dividing the number of features present by the total possible within a category to produce a percentage. This allows direct comparison when categories have different numbers of features within them and has been used frequently to measure adherence to strategies or the functionality of websites (Vaccari 2008; Lilleker and Koc-Michalska 2013).

Having provided an overview of adherence to the four elements of a hypermedia strategy we develop our analysis of the websites using our derivation of the Ferber et al. (2007) six-part model of interactivity. The model, employed in previous studies of interactivity (Jackson and Lilleker 2009; Lilleker and Malagon 2010; Lilleker and Jackson 2011), differentiates between three modes of communication: one-way, two-way and three-way. Each mode of communication can also offer varying levels of user control. One-way communication can range from the purely monologic to presenting user feedback and evidencing some form of private interaction. Two-way communication ranges from responsive dialogue, a reactive response, to more conversational mutual discourse. Three-way communication is divided into controlled response and public discourse, the latter being completely open and participatory and offering the best evidence of a relationship marketing approach. The features of websites are classified across a scale for the mode of communication and the levels of user control they offer within their context. Drawing on the dichotomy between low user control and the levels of interactivity, we assess each campaign based on categorizing communication direction and control within marketing paradigms. This element of the analysis focuses on the extent to which the website and linked features facilitated interaction (Jackson et al. 2012).

Table 9.1 presents our three methodological approaches. Our content analysis is essentially an empirical tool, whereas the second and third are theoretically driven, which we have operationalized. There is clearly a difference between the data we are looking at to test Howard's hypermedia campaign and Ferber et al.'s model of interactivity. However, there are some aspects of the coding sheet in the content analysis that are also to be found when testing the other two models. That there is some overlap is not surprising given that we are essentially focusing on one main concept, interactivity, from three different angles, which aids triangulation of data and a richer understanding of the extent to which a mixed approach to marketing was evidenced. The results from our analysis are discussed below.

TABLE 9.1 Components for Testing the Concepts of Interactivity

Approach	Core Components	Marketing Approaches
Content Analysis	Information Flows (Vertical or Horizontal)	Transactional
	Interaction (Synchronous or Asynchronous)	Relational
Hypermedia	Informing	Transactional
	Targeting	Mixed
	Harvesting Data	Mixed
	Interactive	Relational
Interactivity Model	One-way communication	Transactional
	Two-way communication	Mixed
	Three-way communication	Relational

Empirical Illustration: Branding and Relationship Building in Comparative Perspective

The data derived from the operationalization of hypermedia campaigning demonstrate the innovative nature of the Obama campaign in 2008. While we do not have longitudinal data to support this hypothesis, studies indicate that previous elections made shallow use of the Internet, with the candidates largely relying on purely transmitting information (Foot and Schneider 2006). The low adoption of online communication was coupled with the fact that in 2004 there were no widely used social media that could be incorporated into campaign communication. The use of the Meetup website by Howard Dean, Democratic challenger in the primaries, was a conceptual game changer demonstrating that online activists could be harnessed, and such environments provided a means for gaining small donations from large numbers, as opposed to targeting rich individuals or corporations to gain large sums. Obama turned this into a strategy across a wide range of features and online platforms.

As the data presented in Figure 9.2 show, this did not mean that features that transmit persuasive information were in any way scaled back, and this is the case for all candidates across the two elections. Rather, the data show a rebalancing of the use of transactional and relational features. Obama's website incorporated more features that facilitated interaction than transmission, with the sheer number of opportunities to co-create campaign communication overshadowing any other candidate or party in any forthcoming election to date (see for international comparison Lilleker and Jackson 2011). Obama's campaign team also used a highly sophisticated targeting strategy, utilizing social networking sites for minority groups, bespoke web content and email. The site also incorporated a range of features that facilitated harvesting data, the heart of which was the bespoke MyBO social network housed within his website.

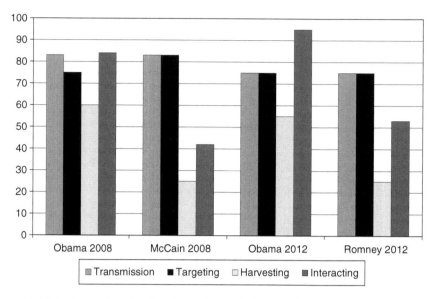

FIGURE 9.2 Comparing the Candidates' Use of Hypermedia Campaigning in 2008 and 2012

Obama's interactive campaign strategy was largely replicated in 2012, though there were strategic differences. While slightly more interactive features were included within the website, the tools that facilitated signing up and donating were prioritized. Furthermore, while in 2008 the front page was a news feed that permitted comments from those subscribed to the MyBO network, in 2012 the site prioritized a defense of his record as president. The site also contained a large amount of negative campaign material attacking his opponent Mitt Romney; the message of "Change," which focused on systemic reform of US politics, was also replaced with "Hope" for a better future, focusing more on economic than political reform. However, despite the transition from challenger to incumbent, Obama remained a highly interactive brand that was accessible across multiple platforms and permitted various forms of access. The Obama brand was a co-created brand. Obama supporters were encouraged to extend the reach of the brand, share messages via their own social networks and work on behalf of the campaign.

The McCain site of 2008 was widely criticized, as was McCain's ability to master new technologies. The McCain web presence largely reflects these criticisms. The site was largely designed to transmit messages; bespoke pages were created for specific groups but there was little of the sophisticated targeting that Obama was concurrently employing. McCain's strategy was closer to that of the 2004 Bush campaign than the 2008 or 2012 Obama campaign. Harvesting data appeared to be a very low priority with limited use of sign-ups, suggesting there was no back-end support to manage those data. McCain's campaign team did not eschew interactive features completely; rather, they avoided public interaction. Social network platforms were used, and the site contained a small weblog that permitted comments, but largely email was the only mechanism that permitted interaction with the campaign. In 2008 Obama's campaign team ensured they responded to most questions, although Obama himself rarely contributed.

The gap in technology use in 2008, and also the gap in donations, with Obama receiving a large amount of small donations from his support network, was largely replicated in 2012. The front end of the Romney website did offer the opportunity to sign up and donate, but largely that was the end of the similarity. Romney's site in style and functionality replicated that of McCain, though in places the appearance of the site was reminiscent of that of Obama. Romney exactly mirrored Obama's use of features facilitating transmission and targeting, but replicated McCain's strategy for harvesting data and provided few more opportunities to interact. It would thus appear that Romney attempted to position himself as being a sophisticated user of technology, but used his online presences largely to transmit persuasive messages. Interactive features were much more ephemeral aspects of the website, pushed to the fringes, as opposed to being central to the brand.

Focusing on both the modes of communication and the levels of user control offered, we are able to view nuances within the strategies of each campaign (Figure 9.3). The Obama website in both 2008 and 2012 used a wide range of features that transmit information, and the increase in 2012 reflects the more complex defensive, persuasive and negative messages on which his campaign centered. In both elections Obama recognized the value of using a monologic style of communication. The differences between McCain and Romney are marginal, although the storage of press releases on the site that characterized McCain's was not a feature employed by Romney. The features that support two-way and three-way modes of communication are where the real differences lie between the Democratic and Republican candidates. Obama offered various ways in which visitors could leave feedback and gain a response, though much two-way communication was around campaign activism rather than the development of campaign messages or policy proposals. Romney offered few ways for visitors to leave feedback, all of which employed wholly private channels, and often it was unclear who would be receiving messages; for example, the ability to email the campaign in itself offers little sense of who might read the message or if a response might be forthcoming, particularly in an era where automated responses are widely used to manage incoming emails. The divide is magnified for three-way communication. While Obama did not offer every possible means for users to take control of his site, one can also understand why a candidate would not allow that. However, the use of forums, chat areas, blog tools and social networks meant there were multiple means by which site visitors could engage in dialogue with one another and members of the campaign team. In the case of the official Twitter feed, Obama signed his tweets BO to signify which were from him rather than his team. Tweets offer one form of public interactivity as they can each be responded to, and re-tweeted. Romney relied largely on encouraging site visitors

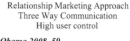

	Relationship Marketing Approach Three Way Communication High user control
	Obama 2008–59 *Obama 2012–52* *McCain 2008–27* *Romney 2012–16*
Obama 2008–78 *Obama 2012–69* *McCain 2008–59* *Romney 2012–37*	
Obama 2012–88 *Obama 2008–82* *Romney 2012–61* *McCain 2008–56*	
Transactional Marketing Approach One Way Communication Low user control	

FIGURE 9.3 Communication Style within Webspaces: Comparing Average Use of the Internet by Candidates 2008–2012

to share material; were it not for his use of Facebook and Twitter the campaign would have had virtually no participatory three-way communication opportunities at all. Therefore, in 2012 both candidates wanted supporters to create a buzz and extend messages online, but only Obama invited the broader range of contributions from his network that suggest a developed relationship marketing approach.

Our analysis thus suggests that online political marketing in the United States followed two divergent paths between 2004 and 2012. Howard Dean gave insights into the power of a relationship marketing approach to online campaigning, and embedded his thinking into Democratic Party strategy during his time as chairman of the Democratic National Committee. Obama embraced and developed the Dean model, bringing into his campaign team key digital enthusiasts to create a hypermedia campaigning to meet the objectives of a serious presidential campaign. It would have appeared strange had Obama retrenched in 2012 and rejected the use of interactivity. Hence, he continued to forge ahead with a campaign style that adhered to a relationship marketing paradigm.

The Obama model has been replicated to some extent within many election campaigns, but largely at a superficial level (Lilleker and Jackson 2011). The appearance is replicated, but not the substance. This is true of the Romney campaign. The i-branding showed sophistication, but it is not an interactive brand. Thus the Republican candidates appear locked within a transactional paradigm involving the transmission of persuasive messages designed to win over floating voters within the context on a single contest. This may be logical from a transactional marketing perspective, particularly given the candidate-centered nature of US politics, coupled with the fact that large swathes of the electorate are reasonably loyal in their allegiances. However, the transactional approach does not encourage long-term loyalty; within our discussion we assess the extent to which this is desirable within a political context and how online relationship marketing may have the potential to shift voter dynamics as well as their expectations.

Conclusions for Research and Practice

Our analysis of relationship marketing within online communications during the US 2008 and 2012 election campaigns offers a mixed picture; there are not necessarily common traits applicable to all campaigns. Rather, any trends are to be found within each individual candidate's campaign, so our conclusions have to be specific to each politician rather than to the election campaign as a whole. We found that there was a lack of steady evolution across the contests. Rather, there was an evolution in the use of interactivity within the Obama campaign, but we largely found stasis between the McCain and Romney campaigns. We suggest that these differences in online marketing behavior may have significant impacts in the future.

Given the clear link between i-branding and online marketing in general, we argue that the branding strategies of each candidate reflect his adherence or lack thereof to a relationship marketing approach. Only Obama's campaign built a brand based on an interactive web experience, being accessible, based around a social movement and permitting co-creation. In contrast, the McCain and Romney campaigns provided a controlled experience designed to sell the candidate and his platform. Moreover, as we shall see, only Obama offered the mixed-marketing approach that is at the heart of i-branding, whereas Republican candidates' campaigns provided a single, and transactional, marketing approach.

In terms of the different elements of a hypermedia campaign, there is evidence of the use of transmission across all campaigns by all candidates, so they sought to appeal to the passively engaged. We also find that targeting was equally used by all candidates as a strategy, suggesting a partial move towards a mixed approach that is designed to appeal to specific voter segments. There is, however, a clear difference in harvesting; only Obama encouraged sign-ups for receipt of communication across multiple platforms. The divergence here is mirrored for interactivity, which is also largely the preserve of Obama. Had social media not existed there would have been no potential to interact with either Republican candidate. Importantly, Obama and his wife Michelle did use platforms (shown by the use of the BO and MO signatures to specific posts), although the posts were largely informative or thanking supporters as opposed to encouraging conversation. Therefore, even for Obama interaction is more about mobilizing and then responding after mobilization has taken place and a successful event in the campaign has been staged. In summary, all candidates meet two of the four components of the hypermedia campaign, but only Obama could be argued to meet all four, and even then there is a limitation to how he used interaction.

Our political loyalty ladder is a useful metaphor for understanding how relationship marketing helped address any prior organizational weaknesses for the Democrats. Obama encouraged the passively engaged to become more active, in choosing to receive communication via mobile and digital platforms, which were designed to move visitors to climb the loyalty ladder and get closer to the campaign. In particular, Obama sought to convert information seekers and passive supporters into the more campaign-active community members and evangelists. The political loyalty ladder applies only to Obama's web presence, where the intention is to get visitors within the broad grassroots organization to become more directly involved. This is achieved by presenting points of entry into the campaign, persuasive messages and action that can be completed to reach shared outcomes. For Romney, the points of entry are read or donate; there are no opportunities for other means of engagement, and so he was talking primarily to information seekers and passive supporters.

Our data suggest that there have been some changes in the hypermedia campaign from 2008 to 2012 that have implications for Henneberg and O'Shaughnessy's idea of micro and macro marketing. Of the four components of Howard's (2006) model, two have decreased in popularity across both the Democratic and Republican candidates' websites, one has increased, and one does not display a consistent trend. For both candidates the use of features designed to allow transmission and targeting has gone down, but interactivity has increased for both from one election cycle to the next. However, beyond this broad-brush trend in the increase in interactivity, there hides a change in use. The nature of interactivity is less concerned with developing dialogue and conversations, and more about interacting with the campaign, such as through fundraising. Therefore, the use of hypermedia campaigning appears to push US presidential candidates towards more consideration of the campaigning benefits of the Internet, and less the wider potential benefits on the body politic of idea sharing.

Clearly Obama was much more likely to apply a relationship marketing approach. His average use of interactive features was more than twice that of McCain and three times that of Romney. Obama's usage of relationship marketing increased in 2012, suggesting an upward trend. This "headline" is perhaps not surprising, but there is an important story hidden by it. Obama is also more likely to use features that adhere to transactional marketing, and this also increased from 2008 to 2012. This suggests that within the marketing communication mix the balance has shifted slightly towards a transactional approach and away from relationship marketing. While the gap between McCain and Romney is not as great with relationship marketing, it is interesting that Obama emerges with a clear lead in both categories. Therefore, rather than concluding that Obama is more likely than his two opponents to use relationship marketing, we can broaden this to say that he is more likely to use marketing in general.

The literature suggests that relationship marketing is more likely to exist in party-dominated countries like the UK, and less so in candidate-centered countries. This is because parties have a membership that needs to be recruited, retained and mobilized (Johansen 2012). However, the dichotomy is not that simple. Both the Democratic and Republican party have members, supporters and loyal voters whom the party and their candidates need to mobilize. Obama appears to have been the first to develop a toolkit for successfully achieving this within the context of both a challenger and incumbent contest, creating a powerful offline and i-brand designed to create enthusiasm and channel that enthusiasm into activism. After 2008, both commentators and campaigners around the world looked to learn the lessons from his campaign. There was a discussion of an "Obamafication" of campaigning, yet maybe Obama's long-term effect is very different from supporting an Americanization hypothesis. Rather, 2008 and especially 2012 suggest that cumulatively Obama may have created a hybrid model between candidate-centered persuasive communication and party-centered mobilization tactics. In the former the aim is to persuade citizens to vote, whereas with the latter parties seek to reach voters indirectly by mobilizing their activists. Table 9.2 suggests that a hybrid model targets citizens seeking not just their vote, but also converting them into activists. In 2008 there was a strategy to build a movement for change around his campaign that was sustained through to 2012; but will this movement, and the communication that nurtured it, expire with the Obama presidency? Can another candidate, perhaps one without the charisma, style and brand narrative of Obama (Escobar 2011), capture public opinion and harness online activism to the same extent?

This study has largely focused on one election, while being aware of what happened before it, yet we also need to consider what, if anything, we can read into this election in terms of the potential longer-term trends. It is possible that we are witnessing the early stages of a campaigning schism in US politics centered on Party. Or an alternative is that the experience of the 2008 and 2012 elections will encourage the Republicans to learn key lessons for their future use of online political marketing. One possible interpretation is that in 2008 Obama was an

TABLE 9.2 The Hybrid Approach to Political Marketing

Approach	Characteristics	Target	Marketing Aim
Party-Centered	Mobilization	Activists, members and supporters	To generate activity that helps to convert voters
Candidate-Centered	Persuasive communication	Voters	To get votes directly
Hybrid	Mobilization and persuasive communication	Voters	To both encourage them to vote, but also to become part of the campaign

outsider who was encouraged to identify and use different communication channels and developed stylistic innovations, whereas McCain was the more established traditional politician who relied on the channels he had always used. However, in 2012 Obama was the incumbent, implying that he might not need the Internet as much, whereas his challenger Romney was now the outsider. Yet Romney was only marginally more likely to make use of the Internet than McCain. This might imply a growing campaign gap between the Democrats and the Republicans. Or are we witnessing a typical ebb and flow in campaigning advances, so the gains in relationship marketing are specific to Obama and will recede after him?

Typically political actors learn from, adopt and adapt their opponents' innovations. This would support the idea of an ebb and flow, that with a different candidate and campaign team the online nature of future campaigns may be fundamentally different. An alternative hypothesis is that we are witnessing a surge where one side, the Democrats, is building a campaigning advantage in marketing terms. Both of these ideas would support Bai's (2007) view that the Democrats' national organization had problems prior to the 2008 election, and that a local grassroots organization was built from the bottom up to fill the vacuum. Vaccari (2008) takes this a stage further by noting that a key component of this activity was at the "netroots," namely online activism. Obama may not have been the originator of these two complementary campaigning trends, but as a local campaigner by profession he clearly adopted, adapted and improved them. To assess this Figure 9.4 suggests that we need to consider how the candidates adhere across three scaled dimensions. The first is the communication style campaigns adopt and then the marketing approach; these are measured against systemic factors and then candidates' behavior. This suggests that there is certainly a growing gap between Obama and the Republican candidates. We note that with the first two columns, the communication style and marketing model are not mutually exclusive; a candidate could follow each. It is possible for a candidate to cherry pick what suits him or her. This may support our earlier idea of a growing hybrid system developing in the US campaigning environment.

We can identify two types of online relationship marketing. The first we classify as "false" relationship marketing. Here campaigners are only interested in how they can use web technologies to promote their message, mobilize supporters and generate new resources. The discussion of policy and ideas is of little interest to them; using interactive features, it appears, is seen as a means to an end, with interaction beyond supporting the campaign an unwanted side effect that will have no impact upon policy positioning. This partially explains the campaigns of each candidate across both contests, though clearly McCain and Romney adhered best to this paradigm. An alternative approach is "real" relationship marketing, which either overtly seeks citizen's interaction, or interactions are at least a welcome by-product that can contribute to creating a better politics; this seems closest to the reality of Obama's campaign style. It is argued that consultative processes can lead to a form of deliberative democracy (Lees-Marshment 2011),

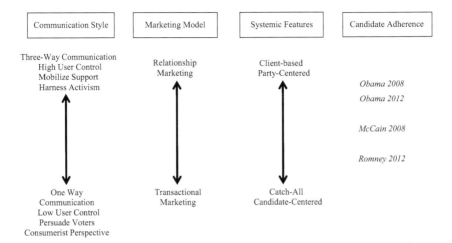

FIGURE 9.4 Mapping Candidates' Online Communication Styles and Marketing Approach within Systemic Contexts

though there is little evidence of this being encouraged even within the highly interactive spaces provided for Obama's online community. What may be key with "real" relationship marketing is to design web presences around visitors with whom relationships are most desirable and most likely to be reciprocal. Visitors to political sites, in particular those willing to engage in some form of participation within party or candidate sites, are most likely to be core activists. Having encouraged interaction, and gained electorally, the cost for candidates might be to give up some of their political autonomy to a decentralized online audience of activists; hence we might suggest that moving towards an online relationship marketing strategy may signal the death of transactional political marketing within online environments.

References

Bai, M. (2007). *The argument: Inside the battle to remake democratic politics.* New York, NY: Penguin.
Bannon, D. (2005). Relationship marketing and the political process. *Journal of Political Marketing,* 4(2–3), 73–90.
Booms, B., & Bitner, M. (1982). Marketing strategies and organisation structures for service firms. In J. Donnelly & W. George (Eds.), *Marketing of services* (pp. 47–51). Chicago, IL: American Marketing Association.
Bowers-Brown, J. (2003). A marriage made in cyberspace? Political marketing and the UK party websites. In R. Gibson, P. Nixon, & S. Wards (Eds.), *Political parties and the Internet: Net gain?* (pp. 98–119). London, UK: Routledge.
Boynton, B. (2009). Going viral—the dynamics of attention, in conference proceedings: YouTube and the 2008 election cycle. *The Journal of Information Technology and Politics Annual Conference at ScholarWorks@UMass Amherst,* 11–38.

Christopher, M., Payne, A., & Ballantyne, D. (2002). *Relationship marketing: Creating stakeholder value*. Oxford, UK: Butterworth-Heinemann.
Davis, A. (2010). *Political communication and social theory*. London, UK: Routledge.
Dean, D., & Croft, R. (2001). Friends and relations: Long term approaches to political campaigning. *European Journal of Marketing, 35*(11–12), 1197–1216.
Dermody, J., & Scullion, R. (2001). Delusions of grandeur? Marketing's contribution to "meaningful" Western political consumption. *European Journal of Marketing, 35*(9/10), 1085–1098.
Duncan, T., & Moriarty, S. (1997). *Driving brand value*. New York, NY: McGraw-Hill.
Escobar, O. (2011). Suspending disbelief: Obama and the role of emotions in political communication. In M. Engelken-Jorge, P. Ibarra Güell, & C. Moreno del Rio (Eds.), *Politics and emotions: The Obama phenomenon* (pp. 109–128). Wiesbaden, DE: VS Verlag.
Ferber, P., Foltz, F., & Pugliese, R. (2007). Cyberdemocracy and online politics: A new model of interactivity. *Bulletin of Science, Technology and Society, 27*(5), 391–400.
Foot, K. A., & Schneider, S. M. (2006). *Web campaigning*. Cambridge, MA: MIT Press.
Gibson, R., & Ward, S. (2000). A proposed methodology for measuring the function and effectiveness of political web-sites. *Social Science Computer Review, 18*(3), 301–319.
Gronroos, C. (1994). From marketing mix to relationship marketing: Towards a paradigm shift in marketing. *Management Decision, 34*(3), 5–14.
Hankinson, G., & Cowking, P. (1993). *Branding in action: Cases and strategies for profitable brand management*. New York, NY: McGraw-Hill.
Henneberg, S. (2002). Understanding political marketing. In N. O'Shaughnessy & S. Henneberg (Eds.), *The idea of political marketing* (pp. 93–171). Westport, CT: Praeger.
Henneberg, S., & O'Shaughnessy, N. (2010). Political relationship marketing: Some macro/micro thoughts. *Journal of Marketing Management, 25*(1), 5–29.
Howard, P. N. (2006). *New media campaigns and the managed citizen*. New York, NY: Cambridge University Press.
Ibeh, K. I. N., Luo, Y., & Dinnie, K. (2005). E-branding strategies of Internet companies: Some preliminary insights from the UK. *Brand Management, 12*(5), 355–373.
Jackson, N. (2005). Party e-newsletters in the UK: A return to direct political communication. *Journal of E-Government, 1*(4), 39–43.
Jackson, N. (2006a). Political parties, their e-newsletters and subscribers: "One-night stand" or a "marriage made in heaven"? In P. Davies & B. I. Newman (Eds.), *Winning elections with political marketing* (pp. 149–175). London: Haworth Press.
Jackson, N. (2006b). Banking online: The use of the Internet by political parties to build relationships with voters. In D. Lilleker, N. Jackson, & R. Scullion, *The marketing of political parties: Political marketing at the 2005 British general election* (pp. 157–184). Manchester, UK: Manchester University Press.
Jackson, N. (2008). MPs and their e-newsletters: Winning votes by promoting constituency service. *Journal of Legislative Studies, 14*(4), 488–499.
Jackson, N., & Lilleker, D. (2009). Building an architecture of participation? Political parties and Web 2.0 in Britain. *Journal of Information Technology and Politics, 6*(3/4), 232–250.
Jackson, N., Lilleker, D., & Schweitzer, E. (2012). Political marketing in an online environment: Direct democracy or demotic branding? In J. Lees-Marshment (Ed.), *Handbook of political marketing* (pp. 286–300). London, UK: Routledge.
Jackson, N. A., & Lilleker, D. G. (2007). Seeking unmediated political information in a mediated environment: The uses and gratifications of political parties' e-newsletters. *Information, Community and Society, 10*(2), 242–264.

James, M.G. (1991). *PRODUSER: PROcess for developing USER interfaces.* San Diego, CA: Academic Press Professional.
Johansen, H. (2005). Political marketing: More than persuasive techniques, an organizational perspective. *Journal of Political Marketing, 4*(4), 85–105.
Johansen, H.P.M. (2012). *Relational political marketing in party-centred democracies: Because we deserve it.* Farnham, UK: Ashgate.
Lees-Marshment, J. (2001). *Political marketing and British political parties: The party's just begun.* Manchester, UK: Manchester University Press.
Lees-Marshment, J. (2011). *The political marketing game.* Basingstoke, UK: Palgrave Macmillan.
Lilleker, D., & Jackson, N. (2011). *Campaigning, elections and the Internet: US, UK, Germany and France.* London, UK: Routledge.
Lilleker, D., & Malagon, C. (2010). Making elections interactive: Online discourse during the 2006 French presidential election. *European Journal of Communication, 25*(1), 25–42.
Lilleker, D.G. (2013). Empowering the citizens? Political communication, coproduction and the harnessed crowd. In R. Scullion, D. Jackson, R. Gerodimos, & D.G. Lilleker (Eds.), *Agents of (dis)empowerment: Media and civic engagement* (pp. 24–38). London, UK: Routledge.
Lilleker, D.G., & Koc-Michalska, K. (2013). Online political communication strategies: MEPs, e-representation and self-representation. *Journal of Information Technology and Politics, 10*(2), 190–207.
Lilleker, D.G., Koc-Michalska, K., Schweitzer, E.J., Jacunski, M., Jackson, N., & Vedel, T. (2011). Informing, engaging, mobilizing or interacting: Searching for a European model of web campaigning. *European Journal of Communication, 26*(3), 195–213.
Lilleker, D.G., & Vedel, T. (2013). The Internet in campaigns and elections. In W.H. Dutton (Ed.), *The Oxford handbook of Internet studies* (pp. 401–420). Oxford, UK: Oxford University Press.
Madrigal, A. (2012, November 16). When the nerds go marching in. *The Atlantic.* Available at www.theatlantic.com/technology/archive/2012/11/when-the-nerds-go-marching-in/265325/
Mauser, G. (1983). *Political marketing: An approach to campaign strategy.* New York, NY: Praeger.
McCarthy, E.J. (1960). *Basic marketing.* Homewood, IL: Irwin.
McMillan, S. (2002). A four-part model of cyber-interactivity: Some places are more interactive than others. *New Media and Society, 14*(2), 271–291.
Morgan, R., & Hunt, S. (1994). The commitment-trust theory of relationship marketing. *Journal of Marketing, 58*(3), 20–38.
Norris, P. (2003). Preaching to the converted? Pluralism, participation and party websites. *Party Politics, 9*(1), 21–45.
Norris, P., & Curtice, J. (2008). Getting the message out: A two-step model of the role of the Internet in campaign communication flows during the 2005 British General Election. *Journal of Information Technology and Politics, 4*(4), 3–13.
O'Malley, L., Petterson, M., & Evans, M. (1999). *Exploring direct marketing.* London, UK: International Thompson Business Press.
Rafaeli, S. (1988). Interactivity: From new media to communication. In R.P. Hawkins, J.M. Wiemann, & S. Pingree (Eds.), *Sage annual review of communication research: Advancing communication science* (Vol. 16, pp. 110–134). Beverly Hills, CA: Sage.
Reichheld, F., & Sasser, W. (1990). Zero defects: Quality comes to service. *Harvard Business Review, 66*(5), 105–11.

Simmons, G. (2007). "i-branding": Developing the internet as a branding tool. *Marketing Intelligence and Planning, 25*(2), 544–562.

Simmons, G. (2008). Marketing to postmodern consumer: Introducing the Internet chameleon. *Marketing Intelligence and Planning, 25*(6), 299–310.

Stromer-Galley, J. (2004). Interactivity-as-product and interactivity-as-process. *The Information Society, 20*(5), 391–394.

Sweetser, K. (2011). Digital political public relations. In J. Strombach & S. Kiousis (Eds.), *Political public relations: Principles and applications* (pp. 293–313). London, UK: Routledge.

Vaccari, C. (2008). Research note: Italian parties' websites in the 2006 elections. *European Journal of Communication, 23*(1), 69–77.

Wring, D. (2001). Labouring the point: Operation victory and the battle for a second term. *Journal of Marketing Management, 17*(9–10), 913–27.

Zineldin, M., & Philipson, S. (2007). Kotler and Borden are not dead: Myth of relationship marketing and truth of the 4Ps. *Journal of Consumer Marketing, 24*(4), 229–241.

10
RELATIONSHIP MARKETING IN SOCIAL MEDIA PRACTICE

Perspectives, Limitations and Potential

Christine B. Williams and Girish J. "Jeff" Gulati

Overview of the Topic

The last two election cycles have seen record numbers of Americans going online for political news, to view official campaign videos, and to use Facebook and other online social networking sites to engage in the campaign (Smith 2009, 2011). At the same time, candidates for U.S. Congress have made significant strides incorporating Web sites and, most recently, social media into their campaigns. By 2012, 97% of the major party candidates had a campaign Web site, 95% had a Facebook presence, and 90% had a Twitter account, the most recent addition to social media campaign tools. This embrace of social media by a large majority of candidates running for Congress is changing the way that campaigns are managed, how money is raised, resources are allocated, and the means candidates use to communicate with the electorate and with their supporters and staff. Ultimately, social media has the potential to alter not only the dynamics of campaigns but also the nature of democratic elections.

The reasons and purposes for which candidates adopt new technologies are central to this investigation. Given near universal adoption of these new technologies by candidates for Congress in 2012, we pay particular attention to the latter stages in marketing process models: the targets, goals and plans that underlie these decisions and activities. Taken together, do they evidence a marketing strategy or orientation? A political marketing perspective further leads us to question how these new technologies are being used (implementation stage) and their consequences (evaluation). More specifically, it gives rise to a set of interrelated questions:

- Is the "permanent campaign" evident in these campaigns' use of new technology, or is it a "one-off" application with limited or unspecified objectives and motivation?

- What kinds of communication do these new technologies afford campaigns in terms of purpose (e.g., seeking feedback) and direction (one way or two way)?
- Are these new technologies directed at building networks and relationships between candidates and the electorate or segments thereof?
- Do campaigns' applications of new technologies evidence professionalism, i.e., are they holistic and strategic in their approach? More specifically, have campaigns: (a) specified their objectives; (b) identified their target audience; (c) reached clarity about their goals and how to achieve them; (d) identified the best delivery medium or media for each of the above and chosen their message accordingly; and (e) assessed their success?

Review of Previous Literature

Market intelligence, targeting, relationship marketing and strategy are common themes in political marketing research. However, few works apply these constructs to social media specifically, and as yet we do not have many quantitative or qualitative studies examining whether, to what extent, and in what ways campaigns' social media decisions and activities are consistent with them. This research seeks to address these gaps in the literature by integrating constructs from political marketing theory and applying them to the analysis of social media decisions and activities by candidates for the U.S. Congress.

In addition, other disciplines and their literatures offer insights into how candidates make decisions about whether and how to use social media in their marketing. For example, studies of the diffusion of technology focus on two sets of motivating factors: the external environment and internal assessment. In the early years, campaign Web site adoption was related to constituency attributes such as education, income, ethnicity, age, and urbanization (Chadwick 2006; Klotz 2004; Mossberger et al. 2003) as well as to political conditions such as the electoral marginality and partisanship of the constituency (Adler et al. 1998) and status of the candidate contesting the seat (incumbent, challenger, open) (Kamarck 2002; Xenos and Foot 2005; Foot and Schneider 2006; Hernnson et al. 2007). Although less important today, electoral attributes remain important determinants of the degree to which campaigns provide more sophisticated content and use their Web sites to engage and mobilize supporters (Gulati and Williams 2007), important concerns of political marketing research. With respect to newer technologies and social media specifically, the predictors vary by platform: incumbency explains Facebook adoption but challenger and open-seat candidacy status explain Twitter adoption, and competitiveness of the race is not important for either one (Gulati and Williams 2010). These divergent findings illustrate inherent limitations in using aggregate quantitative data to understand questions of interest in political marketing research.

Internal assessment factors typically involve resources. For example, diffusion of innovation research relates adoption decisions to the size and age of the business, its IT support and budget, and technology experience (e.g., Goode and Stevens 2000). For campaigns, financially disadvantaged candidates were less likely to have a campaign Web site in the early days of Internet campaigning (Gibson et al. 2003), but funding proved less of a barrier subsequently. Financial resources and major party status still differentiate which campaign Web sites have the latest technology and features (Foot and Schneider 2006), and for social media, which candidates were most likely to have adopted Facebook (Williams and Gulati 2013) and Twitter (Gulati and Williams 2011). Experience also affects campaigns' internal assessments: familiarity with technology and earlier generations of online media increased the likelihood of adopting the next new tool (Gulati and Williams 2011). These studies point directions to probe in our interviews with campaign staff and presage some themes that are likely to emerge.

Jackson (2003) is illustrative of studies that investigate post-adoption behaviors. His examination of 186 Web sites for MPs in the UK found they were being used primarily for one-way communication and as a more efficient means of delivering existing functionality, not leveraging the technology's unique capabilities. Consistent with previous work, resources proved a key factor limiting their numbers, quality and scope. Subsequent research (Jackson 2011) ascertained MPs' motivation, perception of benefits and assessment of the impact of Web site adoption. Respondents expressed uncertainty or perceived limited tangible benefits from their Web presence. Most viewed it as a means of providing information to constituents and promoting the MP's activities on their behalf. Those using it to mobilize activists increased from 2001 to 2005 but their sites did not constitute a major source of campaign resources (donations or volunteers). Soliciting constituent feedback was not highly valued given indirect benefits and increased workload; with rare exceptions long-term relationship building was not sought. The upshot of research in this vein is that despite the need for two-way e-marketing, political actors have yet to embrace it. Since interactivity is a defining characteristic of social media, it is important to investigate these political marketing questions in this new domain.

Theoretical Framework

Relationship marketing provides the theoretical framework that underpins this study. That framework describes a process of mutual exchange whereby a service-centered campaign establishes partnerships with voters for mutual exchange. The relationship is interactive and long term (Grönroos 1998). We are particularly interested in ascertaining whether and what marketing strategy these congressional campaigns are pursuing. A strategic campaign has a marketing map (Kotler and Kotler 1999) that defines its environment and conducts research for the purpose of generating market intelligence for an internal and external assessment of its position. The campaign then develops an actionable plan to achieve its goals by segmenting the voting market and targeting each segment with messages that position the candidates' image and platform in ways that are responsive to the needs, aspirations and preferences of each group.

Kotler and Kotler (1999) propose a marketing process model with six sequential steps: environmental research, assessment, market segmentation, goal setting and strategic planning, tool development and implementation. Mauser (1983) delineates a streamlined three-stage process while Lees-Marshment (2003) specifies a more comprehensive and granular eight-stage model. Newman (1994: 12) provides a useful sequential schematic illustrating the various stages and their constituent steps. All conceptualize the adoption decision as rooted in the initial stages of the process: research and assessment of the political environment. The activities surrounding implementation and use are rooted in the latter stages of the process: market segmentation, goal setting and strategic planning, tool development and implementation; evaluation follows last and leads to adjustments mid-course or in the next campaign.

Drawing on this framework and the research questions it raises, our analysis organizes the interview data into three of the topic areas described above: see Table 10.1. Within each topic several themes emerge, which we describe below in the interview analysis.

There are three approaches campaigns can take in their marketing: product orientation, sales orientation and marketing orientation (Lees-Marshment 2003). Political parties and candidates use these in combination or at different times. Product orientation focuses on their own or party platform and issue positions while a sales orientation is focused on using market research to develop and implement advertising and communication techniques that will persuade voters. Market orientation, in contrast, uses that intelligence not merely to identify voters' needs and wants (assessment), but to respond to and meet those demands (for each target group). This latter approach embraces the principles of relationship marketing.

A premise of this chapter is that assessment, market segmentation, goal setting and strategic planning will be most effective if they reflect relationship marketing principles. Briefly stated, campaigns accomplish that objective by the mutual exchange of information through interactive communication to the benefit of

TABLE 10.1 Framework for Assessing Practitioners' Perspectives on Relationship Marketing in Social Media

1. **Assessment**: What are the factors that campaigns consider in assessing the costs and benefits of adopting social media? How do they describe their motivations for, and perceptions about, social media use?
2. **Market Segmentation**: How do campaigns define their target audiences and which segments of the electorate do they want to reach through social media?
3. **Goal Setting and Strategic Planning**: What are the goals and plan campaigns pursue in adopting social media?

both the voter and candidate (party) and in the service of developing a long-term relationship. The interview analysis that follows considers whether and to what degree campaigns evidence these principles.

Empirical Illustration

The Candidate Interview Data

To understand how congressional candidates use Facebook and their underlying motives and strategic goals for doing so, we conducted interviews with representatives from 91 different campaigns for the U.S. House of Representatives who had first-hand knowledge of the campaign's Internet strategy and operations between October 15 and December 14, 2012. We restricted our interviews and analysis to House candidates primarily because there are more candidates running for the House (N = 832) than the Senate (N = 66). The larger sample size provides a much greater variety of candidates in terms of electoral competition, demographics, resources and quality, and thus allows an opportunity to compare the motives and goals of theoretically interesting subgroups.

Using a semi-structured interview protocol developed by the authors, the interviews were conducted by 28 student assistants enrolled in a class on campaigns and elections. Each assistant was randomly assigned approximately 15 races, yielding a list of approximately 29 candidates to interview. Contact information was obtained from the candidates' Web sites, social media pages, other third-party sources, and in some cases, by browsing the candidate's Facebook page. At least one attempt was made to contact each candidate's campaign either by e-mail or phone, but nearly all of the interviews were conducted over the phone.

All interviewers asked the respondents to explain why their candidates were using social media and which specific applications and features they were using, and to describe how they were integrating these into their larger strategy. Candidates who had not adopted social media also were interviewed and asked why they had not done so. In semi-structured interviews every respondent does not answer every question or all of the same questions, nor is the wording and format precisely the same when they do. Thus the number of responses and the respondents' identities vary by question in our interview data. For this reason, our analysis characterizes the data by central tendencies rather than by exact count or percentages, and we provide excerpts to illustrate the range of responses for each theme.

Although our choice of qualitative methodology is designed to elicit an in-depth understanding of why (and how) some campaigns chose to use (or not use) Facebook, we did strive to obtain a representative sample. In our sample, 51.6% of respondents were from Democratic campaigns, while 50.5% of the candidates in the population were Democrats. Incumbents comprised 44% of our sample and 43.6% of the population. Our sample was similar to the population in terms of gender, but included a slightly higher percentage of minorities. Whereas 20%

of our respondents were women and 24% of our respondents were non-white, 19.6% of all candidates were women and 16.2% were non-white.

Moving beyond candidate demographics to attributes of their election contests, our respondents included 40.7% challengers (vs. 42.4% in the population) and 15.4% were candidates running in open seats (vs. 14% in the population). Only 22.4% of the challengers and open-seat candidates in our sample (vs. 19.2% in the population) could be categorized as "quality challengers," which we define as candidates who previously have been elected to the state legislature or a major statewide office or were previous members of Congress (Jacobson 2012). In terms of money raised, the candidates in our sample raised an average of $1.37 million, while the entire population of candidates overall raised an average of $1.16 million. Among non-incumbents, the average amount raised by candidates in the sample was $862,000, compared to $664,000 by the entire population of non-incumbents. The overall similarity between our interview respondents and the population of 2012 congressional campaigns gives us confidence that we have a representative sample from which to generalize.

Interview Analysis

Assessment

We asked campaigns whether they viewed social media as necessary or important to winning, and the strategic purposes for which they were being employed. The responses elicited several themes: Necessary/Important (see Table 10.2), Cost Calculus, Situation Specific, and Opponent's Actions. Necessary/Important was the dominant assessment comment, followed by Cost Calculus, Situation Specific and Opponent's Actions. When we differentiated between positive and negative assessments, there were three times as many positive as negative comments. This is

TABLE 10.2 Necessary/Important (Dominant Theme)

Positive examples (predominant)
- "Merely having one is a key part of today's election. When voters can't find their candidates on social media it is sometimes off-putting and they may go as far as to become wary because there is no page for voters to check." Griffith, VA 9th
- "I have found the power of social media to be increasing with each election season and it has come to a point where it is an essential part to any campaign." Hanabusa, H 1st

Negative examples
- "The virtual worlds of Facebook and Twitter only capture a small percentage of the actual voting population. . . . We didn't feel it was necessary to waste energy in a social realm when we could be running a stronger ground campaign." Wyman, TX 31st
- "Although we were able to reach out to a small percentage of voters who use social media, that didn't make a difference in the election outcome." Coffman, CO 6th

a major change from 2010, when by a 2 to 1 margin campaigns were negative or at least cautious in their strategic evaluations of social media.

This shift in the tenor and distribution of comments on the role of social media in campaigns shows that by 2012 Facebook was no longer a novelty and had moved beyond experimentation. For incumbents, this was not their first time using the medium, and candidates often indicated they also had existing personal pages and/or official congressional profile pages on Facebook, potentially three different accounts simultaneously. There were no wait-and-see comments this election cycle, and a number of campaigns said they wished they had used it more this time or they planned to use it to a greater extent in the next election. Nevertheless, the comments about social media's necessity or importance are very general—mere assertions that lack supporting reasons, explanation or evidence. Thus our 2010 conclusion (Williams and Gulati 2012) holds: we still do not see standardization in how campaigns view their role, nor evidence that social media have been integrated into a larger campaign strategy or with other, traditional marketing tools. Instead, we find that campaigns recognize social media are here to stay and have become pervasive tools despite a lack of understanding of how to use them or what added value they bring.

Turning to our other assessment themes, interviewees' comments evidence a similar positivity. On the occasions when cost considerations were mentioned, they were a positive motivator twice as often as a negative one. See Table 10.3.

Finally, although infrequent, situation-specific assessments prompting adoption outnumbered their opposite two to one. See Table 10.4. In 2010, campaigns paid more attention to what their opponents were doing with social media than in 2012, although less than half cited it as motivating their own adoption (Williams and Gulati 2012). In 2012, campaigns rarely mentioned their opponents' social media behavior at all, and in only two cases said it factored into their decisions. No one indicated that an opponent's social media activity prompted non-adoption or diminished use.

TABLE 10.3 Cost Calculus (Infrequent)

Positive examples (predominant)
- "Social media is the best way to campaign because it is free." Kirkpatrick, AZ 1st
- "Because [my opponent] is able to raise so much money, I need to find alternative ways to sway voters, and Twitter and Facebook are nearly my only opportunity to do so." Enderle, MI 8th
- The campaign was being outspent 20:1 by their competitor and social media provided a low cost platform capable of reaching dedicated supporters." Sheldon, MA 9th

Negative example
- "If people like or are a follower of your Facebook page, they are already inclined to vote for you. With a limited budget we don't want to waste time in a social media campaign that will be less effective than door to door." Concepcion, IL 4th

TABLE 10.4 Situation Specific (Infrequent)

Positive motivator examples (predominant)
- "The candidate is running against an incumbent and behind in the polls so needs to use every means to reach voters." Snow, FL 12th
- "The team needed to do a good job spreading the word on social media because the candidate had lost much of his district through redistricting following the 2010 census." Heck, NV 3rd
- "The candidate's past career as a radio talk show host, PR executive and TV news reporter familiarized him with social media, which he could use to advantage over his competitors. Because he already had a lot of friends on Facebook and followers on Twitter he did not have to build a fan base to campaign on social media." Radel, FL 19th
- "Our staff thought it was a good idea; a volunteer approached us to run the page." Ford, AL 2nd

Inhibitor examples
- "The candidate is 89, the oldest in Congress, and social media does not fit with that image." Hall, TX 4th
- "The candidate won in such a landslide that social media was almost irrelevant when it came to affecting the outcome of the election." McClintock, CA 4th

TABLE 10.5 Opponent's Actions (Rare)

Positive motivator example
- "They have it, so we have it." Amouzouvik, TN 7th
- "Our opponent is very active, so we have to be on social media." Vela, TX 34th

Thus we see that although campaigns now assess social media in positive terms, they base their assessment on generalities. For this first topic, our interviewees raise specific considerations of cost, situational parameters or opponents' actions (see Table 10.5) infrequently. The analysis turns next to the question of how campaigns define their target audiences and which segments of the electorate they want to reach through social media.

Market Segmentation: Target Groups

Market segmentation divides the electorate into subgroups based on criteria such as partisanship, likelihood of voting, and demographics and tailors a strategy accordingly (Cwalina et al. 2011). A slight majority of campaigns we interviewed indicated that they were targeting a specific group, with some variation in which one. Just under half indicated that they were using social media to target everyone or no one in particular.

In these interview data, the specifically identified target groups divide evenly between youth (see Table 10.6) and the campaign's supporters and/or volunteers. This is a change from 2010. In that election cycle the single-target young voters

TABLE 10.6 Target: Specifically Identified (Just over Half)

Youth (almost half of specifically identified target groups)
- "They used Facebook and Twitter largely to gain the youth vote because there are sixteen colleges in their district." Boland, WI 3rd
- "It was particularly useful in reaching out to the younger generation because they use social media pages the most." Reilly, GA 7th
- "He is a young candidate (34) so he looked to connect with the young voters to gain an advantage." Knowles, MD 3rd

TABLE 10.7 Target: (Continued)

Supporters/volunteers (almost half of specifically identified target groups)
- "Social media made it easier not only to connect with supporters, but to manage the volunteers and stay connected with them all the time." Lamb, NY 22nd
- "Social media is a great, evolving tool to keep track of supporters." Cramer, ND 1st

received more mentions than everyone/no one, and mentions of supporters and volunteers or partisan loyalists were extremely rare. The current year's responses reflect a new reality: social media are no longer the exclusive province of young voters, although they still dominate. More telling, older voters are the most rapidly expanding consumers of social media (Zickuhr and Madden 2012). Indeed, a 2013 survey by SurveyMonkey and iAquire showed that 65% of Facebook users and 55% of Twitter users are now over the age of 30 (Melin 2013).

The increase in mentions of supporters and/or volunteers as a target group has increased significantly from rare mentions to equal billing with the youth target category. See Table 10.7. This change from 2010 reflects a different reality. Most campaigns attract relatively few followers (i.e., visitors who "like" the profile page). The median number of followers is 1,793, although the range is large, with a minimum of 2 and maximum of 319,718. Campaigns are now recognizing the limitations of their social media outreach efforts and are tailoring communications to their actual audience. The 2012 uptick for this target group also reflects a second reality: the proportion of undecided voters was markedly lower in 2012 than in either 2010 or 2008 (Epstein 2012; Hughey-Burns 2010), prompting campaigns to focus largely on appealing to their base (Hughey-Burns 2010).

On the other hand, political party loyalists or affinity groups were rarely mentioned as targets either in 2012 or in 2010. One campaign to do so singled out three voting blocs that generally support Democratic candidates, as shown in the first interview excerpt. Partisans are the chief target of primary market segmentation in political campaigns (e.g., Baines 1999). They represent a large, readily identified and accessible group that is predisposed to the candidate's platform and messaging (Rahn 1993), hence an easily actionable target for campaigns to identify and access (Bannon 2004). The second interview excerpt underscores this point. Table 10.8 shows these excerpts.

TABLE 10.8 Target: (Continued)

Partisan or affinity group (rare)
- "They had different affinity groups—Veterans, African Americans, Latinos, or other identifiable voting bloc. Social media would allow you to fit into the group you identified with and this could motivate them to be more involved with the campaign." Horsford, NV 4th
- "It is the most efficient way to get campaign information to the people who want it most rather than waste valuable resources trying to inform or sway voters whose minds can't be changed because they are loyal to the other party." Clyburn, SC 6th

TABLE 10.9 Target: (Continued)

None or anyone/everyone (just under half)
- "The campaign doesn't have a specific set strategy, more trying to reach as many potential voters in the district as possible." Jacobs, MD 2nd
- "We're just attempting to get a broader outreach to people that use social media for news." Tierney, MA 6th
- "It's an enormous district. Our goal is a large audience; must target a lot of people." Messinger, GA 1st

Finally, considering the above target groups separately, none of them receives as many mentions as the response that the campaign is either targeting everyone, or no one in particular. See Table 10.9. That is a reversal from 2010, when youth outpolled the non-identifiers. Besides the changed demographics of social media, diffusion of innovation literature provides another explanation. This is the late-adoption stage, when all but the laggards have a social media presence on the major platforms: Facebook, Twitter, YouTube and/or LinkedIn. But adoption is different than implementation and use. Many of these campaigns have few followers; more important, they themselves are making little use of the medium. The number of posts is small: the median number over the period from Labor Day to Election Day is 27 (an average of 3 per week). Posts range widely from 0 to 122, skewing to the lower end with many campaigns posting 0, 1 or 2 times and hardly any over 100. This suggests that although adoption is nearly universal, implementation and use is still at a very early stage. You need a sizeable audience before you can segment it. Market segmentation requires understanding its constituent parts and the interests of each. Then you act on that information and create differentiated messages. Most campaigns are still struggling with the first step; some are at the second; virtually none are at the third.

These interview excerpts are couched in generalities in much the same way as the earlier comments about assessment. More telling, nearly half of the campaigns did not employ any market segmentation and notably passed up the opportunity to target partisans and affinity groups in their messaging. That said, we find some indication that both the medium and campaigns' understanding of it have matured. In 2010, and to a lesser extent in 2012, our interview data reveal that when campaigns do target a specific constituency they are using social media to try to reach young people. Since Facebook originally restricted membership to college students, and younger people are the most eager and capable of embracing new technology, it follows that campaigns would use social media to communicate to young voters and use it to engage and mobilize them as well. Statistical models showing that median age or percentage of elderly people in the district do not differentiate campaigns that adopt from those that do not (Gulati and Williams 2011) thus present an incomplete picture. Our interviews also show that in 2012 a growing number of campaigns were beginning to recognize the importance of targeting their base—supporters and volunteers who are their followers on Facebook. Taken together, the findings for this topic are mixed. The analysis turns now to our third and final question: What goals and plan do campaigns pursue in adopting social media?

Goals and Plan

To analyze our interview responses describing specific motivations for adopting Facebook, we adopted themes representing Lees-Marshment's product, sales, and market orientations: Research/Polling, Communication (product orientation), Mobilization (sales), and Engagement (market orientation). Communication was the dominant motive, followed by infrequent mentions of Mobilization/Engagement. Research/Polling was rare.

Consistent with a product orientation, the large majority of campaigns (just over two-thirds) sought to inform voters of the candidate's issue positions, educate them about his or her record, and inform them about campaign events. See Table 10.10. This category applies to campaigns whose self-described efforts to reach out and connect with voters were one directional, i.e., pushing content at voters. As noted above, these communications were not targeted and did not appear to be responding to voters' own concerns or preferences.

A sales orientation employs research and polling to understand voters' interests and develops appeals to persuade them to undertake action to assist the campaign

TABLE 10.10 Goals and Plan: Articulated

Communication (predominant)
- "It was geared toward up to date information on events and appearances." Fields, MN 5th
- "We used it just enough, and released information that voters wanted to see—for example, pictures of events and speeches ... things that are relevant to them and things that they care about." Biggert, IL 11th
- "The goal was to build brand awareness for the candidate and get her name out into the limelight of politics." Love, UT 4th
- "The things he posts are mainly informational and about himself." Serrano, NY 15th

TABLE 10.11 Goals and Plan: Articulated (Continued)

Research/polling (rare)
- "They used the feedback/results from the Facebook page to calculate hits, visits, likes, and what pages/issues people generally were concerned with by seeing who was talking about what and how many people who visited his website were directed from the link on his Facebook page." Uppal, CA 4th
- "The main thing we looked at closely was how big and how quick of a following she got during key points of the election, i.e., after local debates, larger press events." Love, UT 4th

TABLE 10.12 Goals and Plan: Articulated (Continued)

Mobilization/engagement (infrequent)
- "Get the word out about current events and ask them to come to these events." Chen, CA 39th
- "It allows constituents to express concerns and ask the candidate questions: that constituent connection was the way to build a strong campaign." Wasserman Schultz, FL 23rd
- "Their goal was to make the Facebook page an interactive one. They wanted people not just to go on the Facebook page, but be active on it." Hirschbiel, VA 2nd
- "I like using Facebook because it is easy for me to contact the voters and for the voters to contact me in a public atmosphere. By answering the question of one voter on Facebook I am actually indirectly speaking to all the voters, which is an amazing opportunity." Paton, AZ 1st

effort and ultimately to vote for the candidate. Only two campaigns indicated that they conducted research on their Facebook profile pages despite the availability of statistics about the number of visitors, and what they liked or posted: see Table 10.11. Indeed, one expressly stated it never used the statistics from Facebook and Twitter for analysis (Tierney, MA 6th).

The mobilizing actions most commonly referenced by campaigns were attending events, donating money and volunteering. Engagement consists of two-way, interactive communication. Some campaigns reported that they made explicit efforts to solicit and respond to voters' feedback, but it was infrequent. See Table 10.12. The finding that a relatively small number of campaigns were following a market orientation in 2012 is similar to what we found in 2010. In that election cycle, the dominant goal of campaigns was to be able to communicate their message to the voting public; the second most common goal was to be able to engage and mobilize their supporters, mostly by increasing attendance at campaign rallies. The failure to use social media to promote event attendance seems a missed opportunity. Interactive communication, on the other hand, is resource intensive and many campaigns avoid it (Stromer-Galley 2000): ours did not have large staffs or dedicated social media staff members who could assist in responding to voters in such personalized communications.

TABLE 10.13 Goals and Plan: Absent (Rare)

- "Social media was just another tool the campaign was utilizing. It was not used with any specific goals or focus." Lee, CA 13th

In addition to those who did not adopt social media in their campaigns, a few campaigns admitted to having no goals or plan despite having established a social media presence. See Table 10.13.

Collectively, our interviews have uncovered some interesting insights not previously gleaned from empirical research using statistical models. One noteworthy finding is that although social media received few positive assessments in the 2010 election cycle, the picture changed in 2012. This time, there was acceptance rather than skepticism that social media constituted a necessary, if not important, campaign tool. On the other hand, the new interviews still did not reveal a nuanced or reasoned assessment of its role.

Finally, we again found that the overarching goal for campaigns in adopting social media was to communicate their message to the voting public; in other words, they had a product orientation. To a lesser extent, campaigns sought to mobilize (sales orientation) and engage (market orientation) their supporters and other voters. We did not, however, find campaigns availing themselves of the market intelligence data social media sites offer. Campaigns that do not conduct such research are unlikely to have the underlying mindset needed to design and implement a plan to respond to voters' needs, aspirations and preferences (Kotler and Kotler 1999). They lack a marketing orientation, which is a necessary prerequisite for being market oriented and adopting the marketing concept (Cwalina et al. 2011: 22).

Conclusions for Research and Practice

At the outset we posed four questions central to the concept of relationship marketing. Regarding the first, we found scant evidence of the "permanent campaign" in these campaigns' use of new technology. In both 2010 and 2012, it seemed to be a "one-off" application with limited or unspecified goals and plan. Second, we asked whether campaigns are seeking feedback and engagement direction from these new technologies. The answer is no. At present, research and polling is not on the radar screen; their focus is on mobilization, particularly turnout (a sales orientation). We then considered whether campaigns are using these new technologies to build networks and relationships. Our interviews showed that engagement is much less common than mobilization, and both are dwarfed by communication. This is doubly ironic given that these are *social* media; the unique features, capabilities and strengths of the medium are largely ignored.

Finally, our last question addressed the extent to which campaigns' applications of new technologies evidence professionalism. Its several components meet this criterion to a limited extent. For the most part, the campaigns express low level, general or non-specific goals; if a group is targeted at all, the chief target audience is youth and, in 2012, also supporters. These data do not address implementation and achievement sufficiently to judge this component, but interviewees did not articulate such strategic planning or a plan for how to integrate social media into it. Virtually none of the campaigns were conducting research on their social media efforts; beyond a handful of anecdotal comments, none mentioned success measures or indicators. Only one campaign hired a professional firm to handle its social media; few dedicated staff to that task, and of those that did, the number was very small.

While other studies have taken a qualitative approach (e.g., see Foot and Schneider 2006; Howard 2006; Jackson 2011), researchers have rarely combined a large-N quantitative study with a large number of in-depth interviews. Our 62 interviews of candidates and staff from congressional campaigns in 2010 (Williams and Gulati 2012) combined with these 91 interviews from 2012 provide a rich explanation for the motivation behind their decisions to adopt social media and its use. Moreover, with two election cycles we gain insights into the dynamics of technology adoption as the medium matures. Statistical models typically do not take into account the learning curve for new technologies. Yet interviewees frequently expressed this concern. Their comments underscore the various impediments campaigns face in adopting and using social media. It is a matter of adjustment, professional advice and experience: "In an ever-changing world, it takes time to adjust to the new technologies out there" (Murphy, PA 18th); "The candidate doesn't totally understand social media so he is not comfortable posting to his own pages or instructing others on how he wants his social media run. It's better for him as well as the campaign to have professionals doing it" (Young, AK 1st); "We are still in the developing stages of using social media effectively (Baechler, WA 4th); "It has been a learning experience integrating social media into the campaigning process" (Hastings, WA 4th).

The evolution of the medium and practice is ripe for additional research. It is likely that in the election cycle two years hence we will see changes in the dominant response categories and evidence that campaigns have become more sophisticated and selective in their use of social media. That maturation of both the medium and of practice is likely to result in more of an orientation to political marketing strategies and techniques.

The major lesson from this study is that campaigns have not as yet tapped the potential of social media as a marketing tool that can be employed strategically to achieve campaign goals. Their conceptualizations focus on selling a political product. To leverage marketing principles and techniques, campaigns should design a social media strategy around three activities, as shown in Table 10.14.

These principles and techniques are not completely absent from our interview data. In a few cases, candidates recognized the need to be more strategic in their use of social media, although a few simply expressed the need or desire to do

TABLE 10.14 Framework for Relationship Marketing Strategy

1. Market intelligence with feedback to the campaign and two-way communication between candidate and voter
2. Market segmentation that targets campaign messages to specific groups
3. Relationship building over the long term

"more" next election. As one campaign expressed it, "We would have liked a more developed social media strategy and to have tied social media closer to our mass media efforts (Sheldon, MA 9th). Although campaigns rarely expressed interest in long-term relationship building, a few did so very explicitly, as these two comments illustrate: "Social media allowed the candidate to build a brand and get her name out there for the future" (Love, UT 4th); "We hoped social media would help boost the candidate's drive to win the Wisconsin 1st and begin to build a brand for 'later'" (Ryan, WI 1st).

Overall, however, in 2012 the congressional campaigns that recognize the value in subscribing to these three principles are exceptions; they represent the vanguard who will become role models for best practice. Yet there is reason to believe innovation will disseminate quickly. Often each party's candidates employ the same set of professional firms, and these practitioners as well as their clients pay attention to successful implementations of new technologies. For example, one interviewee reported closely following President Obama's social media campaign (Messinger, GA 1st). In social media we see the potential to change the dynamics of campaigns as well as the relationship between those who hold or seek elective office and the voting public. We are far short of realizing that potential in 2012, but some of our interviews provide indications of steps being taken in that direction.

References

Adler, E.S., Gent, C.E., & Overmeyer, C.B. (1998). The home style homepage: Legislator use of the World Wide Web for constituency contact. *Legislative Studies Quarterly, 23*(4), 585–595.

Baines, P.R. (1999). Voter segmentation and candidate positioning. In B.I. Newman (Ed.), *Handbook of political marketing* (pp. 403–420). Thousand Oaks, CA: Sage.

Bannon, D.P. (2004). Marketing segmentation and political marketing. Paper presented at the annual Conference for Contemporary Political Studies, Political Studies Association, Lincoln University, England, April 6–8.

Chadwick, A. (2006). *Internet politics: States, citizens and new communication technologies.* New York, NY: Oxford University Press.

Cwalina, W., Falkowski, A., & Newman, B.I. (2011). *Political marketing: Theoretical and strategic foundations.* Armonk, NY: M.E. Sharpe.

Epstein, R.J. (2012, August 9). The disappearing undecided voter. *Politico.* Available from www.politico.com/news/stories/0812/79504.html

Foot, K.A., & Schneider, S.M. (2006). *Web campaigning.* Cambridge, MA: MIT Press.

Gibson, R.K., Margolis, M., Resnick, D., & Ward, S.J. (2003). Election campaigning on the WWW in the USA and UK: a comparative analysis. *Party Politics, 9*(1), 47–75.

Goode, S., & Stevens, K. (2000). An analysis of the business characteristics of adopters and non-adopters of world wide web technology. *Information Technology and Management, 1*, 129–154.

Grönroos, C. (1998). Marketing services: The case of a missing product. *Journal of Business and Industrial Marketing, 13*(4/5), 322–338.

Gulati, G.J., & Williams, C.B. (2007). Closing gaps, moving hurdles: Candidate web site communication in the 2006 campaigns for congress. *Social Science Computer Review, 25*(4), 443–465.

Gulati, G.J., & Williams, C.B. (2010). Congressional candidates' use of YouTube in 2008: Its frequency and rationale. *Journal of Information Technology and Politics, 7*(2–3), 93–109.

Gulati, G.J., & Williams, C.B. (2011). Diffusion of innovations and online campaigns: Social media adoption in the 2010 U.S. congressional elections. Paper presented at the 6th General Conference of the European Consortium for Political Research Reykjavik, Iceland, August 26.

Hernnson, P.S., Stokes-Brown, A.K., & Hindman, M. (2007). Campaign politics and the digital divide: Constituency characteristics, strategic considerations, and candidate Internet use in state legislative elections. *Political Research Quarterly, 60*(1), 31–42.

Howard, P.N. (2006). *New media campaigns and the managed citizen*. New York, NY: Cambridge University Press.

Hughey-Burns, C. (2010, October 25). 2010 elections poll roundup: Undecided voters leaning for Republicans. *U.S. News and World Report*. Available from www.usnews.com/news/articles/2010/10/25/2010-elections-poll-roundup-undecided-voters-leaning-for-republicans

Jackson, N. (2003). MPs and Web technologies: An untapped opportunity. *Journal of Public Affairs, 3*(2), 124–137.

Jackson, N. (2011). Perception or reality: How MPs believe the Internet helps them win votes. *Journal of Political Marketing, 10*(3), 230–250.

Jacobson, G. (2012). *The politics of congressional elections*. Upper Saddle River, NJ: Pearson Education.

Kamarck, E.C. (2002). Political campaigning on the Internet: Business as usual? In E.C. Kamarck & J.S. Nye, Jr. (Eds.), *Governance.com: Democracy in the information age* (pp. 81–103). Washington, DC: Brookings Institution.

Klotz, R.J. (2004). *The politics of Internet communication*. New York, NY: Rowman and Littlefield.

Kotler, P., & Kotler, N. (1999). Political marketing: Generating effective candidates, campaigns, and causes. In B.I. Newman (Ed.), *Handbook of political marketing* (pp. 3–18). Thousand Oaks, CA: Sage.

Lees-Marshment, J. (2003). Political marketing: How to reach that pot of gold. *Journal of Political Marketing, 2*(1), 1–32.

Mauser, G. (1983). *Political marketing: An approach to campaign strategy*. New York, NY: Praeger.

Melin, G. (2013). Age demographics and social media behavior. Available from www.spiral16.com/blog/2013/04/age-demographics-and-social-media-behavior-infographic/

Mossberger, K., Tolbert, C.J., & Stansbury, M. (2003). *Virtual inequality: Beyond the digital divide*. Washington, DC: Georgetown University Press.

Newman, B.I. (1994). *The marketing of the president: Political marketing as campaign strategy*. Thousand Oaks, CA: Sage.

Rahn, W. (1993). The role of partisan stereotypes in information processing about political candidates. *American Journal of Political Science, 37*(2), 472–496.

Smith, A. (2009, April 15). *The Internet's role in campaign 2008*. Pew Internet and American Life Project, Washington, DC.

Smith, A. (2011, March 17). *The Internet and campaign 2010*. Pew Internet and American Life Project, Washington, DC.

Stromer-Galley, J. (2000). On-line interaction and why candidates avoid it. *Journal of Communication, 50*(4), 111–132.

Williams, C.B., & Gulati, G.J. (2012). A campaign perspective on social media strategy by Congressional candidates in 2010. Paper presented at the annual meeting of the Midwest Political Science Association, Chicago, IL, April 11–15.

Williams, C.B., & Gulati, G.J. (2013). Social networks in political campaigns: Facebook and the congressional elections of 2006 and 2008. *New Media and Society, 15*, 53–72.

Xenos, M., & Foot, K. (2005). Politics as usual or politics unusual? Position-taking and dialogue on campaign web sites in the 2002 U.S. Elections. *Journal of Communication, 55*, 169–185.

Zickuhr, K., & Madden, M. (2012). *Older adults and Internet use*. Pew Internet and American Life Project. Available from www.pewinternet.org/~/media//Files/Reports/2012/PIP_Older_adults_and_internet_use.pdf

11

MAMA GRIZZLIES

Republican Female Candidates and the Political Marketing Dilemma

Robert Busby

> *Fundamentally, the mama-grizzly phenomenon is not really a movement or even a political term that represents a fully coherent set of ideas. It's mostly a marketing tool, meant to draw attention to Americans' broad dissatisfaction with the way things are.*
> —Miller 2010

Overview of the Topic

The appearance of a new political brand of candidate in the United States in the period from 2008 onwards heralded a wave of media and popular interest in the emergence of female Republican candidates with a distinctive political profile. The Mama Grizzly, denoting a female who will aggressively defend her territory and family, was the term used to profile a number of female Republican candidates in the 2010 and 2012 elections. While not all female Republican candidates were branded with this term, media concentration on those who were ensured that there existed a popular understanding of a new breed of candidate. At the center of the branding exercise was ongoing activity by Sarah Palin. She endorsed individuals whom she believed encapsulated this political product. The use of the brand title was greeted with serious consideration about its impact on the political status quo, alongside amusement that the packaging of a candidate, in a time of serious economic difficulty, could be reduced to simplistic terminology.

The debate about the meaning of the Mama Grizzly brand was evident from a range of perspectives. First, in part the emergence of the Tea Party, a movement with a significant female membership fueled the popularity of branding political candidates who reflected a populist political mandate (Vogel 2010). The Mama Grizzly brand of right-wing Republicans dovetailed well with the Tea Party;

indeed Michele Bachmann was identified strongly with both, being considered an instrumental part of the brand and having created a Tea Party caucus in the Congress. Second, there was division over the exact meaning of the brand. Was it conservative and feminine, or feminist and conservative? The concept of feminism and how it was embraced by the New Right was an issue that had been debated since the 1970s. The portrayal of the Mama Grizzly movement with a strong emphasis on gender considerations created a dispute about the ownership of the feminist concept and how it might be manifested in contemporary society. The flexibility of the brand identity meant that applicability across a range of female Republican candidates was evident, yet few seemed eager to take up the product title in a simplistic form, it being subject to a range of individual reinterpretations. Instrumental to this was Sarah Palin, who identified the nature of the Mama Grizzlies in May 2010. She argued that they were "common-sense conservative women, banding together and rising up" with a political objective of creating "an emerging, conservative feminist identity" (Atal 2010). Third, media coverage of Republican female candidates centered strongly on the Mama Grizzly. The brand concept was emotive, the candidates alluring and the radical views entertained by some, particularly Delaware Senate candidate Christine O'Donnell and Nevada Senate candidate Sharron Angle, ensured that on going coverage of both political positioning and personal issues was pronounced. Fourth, although not necessarily successful in head-to-head races with Democratic candidates, the success of a range of women in Republican primary races, replete with Tea Party support, meant that there were a sufficient number of women candidates present so as to cast this as more than simply an individual and aggrandized piece of political marketing by Palin. There was actually substance to the product. Lastly, the core thrust of many of the arguments was about the nature of feminism. Significant discussion ensued in media and academic circles about whether the Mama Grizzly could embrace the history of that movement in the United States, or whether this was simply an exercise in opportunistic marketing. Initial evidence suggested that more men than women were voting for the candidates with this political brand, erring away from suggestions that the interpretation of feminism and meaning of the movement addressed its desired political target market.

Consideration of the Mama Grizzly movement is important for political marketing and assists in an improved understanding of the integration of branding, political mobilization and gender. The emergence of a new sub-brand that acted as an appendage to the Republican party suggests that it is possible to brand sections of a political party that may have felt underrepresented or marginalized in the political debate. It also suggests problems in locating accurately the position and role of women in the social conservative movement and attracting women to that position in any numbers. The branding message, while being prominent, did not mobilize female voters to the Republican cause, in part because of inherent conflicts and contradictions within the brand and the tight ideological remit to which it appeared to refer. This chapter considers how sub-branding of an ideological position using a gender remit has distinctive limitations both in the theoretical construct of branding and with the application of it to contemporary electoral politics. The utilization of the Mama Grizzly brand highlights that the ownership of the brand, the definition of ideological issues relating to the Republican party, and the use of gender as a marketing tool poses problems for the contemporary right, especially those of a social conservative orientation.

Review of the Previous Literature

The emergence of women as one of the most important voting blocks in politics impacts clearly on how they, as a voting segment, are marketed to. Gender is one of the most frequently used criteria for marketing purposes in the commercial realm, and in politics the emergence of this has not gone unnoticed. The vast majority of research into gender and marketing comes in the way of consumer-oriented material that considers women as the focal point for domestic consumption choices, and thereafter how feminism and the changing role of women might impact upon changing understandings of this stereotypical role. In the field of management and leadership there are evidently differences in the manner in which men and women approach the subject. In terms of favored models of political marketing, women tend to be more democratically oriented and men tend towards a more authoritarian model of leadership (Vinnicombe & Colwill 1995).

Consideration has been given to how gender is portrayed as a feature of political communication and advertising. How a simple market division such as gender is depicted is clearly an important part of marketing and creating a social and emotional connection with prospective voters. Chang and Hitchon have identified that category-based understanding of gender may influence perceptions of candidates, the consumer using assumptions about gender roles to give an initial shape to their opinions (Chang & Hitchon 2004). They further identify that gender-based associations are important to an understanding of how female candidates are received by consumers, and influence how female candidates advertise themselves. Gender-based associations about the type of policies men and women are best at managing and how gender is received are also considered important. They identified that "campaign strategists who work for female candidates often run into a dilemma: should they package a female candidate as a politician who possess a natural fit with 'women's issues' or should they emphasize that she is capable of handling 'men's issues'?" (Chang & Hitchon 2004: 198). Female candidates are increasingly advancing toughness as a campaign position, in part, one might assume, to demonstrate that they can compete on issues bracketed as masculine in their orientation. This fits in well with the aggressive positioning by the Mama Grizzly movement and with a broader concept of the Republican Party. However, this goes against earlier political research that suggested that voters are likely to see female candidates as more competent than male candidates when they address issues traditionally associated with the female gender, such as health and education (Huddy & Terkildsen 1993). McGinley identified that for all selected female figures in the 2008 presidential election, Palin, Clinton and Michelle Obama, there were problems of a correlation between femininity and the display of masculine toughness perceived as necessary to court a prominent office (McGinley 2009). Similar conclusions were prominent in research undertaken by Powell and Butterfield, with voters identifying masculine traits as preferable in models of leadership (Powell & Butterfield 2011). The development of a marketing strategy that breaks away from preconceived gender interpretations, and the identification of a target market founded on gender, becomes all the more difficult for female candidates (McGinley 2009).

The gender-oriented view of the consumer has impacted upon how candidates understand political branding and candidate packaging so that they can exploit consumer preferences. There are dilemmas here. Herrnson, Lay and Stokes addressed the extent to which a perception of compassion influenced voter choice. Women voters were more likely to vote for candidates who were "kinder and gentler," and "warm and expressive candidates" were perceived to be better at addressing compassionate issues (Herrnson et al. 2003). Changing approaches by female candidates as to whether to present themselves in this light presents questions as to whether the Mama Grizzly brand worked to deviate from ideas of compassion and advanced an aggressive posture, or served to underscore a caring protective family remit as part and parcel of a gender-construed brand. Herrnson, Lay and Stokes found that gender-construed campaign strategies were effective in shaping electoral support. "When women choose to capitalize on gender stereotypes by focussing on issues that are favourably associated with women candidates and targeting women or other social groups, they improve their prospects of electoral success" (Herrnson et al. 2003).

The means of communicating the political brand is important in the contemporary era, and in the case studies considered later in this chapter it is particularly significant, as the primary spokesperson for the Mama Grizzly brand, Sarah Palin, generally eschewed mainstream mass media in favor of personal addresses and the use of the Internet. The use of the web in particular has become a focal point for study, in part because it opens up the opportunity for more elongated discussion of women's issues, and the audience comes to the web page seeking further detail of the position and identity of the candidate rather than the mass-marketing approach evident in television advertising (Carlson 2003). There is no meaningful divide in web use between genders in the contemporary era and this gives some parity for candidates in seeking to use it as a medium through which to communicate with voters of both genders. Consideration, however, must be given to the way in which the Tea Party brand was established, primarily through women's use of the Internet as a vehicle through which to organize thought and to mobilize those discontented with Obama. That this was done in a private realm of the home lent credence to the notion of individual private action over public rhetoric and gave the Tea Party an organization remit firmly associated with the action of women as opinion leaders.

Work already undertaken on media coverage of women on the political right has focused on the nature of conservatism and its use, or manipulation, of feminism. Schreiber considered that there was an inherent conflict between feminist conservative elements and liberal feminist groups about how to address women's issues, and this conflict was not commonly brought to the fore by mainstream print media (Schreiber 2010). Within academic circles there had been prominent discussion regarding the congruence of the new conservative right in American politics and the concept of feminism. From the rise of the New Right in the early 1980s there had been tensions between those who considered themselves as advocating social reform on behalf of all women, to an understanding that the New Right had its own conceptions of the position and status of women in society (Stacey 1983). The Mama Grizzly brand simply served as a continuity of this tension. The adoption of the concept of feminism to underscore a brand identity gave it an established historical meaning that served to suggest a deeper ideological platform, yet the divisions within the feminist movement and differing interpretations about this ideology brought doubt as to how the Mama Grizzly brand could entertain widespread female support.

The emergence of female candidates as focal points for media and popular attention has been increasingly evident in academic discussion and in wider circles. From the efforts to advance women candidates in order to address prominent gender divides in representation in 1992, entitled the "Year of the Woman," a not especially successful venture, there have been some significant studies of how modern female politicians market themselves to the electorate. Of note, and of particular value given the ideological divide, was the presence of Hillary Clinton and Sarah Palin in the 2008 election. JoEllen Lind, in a study of young female voters and the attraction of Clinton or Palin in 2008, found that neither candidate entertained the support of this voting segment and those between 18 and 29 did not take gender as a prime motivating factor in making political choices (Lind 2009). Indeed in the close Democratic primary race between Hillary Clinton and Barack Obama, Obama gained the support of young women. Research has also considered the presentation by the mass media of contemporary female candidates. Again focusing on Clinton and Palin, Avineri considered how language and gender portrayal affected the presentation of female candidates, and how emotion, perceptions of authority and temperament were tied to female candidates in particular. While Clinton was studied for her own emotions, Obama was evaluated on how he created an emotional response in others, giving a distinctive gender-skewed political identity to the candidates (Avineri 2009). This is important in the study of political marketing. Considerable attention has been given to the creation of brand authenticity in order to grant the brand legitimacy, and whether female candidates have had to conform to preconceived gender understandings and displays of emotion to gain political support. The alternative approach is to create impressions of managerial authority, which goes against existing voter understandings of gender and creates a dilemma about branding, market positioning and voter targeting.

The existing literature on female political candidates suggests a dilemma for the Mama Grizzly concept. It advocates a strong and aggressive remit that goes against research findings that care and compassion from female candidates can resonate effectively with the voter. Yet as the nature of the contemporary Republican right-wing female candidate is one where the brand epitomizes authority and strength, then it may give greater congruence with the leadership categories that appear most demanded by the voter in looking for political leadership from a masculine perspective. It also fits well into perceptions of the Republican Party as one embedded with principled views of strength and conviction.

Theoretical Framework

At the heart of the Mama Grizzly concept is the branding of a niche element of the Republican Party on grounds of both ideology and gender. Branding requires that the idea conjured by the branding concept matches that of the delivery of the product, that it is what it claims to be. Branding concepts come in a range of forms, with attributes that assist in forming an understanding of the political concept, to allow consumers to understand political positions, to cater to niche political needs, and to allow a smooth transition during times of political change (Cosgrove 2012). Additionally integrity is a value that has a strong place in recent American political marketing and in creating a workable political image (Newman 2001). French and Smith argue that the usefulness of the political brand is to allow consumers to learn about political positioning and to see how voters react to political parties (French & Smith 2010). In terms of the use of the Mama Grizzly brand this is important in consideration of how a new brand is accommodated into an existing political framework. Cosgrove suggests that there is brand hierarchy, with top brand levels that are overarching and below these, sub-brands that serve to earmark specific marketing positions. This is important in this area of political marketing, as the Mama Grizzly brand was both a sub-brand of the Republican Party, was gender specific and was oriented around social conservative understandings of the party's ideology. The very nature of the Mama Grizzly brand and its person-centered quality is important in branding and consumer relations. Fournier identified that the personalizing of brands adds legitimacy to their worth (Fournier 1998). This is underscored by the infusion of the brand with value, that it actually means something and creates a relationship with the voter. Phipps, Brace-Govan and Jevons argue that branding works on two levels, the corporate level but also where there is individual interaction between the advocate of the brand and the consumer (Phipps et al. 2010). The use of the family as a focal point for discussion of the Mama Grizzly brand was important in this context as it could create strong bonds of social and emotional association, which could then be exploited politically. A further value of political branding is that it acts as a shortcut, simplifying a concept into a manageable framework for the consumer, frequently in the contemporary period identifying personal characteristics as much as those that are ideological or policy based (Guzman & Sierra 2009). Needham suggests that brands, when thought of in terms of political parties, offer opportunities to instill loyalty and to simplify the political spectrum in a time when the complexity of politics may overwhelm the voter (Needham 2006). The Mama Grizzly brand was simple, defensive, reactionary and gender oriented, and could be conveyed easily on television advertisements via emotive visual imagery. Furthermore, it appeared at a time when the ability of any individual to influence the economy appeared minimal.

Accurate and representative media coverage of female candidates is important to the communication of the brand. Wasburn and Wasburn, considering contemporary female candidates who have run for office, identified five areas that differentiated female candidates from male counterparts on grounds of gender coverage. They receive less attention than male candidates, consideration of appearance and family circumstances is more pronounced, coverage of leadership ability tends to be negative, women's issues are brought to the fore, and the influence of a woman on the political office she might be elected to is subject to pronounced debate (Wasburn & Wasburn 2011). That the Mama Grizzly concept, and the candidates who were branded as such, received so much coverage can be used as a benchmark against which to test the resonance of the movement and the extent to which a female-oriented brand correlated with past experiences.

Targeted messaging is an important remit in the field of political marketing, and the use of the concept of motherhood could be targeted in a similar form to that found in the commercial market sphere. Voters are targeted in a range of different ways, in social, emotional and rational forms (Newman 1999). Identifying target markets is important in refining campaign messages, in ensuring the campaign is cost efficient and in mobilizing defined voting blocs. Identification of target groups can also rest upon an appeal to behavioral traits, lifestyle choices and social concerns (Smith & Saunders 1990). Sub-groups can also be the subject of narrow targeted campaign strategies (Penn & Zalesne 2007). With respect to the Mama Grizzly movement the initial target appeared to be women, but with a strong social conservative remit. The use of the family as a focal point of the discussion correlated well with social and emotional identification of a sub-group with specific lifestyle choices and defined social demands. However, there were problems here in the use of branding. Some of the Mama Grizzly candidates had no children of their own, and there seemed to be some variance about how, as a complete package, the Mama Grizzly candidates could be a singular brand. Individually they could claim to have the appropriate credentials, but collectively the coherence of the brand appeared to be more suspect.

The dilemma of gender, branding and Republican politics has theoretical underpinnings that in part highlight the objectives of the individuals who courted the brand and the challenges of establishing a new brand as part of the political party spectrum. In looking at how gender might inform political branding, it is clear that there are differences between men and women as political consumers, both in terms of political policy preferences and in the types of characteristics desired when looking at political candidates. Republican female candidates in theory need to aspire to build an emotional and rationale connection with voters. In doing this the brand needs to be consistently applied. It appeared that the Mama Grizzly brand represented women in part, but as a sub-brand of the Republican Party it came across as aggressive, confused in part as to its true identity and unable to forge strong bonds across a gender-targeted market. Additionally there are issues about leadership and the conveyance of a brand message. Palin's position as the anointer of Mama Grizzly candidates gave the movement a populist mandate, that women who felt neglected or underrepresented were politically mobilized, yet it frequently appeared as though the movement had a singular leader and that the brand was a mask for the self-promotion of Palin as a political leader of influence, even though she held no political office at the time. It is clear that gender mobilization for the Republican Party was, and remains, a problem. Several themes come to the fore in looking to develop an understanding of how the GOP might address female political concerns, and the theoretical objectives entertained by the Mama Grizzly movement.

The Mama Grizzly Mandate

Figure 11.1 gives an indication of the dynamic interaction of the brand identity and how it serves to cater to a range of diverse identities related to gender and lifestyle considerations.

Party brand association: The sub-brand must complement the party brand without appearing to replace it or to challenge its core ideological values. As such the brand must not displace existing understandings of the party position, else it risks the contamination of messages emanating from the party hierarchy.

Target market: A brand must target a market, yet be sufficiently flexible so as not to offer itself to a narrow niche group that might not have sufficient mobilization to influence the outcome of an electoral contest.

Gender orientation: With the contemporary importance of the female vote a Republican brand must target women in such a form that it is seen to represent gender interests, replete with an ability to accommodate individual variations in lifestyle choice.

Serious social and emotional connections: The brand needs to create social and emotional connections to the voter without appearing to be lightweight in its consideration of political issues. A delicate balance has to be drawn between marketing politics vs. a lifestyle.

Universal appeal vs. target markets: The brand needs to have universality, but also niche targets—corresponding with different policy issues affecting demographic themes such as age, parenthood, marriage, income and other variables that affect voting behavior. The problems in this realm are evident, as the brand could serve

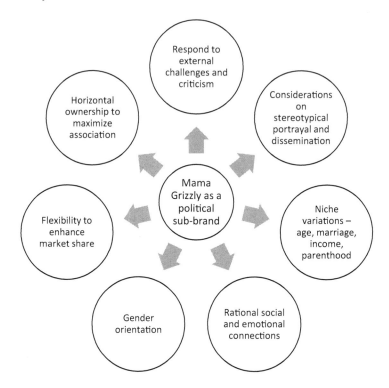

FIGURE 11.1 Model of Mama Grizzly as a Political Sub-Brand

to express messages of exclusion as much as inclusion and thereby work against its intended goals.

Media portrayals and stereotyping: The brand needs to address and accommodate media portrayals of gender in politics, particularly those that stereotype on the grounds of physical appearance.

Leadership and brand management: The brand has to counteract external challenges to its identity through leadership and brand management. The abrasive association between the New Right and the debate over the meaning of feminism is testament to the need for ownership of the brand to be necessary.

Horizontal ownership: Disseminate the brand to allow a concept of horizontal ownership—promoting variations as needed in a federal political system, and allowing for longevity and best practice. Narrow leadership of the brand serves to allow voters to decide on its meaning based on perceptions of whether the brand advocate is a person who is politically persuasive.

Mama Grizzly as a Political Sub-Brand

The problems of establishing a brand in an already complex political market are evident, particularly in suggesting that a gender-oriented brand can serve to mobilize a segment of the populace rather than serve as an issue to exclude segments of the populace. In other words, in seeking to attract conservative women does it alienate other consumer groups? There are other theoretical issues that suggest problems in establishing a gender-oriented brand rooted in a tight ideological niche. It appears unlikely that a brand positioned in this form will attract new converts to it. Rather, it could really only serve to mobilize voters who entertained socially conservative credentials but did not vote regularly. Liberal-oriented women, swing voters and Democrats would be unlikely to be attracted by the ideological positioning of the brand. As such, the message of the brand in this instance appears to be more of a rallying call to the converted, rather than a product that could attract a new market.

Empirical Illustration

The Mama Grizzly brand developed as a consequence of remarks made by Sarah Palin about the appearance of socially conservative female candidates who were opposed to a range of policies emanating from Washington. The term was first used by Palin during her run as vice-presidential candidate in 2008. In May 2010 she used the term when addressing a pro-life women's group and forged a definitive brand: "Mama bears not only [forage] for themselves to prepare for winter, they [work] twice as hard to slay salmon for their cubs, too" (Miller 2010). The address focused very strongly on women as a target audience and at the center point of the brand. "The mama grizzlies, they rear up, and if you thought pit bulls were tough, well you don't want to mess with the mama grizzlies ... and that's what we're seeing with all these women who are banding together, rising up, saying, 'No, this isn't right for our kids'" (Gay 2010). Palin had already used the concept of the pit bull in the 2008 election, and the Mama Grizzly construct built upon this notion of defensive ferocity. An increase in the number of female Republican candidates in 2010 appeared to endorse Palin's notions of change, either as candidates anointed by Palin as being Mama Grizzlies, or in advancing their own interpretations of the cause of contemporary women. Victoria Budson, executive director of the Women and Public Policy Program at Harvard's Kennedy School of Government, observed, "This is a time of great political investment in change.... And people who are marketing themselves as agents of change are doing incredibly well—particularly in the Republican party" (Gay 2010). One of the motivating factors involved in seeking to push female candidates to the fore was the lack of female representation in the Congress. Seventy-two women served in the House of Representatives in advance of the 2010 election. In 2012, 73 women were present in the House, making up only 16.8% of its membership. However, there was a disparity in terms of partisanship, with 49 women being Democrat and a mere 24 being Republican (Center for American Women and Politics [CAWP] 2012).

The policy positions held by those who were earmarked as Mama Grizzly candidates were those in the social conservative realm. They opposed the stimulus package, health care reform, abortion and same-sex marriage, were pro border security, advocated prayer in schools and were supportive of "stop and search" in Arizona. The positions held by most Mama Grizzly candidates were considered to be immovable, with some, like Nevada Senate candidate Sharron Angle, opposing abortion in all circumstances, including rape (Clift 2010). Additionally, the appeal to women in the domestic sphere as a whole was narrowly defined by Angle: "in a traditional home, one parent stays home with the children and the other provides the financial support for that family" (Atal 2010). In this context the Mama Grizzly brand was clearly a political product that would have limited flexibility within the market, and could serve to isolate candidates rather than give them an attractive position in the marketplace. It relied wholly on individuals moving to embrace its message rather than seeking to maximize its market presence by embracing issues that were considered salient or popular during election cycles. This may have been, in economic terms, a pertinent approach in seeking to harbor the discontent of those affected by the economic downturn; however, on the social conservative issues the matters of principle that were entertained were present irrespective of the state of the economy.

Who were the most prominent Mama Grizzly candidates across 2010 and 2012?

Nikki Hayley—Gubernatorial race South Carolina
Susana Martinez—Gubernatorial race in New Mexico
Kristi Noem—House of Representatives race in South Dakota
Carly Fiorina—Senate race in California
Sharron Angle—Senate race in Nevada
Sarah Steelman—Senate race in Missouri
Christine O'Donnell—Senate race in Delaware

One of the core debates about the Mama Grizzly brand was what it actually meant to women. It created a pronounced rift over who was in command of a feminist label and how conservative women might position themselves in contemporary American politics. In the first instance it appeared to be Palin who identified who was a Mama Grizzly and what it meant. Her position as a market leader in this context gave her a power that far exceeded her position as an individual who held no elected office. It was of course entirely possible that the Mama Grizzly brand was simply a vehicle through which Palin could keep her own position in politics to the fore, the absence of her own running for congressional office. Palin's pivotal position suggested that this was a personal brand as much as it was a collective product. However, there were individuals who entertained their own interpretations of the product. Nikki Hayley, running in South Carolina, offered her own more expansive interpretation of the brand: "I wear it with pride because a mama grizzly is someone who looks after her state like they would look after her family" (Fifield 2010). Hayley's supporters had t-shirts that adopted a phrase from former

British prime minister Margaret Thatcher: "If you want something said, ask a man. If you want something done, ask a woman." The evolution of a debate about the meaning of the Mama Grizzly spread into a broader gender argument about the contemporary nature of feminism and how it integrated into a fragile political framework under strain on account of economic conditions.

The irony of the Palin-inspired brand of the Mama Grizzly was that while it appeared to be a product designed for and aimed at women, with prominent and confident female candidates running for office, it appeared also to have inherent contradictions. While rallying socially conservative Republican women to her cause Palin also targeted Democrats whom she considered to be particularly vulnerable to Republican challenges. Of 17 House Democrats she listed in March 2010, 5 were women (Hunt 2010). Yet Palin and those who supported her concept of feminism narrowly defined it in an ideological sphere that appeared to set the political product against those who might have been considered to be part of the target market. Palin's concept of feminism appeared to be one that split the women's movement rather than unifying it behind a single identifiable political cause. Palin stated, "I kinda feel a connection to that tough, gun totin' pioneer feminism. For far too long when people heard the word feminist, they thought of the faculty lounge at some East Coast woman's college. . . . And no offence to them, they have their opinion and their voice and God bless 'em, that's great, but that's not the only voice of women in America" (Hunt 2010). This received criticism from female Democrats who argued that rather than increasing the number of women in politics, or infusing a new momentum to the women's movement in a broader context, Palin was utilizing the women's movement for her own narrow political end. This indeed appeared to be a problem for the brand. Palin's political position and reputation were well known by 2010. It was unlikely that she could wholly separate herself from the brand identity, even if she wanted to do so. As a consequence in part the brand appeared to be a promotional vehicle to demonstrate Palin's influence upon the party, and given the way in which she split opinion this was not necessarily beneficial for the brand or for the lure of the Republican Party.

One of the reasons for the prominence of the Grizzly brand was focused media attention on individuals who made for good media coverage. The brand was given market exposure but often in areas where it was portrayed by the media as a liability rather than an asset to the Republican movement. This was further exacerbated by coverage on the web. The most notable coverage was that afforded to Christine O'Donnell, a former marketing consultant running in a senatorial race in Delaware. O'Donnell was a surprise victor in the Republican primary race in the state and had the Mama Grizzly endorsement. However, she suffered from negative media coverage, largely on account of reports of her having "dabbled in witchcraft" when she was younger (Catanese 2010). A television advertisement that featured O'Donnell forwarded a disclaimer in which she announced "I am not a witch." This retort was greeted with much humor in the media, and crippled O'Donnell's campaign. It also lent strong negative gender bias to her candidacy, which appeared to suffer detrimentally from this factor. There were also issues advanced that appeared to suggest that ideologically and in terms of class there were strong negative interpretations of O'Donnell (Knickerbocker 2010). Furthermore, O'Donnell had no children of her own at the time of the election. This appeared to go against the central thrust of the brand meaning, that the Mama Grizzly acted to protect the interests of her own offspring and that the candidates could associate directly with mothers across America, thus detracting from the credibility of the brand.

The year 2010 was identified, reflective of 1992, as the "Year of the Woman" in politics. Particularly for Republicans, the aspiration was to have an increase in the number of women elected, and to try to court the female vote, a vote that had shown increasing majorities for Democratic candidates in recent elections. This underscored the importance of the female vote. However, the Mama Grizzly brand appeared to alienate a significant proportion of female voters. Instead the overarching feature was that Mama Grizzlies won more male white votes than female votes, which would err towards the dominance of femininity over feminism. Nikki Hayley, elected as governor of South Carolina, fell into this bracket, although she still managed to win her race. In Delaware Christine O'Donnell lost the female vote by 25 percentage points and in Nevada Sharron Angle trailed Harry Reid by 11% of the women's vote (Stanley 2010). Even within Republican races there were dilemmas regarding gender. In the Republican New Hampshire primary of 2012, Kelly Ayotte, a candidate identified as a Mama Grizzly by Palin, won half of the Republican male vote and only one-third of the female vote (Atal 2010).

Although the candidates Palin endorsed had mixed fortunes, the outcome of the 2010 election cycle was one that was generally marked by disappointment for those who adopted the Grizzly brand. The emergence of a fractious gender component within the Republican Party was evident, as was the media's willingness to push negative impressions of the Grizzly brand to the fore on the grounds that the candidates came across as unorthodox and outside political convention. Ordinarily this prominence would be beneficial. As identified by *The Nation*, "[O]ne of the oddities of these midterms was the inverse relationship between O'Donnell's standing in the polls and her prominence in the press: even as she trailed her Democratic rival by double digits, she was the single most covered candidate in the election . . ." (Reed 2010).

Communicating the brand is an important part of political marketing and the use of new media and innovative marketing strategies by the Mama Grizzlies is an interesting dynamic with respect to how the Internet was utilized. In June 2010 Palin's political action committee had produced an Internet advertisement in a conventional form to the type of political ad found on mainstream television. It was entitled "Mama Grizzlies" and specifically focused on an instinctive reflex of women to act to protect their offspring, with the emotive words that "moms kind of just know when there's something wrong" (Miller 2010). As of the end of 2012 it had received over half a million hits. Palin's use of new media is marked. At the end of the 2010 campaign period she had just over 2.5 million "fans" on Facebook. Speaker of the House Nancy Pelosi had 36,000. On Twitter Palin had a significant following, but lagged behind both President Obama and former presidential candidate John McCain (Russell 2010).

In seeking to communicate with and target sub-groups within political campaigns, the efforts of Michele Bachmann to court supporters is of note. Bachmann engaged in geo-targeting in the 2012 campaign, working with Google to send ad messages directly to smartphones at a Minnesota state fair. Google offers a range of options for voter targeting, looking at how cities search the web, following individuals who have looked at a candidate's web site, and then using advertising to follow the user as they surf the web, a strategy labeled "retargeting" (Bierschbach 2011). Yet Bachmann, in running for the presidential office in the Republican primary race of 2012, had a disastrous short-lived campaign. One of the core features of her campaign was that even among Republican voters, despite being the only woman in the race, she only received 7.2% of the female vote, far in arrears in comparison with her male counterparts (Grier 2012). In branding a female candidate as one who can reach out and target sections of the female vote, either in a mass market or in niche marketing, female Republicans appear to have significant problems in mobilizing the female consumer.

At the heart of the debate involving those termed Mama Grizzlies was the overall packaging of the brand—was it a conservative feminist movement that tried to advance the position of women in the contemporary home and workplace, or was it a feminine conservative movement where the gender appeal of the candidates gave them a marketing profile that was disproportionate to their electoral impact? That the Tea Party, of which many Mama Grizzlies were vociferous supporters, was strongly composed of women, and indeed largely led by women, lent credence to the notion that there was the potential for a resurgent women's movement, if encased by an ideological shell in the United States (Vogel 2010). *The New Statesman* cited Kathleen Blee from the University of Pittsburgh who considered the Tea Party's interpretation of feminism as a "terrible distortion.... [I]t strips most of the meaning away from feminism.... They don't support equal rights, they don't support abortion—you name the feminist issues, they are on the other side" (Miles 2010).

Conclusions for Research and Practice

At the heart of the Mama Grizzly movement was the identity of the brand. It was a positive and dynamic marketing ploy in several respects. First, it was delivered by a market leader, defined on her terms via candidate endorsement and eagerly disseminated by the media. Second, it appeared to target a range of easily identifiable markets—women as a broad gender component, women who were pressed socially and economically in the midst of an economic downturn, and women who had an ideological disposition towards social conservatism. Strategically it offered a number of lessons about branding, gender and political marketing.

The pinpointing of women as a target market has obvious electoral benefits as the importance of women in terms of numbers and turnout has an increasingly important role to play in shaping the outcome of elections. Several contemporary elections have been deemed important in advancing the interests of female candidates: 2008 catapulted Clinton and Palin to the fore, and 2010 was significant in that the media in particular gave disproportionate coverage to a broad range of female candidates. Consumers were served political products from a range of different ideological positions and while several variables are evident in shaping voter choice branding, product placement and target market considerations were significant in explaining the prominence of the Mama Grizzly and its mixed reception by the voter.

The gender considerations that accompanied the brand from the outset suggested overtly that women in particular faced important economic and social considerations in a time of economic downturn. The idea of the "pink elephants" gave specific vent to an identification with a target market. Several factors however appear to undermine the appeal of this type of political branding. First, on account of the offering being a political product that is largely immovable within the political market, expectations that women might be attracted to the brand proved erroneous. In large part only those who were already ideologically oriented to a social conservative mandate were drawn towards the Mama Grizzly as a brand. Second, the concept of gender as a strategic market division in political marketing is one that needs further exploration. Evidence suggests that consumers, while identifying masculine traits as important to political leadership, want female political candidates to show emotional and behavioral traits that would be considered feminine, going so far as to look to women to address issues that would be considered "female" in terms of policy considerations. Using a brand that identifies an aggressive Mama Grizzly at its forefront appears to go against existing research into what voters want. Third, the presentation of the Mama Grizzly brand brought about an intra-gender schism about the occupation of preexisting market positions with regard to gender. The notion of feminism and its ideological positioning created an intra-market debate that highlighted many of the product placement problems faced by female candidates in contemporary elections. Attention was given to how candidates looked and were packaged, ultimately leading to debate about what the brand was, conservative and feminist, or feminine and conservative? This evidently highlights a lack of appropriate market research into how the brand might be received, and the overt discussion in the media as to what the brand meant diluted its impact and raised significant questions as to its ownership.

Other lessons are evident from the Mama Grizzly experience. That the most prominent Mama Grizzly candidates received more votes from male voters than female voters raises a range of questions as to the usefulness of gender considerations as a core political market strategy. Gender stereotypes appeared to be pressed upon Mama Grizzly candidates, as much as they were advocated by them. In part this was attributable to the public advocacy of Palin. Having pushed themselves forward primarily on account of gender, they were, particularly in the case of O'Donnell, subject to popular and media evaluations through a gender-skewed prism.

At face value the Mama Grizzly brand appeared to conform to many of the core remits of political marketing. It had market impact, it was advocated by a market leader, it had a specific target market when initially conceived, and those who advocated it appeared to be both authentic in their support for it and legitimate purveyors of the product. The outcome of the Mama Grizzly construct of 2010 was one in which marketing principles were in operation, yet the targeted consumer market was unmoved by the product-based construct of the political offerings.

References

Atal, M. (2010, November 3). Why don't grizzlies get the women's vote? *Forbes.com*. Available at www.forbes.com

Avineri, N. (2009). *Language and gender: The mass media's portrayal of two U.S. presidential candidates*, Thinking Gender Papers, UCLA Center for the Study of Women, UCLA. Available at http:eschloarship.org/uc/item/08z6q11f

Bierschbach, B. (2011, October 5). Geo-targeting will play big role in 2012 elections. *Politics in Minnesota*. Available at www.politicsinminnesota.com

Carlson, T. (2003, August). It's a man's world? Male and female campaigning on the internet. Kristiansand, Norway, Conference for Media and Communication Research.

Catanese, D. (2010). DeMint PAC hits the air for O'Donnell. *Politico*. Available at www.politico.com

Center for American Women and Politics (CAWP). (2012). *Women in the U.S. House of Representatives 2012*. Available at www.cawp.com

Chang, C., & Hitchon, J.C.B. (2004). When does gender count? Further insights into gender schematic processing of female candidates' political advertisements. *Sex Roles, 51*(3/4), 197–208.

Clift, E. (2010, July 16). Are Sarah Palin's "Mama Grizzlies" feminist? *Newsweek*. Available at www.newsweek.com/are-sarah-palins-mama-grizzlies-feminist-74903

Cosgrove, K.M. (2012). Political branding in the modern age: Effective strategies, tools and techniques. In J. Lees-Marshment (Ed.), *Routledge handbook of political marketing* (pp. 107–123). New York, NY: Routledge.

Fifield, A. (2010). Mama Grizzlies make grab for votes. *Financial Times*. Available at www.ft.com

Fournier, S. (1998). Consumers and their brands: Developing relationship theory in consumer research. *Journal of Consumer Research, 24*(March), 343–373.

French, A. & Smith, G. (2010). Measuring political brand equity: A consumer oriented approach. *European Journal of Marketing, 44*(3/4), 460–477.

Gay, M. (2010). Mama bear: How Sarah Palin has inspired an army of Republican women to run for office. *Washington Monthly*, July–August, p. 9.

Grier, P. (2012). Why did Michele Bachmann's campaign crater? *Christian Science Monitor*. Available at www.csmonitor.com

Guzman, F., & Sierra, V. (2009). A political candidate's brand image scale: Are political candidates brands? *Journal of Brand Management*, 17(3), 207–217. Available at www.palgrave-journals.com/bm

Herrnson, P.S., Lay, J.C., & Stokes, A.K. (2003). Women running "as women": Candidate gender, campaign issues, and voter-targeting strategies. *Journal of Politics*, 65(1), 244–255.

Huddy, L., & Terkildsen, N. (1993). Gender stereotypes and the perception of male and female candidates. *American Journal of Political Science*, 37(1), 119–147.

Hunt, K. (2010). Sister sledgehammer: Sarah Palin takes aim at Dem women. *Politico*. Available at www.politico.com

Knickerbocker, B. (2010). Class as a way of understanding Christine O'Donnell and the Tea Party. *Christian Science Monitor*. Available at www.csmonitor.com

Lind, J. (2009). *Valparaison University School of Law: Legal Studies Research Paper Series*. Social Science Research Network. Available at http://ssrn.com/abstract=1397620

McGinley, A.C. (2009). *Hillary Clinton, Sarah Palin, and Michelle Obama: Performing gender, race, and class on the campaign trail*. Social Science Research Network. Available at http://ssrn.com/abstract=1375743

Miles, A. (2010). What Tea Party women want. *New Statesman*. Available at www.newstatesman.com

Miller, L. (2010, September 27). What does Mama Grizzly really mean? *Newsweek*, Available at www.newsweek.com/what-does-mama-grizzly-really-mean-72001

Needham, C. (2006). Brands and political loyalty. *Brand Management*, 13(3), 178–187.

Newman, B.I. (1999). *The mass marketing of politics: Democracy in an age of manufactured images*. London, UK: Sage.

Newman, B.I. (2001). Image-manufacturing in the USA: Recent presidential elections and beyond. *European Journal of Marketing*, 35(9/10), 966–970.

Penn, M., & Zalesne, E. (2007). *Micro-trends: The small forces behind tomorrow's big changes*. London, UK: Twelve.

Phipps, M., Brace-Govan, J., & Jevons, C. (2010). The duality of political brand equity. *European Journal of Marketing*, 44(3/4), 496–514.

Powell, G.N., & Butterfield, D.A. (2011). Sex, gender, and the US presidency: Ready for a female president? *Gender in Management*, 26(6), 394–407.

Reed, B. (2010). Mama Grizzlies die hard. *The Nation*. Available at www.thenation.com

Russell, A. (2010). Which came first: Sarah Palin or Facebook? *National Journal*. Available at www.nationaljournal.com

Schreiber, R. (2010). Who speaks for women? Print media portrayals of feminist and conservative women's advocacy. *Political Communication*, 27(4), 432–452.

Smith, G., & Saunders, J. (1990). The application of marketing to British politics. *Journal of Marketing*, 5(3), 295–306.

Stacey, J. (1983). The new conservative feminism. *Feminist Studies*, 9(3), 559–583.

Stanley, T. (2010). Why women didn't like the Mama Grizzlies. *The New Republic*. Available at www.tnr.com

Vinnicombe, S., & Colwill, N. (1995). *The essence of women in management*. London, UK: Prentice Hall.

Vogel, K.P. (2010). Face of the Tea Party is female. *Politico*. Available at www.politico.com

Wasburn, P.C., & Wasburn, M.H. (2011). Media coverage of women in politics: The curious case of Sarah Palin. *Media, Culture & Society, 33*(7), 1027–1041.

12

THE MARKET RESEARCH, TESTING AND TARGETING BEHIND AMERICAN POLITICAL ADVERTISING

Travis N. Ridout

Overview of the Topic

Some political ads are seared into the collective memory of Americans. One of the most memorable aired in 1988 and featured the story of a convicted criminal named Willie Horton. While Michael Dukakis, the Democratic Party's presidential nominee that year, was governor of Massachusetts, Horton was released from prison on a weekend furlough program and never returned. A year later, he twice raped a woman after beating up her fiancé.

The ad, sponsored by the National Security Political Action Committee, told the story of Horton and ended with the statement: "Weekend Prison Passes. Dukakis on Crime." The ad became an issue in the campaign, with some observers calling the ad racist. Many also give the ad—and the ensuing conversations about Dukakis's weakness on the crime issue—credit for shifting the momentum in the race and wiping out Dukakis's double-digit lead.

What is important to remember, though, is that the ad's effectiveness did not just happen by chance. It was thoroughly market researched. In his book *Road Show*, which recounts the 1988 campaign, Simon (1990) describes the focus group sessions conducted by a marketing company hired by the Bush campaign.[1] The company gathered two groups of Reagan voters in Paramus, New Jersey, who said they were going to vote for Dukakis in 1988. Most were white, urban and of Southern European ethnicity. Watching them behind a two-way mirror were many of George H.W. Bush's top campaign people: Lee Atwater, Roger Ailes and pollster Bob Teeter. When the moderator told the focus group participants about the Massachusetts prison furlough program, most were surprised, and many were incensed. By the end of the 90-minute session, fully half of the participants had switched their votes from Dukakis to Bush. The Bush campaign had found its issue: Willie Horton.

The extensive research that identified Willie Horton as a campaign issue is not unusual. Indeed, many political advertisements go through a comprehensive research process before being put on the air, with political consultants employing some of the most advanced techniques in the market research field. Not only does sophisticated research affect the content and design of the advertisement but its deployment as well. Nowadays, political ads are targeted toward very specific audiences, using multiple channels, in a highly sophisticated fashion. Yet, surprisingly, this story has not received much attention in the literature on political marketing. My aim in this chapter is to correct that lack of attention by focusing specifically on how techniques from marketing are used in both 1) the design of political advertising and 2) the targeting of such ads. Although I will use examples from various election campaigns, I will focus specifically on the 2012 presidential race.

Review of Previous Literature: Political Advertising and Political Marketing

As a research topic, political advertising has received considerable attention, much of this coming from political scientists and scholars of mass communication. There have been particularly extensive scholarly debates on the extent to which political advertising shifts voters' choices and whether negative advertising leads to lower voter turnout and more negative attitudes toward the political system. Other research has focused more on describing the content of advertising and its sponsorship in today's "anything goes" regulatory environment. Very little research on political advertising, however, has taken a marketing perspective, perhaps because many of the important decisions about creating and deploying advertisements are made behind the scenes.

The one exception to this rule is in the study of how political campaigns target their advertising to particular audiences, and interest in this topic appears to be growing (Gordon et al. 2012). One area of inquiry is how campaigns distribute advertising dollars across the states (Gordon and Hartmann 2013; Shacher 2009). Other research has focused on the allocation of dollars across types of television programs. For instance, Lovett and Peress (2012) combined information on the audience characteristics of various television programs with data on candidate ad buys during those programs to determine whether campaigns largely target base voters, which would be implied if competing candidates targeted different programs, or are aiming their messages at persuadable voters, which would be implied if competing candidates targeted the same television programs. Their evidence supported the idea that advertising is largely aimed at swing voters. Ridout et al. (2012) examined the program audiences that candidates targeted in the 2000, 2004 and 2008 presidential campaigns, finding that the extent to which campaigns followed a "base" or "persuadable" strategy varied by year. They also reinforced the point that audiences for various types of television programming vary considerably not only in their partisan leanings but also in their propensity to vote. Thus, efficient campaigning demands not only avoiding audiences predisposed against the candidate but avoiding audiences who are unlikely to vote, too.

One of the few scholars to have taken an explicit marketing perspective to the study of political advertising is Robinson (2006, 2010). Robinson examined political advertising in New Zealand to see if it displayed a "market orientation," arguing that those parties who display this orientation in their advertising have more electoral success. A market-oriented party's advertising, according to Robinson, should display several characteristics. First, it should identify its targeted audience by displaying images of that audience in its advertising. Second, it should "sense and respond to voter needs." This could be done through images of a party leader interacting with voters or using "caring" images or words. Third, advertising should evoke the party's history and voters' associations with the party. It should talk about promises kept and employ messages that have been consistent over the party's history. Fourth, the party's advertising should offer something to the voter, whether it be a new policy or a leadership characteristic; something should be offered in exchange for the person's vote. Finally, a market-oriented party should feature a competitor orientation. This includes identifying and sometimes attacking competitors in advertising, adopting the policies of smaller parties and showing openness to building coalitions with other parties.

One caveat is that Robinson has used her theory to study political advertising in New Zealand, which has more party-centered politics than the United States. In the United States, political parties—especially very recently—have taken a back seat to the candidates and outside interest groups when it comes to political advertising. Still, on its face, the theory would seem to work for studying the market orientation of campaigns in the United States, with perhaps some minor modifications, e.g., party associations and myths might be better examined as candidate associations and myths. Applying Robinson's theory in the United States would have another advantage; the hundreds of campaigns conducted each year would provide a large sample size for testing the relationship between market orientation and electoral success.

Theoretical Framework

My basic assumption is that campaigns have one central goal: winning. Winning involves both 1) persuading voters to make them supporters and 2) getting existing supporters to the polls. Moreover, I assume that campaigns want to carry out these tasks in the most efficient and cost-effective way possible.

The most efficient way to achieve these goals, however, has changed over time as a result of large changes in the American media landscape and political marketplace. These changes, in turn, have influenced how campaigns have targeted their advertising and developed their messages. The first change was a proliferation of media options. In the golden era of network television in the 1950s, 1960s and

1970s, most people had access to just three or four television channels, but now most people have access to hundreds of television channels. This has resulted in a fragmentation of the viewing audiences. Whereas a campaign in the 1960s could access a sizeable percentage of the American public by running an ad during a network news broadcast (Bennett and Iyengar 2008), that is no longer true. In 2009, only 26 percent of American households with televisions had them tuned to a network affiliate during prime time compared to 36 percent watching basic cable (Gorman 2010).

Second, while the ranks of political independents rose in the 1960s and early 1970s (Niemi and Weisberg 1976), the number of Americans identifying as political independents has decreased considerably since then (Bartels 1996), resulting in a more partisan electorate. It is an electorate with relatively few voters open to persuasion. Thus, ad appeals made to a general population are likely to reach many who are unreceptive to the message. The efficient use of campaign resources demands that campaigns target their messages to specific rather than general audiences nowadays.

In sum, the changing media environment and the changing electorate mean that political advertising is moving away from being a mass medium. Ads are no longer designed to speak to a broad swath of the American public but are designed to speak to, and to be delivered to, specific subgroups of voters.

These changes to the media environment and the electorate have influenced the way in which ads have been targeted. In an interview, Will Feltus of National Media described four generations of targeting. The first generation of targeting involved focusing ad buys on broad demographic groups defined by age and sex. Traditionally, when it came to political advertising, campaigns sought ratings points in the 35-plus age group, as older people were more likely to vote. Some campaigns, however, shifted to buying ratings points for the 35–64 age group, not wanting to overbuy old people. Such age/sex targeting is still used heavily for consumer products, but it has less utility for political advertisers because age and sex are not highly predictive of people's political leanings.

Such targeting was evident in the Democratic National Committee's (DNC) ad buying in the 1964 presidential campaign. Mann (2011: 126) reprints an advertising strategy memorandum from the Doyle, Dane, Bernbach (DDB) advertising agency to their client, the DNC. DDB recommended spending just under $2 million on network television, focusing on the evening programs "because of our need to reach equally men and women" (Mann 2011: 127). Nonetheless, they did recommend some limited daytime advertising in order to better reach women. Thus, gender was the only way in which segmentation of the electorate was mentioned. DDB also recommended spending $4.3 million on local television, with not all states receiving equal allocations. Under DDB's media plan, markets in 28 states would receive 400 rating points per week, markets in Missouri would receive 300 ratings points per week, markets in 9 other states "considered to be of secondary importance" would receive 200 ratings points each week, and markets in 8 states would receive 100 ratings points each week. Thus, advertising was aimed at a much wider audience in 1964 than it is today. The only mention of market segmentation was gender, national network television ensured that audiences everywhere were hearing the DNC's message, and local television was utilized, though to varying degrees, in 46 of the 50 states.

The second generation of ad targeting began in full force in 2004 when the Republican National Committee and the Bush campaign began to analyze survey data to find out which television programs their base voters were watching. By buying ads during those programs, instead of just buying "ratings points" of those aged 35–64, Republicans wasted fewer of their dollars on ads that reached audiences that were very unlikely to ever vote for a Republican. In analyzing the data, Republicans found some unexpected patterns. For instance, they discovered that *Will and Grace*, a sitcom featuring two gay characters, was a favorite of Republican voters, especially young Republican women (Seeyle 2004). These data yielded other insights that were helpful to the parties as they placed their advertisements. For instance, almost all genres of programming had audiences that skewed Democratic, but the most Republican audiences could be found watching sporting events and network news (Ridout et al. 2012). By contrast, the audiences for daytime talk shows, court shows and daytime soap operas all skewed heavily Democratic (Ridout et al. 2012).

This second generation of targeting gave way to a third generation about two years ago, according to Feltus, when campaigns started using detailed data on people's television viewing habits that were obtained from the set-top boxes that satellite television providers have. This information does not reveal who is watching, but campaigns have been able to use information provided by third parties, such as Target Point Consulting, to match these detailed television watching habits with consumer information and the campaign's own voter file. Having this information has allowed campaigns to reach specific categories of voters with their messages.

The fourth generation of ad targeting is something that is still on the horizon: individually addressable ads. This means that a campaign could send a particular ad to the television at 201 Maple Street, send a different ad to 203 Maple Street and send no ad to 205 Maple Street—all based on what the campaign knew about the political preferences and voting habits of the residents in those homes. According to National Media's Feltus, such targeting is technologically possible today, provided that residents are watching television through a satellite provider such as Direct TV. But it may be some time before political campaigns take advantage of this possibility given that campaigns may find it expensive and impractical to make so many custom versions of a political ad.

In addition to this broader historical framework, which has influenced the ways in which ads have been targeted, I rely upon Johnson's (2007) framework for discussing the creation of political commercials. Johnson divides the process into nine phases, which are summarized in Figure 12.1.

1. **Research.** Campaigns typically have relied upon four different types of research: obtaining information about the candidates, such as their accomplishments and desirable characteristics; focus group analysis that delves into people's sentiments about the political culture, views about which issues are important and impressions of the candidates; a benchmark survey to provide more detailed information about attitudes toward the candidate and issues; and finally targeting analysis of the voter groups likely to vote for the candidate.
2. **Buying decisions.** When buying ad time, the goal of campaigns has been to reach the largest segment of the target audience at the lowest price. This often has meant buying multiple media channels.
3. **Ad concept.** Deciding the message of the ad typically has been left to a senior media consultant with input from others on the campaign, including the candidate and pollsters.
4. **Ad creation.** Often in-house production staff has been used to produce the advertisement. Some ads can be produced quickly, but for others extensive filming may be involved, especially if the candidate is featured.
5. **Ad testing.** Focus groups have been used to evaluate the ad, or multiple versions of the ad, to help identify problems or areas of confusion for audiences.
6. **Final Production.** Campaigns create final versions of the ad, including all music, voiceovers, lighting features and transitions.
7. **Launching the ad.** This stage has involved holding a news conference to try to gain free media coverage of the advertisement—and the claims made therein.
8. **Airing the ad.** The ad finally appears on television.
9. **Impact analysis.** Campaigns have attempted to gauge the impact of the ad, often through polling. They have assessed whether people's recognition of the candidate has increased or evaluations of the candidate have improved, and these data can help in creating future advertisements.

FIGURE 12.1 Johnson's Framework for Developing and Marketing Political Advertising

Empirical Illustration: Designing and Targeting Political Advertising

This section will discuss the design and targeting of political advertising in more depth, mixing further theoretical detail with a range of empirical examples from American electoral history. This will be followed by a focused analysis of ads aired during the 2012 presidential race.

Following the stages outlined by Johnson (2007), campaigns have begun the process of designing and marketing political advertising with research. Campaigns have conducted research into their own candidates to figure out what their brands are, and they also have conducted research to determine which themes resonate best with the electorate. This has been accomplished through survey research or focus group analysis, such as was done by the Bush team in deciding whether to make Willie Horton an issue in 1988. Campaigns also have conducted research into the electorate: What are the key segments of the electorate that need to be targeted?

The next step for campaigns has been to develop the ad concept. Developing the concept typically has involved a mix of art and science, according to Johnson.

While the detailed research conducted in the first phase should inform the ad concept, campaigns also have relied upon the experience and judgment of media consultants, campaign managers and sometimes even the candidates.

Then ad creation begins. The media firm's in-house production staff typically has handled the logistics, but sometimes they may need to hire on additional people for the shoot, such as videographers or actors. In 2000, for instance, the Gore presidential campaign assembled 20 cast and crew members and 20 vehicles (and even a camel!) on a Texas ranch in order to film a lengthy commercial called "The Ballad of George W. Bush" (Peters 2012). Incidentally, the Gore team eventually decided not to air the ad in spite of all of the resources that had been invested in creating it. Sometimes, the media firm has created multiple versions of the same ad. This has been done to 1) allow for testing of which ad resonates better with audiences or 2) to allow the campaign to air similar, but targeted, ads to different audiences. For example, in 2012 the Romney campaign made several versions of an ad called "A Better Future." The ad mentioned the names of various swing states, with the Ohio ad discussing manufacturing, the Colorado ad discussing defense jobs, the Virginia ad discussing energy and the Iowa ad discussing the deficit.

The fourth step is testing the ad. Testing alerts the campaign to ad messages that may be confusing to viewers or words that voters might find objectionable, which allows the campaign to iron out problems in the final version of the ad. Johnson (2007) noted that typically multiple versions of the ad have been tested, allowing the campaign to identify the most effective version. Typically, ad testing has been done through focus groups, gatherings of 8–12 individuals chosen to watch the ads and offer their comments on them. Sometimes the testing has used dials that allow a participant to show approval or disapproval of the ad as it is aired (Peters 2012). Not only has this allowed campaigns to pinpoint the timing of problem areas in an ad, but it also has allowed the participants to remain anonymous, which may lead them to be more honest in their evaluations.

One of the most effective negative ads from 2012, according to the well-known political marking firm Luntz Global, was an ad aired by Americans for Prosperity, a Republican group. Luntz's focus groups, which were composed of 2008 Obama voters who were on the fence in 2012, particularly liked the AFP ad because it featured a variety of ordinary people who had voted for Obama in 2008. They talked about the high hopes they had had for Obama and how he had failed to live up to those hopes (Conroy 2012). One of the most effective attacks against Romney came in a 60-second spot aired by Priorities USA. It featured a man who worked at a factory that was acquired by Romney's Bain Capital. The man recounted how he was ordered to build a stage that was used by company managers to announce layoffs.

Other methods, in addition to focus groups, have been used to test ads. Recently, some firms have entered the business of testing political ads online. Ace Metrix, for instance, asked a sample of 500 online respondents for their assessments of each ad aired during the 2012 presidential race. Respondents were chosen to be representative of the U.S. population. The company found that the Priorities USA "Stage" ad mentioned earlier was the most persuasive of the 2012 presidential race.[2] The least effective ad was one aimed at Latinos that featured Marc Anthony declaring that Obama "has our back." Although a general audience found the ad unpersuasive, it may have scored much more highly among Latinos. Given the large sample sizes used by the company, a campaign could examine the relative effectiveness of an ad among various demographic groups.

Sometimes, however, speed is essential, and thus ad testing has been skipped. The Strategy Group, a Republican firm, has boasted that it can produce a television advertisement within two hours (Rosin 2012). Such rapid ad production usually has been done when a campaign believes it must respond quickly to an attack made by an opponent. Alternatively, ad creators sometimes have relied upon political instinct. Johnson (2007) told the story of Bob Dole's campaign during the 1996 Republican presidential primaries. At one point, Dole's team brought in a new media consultant, Don Sipple, who believed that the campaign needed to rapidly change course. Sipple scrapped all of Dole's negative ads and designed a new one overnight for broadcast the next day. The only person on whom the ad was tested was Sipple's wife (who liked it).

After completing ad testing, campaigns have begun final production on their ads. Campaigns fix messages that voters found confusing, tweak words, modify pacing and change music. Then the ad is launched. Although sometimes the ad will be shipped to the television station as quickly as possible, campaigns typically have made the airing of a new ad a media event so as to garner as much free coverage as possible. Thus, campaigns have invited journalists to a pre-viewing news conference during which the journalists are given additional information about the ad's message and invited to ask questions. This appears to be an effective way to garner additional attention as research demonstrates that media coverage of advertising has increased in recent years (West 2005) and constitutes a substantial percentage of overall campaign coverage, up to 50 percent in some races (Fowler and Ridout 2009). Sometimes a campaign has produced an ad, launched it to the news media and then spent little to no money airing it. These have been called "shadow" ads. For example, in late summer 2003, Democrat Howard Dean's campaign aired an ad in Austin, Texas, that was critical of President George W. Bush. Although Dean claimed that the ad was aired to generate support in Texas (King 2003), it is more plausible that the ad was aired to generate news coverage, as it coincided with a trip by President Bush to his ranch in Texas. Nowadays, generating such coverage of advertising has become even easier because campaigns have started designing web-only ads to respond to major campaign events.

The final stage of the ad process, according to Johnson, is assessing the impact of the advertisements. This typically has been done through polling to see if knowledge or evaluations of the candidate have changed during the time during which the ad aired.

Ad Targeting in 2012

One decision a campaign must make is how to reach an ad's intended audience. Some of these targeted groups, such as women, young people or Latino voters, are large demographic segments of the population. Some of these segments are narrower, such as people who watch the Hallmark channel, Cubans living in South Florida, or people who care passionately about free trade. In this section, I will provide examples from the 2012 presidential campaign of how various groups were targeted, focusing both on the choice of medium as a way to efficiently reach specific groups and the messages employed to appeal to these groups.

Just over $1 billion was spent on television advertising in the presidential race from January 1, 2012, through Election Day, as Table 12.1 shows. But these advertising dollars were divided among many different television outlets. The most popular outlet in 2012, by far, was local broadcast television, which accounted for $887 million in spending. Local broadcast television has the advantage of offering a more narrow geographic reach and thus more efficiency. Ads can be aired only in those battleground state media markets, and the messages can be customized geographically as well. In 2012, for instance, the Obama campaign aired an ad only in Ohio media markets that lauded the success of the government's bailout of the auto industry. It proclaimed, "Ohio auto workers are leading the recovery."

The campaigns spent another $62 million on local cable advertising. The chief advantage of local cable television is that it offers campaigns the narrowest geographic reach. Ads can be aired on individual cable systems, which generally serve only a single city or metropolitan area, and some cable systems offer the possibility of delivering an advertisement only to certain neighborhoods in a city. This makes local cable especially attractive for candidates running for mayor or county commissioner. Advertising on local cable television has increased dramatically in the past decade. Tim Kay, the head of political advertising at NCC (National Cable Communications) Media, which handles the bulk of the local cable buys, said in an interview that his business has grown from $40 million in 2002 to

TABLE 12.1 Volume of and Spending on Presidential Advertising by Type of Television (January 1, 2012–Election Day)

Type	Number of Spots	Est. Spending
Local Broadcast	1,420,758	$886,509,230
Local Cable	N/A	62,091,310
National Cable	11,773	29,275,710
National Network	355	35,033,740
Total		1,012,909,990

Data on local broadcast, national cable and national network ad airings and spending come from Kantar Media-CMAG, with analysis by the Wesleyan Media Project. Data on local cable spending come from Tim Kay at NCC Media. Figures include spending by candidate campaigns, parties and outside groups airing ads on behalf of candidates.

$400 million in 2012 (Kay 2012). That growth stems from several factors. One is the consolidation of the cable television industry, which has made it easier for advertisers to coordinate with those who sell advertising. A second factor is the increasing segmentation of viewing audiences, which has made it more difficult to reach a mass audience on broadcast television and has highlighted the ability of local cable to reach niche audiences. A third factor contributing to the growth of advertising on local cable is the development of cable interconnects in the late 1990s, which have allowed ads to be distributed to several cable systems within a geographic area. This means that ad buyers can deal with fewer cable companies.

The campaigns spent only about $35 million of the $1 billion total on national network television advertising (e.g., ABC, CBS, FOX, NBC). Because of the high prices on national network television, the campaigns purchased only 355 airings. One advantage of network television is that it gives campaigns access to a wide audience that spans the 50 states. Of course, network television only makes sense in campaigns for president, which are national, and even then such purchases may not be very efficient, as the number of swing states has declined to a dozen or fewer in recent campaigns.

Finally, the campaigns spent $29 million on ads on national cable channels. National cable television also offers a large geographic reach like national network television, but because of audience segmentation, one can reach narrower segments of the audience (e.g., sports enthusiasts, who tend to be more Republican, may watch ESPN or the Golf Network). Obama and his allies distributed their advertising across these channels quite differently than Romney and his allies. For instance, Democrats spent more than twice as much on national cable as did Republicans ($20.3 million to $9.0 million), while Republican sponsors spent nearly twice as much as Democratic sponsors on national network ads ($22.9 million to $12.1 million).

The Obama campaign used third-generation targeting in 2012, allowing it to target two types of voters: undecided, swing voters and Obama supporters who did not frequently vote (Eggen and Farnam 2012). This led the campaign to depart somewhat from the traditional strategy of buying local television news. Instead, they made some unorthodox ad buys, including placing ads on the Family Channel, the Food Network and the Hallmark Channel (Eggen and Farnam 2012). Moreover, the Obama team discovered that there were a large number of politically interested registered voters who had not viewed the debates. The reason? They were too busy raising young children, and so the Obama team would air ads on cartoons such as SpongeBob in order to reach those busy parents (Murphy 2012).

Table 12.2 shows the national cable networks on which the Obama campaign aired ads in 2012 and the volume of advertising on each, sorted by the number of ads aired. Unfortunately, data on local cable buys are not available, but the table does reveal the diversity of audiences that that Obama campaign targeted. At the top of the list was TV Land, a network that largely airs classic comedy shows. This was followed by CNN, SyFy, USA and TNT.

TABLE 12.2 Obama Campaign Ad Buys by Cable Network

Network	Ads
TV Land	1712
CNN	820
SyFy	790
USA	568
TNT	552
ESPN	425
MSNBC	413
Headline News	387
CNBC	381
MTV	281
Comedy Central	274
History Channel	269
Lifetime	269
TBS	255
BET	234
FX	222
Nat'l Geographic Channel	205
Spike	165
A&E	145
TruTV	103
AMC	74
Hallmark	69
Fox News	33
Discovery Channel	14
ESPN2	14
Bravo	13
Adult Swim	7
MTV2	1
VH-1	1

Data from Kantar Media-CMAG, with analysis by the Wesleyan Media Project.

Helping the Obama team decide when and where to air ads was a software program dubbed Optimizer. Murphy (2012) described the program as one that searched through large volumes of information about the pricing of television advertising—across various local and national channels—in order to find the most efficient ad buys. Moreover, the system allowed the campaign to predict the price of advertising on various outlets at various points in time in order to more efficiently allocate advertising dollars.

By contrast, the Romney campaign—and most of its interest group supporters—was panned after the election for its inefficient purchases of advertising. One analyst who looked at the Romney campaign's purchasing decisions called it "campaign malpractice" (Hamburger 2012). The crux of the problem, according to

The Washington Post's Tom Hamburger, was this: "Obama and his allies spent less on advertising than Romney and his allies but got far more—in the number of ads broadcast, in visibility in key markets and in targeting critical demographic groups, such as the working class and younger voters in swing states." It would be difficult to argue that efficient allocation of advertising dollars led to Obama's victory in 2012, but it is certainly plausible that his campaign's "smarter" ad buys increased his margin by a percentage point or maybe even two.

In addition to making targeting decisions about the best channels for their advertising, the campaigns also designed their ads to appeal to specific demographic groups. During the 2012 presidential campaign, one highly sought-after group was Latino voters. According to data from the Wesleyan Media Project, just under 2 percent of total general election ad airings were in Spanish. The Romney and Obama campaigns paid similar attention to Latino voters; for each campaign, about 1.8 percent of total ad airings were Spanish language. Almost all of these Spanish-language ads aired in swing-state media markets with large Latino populations: Denver, Colorado; El Paso, Texas (which reached New Mexico); Las Vegas, Nevada; Miami, Tampa and Orlando, Florida; Raleigh, North Carolina; and Washington, D.C. (which reached Virginia).

Not only were these attempts to appeal to Latino voters in Spanish, but many of them spoke of issues designed to appeal specifically to Latino voters. For instance, one Romney ad featured Romney's son, Craig, speaking in Spanish. Craig Romney said that his father "values that we are a nation of immigrants" and spoke of his grandfather, George, having been born in Mexico. Another Romney ad was designed to speak to an even more specific population: conservative Cuban-Americans living in South Florida. The ad, which aired in Miami the week before Election Day, tried to link Barack Obama to two leftist governments in Latin America. The ad pointed to "endorsements" of Obama by both then Venezuelan president Hugo Chavez, and the daughter of Raul Castro, the leader of Cuba (Hernandez-Arthur and Liptak 2012).

The Obama campaign, which had generated a sizeable lead in the polls among Latinos, focused some of its Spanish-language advertising on ensuring that Latinos turned out to vote. One ad, which was released two days before Election Day, featured first lady Michelle Obama sitting on a couch talking with Cristina Saralegui, the host of a Spanish-language talk show (Cohn 2012). Saralegui asked Mrs. Obama, in Spanish, why it was critical for Latinos to vote. Mrs. Obama said that much was at stake, pointing to several pressing issues, among them comprehensive immigration reform.

Other ads made explicit appeals to women voters. The ad "Dear Daughter," which was released by the Romney campaign, featured soft images of a young woman holding her baby daughter. The female announcer began: "Dear daughter. Welcome to America. Your share of Obama's debt is over 50,000 dollars. And it grows every day." She continued to discuss how Obama's policies have increased poverty and unemployment for women. Indeed, the word "woman" or "daughter" was used seven times during the 30-second ad.

In this ad and others, the Romney campaign tried to connect women's issues to economic concerns. That may have been in response to a perception that Romney could competently handle such issues and also an attempt to answer a critique that the Republican Party was not responding to the changing concerns of women voters. As Hanna Rosin described it: "Instead of acknowledging the prevalence of divorce and single-parent homes in some way, the GOP's candidates continue to project photos and postcards of perfect Republican families, each husband matched to a beaming wife and two children—in short, the Romneys at Christmas. If you're a single mom in Alabama struggling to work and take care of a kid alone, it can be grating to have to take in three generations of Romney perfection" (Rosin 2012).

The Obama campaign similarly targeted women voters with an ad released in June that made reference to the Lily Ledbetter Fair Pay Act. The female narrator stated: "The son of a single mom. Proud father of two daughters. President Obama knows that women being paid 77 cents on the dollar for doing the same work as men isn't just unfair; it hurts families." The ad included images of women performing both blue-collar and white-collar jobs along with photos of Obama as a boy with his mother and Obama with his daughters.

Another Obama ad that was aimed at women went straight for the jugular. The ad featured two women, Dawn and Alex, who criticized Romney for his stands on women's health issues. As Alex put it, "This is not the 1950s. Contraception is so important. It's about a woman being able to make decisions." Dawn replied, "I don't remember anyone as extreme as Romney." The ad went on to note that Romney opposed requiring employers to cover contraception and showed video of Romney saying he would "cut off funding for Planned Parenthood."

The candidates' television advertising in 2012 generally targeted fairly large demographic groups, such as women and Latinos. But their online advertising often targeted much narrower groups. For instance, the Obama campaign released an online video on July 4 that spoke of all he had done as president for veterans. Another Obama video directly addressed the LGBT community.

The examples provided in this section clearly illustrate that American presidential campaigns lean heavily on lessons gleaned from the field of political marketing in both the design of their ads and their targeting to particular audiences. The activities of the 2012 presidential campaigns point out just how sophisticated their use of these techniques has become.

Conclusions for Research and Practice

Surprisingly, those who study political advertising have not shown all that much familiarity with the field of political marketing. This has been a real oversight, as this chapter has pointed to two ways in which political marketing might contribute to an understanding of political advertising: in the development of the ad and its message and in the targeting of advertising to specific audiences. I have illustrated these potential contributions by providing examples from past campaigns and a wealth of data and vignettes from the 2012 presidential campaign. In today's world of segmented television audiences, sending a single message to a mass audience will not be as effective as sending targeted messages to specific audiences. Yet much research on the topic remains to be done.

One thing that may foster research on advertising that uses a political marketing approach is the increasing availability of data. Thanks to the Wisconsin Advertising Project, and its successor, the Wesleyan Media Project, academics now have access to detailed data on both the content of political advertising in American electoral campaigns and where and when those ads were aired. These data have appeared in scores of studies on political advertising in the past decade. Still, the academic community lacks data on ad placements on local cable stations, which make up an increasing, though still fairly small, fraction of overall ad spending in the United States. Local cable attracted an estimated $624 million in political spending in 2012 (Kay 2012) compared to the $3.8 billion spent on local broadcast, national network and national cable. Unfortunately, no one currently systematically tracks local cable airings at any level of detail (Kay 2012).

Another positive development in the study of political advertising is that scholars and practitioners have started to team up to examine the effectiveness of political advertising. For example, Issenberg (2012) reported on a group of political scientists who collaborated with the campaign of Texas Governor Rick Perry in 2006 in order to study the impact of advertising. The campaign allowed the scholars to randomly assign political advertising to various media markets and at various volumes. This was combined with public opinion polling in these areas to assess the advertising's impact, which was found to be strong but short lived (Gerber et al. 2011).

One other area ripe for more research is how the content of political advertising varies with audience characteristics. Does matching ad content (for instance, the spokesperson, the voiceover announcer or the message) to the characteristics of certain targeted voters make the ad more effective? Based on studies of consumer products, scholars suspect that such strategies must make a difference, but by how much? Certainly, the literature in marketing can provide those who study advertising with some guidance on these questions, but it also may be useful to develop additional theories that would be useful in the more specific realm of *political* marketing.

There is also much that practitioners—those who design the ads and their messages and those who buy the airtime—can learn from the field of political marketing. To make advertising truly effective, campaigns must design ads to fit the candidate's overall brand and message and develop a strategy to reach specific groups of targeted voters.

Acknowledgment

I thank Michael Franz for his suggestions on this chapter and Crystal Ebert for her research assistance.

Notes

1 The most famous "Willie Horton" ad was aired by the National Security Political Action Committee, an independent expenditure committee that legally was not allowed to coordinate with the Bush campaign. The Bush campaign did, however, air a similar ad that attacked Dukakis over the prison furlough program, and Bush had mentioned Willie Horton in a speech.
2 "Ace Metrix Announces the Most Effective TV Ads of the 2012 Election." Available at www.acemetrix.com/news/press-releases/ace-metrix-announces-the-most-effective-tv-ads-of-the-2012-election/. Accessed on 15 February 2013.

References

Bartels, L. M. (1996). Partisanship and voting behavior, 1952–1996. *American Journal of Political Science, 44*(1), 35–50.
Bennett, W. L., & Iyengar, S. (2008). A new era of minimal effects? The changing foundations of political communication. *Journal of Communication, 58*(4), 707–731.
Cohn, A. M. (2012, October 24). Michelle Obama appears in first TV ad, targets Latino voters. *The Hill.* Available at http://thehill.com/video/campaign/263865-michelle-obama-appears-in-first-tv-ad-targets-latino-voters
Conroy, S. (2012, August 27). Ad with former Obama backers deemed most effective. *CBS News.* Available at www.cbsnews.com/8301–503544_162–57500797–503544/ad-with-former-obama-backers-deemed-most-effective/
Eggen, D., & Farnam, T. W. (2012, November 14). Obama campaign took unorthodox approach to ad buying. *The Washington Post.* Available at http://articles.washingtonpost.com/2012-11-14/politics/35506961_1_romney-operation-obama-campaign-cable-operators
Fowler, E. F., & Ridout, T. N. (2009). Local television and newspaper coverage of political advertising. *Political Communication, 26*(2), 119–136.
Gerber, A. S., Gimpel, J. G., Green, D. P., & Shaw, D. R. (2011). How large and long-lasting are the persuasive effects of televised campaign ads? Results from a randomized field experiment. *American Political Science Review, 105*(1), 135–150.
Gordon, B. R., & Hartmann, W. R. (2013). Advertising effects in presidential elections. *Marketing Science, 32*(1), 19–35.
Gordon, B. R., Lovett, M. J., Shachar, R., Arceneaux, K., Moorthy, S., Peress, M., Rao, A., Sen, S., Soberman, D., & Urminsky, O. (2012). Marketing and politics: Models, behavior, and policy implications. *Marketing Letters, 23*(2), 391–403.
Gorman, B. (2010, April 12). Where did the primetime broadcast TV audience go? *Zap2it.com.* Available at http://tvbythenumbers.zap2it.com/2010/04/12/where-did-the-primetime-broadcast-tv-audience-go/47976/
Hamburger, T. (2012, December 11). Romney spent more on TV ads but got much less. *The Washington Post.* Available at http://articles.washingtonpost.com/2012-12-11/politics/35767760_1_romney-campaign-officials-obama-campaign-ad-strategy
Hernandez-Arthur, S., & Liptak, K. (2012, November 1). Romney ad pins Obama to Chavez and Castro. *CNN.* Available at http://politicalticker.blogs.cnn.com/2012/11/01/romney-ad-pins-obama-to-chavez-and-castro
Issenberg, S. (2012). *The victory lab: The secret science of winning campaigns.* New York, NY: Crown.

Johnson, D. W. (2007). *No place for amateurs: How political consultants are reshaping American democracy* (2nd ed.). New York, NY: Routledge.

Kay, T. (2012, December 12). Telephone interviewed by Travis Ridout.

King, Larry. (2003, August 4). *Larry King Live*. Interview with Howard Dean. *CNN*. Available at http://transcripts.cnn.com/TRANSCRIPTS/0308/04/lkl.00.html

Lovett, M., & Peress, M. (2012). Targeting political advertising on television. Simon School Working Paper, No. FR 10-32. Available at SSRN: http://ssrn.com/abstract=1649469 or http://dx.doi.org/10.2139/ssrn.1649469

Mann, R. (2011). *Daisy petals and mushroom clouds: LBJ, Barry Goldwater, and the ad that changed American politics*. Baton Rouge, LA: LSU Press.

Murphy, T. (2012, November 15). Under the hood of team Obama's tech operation. *Mother Jones*. Available at www.motherjones.com/politics/2012/11/inside-obama-campaign-tech-operation

Niemi, R. G., & Weisberg, H. (1976). Are parties becoming irrelevant? In R.G. Niemi & H. Weisberg (Eds.), *Controversies in American voting behavior*. San Francisco, CA: W. H. Freeman.

Peters, J. W. (2012, March 22). The selling of a politician, and the ads almost broadcast. *The New York Times*. Available at www.nytimes.com/2012/03/23/us/politics/the-selling-of-a-politician-and-the-ads-almost-broadcast.html

Ridout, T. N., Franz, M. M., Goldstein, K. M., & Feltus, W. J. (2012). Separation by television program: Understanding the targeting of political advertising in presidential elections. *Political Communication, 29*(1), 1–23.

Robinson, C. (2006). *Advertising and the marketing orientation of parties contesting the 1999 and 2002 New Zealand general election campaigns*. (Unpublished doctoral dissertation). Massey University, Palmerston North, New Zealand.

Robinson, C. (2010). Political advertising and the demonstration of market orientation. *European Journal of Marketing, 44*(3/4), 451–460.

Rosin, H. (2012, March 13). Rise of the single-woman voter. *Slate*. Available at www.slate.com/articles/double_x/doublex/2012/03/single_women_are_the_new_swing_voters_but_which_way_do_they_lean_.html

Seeyle, K. Q. (2004, December 6). How to sell a candidate to a Porsche-driving, Leno-loving Nascar fan. *The New York Times*. Available at www.nytimes.com/2004/12/06/politics/06strategy.html?_r=0

Shacher, R. (2009). The political participation puzzle and marketing. *Journal of Marketing Research, 46*(December), 798–815.

Simon, R. (1990). *Road show: In America, anyone can become president, it's one of the risks we take*. New York, NY: Farrar, Straus, Giroux.

West, D.M. (1995). *Air wars: Television advertising in election campaigns, 1952–2004* (4th ed.). Washington, DC: CQ Press.

13
CRISIS-MANAGEMENT, MARKETING, AND MONEY IN US CAMPAIGNS

R. Sam Garrett

Overview of the Topic

Campaign life is rarely certain, even if eventual outcomes are expected. History is replete with examples of unexpected candidate gaffes, poor organization, and hard-hitting attacks from opposing candidates and outside parties or groups that sink even the most established campaigns. The fact that campaign crises occur isn't news. It also isn't surprising that money plays a major role in shaping campaigns. What is unusual, however, is that the interaction of these topics has received little scholarly attention—despite their clear interaction in practical terms, including substantial interest from practitioners and journalists. Even among political marketing scholars, there is little attention to either subject—and virtually none to both—despite a substantial literature on crisis-management in loosely related topics such as commercial marketing.

The chapter extends the existing applied politics literature by considering how changes in campaign finance policy create new opportunities for considering campaign crises and political marketing. Selected events in the 2012 US presidential campaign illustrate key concepts. The chapter doesn't attempt to provide a playbook for all situations that researchers or practitioners might encounter. It also doesn't attempt to establish which side was right or wrong—either ethically or legally—in the cases studied. It does, however, add to the limited scholarly resources to seriously consider the critical events—whether one chooses to label them "crises" or something else—that win and lose elections. The chapter advances the literature by considering how an existing typology of campaign crises can be used to consider political marketing and campaign finance themes.

Review of Previous Literature: Political Marketing and Crisis-Management

Crisis-management is among the most important but least understood topics in campaign politics. Political professionals—the political consultants, professional campaign managers, party and group operatives, campaign staff, and others who make their living from politics—spend their careers anticipating, managing, and sometimes even perpetuating crises (only for the opposition, they hope). In many cases, their expertise is passed down anecdotally and through a few professional training programs. There is, however, little written knowledge and scholarly study of the topic (Garrett 2010). Understanding crisis-management and its connection to political marketing must, therefore, rely on a diverse set of literature.

As one of the editors of this volume explains elsewhere (Lees-Marshment 2009), political marketing is also a discipline in progress. Even within the past decade, scholars have described "contested" definitions of "political marketing" and struggled with the inadequacy of commercial marketing for the political field while nonetheless needing to rely on the commercial literature as a foundation (Johansen 2005: 93; see also Osuagwu 2008: 797). There is, nonetheless, general consensus that, drawing on political science, marketing, and communications literature, political marketing explores not simply how politicians frame messages and reach audiences, but also how those decisions play out in campaigning and governing. As Lees-Marshment (2009: 28) explains, "The key difference [between commercial marketing and political marketing] is that political marketing is now seen as potentially affecting the way politicians, parties, and governments behave, not just how they communicate that behavior." In the United States, microtargeting, for example, is quickly becoming the norm among sophisticated campaigns. Using this practice, political professionals can employ data-mining techniques to segment potential voters based on magazine subscriptions and demographics, and then appeal to them with uniquely tailored mass mailings, e-mail, and other marketing efforts.

Few topics emphasize "applied" or practical political behavior more than campaign management. At one time, there was relatively little mass marketing in political campaigns. Before 1950, in particular, political parties dominated campaigning, which relied more on large-scale get-out-the-vote (GOTV) efforts than advertising. Beginning in the 1960s, the rise of "candidate-centered" campaigning and the growth of television helped establish political consulting as a full-time, dedicated profession (Dulio 2004). Media consultants, particularly important for the purposes of this chapter, write scripts and establish advertising plans. They also provide technical services, such as filming and editing. Over time, "paid media," as commercial advertising is known in the political campaign world, became so important that media consultants became less narrow strategists providing technical broadcasting services and more general advisors. Indeed, today they have arguably replaced professionals actually called "general consultants" in many races (Garrett 2010).

The marriage between strategy and external communication—whether the latter is called "marketing" or something else—is central to campaign management. Political scientists and former political professionals Burton and Shea (2003) explain that a constant mindset emphasizing political victory is perhaps the most important element of a campaign plan. This "strategic thinking," they suggest, is "the capacity to relate the knowledge of political terrain and campaign rules, often by combining a forward-looking plan with a reverse-engineered vision of electoral success" (Burton and Shea 2003: 5). This is not to say that "strategic thinking" can avoid all campaign missteps, but it might help a great deal. Burton and Shea's "vision of electoral success" might simply be called the "campaign plan." As is explained below, experienced political professionals report that major disruptions to the campaign plan are the key indicator of campaign crises.

A limited amount of literature has attempted to bridge the applied politics and political marketing fields. Stephen Medvic, for example, has adapted his "theory of deliberate priming" (Medvic 2001) to political marketing settings (Medvic 2006). As he explains, "deliberate priming is a process whereby campaigns attempt to disseminate a theme by using various messages to appeal to distinct groups of voters" (Medvic 2006: 27). Essentially, Medvic's theory suggests that political consultants use strategic decisions to market tailored policy messages to voters believed to be most persuadable by those messages. Although it might seem obvious that campaigns work to attract particular groups of voters, research such as Medvic's has shown that modern political marketing is not simply the mass-appeal, largely partisan-oriented outreach of the mid-twentieth century or even later. Instead, political operatives are increasingly using marketing techniques to dissect groups of voters into strong and weak supporters with similar but nonetheless unique messages. Even newer works with attention to modern outreach, however, typically emphasize either applied politics or political marketing, but rarely both. Some scholars (Steger, Kelly, and Wrighton 2006) have suggested that this divide persists because influential political behavior literature has found that campaigns have little effect on voters. As is clear in the applied politics literature, however, marketing decisions occupy tremendous time and energy for candidates and political professionals (Garrett 2010).

The Existing Work on Campaign Crises and Crisis-Management

Despite its obvious relevance for everyday campaign life, crisis-management has received little substantial, sustained study in political science. Expanding the search to marketing or communications literature broadens the possibilities, but also makes unifying theory and practice more challenging. Some communications and marketing literature provides general lessons on topics such as corporate-style crisis-management (Fearn-Banks 2007; Coombs 1998), disaster communications

(Guion, Scammon, and Borders 2007), and product recalls (Van Heerde, Helsen, and Dekimpe 2007). Overall, however, just as the "applied politics" and even "political marketing" literature pays little attention to crisis-management, even the traditional marketing literature that explores crisis-management does not emphasize political campaigns.

The applied politics literature in political science, however, offers some starting points for studying political crises and crisis-management. Rather than addressing broader crises, most works that broach the topic explore only ethical "scandals," usually meaning an alleged transgression by the candidate. These works emphasize corruption, particularly as it affects final outcomes, such as a candidate exists from races, votes received, or funds raised (see, for example, Dimock and Jacobson 1995; Groseclose and Krehbiel 1994; Peters and Welch 1978). Even if one is willing to limit research to ethical scandals, despite the fact that scholars called for these and related subjects to be "center stage on the research agenda" almost two decades ago (Welch and Hibbing 1997: 226), the topic has been prominently studied only sporadically. The work that is available rarely relies on practitioner expertise (Garrett 2010).

Broader campaign crises, which do not necessarily involve ethics, have received little attention indeed. *Campaign Crises: Detours on the Road to Congress* (Garrett 2010), as far as this author knows the only book-length treatment of the subject, analyzes more than 100 interviews with political professionals. This research concludes that "[c]ampaign crises are interactive events, which the campaign team believes represent a significant disruption to the campaign strategy or plan" (21).

Because campaign crises can vary substantially, and because little research exists to help diagnose and understand crises, some ambiguity remains. Although most political professionals agree that campaign crises are distinct and clearly identifiable events, a vocal minority suggests instead that all competitive campaigns are constantly in a state that might be regarded as crisis-management. Additional discussion appears elsewhere (Garrett 2010: Chapter 2) but is beyond the scope of this chapter. For the purposes of this chapter and other inquiries, one need not necessarily agree which events were "crises" per se. Because a key element of defining campaign crises is determining whether the campaign in question believes the event is a crisis, interviews with campaign staff and other research would be required to determine precisely how particular events affected the campaigns in question. Even if they were not crises or if one disregards them as crises, however, the value of considering the *potential* for crises is that it provides a framework for understanding key turning points in campaigns.

The point here is that, through crises, campaigns can be studied as more than collections of strategy and tactics; they are also distinct but interrelated critical decisions about critical events. In this case, that means considering how both political marketing and fundraising events can help turn the tide of a race or have a major affect on the outcome. To better understand how, this chapter considers

Garrett's (2010) "crisis typology" with an eye toward political marketing and campaign finance.

Adding Money to the Discussion

Despite the attempt to spur more serious attention to crisis-management in *Campaign Crises*, the book and the limited available other works leave at least one major subject largely unaddressed: campaign finance. *Campaign Crises* notes that unsuccessful fundraising can represent an internal crisis (e.g., threatening the campaign organization's survival), or that unexpectedly successful fundraising by an opposing candidate—or well-funded attacks from an opposing group—can be an external crisis. Nonetheless, political money does not receive substantial attention in the rest of the inquiry. There is a broad and diverse literature on campaign finance in general, but relatively little on the practical effect of campaign finance issues—particularly policy matters—on campaign strategy, marketing, or management. Campaign finance is an entire subfield in and of itself, a review of which is beyond the scope of this chapter, but for a general overview, see, for example, Corrado et al. (2005), La Raja (2008), and Magleby and Corrado (2011).

Money in politics has always been important, but the substantial changes following a major 2010 Supreme Court ruling—*Citizens United v. Federal Election Commission* (FEC)—create new potential for campaign crises related to fundraising and spending. They also provide new opportunities for various outside groups operating both in support of and in opposition to candidates to spend substantial sums and reshape the campaign environment (Herrnson, Deering, and Wilcox 2013).

This chapter takes no position on the heated debate over whether *Citizens United* was good or bad for the democratic process. It also does not address legal details of the decision or most policy implications resulting from it. For the purposes of this chapter, which emphasizes relevant issues for campaign management and political marketing, only some selected details are particularly relevant (see *Citizens United* 2010, *SpeechNow* 2010, and Garrett 2014 for further detail). A brief summary appears in the next section.

The preceding review of the literature suggests that two related areas of study—political marketing and applied politics—each contain important elements for understanding how and why political professionals and others involved in campaigns structure messages and make strategic decisions to win elections. Despite their commonalities, work in each field lamentably often ignores the other. Recent efforts, such as those of the *Journal of Political Marketing* in the past decade (Newman 2012), have made notable progress in bridging the divide between relevant marketing and political fields, and between continents. Given this state of flux, why should this chapter add even more divergent literature by exploring crisis-management and campaign finance? Can these areas of study and practice really help clarify, rather than confuse, our understanding of political marketing, applied politics, or both? This author suggests that the answer is "yes."

Although campaign finance has long been considered in the applied politics literature, some prominent scholarship has recently argued that changes in political money are affecting political marketing in new ways. As *Journal of Political Marketing* editor Bruce Newman (2012: 1) observed upon the journal's tenth anniversary, "As one considers the broad range of activities encompassed by political marketing, the focus still centers on the strategic management of political campaigns. What has changed over the past ten years is the increasing amount of money necessary to pay for the execution of those campaigns." Whether *Citizens United* spurred more money in campaigns has been subject to debate, but it is undisputed that the decision permitted new kinds of spending (independent expenditures) by corporations and unions, and indirectly led to the development of super PACs and clearer permission for certain 501(c) groups to spend money influencing campaigns.

As we will see later in the chapter, campaign finance has always been important for the obvious task of funding campaigns. Raising and spending money to win campaigns perhaps now shares a more symbiotic relationship with political marketing than ever before. Money has always been necessary to transmit campaign messages, but the new media now available to campaigns—whether an increased reliance on avenues such as local cable television advertising or microtargeted e-mail campaigns—both help generate political money and depend on that money for success. Campaign finance policy has also become part of the narrative of campaigning in new ways, as campaigns and various groups frame a vote choice not only as a choice for or against a candidate, but also as a vote for or against particular industries, people, and funding allegedly surrounding those candidates.

Theoretical Framework

Before exploring the crisis typology's implications for the connection between campaign finance and political marketing, a brief review of the relevant dimensions of the typology and gaps in the literature is appropriate. In addition to the emphasis on strategic disruptions discussed above, "[c]ampaign crises may be internal or external, and are usually unexpected. The full complexity of campaign crises is rarely explained by a single event" (Garrett 2010: 37). Furthermore, political professionals most often (in more than 80 percent of interviews) defined crises by emphasizing a "strategic disruption," essentially a major, often unexpected, interruption in the campaign's planned business. As Garrett (2010: 21) explains:

> Even if only for a day (but often much longer), political professionals said that "strategic disruptions" are the essence of campaign crises because they prevent campaigns from doing what they had planned to do, usually in a major way. Examples include candidate deaths, unexpected election recounts, unexpected third-party messages contradicting candidates (e.g., interest-group attack ads), and other events that surprise the campaign

and reshape its environment. Unexpected changes in resources—in time, personnel and money (some of which are impossible to redirect or replace) are often the most damaging element of crises.

Importantly, political professionals' definitions of campaign crises spanned a variety of external, internal, expected, and unexpected events (see the typology of campaign crises in Chapter 2 of Garrett 2010). These included a dozen categories, such as organizational problems and media "feeding frenzies." Most of those are beyond the scope of this chapter. For understanding the connection between political marketing and crises, however, concentrating on strategic disruptions—the most common form of campaign crisis political professionals identified—may be especially fruitful because these typically represent the most serious and all-encompassing crises, thus perhaps requiring the most attention to external communication. Strategic disruptions are particularly important for marketing concerns because they can disrupt a campaign's internal and external message-framing. In many of the worst crises, campaigns lose control of their messages, ultimately compromising the ability to reach the voters they have worked so hard to identify and convince with tailored messages. *Campaign Crises* notes that unsuccessful fundraising can represent an internal crisis (e.g., threatening the campaign organization's survival), or that unexpectedly successful fundraising by an opposing candidate—or well-funded attacks from an opposing group—can be an external threat. With this background in mind, this chapter suggests that greater attention to the connection between political marketing and campaign finance can improve the understanding of campaign crises and crisis-management as follows.

- Legal or policy changes can affect the environment in which campaigns must operate. One of the most controversial areas of campaign finance regulation, for example—the ability of campaigns to "coordinate" their activities with parties or groups—directly affects how or whether campaigns and other entities can share products such as targeting information and agree on advertising strategies.
- In the case of *Citizens United*, new forms of outside political messages (independent expenditures) were permitted. This change permitted corporations, unions and "super PACs" to enter the political marketplace in new ways, including by airing previously prohibited advertisements calling for election or defeat of specific candidates.
- These developments can add uncertainty to the "expected/unexpected" dimension to the "external" dimensions of the crisis typology.
- The presence of additional political messages (marketing) can both help and harm campaigns. "Outside" groups, for example, can provide additional support to campaigns experiencing crises (within legal limits), or can attempt to cause crises for campaigns they oppose. Campaigns therefore face new,

potentially unexpected potential for crises. These developments make targeting voters and executing consistent marketing strategies increasingly difficult.

Empirical Illustration: Campaign Crises and Exploring Connections to Campaign Finance

Relevant developments in US campaign finance law provide a unique opportunity to consider the connection between political marketing, campaign finance, and crisis-management. *Citizens United v. Federal Election Commission* was a major US Supreme Court ruling handed down on January 21, 2010. Arguably the most significant judicial campaign finance decision in at least 30 years, the case represented a watershed moment in the nation's campaign finance law. In brief, *Citizens United* permitted corporations—for the first time in modern history—to spend their treasury funds to explicitly call for election or defeat of political candidates. They could do so through communications known as "independent expenditures," which largely include broadcast political advertisements—the most prominent form of political marketing, perhaps the most overt manifestation of targeting—in competitive federal elections. The communications cannot be coordinated with campaigns. Political action committees (PACs), legally separate entities that are often affiliated with corporations and unions, had engaged in independent expenditures since the 1970s, but *Citizens United* marked the first time a corporation could use its own funds to do so. The decision did not affect a long-standing federal ban on corporate or union campaign contributions using treasury funds. Finally, although *Citizens United* did not address union activity, the case has been widely understood to also permit labor organizations to use their treasury funds to make independent expenditures, too.

In addition to new freedoms for corporations and unions, *Citizens United* and a related case fostered the growth of a new player in the campaign environment called "super PACs." In *SpeechNow v. FEC*, relying on the *Citizens United* precedent, the US Court of Appeals for the D.C. Circuit held in March 2010 that unlimited contributions to PACs that make only independent expenditures were constitutionally protected under the First Amendment. In other words, not only could corporations and unions now directly make independent expenditures, they could also give money to new groups, which came to be called "super PACs," that make independent expenditures.

Citizens United also had implications for three kinds of tax-exempt 501(c) organizations—(c)(4) social welfare groups, (c)(5) unions, and (c)(6) trade associations. These entities engaged in political activities before *Citizens United*, but some observers viewed the decision as giving (c)(4), (5), and (6) organizations more freedom to engage in independent expenditures because typically the groups are incorporated (and, hence, can use corporate treasuries to make independent expenditures). The degree to which these 501(c)s can engage in independent expenditures versus other activities (e.g., conducting more general "social welfare") while maintaining their tax-exempt status remains open to debate.

How might these changes be relevant for understanding campaign crises and crisis-management, particularly when it comes to political marketing? The following examples show that *Citizens United* dramatically changed the campaign environment. The timing of this change meant that campaigns could not fully prepare for the decision or its effects, particularly during the 2010 cycle. In addition, the new players that emerged after *Citizens United* exacerbated the uncertainty surrounding money in politics. Change and uncertainty do not necessarily equate with campaign crises, but they are key indicators of the *potential* for crises. Loss of control of the campaign environment is the essential element of the "strategic disruptions" that political professionals report most often signal campaign crises. It also makes planning political marketing strategy, such as through Medvic's (2001, 2006) "deliberate priming," more challenging.

Especially in presidential campaigns, financial resources play a major role in determining control of the strategic environment. Outside groups can be especially important for sending negative messages about candidates that are viewed as too sensitive for opposing candidates themselves (Garrett 2010). Campaigns and these groups must, therefore, increasingly battle for market share and limited political advertising time. Sometimes their efforts are complementary; at other times, they are adversarial. As a *Washington Times* report observed in July 2012, "With a presidential campaign gone bitterly negative before the opponents have even tapped gloves and a new breed of super PACs freed from old contribution and spending limits set to pour millions of dollars into opposition research, it's a skill set that has never been more relevant" (Hruby 2012). During the 2012 presidential cycle, there was, indeed, plenty of money to spend. As Table 13.1 shows, outside spending—which would include super PAC and 501(c) activity on independent expenditures and electioneering communications, at least—heavily favored Republicans in the presidential race. Most of this money fueled broadcast advertisements. The Obama campaign nonetheless outspent GOP nominee Mitt Romney's campaign.

TABLE 13.1 Spending Affecting the 2012 Presidential Campaign

Democratic-Affiliated Spending		Republican-Affiliated Spending	
Candidates	$683,546,548	Candidates	$433,281,516
National Parties	$292,264,802	National Parties	$386,180,565
"Outside" Groups	$134,841,433	"Outside" Groups	$405,688,417
Total	$1,110,652,783	Total	$1,225,150,498

Source: Author adaptation from Center for Responsive Politics data at www.opensecrets.org/pres12/index.php#out, accessed February 9, 2013

Note: "Outside" spending appears to include non-party and non-candidate entities such as super PACs and 501(c) organizations making independent expenditures or electioneering communications. Data are valid through November 2012.

TABLE 13.2 Top Five Television Advertising Spenders in the 2012 Presidential Race, April 11–October 29, 2012

Spender	Entity Type	Party Affiliation	Estimated Cost	Number of Airings	Number of Markets
Barack Obama	Candidate Campaign	Democratic	$265,981,010	503,255	63
Mitt Romney	Candidate Campaign	Republican	$105,393,980	190,784	78
Restore Our Future, Inc.	Super PAC	Republican	$57,611,970	60,366	64
American Crossroads	Super PAC	Republican	$56,864,790	64,441	60
Crossroads GPS	501(c)(4)	Republican	$45,886,280	74,092	67

Source: Author adaptation from Kantar Media/CMAG with analysis by the Wesleyan Media Project at http://mediaproject.wesleyan.edu/2012/11/02/presidential-ad-war-tops-1m-airings/; the author of this chapter adapted the format and added the "Entity Type" column.
Note: Data include broadcast television and national cable advertising.

Table 13.2 shows that the Obama and Romney campaigns were responsible for most advertising during the final months of the campaign. Republican groups, however, were far more prominent than Priorities USA Action—the only major pro-Obama super PAC (which would have ranked seventh in Table 13.2). Overall, as Table 13.1 shows, outside spending appears to have substantially buoyed the Republican ticket, more than making up for the financial disparity between the Obama and Romney campaigns themselves.

In anticipation of being outpaced, the Obama campaign projected a message of being in financial straits as a result of *Citizens United*, notwithstanding the campaign's record-setting fundraising in 2008. During that cycle, the Democratic nominee's campaign raised a stunning $750 million—financially crushing GOP nominee John McCain. The Republican nominee's campaign raised just more than $350 million but was also prohibited from accepting private funds during the general election after choosing to accept public funds, unlike the Obama campaign.[1] Since that time, however, *Citizens United* had occurred, and there was a widespread assumption that the ruling would benefit Republicans over Democrats because of the former's typically greater fundraising success, particularly among business groups. For the Obama campaign, the policy change became a new marketing theme, both to appeal for funds and to reinforce its image among its base as a champion of regulating money in politics.

Against that backdrop, and in an interesting tactic, the Obama campaign and allied Democratic groups essentially began suggesting publicly that the incumbent's campaign would suffer a crisis—a financial blowout—without massive fundraising success of its own. From a message-framing perspective, the Obama campaign was "turning a negative into a positive" by signaling an impending crisis but also offering a plan to manage that crisis through financial resources. The same applied for other campaigns. For example, a February 2010 fundraising message from the

Democratic Senatorial Campaign Committee (DSCC) signed by then Massachusetts senator John Kerry warned:

> Republicans are counting on big, big corporate money thanks to the conservative Supreme Court's decision. Democrats are depending on you. **The DSCC needs your help to raise $71,074 by tomorrow's FEC deadline. Every dollar you give will help even out the playing field for our candidates.** . . . I know very well what happens when Republicans get their shadowy outside assistance to spread their smears. And they'll have plenty of help this time. . . . [T]hanks to the Citizens United ruling, Democrats must be ready to fight. . . . **[I]f the DSCC doesn't meet each and every fundraising goal, none of that will matter. Our message will be lost in their blizzard of falsehoods, and President Obama will pay the price.**[2] (Democratic Senatorial Campaign Committee 2010)

Although inconsistent with the traditional crisis-management technique of portraying confidence at all costs (Garrett 2010: Chapter 3), the language above suggests that fundraising might provide an exception. Additional discussion of implications for research appears later in this chapter.

The presence of outside money can be challenging for candidates of both major parties, but this was particularly so among Democrats post–*Citizens United*. In responding to the new campaign finance environment, Democratic campaigns also had to balance their financial needs with their traditional public policy themes, prominent in their political marketing, opposing "big money." This was particularly so for the Obama campaign. Although the president had been a prolific fundraiser, he and his campaign had also been criticized for opting out of the presidential public financing program in 2008 and 2012. Despite the program's widely regarded inadequacy, some prominent Democratic groups openly criticized Obama for not at least moving to modernize presidential public financing even as he continued to court high-dollar donors (see, for example, Mayer 2012).

Their potential ideological conflicts notwithstanding, Democrats relied on super PACs and other groups to defend Obama campaign and attack Romney. In a particularly relevant example for the purposes of this chapter, pro-Obama super PAC Priorities USA Action placed heavy emphasis on attempting to debunk the Romney campaign's core message of building American business. Priorities USA Action was especially critical of Romney's tenure at financing firm Bain Capital. In a classic example of attempting to create a crisis by attacking an opponent's perceived strength, one of the super PAC's highest-profile advertisements, called "Stage," featured a former employee of a Bain-acquired firm recalling an episode in which he claimed to have been ordered to build a platform for a company event, only to learn that it was, in fact, a stage to announce layoffs. In the hard-hitting ad, the former employee declared that "it was like building my own coffin ... and it just made me sick" (quoted in Kessler 2012). The ad became one of the most memorable elements of the 2012 campaign. In a likely crisis for the Romney camp, the ad and related efforts consistently made it difficult for the GOP nominee and its allies to execute their planned message strategy that Romney's business experience would be easily embraced during tough economic times.

The "Stage" episode also provides an important example of exploiting opponent weaknesses through speed and clear messaging. As *National Journal* (Roarty 2012) explained, even in the post–*Citizens United* era, good strategic decision-making can outweigh financial advantage from the opposition:

> Mocked much of this campaign as an underfunded cousin to a wave of flush conservative counterparts like American Crossroads, Priorities USA has had an outsized impact on the presidential race. If the Obama campaign has waged a war of attrition against Romney, Priorities USA has been responsible for an array of tactical strikes key to defining him in negative ways—largely before the GOP nominee and his army of super PACs bothered to draw a positive picture of him.

Republican groups both helped and hurt GOP candidates. For example, despite more than $200,000 in independent expenditures, pro–Herman Cain super PAC the 9-9-9 Fund could not save its candidate after allegations of an extramarital affair dogged Cain's campaign.[3] Cain eventually suspended his campaign, having consistently denied wrongdoing (Lamb 2011). This example reminds us that although money can help precipitate or manage crises, it cannot necessarily overcome crises.

For all sides, making strategic decisions became more complex for affected campaigns because FEC regulations governing a concept known as "coordination" limit the extent to which campaigns can communicate with political parties and outside groups if the exchange of information would contain financial value, even if no money was actually exchanged. These regulations are in place to thwart circumventing campaign contribution limits by, for example, a super PAC airing an advertisement in close consultation with a candidate even if the entity is barred from making campaign contributions. Some critics, however, alleged that the coordination limits are easily avoided and that there are insufficient boundaries between campaigns, parties, and groups (see, for example, Corrado et al. 2005).

The policy debate surrounding coordination is beyond the scope of this chapter, but it is not hard to envision implications for crisis-management and political marketing. On one hand, firewalls between groups and campaigns potentially facilitate crises because they prohibit some essential communication that could otherwise be important for strategic advertising decisions. Campaign finance implications aside, for example, the communication literature noted above makes clear that during crises, messages should be consistent. Crises can also reinforce branding messages among various market segments by letting them know how the campaign might be affected and how core constituencies can help. Nonetheless, when multiple groups are competing over the same amount of advertising time and attempting to frame the same message for the same audience, uniformity and coordination would be ideal from a communication perspective, but it is not necessarily feasible or permissible in a campaign setting. Even when groups want to help their candidates, mixed messages and unintended consequences are a common problem.

Conclusions for Research and Practice

The study of campaign crises remains in its infancy. Political marketing is more developed, but still struggling to define concepts and establish relationships with related subfields and other disciplines. Much remains to be learned, and both researchers and practitioners stand to benefit. This chapter builds on the limited available foundation in the literature by considering how changes in the external environment, particularly recent changes in the campaign finance landscape, could affect crisis-management with an eye toward political marketing. The case study illustrations add new insights that do not receive substantial attention in the existing literature. Three themes are particularly noteworthy for future research, as well as for understanding practice. These themes include greater attention to: (1) potential connections between public policy developments and campaign crises; (2) the presence of new actors in the campaign environment that can attempt to create or exploit crises for candidates they oppose, particularly through political advertising; and (3) emerging strategic and tactical considerations.

The limited existing literature does not significantly contemplate the connection between public policy and crisis-management. The post-2010 developments discussed above show that policy changes can have a substantial impact on the campaign environment. Of course, legislative votes and other policy matters have always been a component of campaigning, but a policy issue that dramatically reshapes the campaign environment for all candidates is rare.

For this chapter's interest in theory-building, *Citizens United* provides an opportunity to explore how this major legal development—a public policy change—affected both the "rules" by which political marketers had to abide, and how the presence of new money and spenders—a political change—affected political communication. Importantly, the chapter does not suggest that *Citizens United* was a policy or political crisis. The major change it represented, however, did fundamentally alter the campaign environment—from policy and political perspectives—in ways that are reminiscent of the literature on campaign crises. Research on crisis-management in various areas of public policy (see, for example, Boin and 't Hart 2003; Birkland and Nath 2000), along with work encouraging more research on political marketing in the policy process (Lees-Marshment 2012; Cosgrove 2012), might provide helpful foundations for future research on connections between crisis-management, political marketing, and public policy.

From an electoral perspective, *Citizens United* and its aftermath dramatically changed the campaign environment for every federal candidate (and many state and local candidates). The decision didn't necessarily affect the outcome of elections for all those candidates. Indeed, many observers wondered if the substantial spending among some groups was wasted after their preferred candidates lost, despite super PACs and 501(c) organizations spending more than an estimated $1 billion on advertising. Super PAC American Crossroads and its 501(c)(4) affiliate Crossroads GPS was especially criticized for allegedly making poor investments (Bykowicz and Fitzgerald 2012).[4] The fact that these and other groups' activities were not decisive, however, is likely of little comfort to the candidates they opposed, often through massive broadcast advertising expenditures. Altogether, super PAC American Crossroads and its 501(c)(4) affiliate Crossroads GPS alone reported spending $175.7 million in independent expenditures during the 2012 election cycle.[5]

This brings us to the second point—that super PACs and new, or newly emboldened, 501(c) organizations entered the campaign environment after 2010 (Garrett 2012) and brought with them another source of uncertainty and potential crisis in the campaign environment. Outside spending of various forms has been a component of campaigns since the 1970s. At least since that time, campaigns have had to actively consider the possibility of large opposition spending from these groups or individuals. Indeed, political professionals consider outside attacks as potential crises (Garrett 2010).

Thus, to some extent, the groups that emerged post–*Citizens United* are "more of the same" as has long been the case. Nonetheless, the extent to which super PACs and 501(c)s permit the aggregation of funds should not be underestimated. The financial sway a relatively small number of groups obtained in the short time between 2010 and 2012 has also been well documented (see, for example, Wesleyan Media Project 2012).

Third, typical crisis-management tactics and strategies might require modification with respect to campaign finance issues. Interestingly, although political professionals otherwise report that that they try to avoid signaling potential crises whenever possible (Garrett 2010: Chapter 3), the DSCC fundraising example above suggests that fundraising tactics provide an exception. Even if a campaign did not really believe a financial crisis would occur, it could be advantageous to motivate donors by signaling crises. In addition, although low fundraising totals can signal crises (Garrett 2010), perhaps fundraising *appeals* (but not results) receive tactical latitude.

Practitioners are still learning how to adjust to the post–*Citizens United* environment. It is nonetheless clear that political professionals are keenly aware of the potential new "outside" spending—whether from super PACs or 501(c) organizations—have for shaping and disrupting the campaign environment. This has both offensive and defensive implications. Perhaps most obviously, the post–*Citizens United* environment provides an outlet for super PACs, 501(c)s, or even corporations and unions themselves to support or oppose candidates. Not all opposition for a campaign will rise to crisis. Importantly, however, because political professionals emphasize that they must always be on guard for crises and potential crises (Garrett 2010), it stands to reason that the unlimited new sources of spending post–*Citizens United* will make political professionals all the more vigilant. Particularly if a group chooses to explicitly call for a candidate's election or defeat—as opposed to more general policy advocacy (i.e., "issue advocacy" in campaign finance parlance)—it can make the difference in winning or losing on Election Day.

At the very least, the presence of new money and new players post–*Citizens United* means that political professionals and the candidates they support face a more complex and uncertain campaign environment than in the past. For political marketing purposes, that uncertainty can include everything from when to buy advertising time to identifying groups that might air opposing ads. There is every indication that political professionals are well aware of that potential looking ahead. In fact, just months after the 2012 campaigns concluded, Karl Rove and other prominent Republicans announced the formation of a new super PAC, the Conservative Victory Fund, designed to play a substantial role in vetting future candidates. Tellingly for the purposes of this chapter, much of the motivation behind the group was reportedly to avoid potentially choosing crisis-prone candidates who campaign operatives believed could win primaries but might face difficulty in general elections (see, for example, Zeleny 2013). It appears that the connection between crises, campaigns, and money is ripe for future research.

Disclaimer

The views represented in this chapter are those of the author and not necessarily those of the Congressional Research Service or any institution with which the author is affiliated.

Notes

1 Source: FEC totals in its "2008 Presidential Campaign Finance Map," at www.fec.gov/disclosurep/pnational.do;jsessionid=6C1A0BE6E9067BAA8D21AE40671B1675.worker1, accessed February 9, 2012.
2 Bold text as per original email.
3 As political committees, super PACs report all their receipts and expenditures to the Federal Election Commission (FEC); 501(c) organizations report independent expenditures and other advertisements known as "electioneering communications." However, 501(c) spending that falls outside these categories could go undisclosed.
4 Source: Independent expenditure data come from author analysis of FEC data at www.fec.gov/fecviewer/CandidateCommitteeDetail.do, accessed February 9, 2013.
5 Source: Author totals of independent expenditures reported to the FEC at www.fec.gov/fecviewer/CandidateCommitteeDetail.do, accessed February 9, 2012.

References

Birkland, T.A., & Nath, R. (2000). Business and political dimensions in disaster management. *Journal of Public Policy, 20*(3), 275–303.

Boin, A., & 't Hart, P. (2003). Public leadership in times of crisis: Mission impossible. *Public Administration Review, 63*(5), 544–553.

Burton, M., & Shea, D. (2003). *Campaign Mode: Strategic Vision in Congressional Elections.* Lanham, MD: Rowman & Littlefield.

Bykowicz, J., & Fitzgerald, A. (2012, November 8). Rove biggest super-PAC loser, Trump says waste of money. Bloomberg.com. www.bloomberg.com/news/2012-11-08/rove-biggestsuper-pac-loser-trump-says-waste-of-money.html

Citizens United v. Federal Election Commission. (2010). 130 S.Ct. (slip opinion).

Coombs, W.T. (1998). An analytic framework for crisis situations: Better responses from a better understanding of the situation. *Journal of Public Relations Research, 10*(3), 177–191.

Corrado, A., Mann, T.E., Ortiz, D.R., & Potter, T. (2005). *The new campaign finance sourcebook.* Washington, DC: Brookings Institution Press.

Cosgrove, K.M. (2012). Political branding in the modern age: Effective strategies, tools and techniques. In Jennifer Lees-Marshment (Ed.), *Routledge handbook of political marketing* (pp. 107–123). New York, NY: Routledge.

Democratic Senatorial Campaign Committee. (2010, February 27). The president needs us. Fundraising e-mail signed by John Kerry to listserv.

Dimock, M.A., & Jacobson, G.C. 1995. Checks and choices: The house bank scandal's impact on voters in 1992. *Journal of Politics, 57*(3), 1143–1159.

Dulio, D.A. (2004). *For better or worse? How political consultants are changing elections in the United States.* Albany, NY: SUNY Press.

Fearn-Banks, K. (2007). *Crisis communication: A casebook approach.* Mahwah, NJ: Lawrence Erlbaum Associates.

Garrett, R.S. (2010). *Campaign crises: Detours on the road to Congress.* Boulder, CO: Lynne Rienner Publishers.

Garrett, R.S. (2012). Seriously funny: Understanding campaign finance policy through the Colbert super PAC. *Saint Louis University Law Journal, 56*(3), 711–723.

Garrett, R.S. (2014). Money, politics, and policy: Campaign finance before and after Citizens United. In J.A. Thurber & C.J. Nelson (Eds.), *Campaigns and Elections American Style* (4th ed.). Boulder, CO: Westview.

Groseclose, T., & Krehbiel, K. (1994). Golden parachutes, rubber checks, and strategic retirements from the 102nd House. *American Journal of Political Science, 38,* 75–99.

Guion, D.T., Scammon, D.L., & Borders, A.L. (2007). Weathering the storm: A social marketing perspective on disaster preparedness and response with lessons from Hurricane Katrina. *Journal of Public Policy & Marketing, 26*(1), 20–32.

Herrnson, P.S., Deering, C.J., & Wilcox, C. (Eds.). (2013). *Interest groups unleashed.* Los Angeles, CA: Sage/CQ Press.

Hruby, P. (2012, July 18). Embracing the not-so-dark arts. *The Washington Times,* p. C10.

Johansen, H.P.M. (2005). Political marketing: More than persuasive techniques, an organizational perspective. *Journal of Political Marketing, 4*(4), 85–105.

Kessler, G. (2012, November 11). Did negative ads work in presidential race? *The Washington Post,* p. A31.

Lamb, C. (2011, December 11). Sex claims terminate Hermanator's presidential bid. *Sunday Times* (London), p. 33.

La Raja, R.J. (2008). *Small change: Money, political parties, and campaign finance reform.* Ann Arbor, MI: University of Michigan Press.

Lees-Marshment, J. (2009). *Political marketing: Principles and applications.* New York, NY: Routledge.
Lees-Marshment, J. (2012). Conclusion: New directions in political marketing practice, political marketing and democracy, and future trends. In Jennifer Lees-Marshment (Ed.), *Routledge handbook of political marketing* (pp. 366–386). New York, NY: Routledge.
Magleby, D.B., & Corrado, A. (Eds.). (2011). *Financing the 2008 election.* Washington, DC: Brookings Institution Press.
Mayer, J. (2012, August 27). Schmooze or lose. *The New Yorker,* pp. 24–31.
Medvic, S.K. (2001). *Political consultants in U.S. congressional elections.* Columbus, OH: Ohio State University Press.
Medvic, S.K. (2006). Understanding campaign strategy: "Deliberate priming" and the role of professional political consultants. *Journal of Political Marketing, 5*(1–2), 11–32.
Newman, B.I. (2012). The role of marketing in politics: Ten years later. *Journal of Political Marketing, 11*(1–2), 1–3.
Osuagwu, L. (2008). Political marketing: Conceptualisation, dimensions and research agenda. *Marketing Intelligence & Planning, 26*(7), 793–810.
Peters, J.G., & Welch, S. (1978). Political corruption in America: A search for definitions and a theory. *American Political Science Review, 72*(3), 974–84.
Roarty, A. (2012, September 22). Divide and conquer. *National Journal.* www.nationaljournal.com/magazine/priorities-usa-the-little-pac-that-could-20120920
SpeechNow.org v. FEC. 599 F.3d 686 (D.C. Cir. 2010).
Steger, W.P., Kelly, S.Q., & Wrighton, J.M. (2006). Campaigns and political marketing in political science context. *Journal of Political Marketing, 5*(1–2), 1–10.
Van Heerde, H., Helsen, K., & Dekimpe, M.G. (2007). The impact of a product-harm crisis on marketing effectiveness. *Marketing Science, 26*(2), 230–245.
Welch, S., & Hibbing, J.R. (1997). The effects of charges of corruption on voting behavior in congressional elections, 1982–1990. *Journal of Politics, 59*(1), 226–239.
Wesleyan Media Project. (2012). Presidential ads 70 percent negative in 2012, up from 9 percent in 2008. Press release. http://mediaproject.wesleyan.edu/2012/05/02/jump-in-negativity/
Zeleny, J. (2013, February 7). New Rove effort has G.O.P. aflame. *The New York Times,* p. A15.

14
COMMUNICATING CONTEMPORARY LEADERSHIP IN GOVERNMENT

Barack Obama

Edward Elder

Overview of the Topic

Barack Hussein Obama II was elected the forty-fourth president of the United States on a tidal wave of public support in 2008. Among a sea of compliments, Obama was internationally praised for his political brand and his verbal skills. However, assuming office in January 2009 introduced President Obama to a whole new set of social, political and logistical constraints he did not have to deal with beforehand. Studies in political marketing suggest this underpins the reasoning behind a relatively new trend in Western democracies: political leaders gaining political office using market-oriented behavior, but losing their positive public image once there. It is suggested that being in government drastically intensifies the dilemma between whether leaders should lead or follow the opinions of the public that elected them. Notably, if governing leaders want to lead, and thus achieve notable change, they inevitably have to make many decisions that contradict public opinion. For this reason, among others, governing leaders have found it difficult to maintain high levels of public support over time. However, recent research also suggests that governing leaders may be able to maintain a better, more market-oriented image if they use communication strategies that emphasizes listening, reflexivity and authenticity, while also promoting the attributes associated with strong leadership. This chapter examines if and how contemporary political leaders are adopting new political communication strategies during their time in office in an attempt to alleviate some of the problems faced by their recent predecessors.

To do this, the chapter analyzes President Obama's verbal communication around two major policies introduced during his first term in office: government-funded economic investment through the American Recovery and Reinvestment Act (known as the "Recovery Act"), and health care reform through the Patient

Protection and Affordable Care Act (known as "Obamacare"). The chapter qualitatively analyzes Obama's verbal communication around these policies against a newly developed framework. This framework has been designed with the intention of suggesting how contemporary governing leaders should use communication to highlight the qualities associated with market-oriented behavior.

Review of Previous Literature

The growing importance of a political leader to the overall image and popularity of a political party has been stressed in political academia for some time (Foley 1993; Poguntke and Webb 2005). Subsequently, it has been argued that a market orientation needs to be embodied by a political leader both strategically and in communication (Lees-Marshment 2009: 216). But governing leaders are faced with difficult decisions and constraints not faced when attempting to gain office. This problem is compounded in the United States, where a lack of party unity within the decision-making process places limitations on the power of the president not faced by many other world leaders (Neustadt 1980; Elcock 2001). These variables can hinder the preservation of some traditional market-oriented qualities, most notably staying in touch with the public opinion while simultaneously showing strong leadership characteristics (Lees-Marshment and Lilleker 2005: 15–38; Ormrod 2006: 112–15).

In the field of political leadership, the dominant contemporary position on leadership decision making suggests that the greatest social benefit comes from strong yet open-minded leadership, suggesting that weak leadership contributes to government failures and leads to a lack of creativity and advancement, while foolhardy leadership can cause instability or a catastrophe due to a lack of thinking before acting (Masciulli, Molchanov et al. 2009: 3). However, there are times when governing leaders do have to lead in order to achieve notable change. This may involve making decisions that run counter to the greater public voice. Making such decisions can have a negative impact on a leader's public image, and underpins a general trend of governing political leaders in Western democracies over the past 20 years: gaining power after adopting a market orientation, but losing their positive public image once in office. While the resulting drop in support is not new in the study of political popularity (Heppell 2008), new research in political marketing suggests this has occurred simultaneously with a decline in a governing leader's perceived qualities associated with having a market orientation (Lees-Marshment 2009).

It can be argued that communication and image management are two of the most important aspects of market-oriented behavior (Scammell 1999: 729; Temple and Savigny 2010) and political leadership in general (Elgie 1995; Semetko 1996; Helms 2008). Therefore, it is not surprising that growing evidence suggests that the problems many governing leaders faced in maintaining a market-oriented image were intensified by their use of traditional communication strategies while in office. These strategies were designed to highlight positive leadership attributes while attempting to disregard negative ones—in essence, using communication that suggests, "I am the leader, I have all the information needed to make a decision, you must follow me on this, I will persuade you to see you are wrong and I am right." Such communication strategies lie within the framework of what might be expected from governing leaders' communication (Scammell 2007: 186). Unfortunately, such communication strategies no longer work in an age where the relationship between political elites and the public is more business oriented. Indeed, such communication strategies hinder a governing leader's image of being in touch with the general public, a key component of an effective market-oriented strategy (Lees-Marshment 2008: 525).

Very little attention has been paid to contemporary political communication in the field of political marketing (Lloyd 2009). Where communication is examined, it is often done without great detail (see O'Shaughnessy 1990; O'Cass 1996). Furthermore, it is often done with a focus on political campaign communication (Newman 1994; Steger, Kelly et al. 2006), a common trait throughout the various sub-fields of political science (Nimmo 1970; Kaid and Johnston 2001). However, a few recent studies do help us understand what non-campaign market-oriented communication for a governing leader might look like.

Robinson suggests that a candidate will present his or her market orientation through communication that shows target audience identification; sense and response to voter needs; voter relations management; offer in exchange (what the public get for their vote); and a competitor orientation (Robinson 2006). Lees-Marshment suggests market-oriented governments should demonstrate a sense of and response to voter needs with images; show that they are offering something new; identify and target the competition and show a concern to increase market share; and maintain relationships with traditional voters (Lees-Marshment 2009: 218). Scammell highlights the importance of being less defensive and more open, honest and reflective about the variables of leadership in office. She highlights the positive image that can come from deliberately letting the public vicariously let out their aggressions through media texts rather than at the ballot box, as well as the need for personal conviction and leadership strength, without being stubborn (Scammell 2007: 185–6).

In essence, this recent research suggests that governing leaders do not have to blindly follow public opinion to be perceived as in touch, as long as their communication suggests they are talking with the public, rather than at the public. Such practices also allow governing leaders to show the vital qualities associated with strong, decisive and honest leadership (see Gould 2007: 21), while also allowing the leader to highlight a connection between themselves and the public. Finally, the research highlights the fact that such communication strategies allow a governing leader to be open and honest about the variables of office. This general change in voter-leader communication exchange can be seen in Figure 14.1.

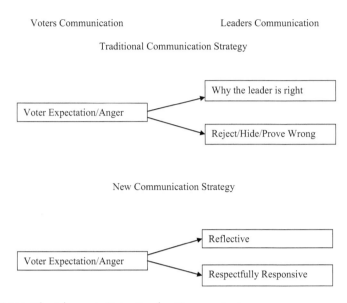

FIGURE 14.1 The Change in Voter-Leader Communication

However, this previous research does not provide a clear and comprehensive framework about communicating market-oriented qualities as a leader in government. Robinson and Scammell's research focuses primarily on campaign communication. But the influence of political marketing extends beyond an election campaign, with many of the techniques associated with political marketing evident throughout the electoral cycle (Ormrod and Savigny 2012: 488). In the field of political communication it has been observed that non-campaign communication often has a very different goal to campaign communication, and therefore must be analyzed differently (Goldstein and Ridout 2004: 208). Also, while Lees-Marshment's framework looks at non-campaign communication, it is not comprehensive. Furthermore, it does not focus on leadership. In relation to an examination of US leadership in particular, this is an important variable. Therefore, further theorizing is needed in order to create an understanding of alternative communication approaches by market-oriented leaders in government.

Theoretical Framework

This section of the chapter outlines a new theoretical framework for how a governing leader might try to communicate with the public in order to show his or her market-oriented qualities. It was designed by synthesizing the relevant aspects of the three previous relevant models, while also being altered on the back of other relevant political marketing, political communication and political leadership literature. This was done to understand what have been the common problems with market-oriented governing leaders' communication, what variables they faced, and how these issues can be resolved. This framework suggests five major qualities a governing leader should try to implicitly and explicitly communicate in order to maintain the image of having market-oriented qualities, as outlined in Table 14.1.

TABLE 14.1 Framework for Market-Oriented Governing Leaders' Communication (Summarized)

Quality Shown through Rhetoric	Communicate through Rhetoric by . . .
Listening	• Respectfully acknowledging concerns and criticisms. • Providing potential solutions for possible public concerns. • Talking about positive working relationships with political elites from both major parties. • Communicating an understanding of target audience.

Leading	• Communicating delivery.
	• Using a consistent message that promotes an image of competence.
	• Communicating ideological positioning.
	• Using words and phrases associated with strength such as:
	  ◦ Determined
	  ◦ Up for the challenge
	  ◦ I will not stand by and let...

Honesty/Authenticity/ Trustworthiness	• Communicating drawbacks of decisions.
	• Communicating a lack of delivery where applicable.
	• Being open about changes in position where applicable.
	• Talking about non-political personality.
	• Being open about scandals where applicable.
	• Communicating an openness to questioning.
	• Using inclusive pronouns such as:
	  ◦ We
	  ◦ Our
	  ◦ Us

Common Goals and Benefits of Decisions	• Focusing communication on how the decision will benefit the target audience rather than focusing on the problem(s) being resolved. • Highlighting an overall goal trying to be achieved that resonates with the target audience. • Communicating where delivery has not been met yet.
Social and Governmental Variables	• Communicating remorse and understanding for the long-term negative effects of decisions. • Talking about other potential options not chosen, and why this was. • Communicating reasoning behind the decisions made. • Outlining the decision making process, including the variables involved.

Listening (Responsive, Reflective and In Touch)

While it is not always possible to follow public opinion, respectfully acknowledging opposing viewpoints through communication may help a governing leader present an image of listening and being in touch (see Lees-Marshment 2011: 91). Therefore, a governing leader should make sure he or she communicates such qualities. Such communication not only implies that a leader has his or her ear to the ground, but should also help promote an emotional connection between the governing leader and the media audience. This may be achieved by respectfully acknowledging and responding to common concerns and criticisms; by providing potential solutions for possible public concerns; by talking about positive working relationships with political elites from both major parties; and through the use of rhetoric that suggests the leader's understanding of the target audience. Such communication techniques may imply that the governing leader is communicating with the public rather than at the public. It may also give the public the opportunity to get any frustrations out in the moment rather than on election day (Gould 2007: 21).

Leadership

While governing leaders need to present themselves as being in touch with public opinion, they also need to show strong leadership characteristics. When governing leaders have blindly followed public opinion too closely they have been criticized accordingly (Langmaid, Trevail, & Hayman 2006: 26). Such practices show a lack of true leadership and mental strength in a position that requires it (Masciulli, Molchanov et al. 2009). Therefore, governing leaders need to communicate mental strength, competence and the ability to make decisions that may be necessary, even if they do not correlate with the greater public voice. Such qualities may be communicated through the use of a consistent message that promotes leadership competence and establishes a clear leadership brand and direction; through communicating delivery in a clear and concise way; through communicating a personal ideological facet to decision making; and by consistently using words and phrases associated with strong leadership characteristics such as "determined," "up for the challenge," and "I will not stand by and let. . . ." Such communication may help imply that a governing leader has the competence and strength to perform well in the job he or she holds. It may also grant the leader the public trust to enact policies that could otherwise be damaging to his or her image (Canes-Wrone, Herron et al. 2001: 533; Fox and Shotts 2009: 1226).

Honesty/Authenticity/Trustworthiness

Market-oriented governing leaders may need to communicate qualities such as being honest, trustworthy and authentic. They also need to communicate personal information that not only presents the governing leader as a politician, but as a personality as well. Such qualities are becoming ever more important to a governing leader's image as the general public becomes less attached to particular parties and ideologies, and judges governing leaders' job-related qualities more on their personal character (Rosenberg, Kahn et al. 1991: 346; Pharr and Putnam 2000). With a market-oriented strategy promoting a closer link between the party and the public it is important to communicate these qualities, as it enables greater trust in a governing leader (Lilleker 2006: 79). This may be achieved by using communication that shows the leader being open about scandals; communicating the leader's non-political personality; talking about the leader's non-political personality; communicating an openness to questioning; communicating the potential drawbacks to decisions; communicating openly about any change in position the leader has had on an issue; and by using inclusive pronouns such as "we" and "us." Such communication strategies may help a governing leader present a personality that the public can connect to, providing the leader with greater public trust.

Common Goals and Benefits of Decisions

A common trend for governing leaders when communicating why a decision has been made is to focus on the problem(s) they are attempting to resolve. However, such communication can easily have negative connotations. As a result, such communication can spawn defensive reactions from segments of the public, especially those groups with a vested interest in the issue of discussion. Therefore, a governing leader should move away from such communication. Instead, a governing leader should choose to highlight the benefits the public should receive as a result of the decision, or potential decision, the governing leader is promoting. The governing leader should also communicate the general goals that they are trying to achieve. Such communication may help the leader give the audience a greater understanding of why the leader feels like he or she has to make a particular decision, while limiting any negative connotations. Also, by communicating end goals that resonate with the public, the governing leader in question has a greater chance of further establishing an emotional connection with the public. Furthermore, a governing leader may also want to communicate information about where he or she has not delivered, or has not delivered yet, in order to manage public expectations.

Social and Governmental Variables

A common trend in governing leaders' communication around potential or confirmed decisions is to communicate the economic or logistical variables involved, especially when decisions go against dominant public opinion. However, such communication is hard to execute successfully. Such communication can easily be (mis)interpreted by the audience as a governing leader expressing a feeling of arrogance—that he or she does not need to listen to public input. However, by giving the public an inside look into the decision-making process, communicating such information effectively can help make the public feel as though they are part of the decision-making process. Such communication once again emphasizes the point that the governing leader in question is talking with members of the public rather than at them. This may be achieved by outlining the decision-making process, including the variables involved; talking about other potential options and why they were not chosen; communicating remorse and understanding for those who may be affected negatively in some way by a decision; and communicating the reasoning behind the decisions made. Such communication may give the public an understanding of why a leader may have made a decision that goes against dominant public opinion, allowing the public to have a greater level of respect for the decision, even if they disagree with it. The next section will apply this framework to the case of President Barack Obama.

Empirical Illustration: Barack Obama

The framework for market-oriented governing leaders' communication was used to analyze the verbal communication of President Barack Obama in over 150 individual media texts. These included speeches/town hall discussions, television interviews, widely circulated quotes in newspapers, and online video blogs. Analysis was concentrated around two key issues during his first term in office: government-funded economic investment through the American Recovery and Reinvestment Act (known as the "Recovery Act") and health care reform through the Patient Protection and Affordable Care Act (known as "Obamacare"). These two issues were chosen because of the attention they garnered and their effect on the public, and because they manifested strong opposition.

Specifically, the analysis took a grounded theory approach. The process involved entering the designed framework into a qualitative data analysis (QDA) computer program. The framework consisted of the five general qualities noted above, as well as multiple "technique" sub-headings under each quality that suggested how that quality might be communicated. Transcripts of Obama's communication in media texts, such as those media texts noted, were also entered into the QDA program. The transcripts were then qualitatively analyzed using the framework, coding any occurrences of the communication techniques suggested, as well as new techniques that occurred often enough to be considered a "common pattern" (Glaser and Strauss 1967).

Through the findings, the case study of this chapter outlines if and how Obama is using communication that highlights the market-oriented qualities he suggested he entered office with (Obama 2008). The following analysis will highlight the most interesting and important findings.

Listening (Responsive, Reflective and In Touch)

In general terms, the analyzed material suggested that Obama effectively used verbal communication to suggest he was in touch with the American general public. However, suggesting a leader is "listening" to the public, in particular, is probably most effectively shown through communication that suggests a respectful acknowledgement of concerns and criticisms. In this area, Obama's communication can best be described as mixed. On the issue of Obamacare, the president's communication often followed the advice of the framework. For example, one of the more prevalent criticisms of Obamacare was that it was a government takeover of American health care. Obama addressed this issue in a number of outlets, including during a town hall meeting in Portsmouth, New Hampshire:

> Now, I recognize . . . you raise a legitimate concern. People say . . . how can a private company compete against the government? And my answer is that if the private insurance companies are providing a good bargain, and if the public option has to be self-sustaining—meaning taxpayers aren't subsidizing it, but it has to run on charging premiums and providing good services and a good network of doctors, just like any other private insurer would do—then I think private insurers should be able to compete. (Obama 2009c)

As a typical example of Barack Obama's communication in response to this criticism, several facets of this piece of communication might promote the idea that Obama respectfully acknowledged public concern. First and foremost, Obama notes the concern, and does not disregard it. Rather, Obama acknowledged the concern as "legitimate." Obama then asked the critical question again, communicating that he was willing to put himself in the place of a person who would ask the question. Furthermore, Obama took the time to explain why he disagreed with this argument. In doing so, Obama may have been communicating some level of respect for the opposing argument without agreeing with it. This communication, and others like it, suggested a healthy level of respect for criticism.

However, on the issue of the Recovery Act, Obama's communication was often much more disregarding of criticism and concerns. A common theme in Obama's communication around the Recovery Act issue suggested those who criticized the plan were doing so for political gain or because they didn't have any better ideas. A short yet useful example can be found in Obama's rhetoric on this issue in an online video blog released on July 11, 2009:

> Now, I realize that when we passed this Recovery Act, there were those who felt that doing nothing was somehow an answer. Today, some of those same critics are already judging the effort a failure although they have yet to offer a plausible alternative. (Obama 2009e)

There are several key indicators in this short quote that suggest Obama had a lack of respect for criticisms about the Recovery Act. Obama almost sarcastically noted that the idea of doing nothing is "somehow" an answer. He also suggested those who criticize the plan "have yet to offer a plausible alternative." Such communication implies that Obama disregarded those who disagreed as either criticizing for the sake of criticizing or having incomprehensible alternative solutions. Obama also called those who criticized the plan "critics" rather than, for example, "people who are worried." The label "critic" in the context of this quote may be interpreted as derogatory, or to at least have a negative connotation. Lastly, Obama noted that these people are "already" judging the effort. Such communication may be interpreted as suggesting that Obama believes the "critics" should not have the right to judge the decision at the time. None of these aspects of this one piece of communication suggest a healthy regard for criticisms and concerns. Such communication was present throughout much of the communication analyzed around this issue. While such communication was often directed at political elites, this was almost never explicitly noted. In doing so, such communication may be interpreted as an insult to members of the public who have concerns about this issue.

Leadership

The analyzed material suggested that Barack Obama successfully used verbal communication to imply having strong leadership characteristics. Notably, around both the issues analyzed, Obama's communication suggested "delivery" was substantial. However, what is even more noteworthy is how comparatively different Obama's communication on delivery was between the two issues.

A major theme in Obama's communication around Obamacare was the message that "we must and will get this done." This is not surprising considering that many of the media texts analyzed around this issue were created prior to the passing of the act. Therefore, during the earlier stages of communication on this issue, a common theme in Obama's communication was his determination to see this act get passed. This can be seen in the quote below, taken from Obama's speech on healthcare reform to Congress in September 2009:

> Now is the season for action. Now is when we must bring the best ideas of both parties together, and show the American people that we can still do what we were sent here to do. Now is the time to deliver on health care. (Obama 2009a)

Such communication was often used in Obama's final remarks during a speech or press conference prior to the bill being passed. In such communication Obama would specifically note his desire to "deliver on health care." Obama would verbally communicate this message with a rather stern tone, thus further implying the determination he felt. Such communication may have helped Obama show leadership characteristics in two specific ways. First, by communicating his determination to pass health care reform, Obama may have implied personal conviction and strength. Such communication may also have helped Obama present himself as a leader who will attempt to deliver on the promises he made prior to being elected. This is especially important in the American context, where being president does not provide the same level of authority to deliver on promises that governing leaders in unitary systems enjoy.

While much of Obama's communication around Obamacare came before the act was passed, most of Obama's communication analyzed around the Recovery Act came after the passing of the initial and most substantial part of the act. As a result, much of Obama's communication in this area directly suggested delivery as a result of the decision Obama and the government made:

> The first thing we had to do was just stop the bleeding, stabilize the financial system. . . . And we have done that. . . . In January . . . we lost 750,000 jobs. . . . Now we've seen eight consecutive months of private sector job growth because of the policies we've put in place. (Obama 2010b)

In the quote above Obama explicitly notes that it is because of the Recovery Act that the American economy was doing better than 18 months earlier. While Obama did not explicitly partner this delivery with himself, he did imply a connection. Obama noted that these were policies "we've put in place." Obviously, when Obama used the term "we" he was including himself in the collective. More importantly, Obama implied his connection to the delivery by implicitly separating and defining two periods of time—the month he took office, when the economic outlook was bad, and a time period when he was in office, when the economic indicators were more encouraging. Such a communication strategy may implicitly suggest that these goals were achieved under Obama's watch, even if he does not explicitly associate the delivery with himself. Such communication by Obama may be decoded as evidence that he is a competent leader, able to deliver in tough situations.

Honesty/Authenticity/Trustworthiness

The analyzed material suggested that Obama's ability to communicate honesty, trustworthiness, and authenticity overall can best be described as mixed. This is because, between the two issues, there was a major difference in the amount of communication that suggested this quality. In the communication analyzed on Obamacare, 7.6 percent of all coded material fits into this category. On the other hand, only 4.3 percent of all coded material on the Recovery Act fits into this category.

This comparative difference was no better seen than in communication on Obama's non-political personality. In communication around the Recovery Act, the analyzed material suggested that Obama spoke little of his non-political personality outside of two backyard town halls in Columbus, Ohio, and Fairfax, Virginia. On the other hand, in a majority of longer media texts dedicated to Obamacare, the president would communicate some aspect of his non-political personality. Obama would often relate this issue back to his own life by linking the issue to the struggles his mother had with the health care system when she was battling cancer:

> And this is personal for me. I'll never forget my own mother, as she fought cancer in her final months, having to worry about whether the insurance company would refuse to pay for her treatment. . . . If it could happen to her, it could happen to any one of us. (Obama 2009d)

By communicating a story that affects him directly, Obama may have been able to get the viewer to feel as though they were gaining a better understanding of Barack Obama as a real person rather than simply a political figure. Such a connection is often linked to feelings about whether that person is trustworthy (Lilleker 2006: 79). Thus, by communicating a real life example of how the issue of discussion actually affects him personally, Obama may have been lending validity to the idea that he can be trusted. In doing so, the American public may be more willing to accept a polarizing policy decision such as Obamacare.

With such potential benefits possibly being available with such communication, it is interesting that such a little proportion of Obama's communication on the Recovery Act did so. This finding may merely be circumstantial. However, it may be due to the fact that a majority of Obama's communication on the Recovery Act came after a decision had been made, while most of the communication analyzed on Obamacare came before the act had been passed. As a result Obama may have felt as though he needed to spend more time selling the benefits of the Recovery Act and where the Obama administration had delivered, rather than focusing on connecting with the public. This difference in communication may also be due to the difference in issue type. While the Recovery Act clearly fits into the realm of an economic issue, Obamacare is very much a social issue. With this being the case, Obama may have been trying to appeal to the general American public on more of an emotive level on the social policy, while trying to explain things more logistically on the economic issue.

Common Goals and Benefits of Decisions

The analyzed material suggested that Barack Obama successfully communicated the benefits of decisions as well as goals that would resonate with the American public. Notably, on each issue Obama was able to use communication to establish a consistent theme of benefits he believed the public would receive, stemming from the decisions made.

However, in communication on both issues, Obama may have communicated the benefits of these decisions more than was necessary, resulting in an overall communication strategy that seemed too "traditional" in comparison to what the framework for market-oriented governing leaders' communication really suggests. In the analysis stage of this research, rhetoric was coded under the heading of "communicating benefits of decisions" more than any other single heading by a large margin; 16.6 percent of all coded material suggested Obama explicitly communicated the benefits of the decisions made. Furthermore, another 9.2 percent of all coded material suggested Obama explicitly communicated the problems that would be fixed with these decisions. That is a total of 25.6 percent of all coded material on "benefits" alone.

It is understandable that Obama would dedicate a large portion of communication to selling the decisions made. However, this overwhelming dedication to such communication seemed to taint many media texts that strongly communicated the market-oriented qualities suggested in the framework. In other words, the lasting impression left on the audience by the media text may have been that it was "Obama selling his decisions" rather than "Obama talking about the issues with the American public."

Such an impression may have been justified. When looking at some of the media texts designed to present Obama as a listening leader, the communication came across as superficial—designed to look market oriented without actually being market oriented. The backyard town hall that Obama hosted in Falls Church, Virginia, is a good example of this. At face value the text presents Obama discussing and answering questions on Obamacare with typical members of the American public in a typical American backyard. However, when looking at the actual details of the verbiage, the elements are not as market oriented as they initially seem. The basic series of events seen in the media text are highlighted in Table 14.2.

TABLE 14.2 Barack Obama—Backyard Town Hall—Falls Church, VA—September 22, 2010, Highlights of Media Text

1. Obama listens to the home owner talk about his struggles with the old health care system and how the reforms have helped and will help him.
2. Obama speaks to audience members about the aspects of the reforms that are about to come into effect and how these reforms will benefit them.
3. Obama calls on several people whom he has talked to in the past to tell their stories about how the reforms have helped them.
4. Obama invites other members of the audience to share their stories or ask any questions, which only serve as triggers for Obama to talk about the benefits of the reforms more.

Source: Obama 2010a

While the communication looked market oriented, it clearly was not. Obama did go out and interact with middle America in a middle-American setting. Yet the text suggests, rightly or wrongly, it was only with middle Americans who agreed with him. In doing so, the actual rhetoric in the text was overwhelmingly being used to sell Obamacare. Such a problem with communication could be found throughout many larger media texts analyzed on both issues of this case study. Such communication does not follow the advice of the framework. In dedicating so much attention to communicating the positive attributes of the policies Obama is essentially tainting his general overall communication strategy. The main goal of the communication still seems to be "selling" the ideals of Obama to the public—in essence, talking at those watching rather than talking with them, implying that Obama is trying to simulate market-oriented behavior rather than actually being market oriented.

Social and Governmental Variables

The analyzed material suggested that Barack Obama was somewhat successful in communicating social and governmental variables. In particular, Obama's communication on both issues analyzed suggested rhetoric on the decision-making process was consistent, but not always substantial. Interestingly, similar to his communication on delivery noted earlier, Obama's communication in this area was comparatively different between the two issues.

On the issue of Obamacare, the president's communication on the decision-making process was often very detailed. For example, when hosting a town hall meeting in Shaker Heights, Ohio, Obama clarified a statement he had made about when the bill would be passed:

> I do think that sometimes people get the idea (that) . . . I had said, let's get this done by August. . . . [W]hat I was referring to is, let's get bills voted out of the House and the Senate by August. That still means that we'd have to come back in the fall; we'd have to reconcile the differences between the Senate bill and the House bill; have a new bill; it would go back to the Senate and the House again to be voted on; then finally come to my desk. Our target date is to get this done by the fall. (Obama 2009b)

Obama's communication outlined the remaining process needed to achieve health care reform. In doing so, Obama highlighted the complexity of the process the bill needed to go through before it could be passed. Furthermore, Obama emphasized the difficulties that come from reconciling bills coming from the House and the Senate. In essence, by communicating these variables in front of the bill being passed, Obama attempted to manage public expectations. Obama gave himself the opportunity to do that by using detailed communication, further highlighted by the following part of the speech (not cited here) where he referred to the length of time it would take to fully implement the bill once it had been passed.

Unfortunately, in communication on the issue of the Recovery Act, while Obama did communicate the decision-making process, it was often much less detailed than communication around Obamacare. For example, when speaking about the issue during a press conference, Obama noted:

> [M]y expectation is that the energy committees or other relevant committees in both the House and the Senate are going to be moving forward a strong energy package. . . . It will be authorized. We'll get it done. And I will sign it. (Obama, quoted in Dinan and Ward 2009)

This quote is indicative of Obama's communication on the decision-making process during media texts dedicated to Recovery Act communication. And, as seen in many of the other examples found, the quote above seems to suggest Obama's main intended message in this communication was that he was "getting the job done" rather than intending to communicate the decision-making process itself. This lack of in-depth communication may have been a result of the fact that most of the communication on this issue came after the initial American Recovery and Reinvestment Act had been passed. As a result, it is possible that Obama felt as though he did not need to communicate the decision-making process in great depth.

Summary of Obama's Market-Oriented Communication

When looking at the analysis of President Barack Obama's verbal communication through the framework for market-oriented governing leaders' communication there are several noteworthy findings. Overall Obama's use of communication that suggested he was in touch with the American public was good. However, in the key area of respecting criticism and concern, Obama's communication was very much dependent on the issue of analysis. What is not considered in this chapter, however, is the role the Republican opposition played in Obama's communication—in other words, what impact the Republican opposition's vocal criticisms played in shaping the public's criticisms and concerns, as well as Obama's responsiveness. Despite this, with the perception of being in touch with the public so important to a market-oriented image, Obama may still want to closer replicate his communication on Obamacare in communication during future polarizing issues' salient periods.

In saying this, Obama was able to communicate delivery in comparatively different ways around each issue. Obama was able to imply determination and personal conviction in his communication, suggesting a desire to deliver Obamacare. On the other hand, Obama was able to imply competent leadership through his communication of delivery on the Recovery Act after the act had been passed. In doing so, of all the areas suggested in the initial framework, this is the area in which Obama followed the intention of the initial framework for market-oriented governing leaders' communication the most.

The fact that so much more of Obama's communication on Obamacare was dedicated to communicating honesty, trustworthiness and authenticity compared to communication on the Recovery Act is telling. In saying that, Obama might be encouraged to highlight more of his non-political personality when talking about economic issues. Such communication can help establish a connection between a governing leader and the audience, helping the governing leader seem more trustworthy. This communication might come at the expense of communication dedicated to explaining the benefits of the decisions being made. Obama was effective in creating a consistent list of benefits around each of the decisions analyzed. However, the domination of such communication seemed to taint many media texts, making those media texts seem like advertisements for Obama's ideals rather than a stimulation or simulation of two-way communication between Obama and the American public. It may help Obama to dedicate less time to selling the decisions and dedicate more time communicating other aspects of his personal character. While doing so would mean less time communicating benefits, Obama's communication in this area may be more effective as a result, as it may be less likely to be interpreted as "selling."

Another interesting finding from the analysis of Obama's communication was that when it came to communicating social and governmental variables, he was more inclined to do so prior to a decision being finalized. While interesting, this is understandable considering this is the time when the public is likely to be interested in how and when a decision is going to be made. In essence, such communication can help a governing leader manage public expectations. This further suggests the framework needs to take into account whether the communication is taking place before or after a decision has been made.

It should be noted that there was very little evidence of communication that suggested Obama was being reflective. This was to be expected considering the communication on these two issues came early on in his time as president. Also, most of the analyzed communication came from a period when the issue was still fresh. Perhaps research into communication on such issues later in Obama's presidency would establish whether or not Obama shows the humbleness and reflective qualities suggested by the limited prior research in this area.

Overall, when analyzing Obama's verbal communication through the framework for market-oriented governing leaders' communication, the findings suggested strong signifiers of market-oriented communication. However, when looking at the most important and noteworthy ways to communicate the market-oriented qualities suggested by the framework for market-oriented governing leaders' communication, Obama's results were mixed.

Conclusions for Research and Practice

Political office introduces governing leaders to a whole new group of social, political and logistical variables. Such variables can drastically change the relationship market-oriented political leaders have with the public. Of note, in making necessary yet unpopular decisions, political leaders risk losing their positive public image. Indeed, the ability to appear to be listening while also being seen as a competent and trustworthy leader is a harder act in government. Growing evidence suggests that traditional communication strategies further exacerbate this problem, especially as the relationship between the political elite and the public becomes more business oriented. Simply telling the public that "I am the leader, I have the information that you don't have, I know best" is no longer an option. Therefore, governing leaders need to change their communication strategies in government in order to adapt to this change in the politician-voter relationship. That is why this chapter highlighted a framework that suggests how market-oriented governing leaders should communicate their market-oriented qualities, even in situations where they have to make polarizing decisions. Designed by synthesizing previous literature, the framework for market-oriented governing leaders' communication suggests a more responsive and reflective style of communication that also promotes their leadership credentials, their authenticity, their shared goals and benefits of decisions, as well as giving the audience an understanding of the variables around any particular decision.

Furthermore, this chapter highlights how important it is that governing leaders don't concentrate too heavily on only one quality. Such communication can taint the perceived purpose of their overall communication strategy, making it seem too "traditional." This finding also highlights the need to actually be market oriented to effectively present market-oriented communication, and thus a market-oriented image. With a lack of evidence found, this chapter also highlights either the inability or the unwillingness of contemporary governing leaders to be truly reflective about their decisions so close to the time of their implementation. While governing leaders are more willing to use non-traditional communication that suggests market-oriented qualities, they still fail to use some of the most useful techniques suggested by the framework. It is encouraging that contemporary governing leaders' overall communication is becoming more market oriented, reflecting their actions before and during their time in office. However, if contemporary market-oriented governing leaders around the world fail to abide by some of the most fundamental suggestions about how to show these market-oriented qualities, they may still face the same degenerative problems former governing leaders faced before they left office.

References

Canes-Wrone, B., Herron, M.C., et al. (2001). Leadership and pandering: A theory of executive policymaking. *American Journal of Political Science, 45*(3), 532–550.
Dinan, S., & Ward, J. (2009, March 25). Obama links budget to recovery. *The Washington Times*. www.washingtontimes.com/news/2009/mar/25/obama-cools-on-climate-change/
Elcock, H. (2001). *Political leadership*. Cheltenham, UK: Edward Elgar.
Elgie, R. (1995). *Political leadership in liberal democracies*. Basingstoke, UK: Macmillan.

Foley, M. (1993). *The rise of the British presidency*. Manchester, UK: Manchester University Press.
Fox, J., & Shotts, K.W. (2009). Delegates or trustees? A theory of political accountability. *The Journal of Politics, 71*, 1225–1237.
Glaser, B.G., & Strauss, A.L. (1967). *The discovery of grounded theory: Strategies for qualitative research*. Chicago, IL: Aldine.
Goldstein, K., & Ridout, T.N. (2004). Measuring the effects of televised political advertising in the United States. *Annual Review of Political Science, 7*, 205–226.
Gould, P. (2007). Labour's political strategy. In D. Wring, J. Green, R. Mortimore, & S. Atkinson (Eds.), *Political communications: The general election campaign of 2005* (pp. 34–45). Basingstoke, UK: Palgrave Macmillan.
Helms, L. (2008). Governing in the media age: The impact of the mass media on executive leadership in contemporary democracies. *Government and Opposition, 43*(1), 26–54.
Heppell, T. (2008). The degenerative tendencies of long-serving governments . . . 1963 . . . 1996 . . . 2008. *Parliamentary Affairs, 61*(4), 578–596.
Kaid, L.L., & Johnston, A. (2001). *Videostyle in presidential campaigns: Style and content of televised political advertising*. Westport, CT: Praeger.
Langmaid, R., Trevail, C., & Hayman, B. (2006). Reconnecting the Prime Minister. Paper presented at the annual conference of the Market Research Society, London, UK.
Lees-Marshment, J. (2008). Managing a market-orientation in government: Cases in the U.K. and New Zealand. In D.W. Johnson (Ed.), *The Routledge handbook of political management* (pp. 524–536). New York, NY: Routledge.
Lees-Marshment, J. (2009). Marketing after the election: The potential and limitations of maintaining a market orientation in government. *Canadian Journal of Communication, 34*, 205–227.
Lees-Marshment, J. (2011). *The political marketing game*. Basingstoke, UK: Palgrave Macmillan.
Lees-Marshment, J., & Lilleker, D.G. (2005). *Political marketing: A comparative perspective*. Manchester, UK: Manchester University Press.
Lilleker, D.G. (2006). *Key concepts in political communication*. London, UK: Sage Publications.
Lloyd, J. (2009). Keeping both the baby and the bathwater: Scoping a new model of political marketing communication. *International Review on Public and Nonprofit Marketing, 6*(2), 119–135.
Masciulli, J., Molchanov, M.A., et al. (2009). *The Ashgate research companion to political leadership*. Farnham, UK: Ashgate.
Neustadt, R.E. (1980). *Presidential power: The politics of leadership from FDR to Carter*. New York, NY: Wiley.
Newman, B.I. (1994). *The marketing of the president: Political marketing as campaign strategy*. Thousand Oaks, CA: Sage Publications.
Nimmo, D.D. (1970). *The political persuaders: The techniques of modern election campaigns*. Englewood Cliffs, NJ: Prentice-Hall.
O'Cass, A. (1996). Political marketing and the marketing concept. *European Journal of Marketing, 30*(10), 45–61.
O'Shaughnessy, N. (1990). *The phenomenon of political marketing*. Basingstoke, UK: Macmillan.
Obama, B. (2008, November 4). Victory speech. Chicago, IL.
Obama, B. (2009a, September 9). Speech to Congress on health care reform. Washington, DC.
Obama, B. (2009b, July 23). Town hall on health care reform. Shaker Heights, OH.
Obama, B. (2009c, August 11). Town hall on health care reform. Portsmouth, NH.
Obama, B. (2009d, August 14). Town hall on health care reform. Belgrade, MT.
Obama, B. (2009e, July 11). Your weekly address—Recovery and the jobs of the future. www.whitehouse.gov

Obama, B. (2010a, September 22). Back yard town hall on health care. Falls Church, VA.
Obama, B. (2010b, September 13). Back yard town hall on the economy. Fairfax, VA.
Ormrod, R.P. (2006). A critique of the Lees-Marshment market oriented party model. *Politics, 26*(2), 110–188.
Ormrod, R.P., & Savigny, H. (2012\). Political market orientation: A framework for understanding relationship structures in political parties. *Party Politics, 18*(4), 487–502.
Pharr, S.J., & Putnam, R.D. (2000). *Disaffected democracies: What's troubling the trilateral countries?* Princeton, NJ: Princeton University Press.
Poguntke, T., & Webb, P. (2005). *The presidentialization of politics: A comparative study of modern democracies.* Oxford, UK: Oxford University Press.
Robinson, C. (2006). *Advertising and the market orientation of political parties contesting the 1999 and 2002 New Zealand general election campaigns.* (Unpublished doctoral dissertation). Massey University, Auckland, New Zealand.
Rosenberg, S.W., Kahn, S., et al. (1991). Creating a political image: Shaping appearance and manipulating the vote. *Political Behavior, 13*(4), 345–367.
Scammell, M. (1999). Political marketing: Lessons for political science. *Political Studies, 47*(4), 718–739.
Scammell, M. (2007). Political brands and consumer citizens: The rebranding of Tony Blair. *The ANNALS of the American Academy of Political and Social Science, 611*(176), 176–192.
Semetko, H.A. (1996). Political balance on television: Campaigns in the United States, Britain and Germany. *The Harvard International Journal of Press/Politics, 1*(1), 51–71.
Steger, W.P., Kelly, S.Q., et al. (2006). *Campaigns and political marketing.* New York, NY: Haworth Press.
Temple, M., & Savigny, H. (2010). Political marketing models: The curious incident of the dog that doesn't bark. *Political Studies, 58*(5), 1049–1064.

15

DOES OBAMA CARE?

Assessing the Delivery of Health Reform in the United States

Brian M. Conley

Overview of the Topic

In the months following its passage in March 2010, the Patient Protection and Affordable Care Act, dubbed "Obamacare" by its supporters and critics alike, emerged as one of President Obama's signature legislative achievements, but also one of his chief political liabilities. Although as an issue, health reform had been an important part of candidate Obama's successful brand message during the 2008 presidential campaign, the health care law was widely seen as having contributed to the Democrats' sweeping losses in the 2010 midterm election. Despite having enacted legislation, an achievement that had eluded leaders in both parties for nearly a century, the Democrats had lost traction on the issue among key voter groups. Public opinion on the issue had shifted, but there is also evidence that how the president talked about health reform changed in the months before and after the law's passage, from an emphasis on controlling health care costs to expanding coverage. The goal of this chapter is to critically analyze how Obama sought to deliver, once in office, on his promise to reform the nation's health care system and the impact it had on popular support for the policy in the lead-up to the midterm 2010 election.

Delivery, as a concept, is fundamental to the type of market-oriented, branded politics that Obama embraced as a presidential candidate in 2008 (Lees-Marshment 2009, 2011; Barber 2007; Esselment 2012; Lee and Woodward 2002; Pare and Berger 2008). As a strategy, branding is defined by not only the promise but also the delivery of a unique and targeted product experience (Cosgrove 2007; Needham 2005). Obama's election in 2008 was seen by many of his supporters as representing the promise of a new, more competent and less partisan politics in Washington, D.C., a politics capable of finding pragmatic and more efficient solutions to the nation's many social and political problems. For many of these voters, few problems were more personal or vexing than those associated with the nation's health care system, particularly the escalating costs of coverage (Jacobs 2008: 1882; Carroll 2007). On the campaign trail, Obama understood this. At rallies across the country, he galvanized support for his candidacy by promising to deliver health reforms that cut costs for families and businesses (Plouffe 2010; Obama 2007). But, once in office, his emphasis shifted, and support for his proposals subsequently declined. Rather than remain focused, as the American public was, on cost reduction, Obama began stressing the need for greater access to health care and the moral imperative of ensuring more people were covered. It was a subtle change, but one that polling data suggest had a corrosive effect on support for Obama's health care proposals, particularly among independent voters (Gallup 2009–2010). Although the speed with which his policies lost favor surprised the president, this turn of events highlights a key insight of political marketing scholars about the importance of managing the delivery process, specifically how policy changes are communicated to and understood by the public. On health reform, Obama delivered, but as the 2010 midterm election results demonstrated, he delivered something that the public either did not want or did not fully understand.

By studying Obama's health care policy as a delivery issue, I hope to examine the extent to which declining public support for health reform followed from changes in how President Obama communicated the reforms to the public. What went wrong for Obama and the Democrats in their delivery of health reform? Was it a delivery failure, a failure to ground what was delivered in what the market wanted or simply a failure to properly manage public perception and to communicate what was delivered? To address these questions, I first examine the political marketing literature on the concept of delivery, before turning to an analysis of Obama's delivery of health reform beginning with his 2008 presidential campaign. Specifically, I will examine what impact, if any, the manner with which Obama communicated delivery had on the public's perception and evaluation of the reforms. To do so, I will track the extent to which an emphasis on either controlling cost or expanding coverage impacted the degree to which voters, particularly political independents, supported the reforms.

Review of Previous Literature

Few observers doubt the importance of making good on campaign promises and pledges once in government. "Success in power is often dependent," notes Esselment, particularly in terms of reelection, "on the ability to implement the identified policy preferences of voters" (2012: 303). This is especially true for more market-oriented parties and elected officials, whose legitimacy and appeal rest upon their responsiveness to the concerns of specific market segments and the delivery of specific product promises. But, while the general premise of delivery may be broadly understood, as a growing body of literature demonstrates, what market-oriented delivery actually entails, and how it is achieved in government, is less well understood. Indeed, among the key insights of this literature is that delivery is a complex process that must be properly managed.

In a market approach, "delivery," Lees-Marshment writes, "is not easy" (2009: 199). Winning elected office may bestow on the victor the resources and legislative power of the state. But it also imposes the demand that you deliver on the unique, and targeted, promises that ground a market approach, regardless of the constraints of government, or face the possibility of defeat in the next election. When delivery works, however, it can serve as the basis of an enduring voter trust and loyalty. As such, it is important to "match ... what you want to do with what you can do," as one Australian Labour Party advisor put it (Lees-Marshment 2011: 170). Delivery, in other words, must be treated as a process that covers not only the governmental sphere—that is, what you do and say in government—but also the electoral sphere, or what you promise on the campaign trail or while in opposition. While delivery ultimately occurs in government, it is critical to understand, scholars argue, that it encompasses not only what is accomplished in government, but also what is promised during the campaign and communicated to the public following passage (Esselment 2012; Lees-Marshment 2009: 199–200, 2011: 167; Arterton 2007: 147).

Delivery, then, is a multi-staged, often protracted process that effectively begins and ends on the campaign trail and has to be managed as such. It is imperative, for instance, as Lees-Marshment argues, that a candidate has a delivery strategy not only for when he gets elected, but also a strategy for what Lees-Marshment describes as "pre-election delivery," "communicating delivery" as well as delivery failure. Determining what the public values or wants, as well as what you want and believe can be delivered, or what your party wants and believes, should not wait until you are elected. Planning ahead helps a party or candidate not only refine key campaign promises and differentiate product offerings, but also, and as importantly, helps manage voter expectations of what is possible (Lees-Marshment 2011: 170; Pare and Berger 2008).

Parties have used a variety of devices, including pledges, contracts and guarantees to at once focus their message, discipline their own members and shape voter expectations. The Republicans' 1994 Contract with America, the Canadian Conservatives' "five commitments" of 2006, as well as Tony Blair's 1997 New Labour "pledges" offer clear, and generally successful, examples of such a strategy (Esselment 2012: 304; Needham 2005: 354; Pare and Berger 2008: 50). But they also highlight, particularly in the Republican and Labour cases, some of the perils involved. Both the Republicans and Labour won majorities in 1994 and 1997, respectively, but neither was able to fully delivery on their stated promises, and in the case of Labour, the party's pledges would, over the course of several subsequent elections, become less and less specific (White and de Chernatory

2002: 49–50; Lees-Marshment 2011: 171). What is clear from these and other examples is that the goal of a pledge or contract or any other pre-election delivery strategy cannot simply be electoral victory in the short run, but rather effective delivery in government, and thus possible reelection in the long run. Moreover, what is promised as part of a pre-election delivery strategy should be neither too ambitious nor too modest. While the Republicans and Labour in the UK may have overreached, there are dangers, as Chris Rudd notes in his study of Helen Clark and the New Zealand Labour Party, of trying to ensure delivery by being too cautious and either leaving no impression on the public or being seen as having no long-term agenda (Rudd 2005: 91).

Pre-election delivery strategies are an essential part of a well-organized market-based delivery strategy. They begin the process of articulating what a candidate or party's delivery priorities are, which is critical to developing a focused delivery strategy once elected. But having a delivery strategy in government is itself not limited, scholars argue, to simply enacting the policy changes you have proposed or promised. Rather, delivery in government should itself be viewed as incorporating a range of activities leading up to and following moments of successful policy delivery. It encompasses, Lees-Marshment argues, not only the challenge of passing and implementing policy change within government, but also effectively "communicating delivery" to voters and other relevant external stakeholders, while simultaneously remaining abreast of how the opposition and the public evaluates your product delivery (2011: 173–179, 181–188).

It is a process that starts, first and foremost, with an appreciation for the unique institutional setting in which the party or elected official is embedded, and the real obstacles, both institutional and political, that they often confronted in efforts to deliver on policy promises. Government, as we noted, is about power, but it is also about constraints, which can be both relatively enduring, such as existing institutional constraints, as well as unexpected, like changing political circumstances or attitudes. In the United States, these variables can have a significant impact on successful delivery. Unlike parliamentary systems, there are real limits on the power that US presidents have over legislators within their own party (Jacobs and Skocpol 2012: 58). Even when government is unified, it is rarely possible, as Arterton notes, for presidents to "dictate . . . policy action" (2007: 147). But, when the federal government is divided—and it has been increasingly polarized politically—presidents can expect to face sustained opposition. Nonetheless, delivery is possible, scholars argue, but it often requires remaining focused on key priorities.

Just as clear delivery priorities help refine a candidate or party's message and shape voter expectations in the pre-election stage, establishing these priorities in government helps focus a party's energy and activities. One strategy that has been used by party leaders in more centralized parliamentary systems has been to create, as Tony Blair did, formal "delivery units" to ensure delivery priorities are acted upon (Esselment 2012; Richards and Smith 2006). By establishing, as

Esselment explains, an agency or body that "links the first minister's office to the bureaucratic level ... and assists in identifying and solving delivery problems, party leaders are able to track their progress on key election promises" (2012: 305). In a presidential system like that in the United States, having clearly stated priorities, especially those that a candidate or party ran on or that form the basis of the president's annual State of the Union address to Congress, can be an important instrument for mobilizing support within the public, party or government for proposed policy changes. This is especially true in instances where a president feels the necessity to "go public," or to pressure Congress to act by appealing not only to elected leaders in Washington but also to their constituents, the American public (Kernell 1997). Priorities communicate seriousness and determine where a president or party leader plans to focus his or her efforts, and if necessary, expend his or her political capital. Among the more costly missteps Jimmy Carter made as president in the late 1970s, for example, was a failure to properly communicate his priorities as the new president to Congress (Light 1982: 230–1). Ronald Reagan, by contrast, learned from his predecessor's mistake and focused his energy during his first year in office on winning support in Congress for his top policy priorities, notably tax cuts. But, as importantly, priorities help with the vital task of communicating delivery success to the public, when it happens.

In politics, it is rarely enough to just deliver, especially in circumstances as contentious and media-driven as contemporary US politics. What you deliver, how it matches what you promised and why it qualifies you for reelection all have to be communicated. On its own, "delivery is not enough," explains Philip Gould, a former advisor to Tony Blair. "You have to communicate what you are doing, why you are doing it, and where you are going," he continued (Needham 2005: 354). All too often, scholars note, presidents or congressional leaders do the hard work of enacting legislation, delivering on what they promised only to discover that the public is unaware of their achievements or is unwilling to believe them. Such was the fate of Bill Clinton in the run-up to the 1994 midterm election. As Dick Morris recounts from conversations with Bill and Hillary Clinton concerning unfavorable polling numbers just prior to the election, each of the "accomplishments of which they were so proud—a smaller budget deficit, more jobs, rising imports—met a solid wall of rejection. Most voters believed they weren't true. Those who agreed they were accurate denied Clinton credit" (1999: 11). The president was flabbergasted, and more than a little agitated, by the polling results, though he would be personally spared the electoral fallout. Morris recommended highlighting "incremental achievements" but he might also have suggested building a narrative that points to specific achievements as evidence that priorities set forth on the campaign trail are being delivered (1999: 13). Legislation is often complex, and in spite of the literal names bills are often given, they do not necessarily tell a specific story or send a certain message. On the contrary, legislation can be treated, and often is by the opposition and the media, as doing something quite different, even counterproductive to what was promised. Indeed, in the absence of a clear communications strategy, what has been delivered can even be described by it supporters in a way that is inconsistent with what was promised.

The solution, scholars argue, is to be specific and explain delivery by focusing on what was promised on the campaign trail, prioritized once elected and ultimately delivered in government. At the same time, it is also critical to assess, and when necessary change, your communication strategy based on how the public actually perceives or evaluates the policy change, or the scope of the opposition. If the public doesn't get the message, or gets a competing message, as occurred with Clinton in 1994, it is politically tantamount to delivery failure. In fact, how delivery is communicated, especially during an election, is often as important to how the public evaluates the policy change as the specifics of the policy itself. But when delivery does not happen—that is, when what was promised and prioritized is not passed, or fully implemented—that too also has to be communicated, scholars assert, rather than denied. In politics, as in the commercial world, it is not uncommon for there to be what researchers describe as a "service delivery gap," where a party or president falls short of delivering what was promised (Lees-Marshment 2011: 179, 2009: 203; Newman 1999). Such service gaps can occur for a variety of reasons, Newman argues, including differences in expectations between the party and the voter and differences between what was delivered and what was advertised, as well as from tangible differences between what was promised and what was delivered, or not delivered (1999: 37–8). Although undesirable, delivery failure, even if only a failure of communication, cannot be ignored.

In the end, delivery is a complex and calculated process that when properly managed can play an important role engendering voter loyalty and thus helping a party or president remain in power. Indeed, delivery on any item in government is significant, but when it relates to a signature issue for a candidate or party it can be transformative, either positively or negatively.

Theoretical Framework

To examine how President Obama managed the delivery of health reform during his first year and half in office, as well as how changes in the way that he communicated delivery may have impacted public evaluations of the reform, I explore how the public responded to each phase of his health care plan using Lees-Marshment's (2009, 2011) delivery model. Specifically, I look at:

1. Obama's pre-election delivery strategy, or how he described the health reforms he would deliver as a candidate. I do so by analyzing:

    How clearly he articulated or described what he would deliver once in office;
    How focused and refined his core delivery promises were;
    The extent to which he adjusted his promises to reflect known political and
        institutional constraints of government; and
    How targeted his promises were at specific market segments.

2. His delivery strategy in government, or how he sought to implement the health reform he had promised on the campaign trail. I do so by examining:

How focused he remained on core delivery priorities, and avoided being distracted either by circumstance or other issues;
The strategies and mechanisms he used to achieved his goals within his stated timeframe; and
How he managed any political opposition that emerged to his delivery priorities.

3. His communication of delivery, or how he explained the policies he enacted as well as addressed the charges of his critics. I do so by studying:

How consistent his pre- and post-delivery communication was of the policy that was enacted;
How compellingly he made the case that what was delivered matched what was promised during the campaign;
How well he countered the charges of the opposition he faced, while communicating what he believed to be the benefits of the policy he delivered;
How targeted his communication of benefits was;
The degree to which he assumed credit for successful policy delivery; and
The extent to which he considered his or his party's reelection prospects in his communication of delivery.

In this way, I hope to identify what Obama promised as a candidate, what was implemented in government and what was communicated to the public. This will help determine what effect a shift in focus, from cost control to expanded coverage, had in undermining public support for reform but also its role in bolstering the Republican call for repeal of the law during the run-up to the 2010 midterm election.

Empirical Illustrations

1. Pre-Election Delivery

From the start of his 2008 presidential campaign, then Senator Obama sought to make reform of the nation's ailing health care system a signature issue of his candidacy. He did so by using of variety of pre-election delivery strategies, including specific targeted promises and timelines that indicated health reform would be a priority of his administration. Indeed, he dedicated the very first policy speech of the campaign, before an audience at the University of Iowa in May 2007, to discussing the issue of health reform and to reiterating his promise to "sign a universal health care plan into law by the end of [his] first term in office" (Obama 2007: 2). But more than that, he focused his pre-election delivery strategy around a specific policy goal: cutting the costs of health care for individuals, families and businesses. While it was imperative to create a health care system that "guarantees coverage for every American," the president explained, it must be done in a way that "brings down the cost of health care and reduces . . . premiums" (Obama

2007: 2). Controlling costs, in Obama's view, was as critical as expanding coverage. In fact, it was only by controlling health care costs, in Obama's view, that the country could achieve anything close to universal coverage. "We often hear the statistic that there are 45 million uninsured Americans," he asserted, "but the biggest reason why they don't have insurance is the same reason why those who have it are struggling to pay their medical bills—it's just too expensive" (Obama 2007: 1).

Obama had considered focusing on the issue of coverage first, recalls David Plouffe, his campaign manager, but ultimately concluded that "before mandating coverage, costs had to be tackled" (Plouffe 2010: 75). His plans for doing so included proposals for reducing waste in the current health care system, improving preventative care in the country, helping businesses with the costs of catastrophic coverage and further regulating the health insurance industry. Some form of universal coverage was Obama's goal—indeed his plan mandated coverage for children—but he would first focus on managing the costs of doing so. In one of the early Democratic primary debates in November 2007, for example, Obama even challenged the idea that a mandate was necessary to achieve expanded coverage, stating: "What I see are people who would love to have health care. They desperately want it. But the problem is they can't afford it" (CNN 2007: 1). As he explained to his staff when they were hashing out the details of their health care proposals the previous May, "I reject the notion that there are millions of Americans walking around out there who don't want coverage." "They want it," he continued, "but can't afford it." The logical policy response, in Obama's mind, was to "attack costs from every angle" (Plouffe 2010: 75). Again, it seemed to Obama that such an approach was the only plausible way to ultimately expand coverage within the confines of the current US health care system, a point he frequently repeated when challenged about a mandate.

It was, by most accounts, a politically cautious position to take, tempered by among other things the Obama team's recognition of both the complexity of the issue and the long history of failed health reform efforts in the country. Moreover, concerns with the mounting cost of coverage were arguably the most persistent public complaint about the nation's health care system (Jacobs 2008: 1882). Although it opened him to criticism from his Democratic primary opponents, notably Hillary Clinton—who claimed Obama's plan not only lacked specifics, but would not achieve universal coverage—such a nuanced approach enabled him to engage both his base of more liberal supporters as well as other groups targeted by the campaign, notably political independents (CNN 2007: 1; Todd and Gawiser 2009: 34; Issenberg 2012). At the time of Obama's announcement, polls showed that upwards of 70% of Democrats favored expanding coverage over controlling cost, but that number dropped to 53% among independents (Quinnipiac 2007). Moreover, at the time, public opinion data indicated that a growing number of Americans were deeply concerned about the rising cost of care. Roughly 60% of respondents in a CBS News 2007 tracking poll reported being "very dissatisfied" with the "cost of health care in this country." By March

2009 the number had risen to 77% (CBS News Poll 2007). Indeed, by early 2009, polling data suggested that cost had for the most part replaced coverage as the "most important health care issue" in the country (NBC News/Wall Street Journal Poll 2009). Although not a particularly bold position politically, Obama's emphasis on costs over coverage was, as scholars advise, highly targeted, did reflect the known challenges of passing reforms and, most importantly, served to tightly focus his pre-election delivery strategy.

2. Delivery Strategy in Government

Once in government, delivering on his promise to reform the nation's health care system remained one of Obama's top policy priorities. The goal of offering "affordable, accessible health care for all Americans" featured prominently in the official agenda Obama and Vice President Joe Biden laid out for their new administration in January 2009 (Obama and Biden 2009). And, overall, Obama's handling of the issue early on would, as his pre-election strategy had, offer a model of how clearly set priorities can help anchor a delivery strategy in government. This was true even as the political dynamics in the country churned and shifted radically in the closing weeks of the campaign following the near collapse of the nation's financial markets in September 2008. Economic concerns consequently dominated the early days of the new administration. In fact, many of Obama's closest advisors, including Vice President Biden and Chief of Staff Rahm Emanuel, urged the president to prioritize jobs and fixing the economy before tackling health reform, which they were concerned, given the history of failed reform efforts, might bog the new administration down in a prolonged and ultimately unsuccessful battle with Congress (Jacobs and Skocpol 2012; Baker 2010). Obama, however, was equally convinced that the issues of economic recovery and health reform were in fact inseparable and that a full economic recovery would not be possible without addressing rising health care costs, and he consequently remained steadfast in his commitment to the issue. Indeed, rather than shift his priorities from health care to the economy, the president sought instead to link the two issues. In his first budget address to Congress in February 2009, for instance, Obama put health care, along with energy and education reform, at the center of his plan for economic recovery (Obama 2009a).

Despite his early resolve, however, Obama's health care delivery strategy, particularly his focus on controlling costs, began to succumb to the centrifugal pressures of government. To start, it became increasingly clear that controlling costs would require nearly universal coverage, or some type of mandate. It was a point made by his budget advisors, but also by a cautiously optimistic, yet still potentially hostile health insurance lobby (Abelson 2009). Moreover, it quickly became clear that virtually any legislation the president proposed would likely face universal opposition—as his economic stimulus package had—from the Republicans. Obama again attempted to adapt, with a variety of different strategies, to the changing political and institutional circumstances, particularly the mounting opposition. He sought, for example, to reach out to potential opponents by hosting not one but two bipartisan health care summits at the White House; by borrowing, whenever possible, reform ideas from Republicans; and by working hard once legislation was being considered in Congress to win even one Republican vote, particularly in the Senate, for reform. At the same time, he decided not to preempt or overly manage the legislative process, as Bill Clinton had done in the early 1990s, and other than to stress the need for cost savings, he left much of the responsibility for drafting legislation to Congress (Cloud 1994).

The process, however, quickly got out of control, as did the level of opposition. Not only were Democratic leaders in Congress unable to meet a White House deadline to vote on legislation by July, but as they struggled to report separate health care bills, the very idea of health reform, and how Obama was managing the process, came under attack from both the left and the right (Wangness 2009). Liberals, for their part, were growing increasingly impatient with the president's inconsistent support for, and apparent willingness to drop, the so-called "public option," or the creation of a government-run insurance program that would compete with private insurance plans within state-run exchanges. "It would be a crushing blow to progressive hopes if Mr. Obama doesn't succeed in getting some form of universal care through Congress," explained Paul Krugman. "But even so, reform isn't worth having if you can only get it on terms so compromised that it's doomed to fail" (Krugman 2009: 1). But it was on the right, in confrontations between conservative Tea Party activists and members of Congress back in their districts in August, that Obama's health care agenda came under the most withering assault. Although many of the charges leveled by Tea Party activists were overly hyperbolic and largely unfounded, including accusations that the president's health care proposals called for the creation of "death panels," they nonetheless dominated the news and made many lawmakers wary about the potential political fallout of health reform.

Obama's response to the growing opposition to health reform would shape not only the legislation that finally passed in early 2010, but also how he communicated what was delivered. Seeking to regain the initiative and to counter the impact the growing opposition might have on support for reform in Congress, Obama would "go public" by again speaking before a joint session of Congress in September to make his case for reform. In the opinion of most commentators, the speech worked. It effectively "nudged congressional committees back to work," write Jacobs and Skocpol, and led to votes in the House and Senate, in November and December respectively (2012: 55). But the speech did something else that ultimately proved counterproductive: it signaled a shift in how Obama described the reforms and what they would deliver for the American public. While his focus had remained on the need to deliver reforms that cut costs, his emphasis now began to change to include not only cost control, but also, as he described it in the speech, the "moral" necessity of ensuring more Americans were covered (Obama

2009b). It was a commitment he reiterated in his January 2010 State of the Union address, one week after losing an effective supermajority in the Senate following the victory of Scott Brown in a Massachusetts special election. Despite the loss, Obama was defiant, telling Congress and the nation that he would "not walk away from" those who did not have or had lost their coverage (Obama 2010a: 9). But, in the process, he began to step away from what had been a consistent emphasis on controlling health care costs. "By the time I'm finished speaking tonight," Obama exclaimed, "more Americans will have lost their health insurance. Millions will lose it this year. Our deficit will grow. Premiums will go up. Patients will be denied the care they need. Small business owners will continue to drop coverage altogether" (Obama 2010a: 9). It was not a dramatic change—expanding coverage had always been an important part of the president's plan and rhetoric—but it was significant enough, especially given the malleability of public opinion on the issue, to further undermine public trust in and understanding of his proposals (Jacobs 2008). More specifically, by complicating his health care message ever so slightly, Obama not only weakened his message targeting, but also the hold on general public opinion his focus on cost had given him concerning the goal of health reform. As Gallup tracking polls highlighted at the time, concerns that Obama's proposed health care reforms would only "worsen" already high health care costs rose by seven points to 49% in the month following his September speech, where it remained through March 2010. Only 21%, over the same period, thought health care costs would "get better" if reforms were passed (Gallup 2009–2010). This trend becomes even more pronounced when we consider how public opinion on the impact reform would have on health care costs was tacking in the months leading up to Obama's speech. The belief that any proposed reforms would increase costs had risen in the early part of 2009, but had begun to drop slightly by midsummer (from 30% to 27%). At the same time, the number of people who thought reform would lead to a controlling of costs, which had begun to decline in the spring, began to rise over the summer (from 34% to 37%). Both trends were reversed in September, however, when the number of people thinking reform would increase cost began to rise, and continued to do so for the remainder of the year and through 2010 (from 27% in September to 42% by March 2011), while over the same time period those believing it would alleviate costs steadily dropped from 37% in September to 24% by March 2011 (Kaiser 2011)—see Figure 15.1.

Public opinion among independents was less volatile, but Obama's shifting rhetoric correlated with a general leveling of support for reform among undecided voters throughout 2010 (Kaiser 2010). Obama had lost his core health care delivery message, but more than that, he inadvertently strengthened one of the Republican opposition's principal charges against the legislation: that it would only increase health care costs for both the average American family and the federal government by requiring everyone to be covered (Jacobs and Mettler 2011: 925). Both trends would only become more pronounced after the passage of the Patient Protection and Affordable Care Act (ACA) in March 2010, as Obama sought to communicate what he had delivered.

Cost of Care: Under the health reform law, do you think the cost of health care for you and your family will get better, worse or will it stay about the same? (February 2009–March 2011)

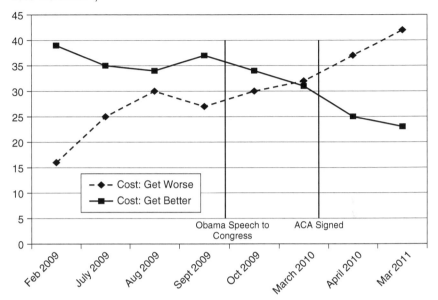

FIGURE 15.1 Public Opinion on the Cost of Health Reform
Source: Kaiser Health Tracking Poll (March 2011): http://kff.org/health-reform/poll-finding/kaiser-health-tracking-poll-march-2011/

3. Communicating Delivery

The passage of the ACA was a momentous occasion for President Obama and the Democrats. Against a backdrop of unprecedented partisanship, raucous protests and a badly weakened economy, none of which Obama had fully anticipated when he first launched his candidacy, the new president delivered on one of his core campaign promises, and essentially within the timeframe he had outlined. But, in spite of the acclaim that surrounded its passage, the law did little to either reverse the ongoing decline in public support for health reform or to remedy the listlessness of the president's health care message. Obama now had a law, but having complicated his position on the question of cost, he did not have a clear, consistent message targeted to appeal to specific market segments. He had inadvertently created precisely the type of "service delivery gap" discussed in the literature that emerges when there is public uncertainty about whether what was delivered matches what was expected. Moreover, as the scale of public opposition to the reforms became evident in the months following passage, and especially with the approach of the 2010 midterm election, neither the president nor the Democratic Party leadership were able to effectively reposition the law or otherwise reclaim the issue of cost (Scherer 2010).

Obama consequently struggled to describe what the law did, its benefits, or, and as importantly, how it delivered on what he had promised during the campaign. He struggled, that is, to defend it. The president continued to emphasize the admixture of cost and coverage. "I will say that any objective observer looking at this bill would say that this is a middle-of-the-road, centrist approach to providing coverage to people and making sure that we are also reducing costs," Obama explained to Matthew Lauer, just after its passage (Obama 2010b: 3). In particular, he and the White House tried to stress what the law did to curb many of the practices that the health insurance industry had traditionally used to deny coverage. Health coverage could no longer be denied because of an administrative error, for instance, because of lifetime limits on certain care options or annual caps on payments, or, and most significantly, due to a preexisting medical condition. The law also expanded Medicaid in the first year and allowed young adults to stay on their parents' insurance plan until the age of 26.

While several individual provisions of the health care law were popular, Obama's arguments for the merits of the reforms were barely perceptible above the clamor of what became the chief line of Republican attack in the 2010 election: repeal, repeal, repeal (Kaiser 2010). If the president's pre- and post-delivery health care message was inconsistent, and left many Americans uncertain about how the ACA would impact their lives at a time of mounting economic distress, the Republicans' repeal message clear: by emphasizing coverage, the president had not only implicitly broken his promise on cost, but he had actually threatened the nation's economic recovery by dramatically increasing government spending (GOP 2010: 6). As they explained in the official 2010 Republican campaign manifesto, *A Pledge to America*, "[T]he American people wanted one thing out of health care reform: lower costs, which President Obama and Democrats in Washington promised, but did not deliver" (2010: 26). What they got instead was a "health care law [that] kills jobs, raises taxes, and increases the cost of health care" (2010: 27). The law, the Republican leadership argued, should be repealed. It was a message intended not only to link the public's economic uncertainty with the new law, but also to cast the Republican repeal effort as a means of cutting costs and creating jobs. Its effects on general public opinion, but particularly on political independents, were significant. As a survey of national polls in the closing weeks of the election found, roughly half of all respondents when asked favored an outright repeal of the law, including 51% of independents (Kaiser 2010; CNN 2010). Moreover, there would be a 17-point swing (from 39% to 56%) in support among independents for Republicans in 2010 compared to the 2006 midterm election (Pew Research Center 2010). Obama had forfeited the issue of cost to the Republicans, and in the process provided them with one of their most effective arguments against the Democrats in their landslide victory in the midterm election. In the context of US politics, health reform was an extraordinary achievement, which Obama could and did rightfully take credit for. But politically it was an accomplishment that was undercut by the inconsistent, and consequently ineffective, manner with which Obama communicated the reforms he had delivered.

Conclusions for Research and Practice

As the historic, yet contested, nature of Obama's health care reform efforts illustrates, having a delivery strategy is as important, if not more, than delivery itself. On its face, the historic significance of the Affordable Care Act was undeniable, but even such a monumental achievement does not by itself communicate delivery on the promises Obama made as a candidate and as the president. On the contrary, delivery, as a market-based electoral and legislative strategy, but also as a strategy for communicating to the public, is something that must be carefully planned and properly managed. Delivery is a story that has to be told, and when necessary defended, beginning with what is promised on the campaign trail and the priorities that are declared in government, and continuing with the communication of what was delivered and how it affirms what had been promised and prioritized. In its earliest stages, Obama's health care delivery strategy exemplified the process of first prioritizing, then seeking to deliver once in government, on a specific campaign promise. But somewhere along the way, in the subsequent delivery and communication of health reform, his management of the process went awry. Despite having delivered on what he promised, bucking nearly a century of policy failure, his reforms were greeted with a mixture of uncertainty and scorn by the public, not to mention sustained Republican opposition. Obama had kept his promise, but what the new law accomplished also needed to be communicated to the public in a way that highlighted the benefits that would result as well as how the law satisfied what was promised and differed from how it was being portrayed by its critics. This Obama did not do. In particular, he did not properly gauge, as he celebrated the law, how it was actually perceived by the public or the traction of the opposition's criticisms. Consequently, he did not effectively counter claims made about the law by the Republicans. On the contrary, he took liberties communicating what the reforms did, emphasizing how they would expand coverage as much as it would control costs and in doing so opened the way for Republican attacks on the law as another example of government overreach and excess in a time of economic uncertainty. Indeed, if Obama's initial focus on cost control highlighted the strategic value of setting clear delivery priorities, the political consequences of his subsequent shift in emphasis, notably the strength of the Republican repeal effort during the 2010 midterm election, demonstrates just how significant a properly managed and executed delivery strategy is to the overall policy process.

But there is evidence that in 2012 Obama learned from his mistakes of 2010. As part of his reelection effort, for example, Obama launched a comprehensive, micro-targeted "Keeping His Word" advertising campaign to, among other things, reposition the ACA as a promise made, and a promise kept. The health care ads highlighted the benefits of the president's health reform agenda, from "protecting a woman's right to choose" to "keeping young adults on their parents' insurance plans ... [and] providing coverage for 2.5 million more young adults since the law passed" (Obama 2012a, 2012b). But the ads particularly emphasized the cost-saving features of the new law, especially for seniors, by, as one ad explained, keeping "America's promise to our seniors and ... shrink[ing] the Medicare doughnut hole in prescription drug coverage" and "reduc[ing] the cost of prescription drugs" (Obama 2012c). That said, for voters principally concerned about cost, the issue's importance continued to be weighed against the goal of expanding coverage. In a marquee campaign ad entitled "The Story of Affordable Care Act," for instance, which celebrated the historic significance of the reforms, particularly the impact the law had on reducing the number of uninsured, no mention is made of any cost saving that may have also resulted (Obama 2012d). It was a lack of focus that, owing to persistent public concerns about the cost of health reform, continued to undermine support, particularly among independents, for the law throughout the 2012 election (Kaiser 2012).

In a market-oriented politics, the importance of a properly managed delivery process cannot be overstated. Delivery links together each phase of a market approach, from market research and product design to segmentation, targeting and communication. Indeed, when faithfully executed, delivery illustrates the full strategic potential of political marketing, not only in terms of delivering policy or political change that reflects the interests of targeted voter groups, but also, in the process, possibly winning their loyalty and enduring support in subsequent elections.

References

Abelson, R. (2009, September 7). President's speech allays some fears in the health insurance industry. *The New York Times.* www.nytimes.com/2009/09/11/health/policy/11insure.html

Arterton, C.F. (2007). Strategy and politics: The example of the United States of America. In T. Fischer, G.P. Schmitz, & M. Seberich (Eds.), *The strategy of politics: Results of a comparative study* (pp. 133–171). Gütersloh, DE: Bertelsmann Stiftung.

Baker, P. (2010, March 8). The limits of Rahmism. *The New York Times.* www.nytimes.com/2010/03/14/magazine/14emanuel-t.html?pagewanted=all

Barber, M. (2007). *Instruction in delivery: Tony Blair, public services and the challenge of achieving targets.* London, UK: Politicos.

Carroll, J. (2007, February 28). Healthcare edges up in public's list of priorities. *Gallup News Service.* www.gallup.com/poll/26725/healthcare-edges-publics-list-priorities.aspx

CBS News Poll. (2007, September 14–16). Health care and the Democratic presidential campaign. www.cbsnews.com/htdocs/pdf/Sep07b-HRC-HEALTH.pdf

CNN. (2007, November 15). Transcript: Democratic debate in Las Vegas. http://transcripts.cnn.com/TRANSCRIPTS/0711/15/se.02.html

CNN. (2010, September 28). Opinion research poll. http://i2.cdn.turner.com/cnn/2010/images/09/28/rel13d1a.pdf

Cosgrove, K. (2007). *Branded conservatives: How the brand brought the right from the fringes to the center of American political life*. New York, NY: Peter Lang.
Cloud, D. (1994). Health care's painful demise cast pall on Clinton agenda. *CQ Weekly* (November 5), 3142–3145.
Esselment, A. (2012). Delivering in government and getting results in minorities and coalitions (pp. 303–315). In Jennifer Lees-Marshment (Ed.), *Routledge handbook of political marketing*. London, UK: Routledge.
Gallup. (2009–2010). Health care system. www.gallup.com/poll/4708/healthcare-System.aspx?#3
GOP. (2010). *Pledge to America*. www.gop.gov/resources/library/documents/solutions/a-pledge-to-america.pdf
Issenberg, S. (2012). *The victory lab: The secret science of winning campaigns*. New York, NY: Crown Publishers.
Jacobs, L. (2008, May 1). 1994 all over again? Public opinion and health care. *The New England Journal of Medicine, 358,* 1881–1883. http://www.nejm.org/doi/full/10.1056/NEJMp0802361
Jacobs, L., & Mettler, S. (2011). Why public opinion changes: The implications for health and health policy. *Journal of Health Politics, Policy and the Law, 36*(6) (December), 917–933.
Jacobs, L.R., & Skocpol, T. (2012). *Health care reform and American politics: What everyone needs to know*. Oxford, UK: Oxford University Press.
Kaiser Public Opinion. (2010). How popular is the idea of repealing health reform? *Kaiser Family Foundation* (October). www.kff.org/kaiserpolls/upload/8114.pdf
Kaiser. (2010). Health tracking poll. *Kaiser Family Foundation* (October). http://kaiserfamilyfoundation.files.wordpress.com/2013/01/8115-f.pdf
Kaiser. (2011). Health tracking poll. *Kaiser Family Foundation* (March). http://kaiserfamilyfoundation.files.wordpress.com/2013/01/8166-t.pdf
Kaiser. (2012). Health Tracking Poll. *Kaiser Family Foundation* (October). http://kaiserfamilyfoundation.files.wordpress.com/2013/01/8381-f.pdf
Kernell, S. (1997). *Going public: New strategies of presidential leadership*. Washington, DC: CQ Press.
Krugman, P. (2009, June 26). Not enough audacity. *The New York Times*. www.nytimes.com/2009/06/26/opinion/26krugman.html?_r=0
Lee, S., & Woodward, R. (2002). Implementing the third way: The delivery of public services under the Blair government. *Public Money and Management* (October–December), 49–56.
Lees-Marshment, J. (2009). *Political marketing: Principles and applications*. London, UK: Routledge.
Lees-Marshment, J. (2011). *The political marketing game*. New York, NY: Palgrave Macmillan.
Light, P.C. (1982). *The president's agenda*. Baltimore, MD: John Hopkins University Press.
Morris, D. (1999). *Behind the Oval Office: Getting reelected against all odds*. Los Angeles, CA: Renaissance Books.
NBC News/Wall Street Journal Poll. (2009, February 26–March 1). http://s.wsj.net/public/resources/documents/WSJ_NewsPoll_030307).pdf
Needham, C. (2005). Brand leaders: Clinton, Blair and the limitations of the permanent campaign. *Political Studies, 53,* 343–361.
Newman, B.I. (1999). *The mass marketing of politics: Democracy in an age of manufactured images*. Thousand Oaks, CA: Sage Publications.
Obama, B. (2007, May 29). Remarks on health care at the University of Iowa. The American Presidency Project. www.presidency.ucsb.edu/ws/index.php?pid=76987
Obama, B. (2009a, February 24). Remarks of President Barack Obama, address to joint session of Congress. www.whitehouse.gov/video/EVR022409#transcript

Obama, B. (2009b, September 9). Remarks of President Obama to a joint session of Congress on health care. www.whitehouse.gov/video/President-Obama-Address-to-Congress-on-Health-Insurance-Reform#transcript

Obama, B. (2010a, January 27). Remarks by the president in the state of the union. www.whitehouse.gov/photos-and-video/video/2010-state-union-address#transcript

Obama, B. (2010b, March 29). Interview with Matt Lauer on NBC's *Today*.

Obama, B. (2012a). Keeping his word: Women's health. *Organizing for Action*. www.barackobama.com/video/keeping-his-word/

Obama, B. (2012b). Keeping his word: Health care coverage for young people. *Organizing for Action*. www.barackobama.com/video/keeping-his-word/

Obama, B. (2012c). Keeping his word: Lowering the cost of Medicare prescription drugs. *Organizing for Action*. www.barackobama.com/video/keeping-his-word/

Obama, B. (2012d). The story of the Affordable Care Act: From an unmet promise to the law of the land. *Organizing for Action*. www.barackobama.com/video/issues/health/page/1/top

Obama, B., & Biden, J. (2009, January). The agenda. http://change.gov/agenda/

Pare, D. J., & Berger, F. (2008). Political marketing Canadian style? The Conservative Party and the 2006 federal elections. *Canadian Journal of Communication, 33*(1), 39–63.

Pew Research Center. (2010, November 3). A clear rejection of the status quo, no consensus about future policies. www.pewresearch.org/2010/11/03/a-clear-rejection-of-the-status-quo-no-consensus-about-future-policies/

Plouffe, D. (2010). *The audacity to win*. New York, NY: Penguin Books.

Quinnipiac. (2007, October 23–29). Government should make sure all have health care, U.S. voters tell Quinnipiac University national poll; Sen. Clinton seen as leader on health issue. Quinnipiac University Poll. www.quinnipiac.edu/institutes-centers/polling-institute/search-releases/search-results/release-detail/?What=&strArea=;&strTime=28&ReleaseID=1114

Richards, D., & Smith, M. (2006). Central control and policy implementation in the UK: A case study of the prime minister's delivery unit. *Journal of Comparative Policy Analysis, 8*(4) (December), 325–345.

Rudd, C. (2005). Marketing the message or the messenger? New Zealand Labour Party, 1990–2003. In D. Lilleker & J. Lees-Marshment (Eds.), *Political marketing: A comparative perspective* (79–96). Manchester, UK: Manchester University Press.

Scherer, M. (2010, September 2). How Barack Obama became Mr. Unpopular. *Time*. www.time.com/time/magazine/article/0,9171,2015779,00.html

Todd, C., & Gawiser, S. (2009). *How Barack Obama won*. New York, NY: Vintage Books.

Wangsness, L. (2009, June 21). Health debate shifting to public vs. private. *The Boston Globe*. www.boston.com/news/nation/washington/articles/2009/06/21/healthcare_debate_shifting_to_public_vs_private/

White, J., & de Chernatony, L. (2002). New Labour: A study of the creation, development and demise of a political brand. *Journal of Political Marketing, 1*(2–3), 45–52.

16
US POLITICAL MARKETING TRENDS AND IMPLICATIONS

Jennifer Lees-Marshment, Brian M. Conley, and Kenneth Cosgrove

Political Marketing in the United States has demonstrated the far-reaching permeation of politics and government by marketing methods such as branding, market-oriented strategy, research, targeting, relationship marketing, and delivery management by government, parties, and candidates at the federal, congressional, and state level. Political marketing offers politicians and political organizations tools to better understand, respond to, organize, and communicate with their public—whether voters or volunteers—in order to win power but also, once in office, to implement policy. The first book dedicated to researching political marketing in the United States itself, this volume conveys the wide-ranging and multifaceted nature of how marketing influences politics. It demonstrates the distinctiveness of political marketing from campaigning and advertising, and showcases new trends—such as how different areas of political marketing overlap each other in practice. Experimental market testing of communication will always be limited in its effectiveness by the quality of the political brand; using online forms of communication is less impactful without the integration of relationship marketing concepts; and delivery marketing is necessary but constrained by the realities of government. But despite the complexities and challenges, practitioners will continue to use political marketing in every area of politics, and it is important that academic researchers study and understand their activities. Political marketing as an academic discipline offers objective, independent, and wide-ranging analysis of their activities that is not intended to support a particular party or point of view, or drive a news cycle. This concluding chapter will collate and synthesize the findings from the individual chapters as to the trends they show in US political marketing before discussing the democratic implications of political marketing and commenting on the potential for future research.

Trends in US Political Marketing

Political marketing methods and approaches are underlying political behavior in all areas and levels of the US political system by candidates, parties, and governments. The chapters in this book explored targeting, utilizing research databases, the use of social media by populism movements, marketing in primary elections, marketing policy by influencing candidates, celebrity marketing, personal political branding at state level, online brand management and relationship marketing, marketing and gender, research-led and targeted political advertising, crisis-management in campaigns, communicating leadership in government, and delivery marketing.

Voter targeting is crucial to maximize effectiveness of political communication and policy development. Burton and Miracle note the $25 million investment into data analysis in the 2012 Obama re-election campaign to maximize the efficiency of campaign expenditures but also how targeting in the United States has a long electoral history, dating back to the 1930s. The collection and processing of data may become more sophisticated over time, but the basic principle is that the electorate should be broken down into groups and prioritized by levels of support, persuadability, likelihood of mobilization, and cost of contact. Furthermore, the exploration of the historical development of voter targeting by Burton and Miracle and how the growing ability of individual candidates to use it instead of it being the prerogative of traditional party organizations has impacted on party power and has interesting implications for the use of political marketing techniques and democracy. It suggests that tools that originate as highly skilled and expensive and therefore only available for elites will, over time, become available to all regardless of resources or power. This makes political marketing a more democratic activity. As political marketing techniques—and with them, political power in terms of votes, public support, issue dominance, and policy change—become more available to the masses, it could help minorities or those under-represented challenge incumbent traditional elites.

The use of research in political marketing was highly visible in the 2012 election, as stories about the resources the Obama campaign invested in creating and utilizing databases to enable the testing of ads, targeted communication, and get out the vote appeared regularly in the media. The implications of the Spiller and Bergner chapter are that a governance model of market-oriented database political marketing to maintain volunteer support is needed that is distinct from that used in campaigning. Obama met many challenges utilizing his campaigning database once in power. In government, parties and political leaders need to continue to carry out listening exercises with volunteers, asking volunteers for constructive feedback on how the politician/party is doing in government, to convey any problems on the ground, and to make suggestions for anything the government needs to do to reach its goals. The database system needs to be adjusted and developed as new technology becomes available, and the campaign's grassroots support networks to mobilize voters need to be maintained, segmenting the supporter database to identify different needs, goals, and potential contributions. Effective internal communication with volunteers through the database is needed to explain and justify any changes to election promises, convey progress on delivery in government, and create a loyalty rewards program to motivate campaign volunteers to carry on their work in government, to develop a long-term relationship between volunteers and the president in power. Volunteers can then be asked to get involved with campaigning in power to help obtain support on legislation the president wants to enact, such as communicating the constraints of government to dissatisfied voters and explaining why it is important to continue to campaign for the president. If this is carried out, then re-election campaigning will be much easier and more effective—but so will governing itself.

Turcotte and Raynauld's chapter on the populist Tea Party shows how online communication may be used to enable populist political movements such as the Tea Party to engage in marketed messages among the grassroots. For political movements themselves it shows that they can use Twitter to generate highly targeted, emotive communication among individuals on the grassroots level and build up grassroots support in a way we have not seen before. However, it led to non-traditional forms of populist organization because social media enables and encourages followers to communicate instead of relying on one charismatic leader, as normally happens in populist movements. In this case there was a hyper-decentralized network of individuals and organizations creating and communicating for the movement. Therefore, other movements that are not right wing/populist may also use political marketing in a more positive sense to bring attention to, and increase support for, neglected issues among the general public and elites—such as interest groups advocating gay marriage, or wanting to raise awareness of child trafficking or increase public support for policy measures such as emissions trading schemes and carbon taxes to halt climate change. While the case shows mobilization of existing concerns on emotive salient issues, more mature, thoughtful marketing might help to stimulate opinion change on issues such as tackling child obesity.

Furthermore, the chapter shows that different elements of political marketing—segmentation, targeting, internal marketing, e-marketing—can be combined to create powerful volunteer support-building mechanisms on key political issues, which might be used by parties, interest groups, and movements. They are not always led by elites, but are bottom-up forms of communication. Thus Turcotte and Raynauld argue that the Tea Party movement constitutes the materialization of an insurgent political marketing technique that has the potential to redefine the structure of political mobilization, engagement, and organizing in the near future. This creates potential but also challenges in political marketing communication. While the obvious threat of the Tea Party was to the Democrats and Obama, in the future it is also potentially a threat to the Republican Party as it makes maintaining a clear brand very hard. The Tea Party may have made it very hard for a moderate energetic new market-oriented leader of the Republicans to build support from independents in the future and so damaged the Republican chances of recovery also.

To date there has been no dedicated analysis of political marketing in primary elections, a gap that Bendle and Nastasoiu fill, noting how the US primaries present obstacles to candidates by requiring them to meet the demands of the internal market (party supporters), whose views are generally divergent from, and more ideological than, the external market (voters). They found that candidate strategies differ, and despite the importance of the primaries, the general election is the ultimate market. They suggest that strong candidates can resolve the internal/external market dilemma by focusing on supporters' desire to stop the other party, while weaker candidates need to convey what only they personally can offer. Otherwise candidates who are successful in getting their party's nomination will find it difficult to reposition after a primary.

Miller's chapter suggests that both the success and decline of the Tea Party was in part due to using branding; it helped citizens understand the goals and functions of the movement through memorable beliefs and tactics and played on the beliefs of individual Americans related to spending and taxing. While it was not a party itself it influenced political parties, but might have been able to have more impact if it had utilized branding in full. Nonetheless the chapter suggested that political movements might even be able to utilize branding more easily than parties as they have a more focused, niche market. Now that a wider range of political organizations are using political marketing, it may be that this empowers non-party organizations to compete with established political parties as they can use branding to generate support quickly. Democratically, this could mean that unheard voices get representation more quickly—or it could imply that more radical movements get support too quickly, threatening established democratic structures. Strategically, in the age of super PACs, it may mean that candidates are faced with a choice between taking this outside money but surrendering some of their branding or eschewing it to gain a tighter brand at the cost of financial resources that could be used to build impressions.

Marland and Lalancette explore how celebrity endorsement is an important tool of political marketing, and offers a range of benefits to politicians. It attracts an audience in an environment that is very fragmented and difficult to influence otherwise; and celebrities appeal to target markets including those whom political elites find it hard to connect with—the young, disaffected, and floating voters. There are two types of celebrity endorsers—those who publicize in a general sense and those who help fundraise. Celebrity endorsement is widely used in US politics but there are potential hazards that researchers and strategists should be aware of in terms of compatibility with brand; strategists have to ensure that the celebrities chosen—who have their own commercial brands of course—fit with and support the political product, adding, not detracting, credibility and appeal. Marland and Lalancette show that to achieve full potential of celebrity endorsement, other aspects of political marketing, such as the brand, need to be effective too. Political marketing now offers a wide range of tools, but the interplay between them—in this case celebrity endorsement and branding—is important for it to really succeed.

Moving afield to the sub-national level, Cosgrove argued that candidates can win elections by building brands out of their unique traits; populist issues; and a sense of outrage at current corruption, underperformance, or dysfunction. The chapter presented a theory of personal political branding at the state level, demonstrating how individual politicians at any level of government can create individualized brands, drawing on research including segmentation to identify new emerging segments that they might appeal to that other candidates have not. They also need to ensure that their brand has policies that appeal to new and core voters and reassure voters they can switch to the new brand. Personal branding allows the candidate to sell him- or herself to the voters instead of trying to sell a party and can therefore enable candidates to win in states where their party does not normally succeed. The choice to develop a personal brand is a strategic decision that might well have future career consequences. For example, Mitt Romney's 2012 presidential campaign was impacted by the personal brand he had built during his time as a Massachusetts politician. A wise strategic decision years earlier at the sub-national level can become a strategic liability years later in a presidential race with a very different market.

The main messages from the analysis of online communication in relation to relationship marketing and branding principles by Lilleker and Jackson are that effective e-marketing is interactive and builds relationships that help support the brand; this is what helped Obama succeed in 2008, and he increased interactivity in 2012. Practitioners should therefore make sure that they build this into their designs and avoid less effective one-way, false communication mechanisms, and academics need to assess these criteria when researching online communication. However, to date, practice in US presidential politics has been mixed; the McCain and Romney campaigns failed to use interactivity to its full potential, using online communication to sell their product instead of involving voters in its creation and dissemination. The fact that Obama won the election may suggest that political marketing as a whole will move toward a more relational than transactional approach. Lilleker and Jackson also found that Obama's campaign sought to move volunteers up the political loyalty ladder from being passively engaged to becoming active community members and evangelists. It also helped maintain and enhance the president's relationship with his supporters, demonstrating the importance of relationship marketing. This might have democratic positives by increasing deliberation within political communication and democratic engagement in participation, though it is not without practical problems as it reduces elite control.

Williams and Gulati's critique of the relationship-marketing effectiveness of congressional politicians' social media found that it contains many weaknesses; e-marketing is not being used permanently to build relationships, or interactively, or to build social networks. This indicates that non-presidential campaigns face challenges in using the full potential of e-marketing. While some candidates and staff recognized the need to use social media more strategically, most need to improve their effectiveness and integrate marketing principles within their online communication, such as conducting market intelligence with feedback to the campaign and two-way communication between candidate and voter, segmenting the market to target campaign messages to specific groups, and building long-term relationships.

Busby's analysis of female conservative candidates noted how the Mama Grizzly brand was designed to appeal to specific market segments—women generally, women suffering economically, and women who were socially conservative. However, the "pink elephant" brand failed to attract women. Busby argues that this was because while women voters desire masculine traits because they are important to show leadership, they also want female political candidates to show emotional and behavioral traits that would be considered feminine, especially in policy terms, so the socially conservative aggressive Mama Grizzly brand works against existing research into what voters want. Most prominent Mama Grizzly candidates received more votes from male voters than female voters, so gender may not be as useful a part of political marketing strategy as we might think when looking at the pink elephant case.

Ridout's exploration of the marketing behind the advertisements makes it clear that market research is fundamental to the development of effective ads: the message and medium are designed to suit targets derived from segmentation to maximize resource effectiveness, and the ads are also tested before launch to ensure they will achieve the goals. His chapter addresses an oversight in existing political advertising by helping to understand what goes into an ad, rather than just researching it once it is completed. Increasingly, ads will be subject to increased testing before release, through experimental and analytic marketing research. Like Marland and Lalancette, Ridout notes how targeting ads has become very important in today's complex media environment. These findings reiterate our assertion above that political marketing techniques tend to be used in an overlapping fashion that creates a more potent end product. In this case, market research gains power when it is used in conjunction with other tools like advertising. Conversely, advertising by itself is not worth so much, but when it is combined with research and segmentation of the market into target groups and fits the overall brand and candidates' product message, that is when it will be most effective.

Garrett's discussion of crisis-management in campaigns highlights how crisis threatens a whole range of political marketing strategies and makes the point about the power of synergy by looking at what happens when events cause it to fall apart. Branding, positioning, product choices, and communication all need effective planning if they are to respond to market research as political marketing research would advise. In such planning, the availability of resources such as finances is taken into account when formulating the strategy. But if crisis in the form of changes to campaign finances enters the picture and causes uncertainty in the knowledge about the market and resources, then the effectiveness of such a strategy is undermined and a cascade of failures can ensue that speed up a campaign's demise. And in the heat of a campaign, it is difficult to make appropriate strategic choices and candidates may be prone to reverting to more tactical, day-to-day political marketing, which can be less successful. Thus more resources need to be invested in predicting and preparing for potential crisis and risks that might occur in future campaigns. Of course, crisis-management is also needed in government, and the last two chapters focus on political marketing in government.

Elder's theoretical framework of how political leaders can maintain the image of a market-orientation in power by making sure their communication follows certain principles and his analysis of communication by President Obama in his first term show that when leaders become market oriented and get into power, they need to be aware of the challenges they will face in government, and the need to lead yet stay in touch. They need to adopt more reflective forms of communication, especially where they are showing leadership, to maintain public support. So they need to convey that they are listening through responsiveness and reflectiveness; they need to show leadership, yet be honest and authentic, and to convey the common goals and benefits of their decisions and the context of social and governmental variables. Modern political leadership, within a marketized environment, thus calls for a more modern form of communication. Leaders cannot just get into power, then do what they like—not even when they had a clear mandate for their proposals. Consider the case of George W. Bush, who ran in both 2000 and 2004, on Social Security reform as a policy offering yet never managed to implement it. More hierarchical and authoritative forms of leadership communication such as "I am the leader, I need to follow my conviction" no longer prove effective. This is an important lesson for political leaders in the United States and indeed all around the world.

The last Democratic president, Bill Clinton, promised to deliver health care reform once elected but was unable to do so, and Conley's chapter on Obama's delivery marketing in his first term demonstrates the importance of delivery marketing in government, both to ensure that promised policy gets legislated and to help build support for re-election. While Obama produced effective delivery ads in time for the 2012 election called "Keeping His Word"—reminding voters of the many things he had succeeded in delivering—it could be argued these came quite late. Conley notes that delivery is a story that has to be told—and sometimes defended—in relation to what is promised on the campaign trail. Obama's health care delivery strategy failed to reap the rewards for successful delivery. Delivery, while at the end of the political marketing process, actually connects with the beginning—the next election—and politicians in power often neglect this. However, delivery marketing is not easy, given the constraints and pressures of governing, and this was conveyed in the mini documentary/advertisement produced by the Obama camp called "The Road We've Traveled." This is a groundbreaking piece of communication that discussed the difficulties of being president to help remind voters so their judgment on performance could be conducted within the right context. It is hard to get credit from voters for successful delivery, and more research needs to be conducted on this, integrating further business concepts such as reputation management. Nonetheless, more effective delivery marketing could build a long-term buffer of support and avoid the anxiety around re-election that occurred in the 2012 election. As Conley concludes, "[I]n a market-oriented politics, the importance of a properly managed delivery process cannot be overstated."

The chapters therefore demonstrated the scope and range of political marketing, but also discussed how each element of political marketing—from the four areas of researching, strategizing, organizing, and communication—connects with and influences the others.

The Implications of Political Marketing for Democracy

The implications of political marketing have been discussed in the field by several scholars. Here we build on the themes in such literature and discuss the implications for democracy in the US context.

The Positives of Political Marketing

Political marketing offers the potential to enhance social connectedness, increase participation, and strengthen democratic institutions in the United States. It does so because it manages to take the esoteric world of public affairs and make it accessible to the public. Further political marketing encourages the public and the elite to interact much in the way that Eddie Bernays thought would be possible when writing in the early-to-middle part of the twentieth century. Bernays believed in an elite-led dialogue with the population as a way to build a strong society and good governance. Political marketing offers the potential to transform Bernays's more managerial, elite-driven vision into a representative participatory conversation that increases the political system's legitimacy and social connectedness (for an in-depth discussion of Bernays, see either Ewen 1996 or Tye 2002). Through well-constructed surveys and focus groups, public attitudes can be measured and marketing campaigns can be constructed in response to the public's perceived needs. Through political marketing and branding, people can come to feel stronger connections with politicians and public affairs than might well otherwise be the case in a society of 330 million people in which economics, not public life, is generally the focus of activity. As the chapter on the evolution of voter targeting shows, political marketing develops strategic literacy, which has helped to undermine old-boy networks, including those entrenched in political party organizations.

In addition, political marketing allows politicians to cut through the clutter of contemporary American life. This has never been a country for those who wanted a lot of quiet and this it remains. Americans are bombarded with messages from dawn until dusk about all sorts of products. In addition, there are many, many sports and entertainment options that exist in modern America that were not dreamed of even into the early years of the twentieth century. The modern citizen can receive all of his or her information about politics from dead-tree media like newspapers, magazines, and books; from terrestrial broadcast radio and television; or from a host of Internet-based competitors, many of which empower citizens to become the producers of content. Political marketing is a particularly valuable activity for the citizen given the infotainment culture that exists in the United States because it allows the candidates to understand what the voters want systematically and to explain themselves and their ideas to the voters in formats that the voters will actually access. As Neil Postman noted (1985), much of modern American culture can be summed up as a quest for more entertainment rather than more engagement. Consider the amount of professional sporting activity that Americans can regularly see on their televisions—for example, they can see college football for up to 18 hours on a Saturday, followed by 11 hours of professional football on Sunday, followed by another program on Monday nights and a college game most nights of the week. People can easily become more attentive citizens of a team's fan base more than the city, state, or country in which they live and know more about the leadership, strategic situation, and future choices of their team than of their country, state, or city. Even if a person develops an interest in public affairs, he or she is faced with specialty cable television channels covering both houses of Congress, endless hours of cable TV news and analysis programs, and a worldwide web full of sites about American political life and public affairs.

As wonderful as this sounds, for the average person, it can be a source of great confusion and information overload. Political marketing can help the public to develop an interest in public affairs, cut through this clutter, and learn about important events facing the country, with branding simplifying but also creating differentiation between products and thus offering voters more choice (see Scammell 2008; O'Cass and Voola 2010). On the elite side, political marketing helps candidates to reach the public by coming to identify what aspects of the political product the public might be interested in and how to communicate them in a way that competes—or co-operates—with such entertainment. Clinton and Obama both liked college basketball, Bush liked major league baseball, and Ronald Reagan reinvigorated the tradition of calling victorious sports teams, something that has continued and expanded to include annual White House visits by a plethora of winning teams throughout his and his successors' administration. Doing these things is a way for political leaders to signal target audiences, to show that they are just like other Americans and that, despite their lofty status, they have common interests and the common touch.

Additionally, political marketing encourages politicians to think about people as members of groups in a way that makes it easier to understand which issues are important to whom and where. It also enables them to discover how to make it desirable and easy for people to volunteer for candidates and parties (Lees-Marshment and Pettitt 2014). Packaging politicians does what Bentley and Truman independently argued group affiliation did for the average citizen a hundred years ago: helps them to make sense out of a very confusing world. Given the amount of organizational decline and decrease in civic engagement in modern America, political marketing can be an important tool through which the public can be encouraged to both pay attention to and participate in politics. In this sense political marketing is a good thing for democracy and the rise of marketed politics illustrates that the public and the politicians have found a way to engage each other in a time of technical change and shifting mores.

The Problems of Political Marketing

Nevertheless, political marketing raises fundamental questions about the health of American democracy because it has the potential to reduce the citizens to the kind of infantile entities of which Barber (2007) has written, produced as an end result of consumerist values. The fact that policy is determined by research into voter demands and the fact of the constraints of needing to communicate it in easily digestible bites for citizens to consume both limits the scope of their choices and forestalls their intellectual ability to consider alternatives (see Paré and Berger 2008). Instead of seeing a wide variety of policy and candidate options, the public is normally presented with whatever candidates and issues a set of political professionals in Washington chooses for them—albeit determined by researching their views. As Paleologos (1997: 1184) argues, "[A] poll-driven society . . . ignores creativity. It overlooks new ideas. It prohibits change and true reform."

Finding new ways to reach, persuade, and mobilize the public has become a full-scale industry employing many professionals. Marketed politics may, as a result, never solve our problems fully because new problems need to be found in order for the political professional to continue being employed as a political professional. In this way, political marketing is engaged in the kind of exchange that Salisbury (1969) noted takes place in the interest group universe in which the group leader develops a set of issues and benefits, then sells those to potential members at a price higher than cost, thus setting members up for continued involvement in political life. So long as the interest group organizer keeps his or her end of the exchange and works on the issues that he or she recruits members with, the organizer is free to do whatever else he or she would like with the rest of his or her professional time. Political marketers are like the group entrepreneurs in that they have to constantly come up with solutions for clients. The clients may be seeking office or they may be seeking a benefit from the government, or to enact a policy preference. Thus, new problems have to be found, new solutions proposed, and new ways to differentiate from either an undesirable present through nostalgia and the promise of renewal or an undesirable past through great hopes for the future must be found. Political marketing might keep us quiet, but the professional incentives of those engaged in doing it ensure that we will never be fully happy. Thus, as Boorstin (1992), writing about the rise of pseudo-events in the 1960s, noted, we become unhappy because we expect more than the world can give us. Thus, just as events have to be created, so too do political problems need to be sold, and the next candidate always has to be better than the last one, just like the next generation of smart phones always has to be better than the last one.

Another challenge that political marketing raises is the question of where problems and solutions to problems come from. As Savigny (2008a: 38–40) notes, preference shaping can be carried out by elites, whether by politicians or the media or politicians influencing the media (see also Temple 2010; Savigny and Temple 2010; Coleman 2007). If Washington, D.C., is a city of solutions in search of problems (Kingdon 2002), then marketing can become the technique through which the solution in search of a problem is sold to the public as the solution to a specific problem. It might be argued that much of what was in the Patriot Act and, indeed, the creation of the Department of Homeland Security were ideas that had been floating around Washington for years. Only with the emergence of a huge problem on 9/11 did the political conditions come into being that allowed these solutions to be marketed to a specific problem. It could be suggested that creating these agencies at this time was done to sell the public on the idea that the government in general and the administration in particular were on top of the situation. Many extant solutions were applied to this problem and packaged for the public through devices like the "Patriot Act," which enabled the government to enhance its domestic surveillance and security efforts in the name of fighting terror and promoting safety. Plus, there were a raft of patriotic ribbons, stickers, and signage that appeared rather quickly after these events. The use of these marketing tools had the effect of shaping a particular discussion, and limited the extent to which dissenters were considered to be expressing legitimate opinions. Political marketing can be employed with the anti-democratic goal of creating acquiescence rather than the democratic one of promoting representation.

By looking at citizens as consumers, political marketing loses the potential to be a civic activity offering the promise of a stronger society in every case, and instead becomes an activity in which attitudes are measured and packages created, and the goal of building social quietude and elite control is maintained (see Lilleker and Scullion 2008: 4; Savigny 2008b). We can see this in the way in which people who attended the most elite educational institutions in the country and are very much members of elite socioeconomic networks strive to be perceived as authentic average people. They usually do so by pointing out some common activity in which they engage or common experiences that they have had. For example, George H. W. Bush talked about his great love of country music and pork rinds; in this way political marketing serves as a tool of the power elite (Mills 1956). Bill Clinton talked about his common background in the small-town South even though he had grown up in the resort town of Hot Springs before leaving for

Georgetown and Oxford, returning only to occupy an academic position in Fayetteville before running for public office. George H.W. Bush was all about using the cowboy image that Reagan developed, yet unlike Reagan, he was never pictured anywhere near a horse (he used a pickup truck as a prop instead). He did, however, have a ranch, just as Reagan had. The difference, one could argue, was that Reagan was the authentic original and Bush was just a guy using a brand. Obama has also tried to convey the same point and to minimize his background as a graduate of Harvard and Columbia. Political marketing, then, has the potential to allow elites to obscure the fact that they are elites at all.

Lastly, it can be argued that the amount of polarization in the country has increased just as political marketing has increased, suggesting that it works against unity and cohesion. Marketers have learned to find the right customers for their products, which in practice often means concentrating on a few subsets of the population and firing all the others. This, in turn, has developed a kind of highly segmented conversation that takes place within but not across audiences, as Turow has described on multiple occasions (see Turow 1998, 2006; Lilleker 2005; Savigny 2008a). In this Americans have, in politics, become like any other group of brand loyalists. An example would be fans of the aforementioned pro sports teams. In the case of the National Hockey League, fans of the Boston Bruins often talk about the Montreal Canadiens but hardly ever to anyone who follows the Habs. This is a somewhat different activity than simply discussing NHL competition in an even-handed fashion. The ability to segment and narrowcast has turned the polity into the equivalent of individual hockey team fan bases. Americans speak within their niches about things they agree upon and about how awful their political opponents are. Thus, politicians find some target, be it welfare queens driving pink Cadillacs (Reagan) or millionaires and billionaires flying around on their corporate jets (Obama), to hit their audience targets on the emotive level that inspires them to act. Just as is true in the hockey example, this is not the same activity as discussing public policy or making choices for the country based on objective evidence.

Striking a Balance: Political Marketing, the Informed Citizen, and Social Organizing

In a closed-loop system in which the public had little ability to impact the decisions politicians made, the dystopian vision above would be very accurate. The American system allows for a great deal of public input. This input can come in the simple form of voting for a candidate for office, or it can take place through the more demanding processes of community and interest group organizing, or through direct contact with elected officials. Were marketing the only thing that mattered, the potential for abuse would be very high indeed—but there are, of course, other forces at work in the American political system that constrain the power of political marketing.

First, increasingly partisan media is more than willing to showcase the faults of the other side. The days of a few big media outlets and politicians to collude to shape public opinion are in the past, and so is political marketing's potential to manipulate the public on an ongoing basis (see Temple 2010; Savigny and Temple 2010; Temple 2013). Much of what constitutes news and the information product in the United States is more of an infotainment product variety accessible through vehicles other than mainstream news and is much more of a collaboratively created product than was once the case. This is not to say that the current media is of higher quality than its predecessor, but rather that it is more ubiquitous and has the ability to be much more disruptive to a political marketing campaign than it once was. Social media's rise has exacerbated the loss of elite control of communication. These channels, because they are ubiquitous, have put the person formerly behind the curtain squarely on the stage, meaning that it is difficult to manipulate anything anymore because there are no shadows. These channels are also disruptive in that they allow many more voices to evaluate political products, then decide to either evangelize for or preach against said products. The result has been the increase in the ability of a campaign's message to be amplified, at the same time that political producer's ability to control the process of this happening becomes more limited than it used to be in the age in which people could be paid to participate in guerilla advertising, to act as the paid representatives of a given product within their demographic and physical communities, or to engage in mass events to drive the marketing message. Now, with suggested posts, retweets, and people making personal statements in public forums, political producers have gained the ability to have more authentic testimonials from spokespeople whom their audience targets really know and who are willing to testify about the greatness of the political product because they chose it themselves. As a result, the ability of a political marketer to simply mislead and manipulate the public is less than it was back in the time of morning dailies and 30-minute nightly newscasts. The rough-and-tumble nature of American media limits the ability of political marketers to tell a consistently misleading story to the public.

Second, Americans have choices and there is partisan competition. In politics, both parties have sporadically incorporated elements of marketing, but only in the first decade of the twenty-first century could it be truly said that both parties were working with full consumer marketing models in the way that commercial producers do. A candidate or party may be able to mislead the people sometimes but, over time, the ability to do so will be limited because marketed politics demands results. Both major parties are now aware of and use political marketing, and have extensive marketing infrastructure. Although the Republicans led the charge on the use of analytical marketing, after their 2000 and 2004 defeats Democrats began looking at and adopting what the Republicans were doing organizationally with marketing (Bai 2008; Berman 2010). This effort bore fruit in 2006 with the election of a Democratic majority in Congress (Peters and Rosenthal 2010) and the election of Barack Obama in 2008. The net benefit for American citizens and democracy has been the development of two parties that are equally well versed in the uses of marketing techniques, meaning that they can target their own audiences and tell their own stories, but also develop counternarratives about what their opponents are claiming. The political marketplace in the United States now more strongly resembles the consumer marketplace. The net result is a voter/consumer who has much clearer, if not more, choices than was once the case and a political entity that knows which consumers it is chasing and how to do so. The result is a more efficient, easier-to-understand process. The public has a better idea of which candidates it should have an interest in and which it should not.

Third, political marketing can also be used by leaders to implement change. In response to the results of research, the second Obama administration sought to utilize professional athletes to act as spokespeople to encourage younger audiences to sign up for health insurance. This campaign was to be modeled on what was done in Massachusetts in 2007 (*New York Times* Editorial Board 2013) in a campaign that featured the Boston Red Sox organization and targeted men between the ages of 19 and 39 (Rowland 2007). The ads in this campaign appeared on Red Sox broadcasts, featured the Red Sox Fenway Ambassadors group talking about having health insurance coverage themselves, a testimonial from a man who suffered an arm injury and made use of the insurance to get treatment,[1] a special night game night focusing on the campaign, and Red Sox logos on health insurance related materials (Rowland 2007; Boston Red Sox 2007). Mounting a campaign like this shows one of the biggest values political marketing adds to American life. This campaign and the one for Obamacare are both educational, in that they teach young people that these exchanges exist and what the benefits of health insurance are, but also help the political marketers achieve an important policy goal: the exchanges will not be viable without enough young, healthy people enrolling to subsidize the older and sicker populations who will likely enroll as well. The policy's success literally depends on the success of the marketing campaign, but it is a marketing campaign that is aimed at encouraging young people to do something that is responsible in personal health and financial terms. While the age of political marketing does come with some potential for manipulation, it also comes with the potential to increase public engagement, achieve societal change, and enhance the depth and length of the relationships that citizens develop with politicians, parties, and policies.

Future Research

Political Marketing in the United States has demonstrated the breadth and scope of marketing in the political sphere, in both parties and groups, campaigns and government, and at the federal, state, and local levels. Political marketing is an underdeveloped field in general in the United States, meaning that there exist a number of potential areas of research that can have a significant impact on the field's development. Marketing offers a wide range of concepts and tools to understand political marketing practice, and while research has explored many of them, there remain many aspects that would benefit from additional scholarship. Williams (2012: 5) identified gaps in areas covered by articles published in the *Journal of Political Marketing's* first 10 years, some of which we would agree warrant attention not just in the journal but in all publications, including the political marketing activities of government leaders or institutions; NGOs lobbying or advocacy activities; and the role of marketing in public relations campaigns and public policy promotion by governmental and nongovernmental actors. The majority of political marketing research focuses on the highest level of government—the presidential level—and thus the field would benefit from an emphasis on political marketing at the congressional level, including how the leadership in both houses markets its platform or caucus to the nation. Of course there is scope for greater analysis of political marketing at the state level, including governors, and also at the local level. As has been shown in this volume, there is a unique political market in each state in terms of who has power, the level of professionalism of the institutions, and the length of term in office, which can each impact both the design and success of a marketing strategy. More exploration and explanation of these differences would be most useful.

Further research that applies concepts from reputation management, public relations, and relationship marketing within government would also be particularly beneficial, as would work adapting consumer behavior concepts to the analysis of voters, volunteers, and activists. There are also areas of business marketing that have never been applied to politics, such as b-to-b (business-to-business) marketing, which could be used to help understand how politicians market themselves to each other within the legislature, for example, or marketing by interest groups wishing to influence legislation.

Emerging research themes that reflect changes in our society include examining the way in which political marketing to visible minorities and by visible minority candidates is conducted, including how political marketing is done in Spanish, but also in Chinese, Brazilian Portuguese, Vietnamese, Haitian Creole, and the many other languages spoken in the country. Marketing along gender lines both to voters and within candidates' campaigns is another area for future discussion, as is how political marketing has been used by sexual minority communities in the United States, specifically the role of marketing in the campaign for marriage and adoption rights.

Of course, the one constant in American politics has always been and continues to be change and innovation. To become a truly mature discipline, political marketing must be willing to look relentlessly at the technological and strategic environmental changes that always take place in US politics. Keeping a close eye on the latest developments in practice is very important. But so too is the normative aspect. Scholarship that explores the potential for politicians and political practitioners to use marketing in a way that enhances societal change, improves trust between politicians and their public, enables more participative forms of organization, and helps elites show political leadership—while remaining aware of the potential negatives that political marketing has for democracy—would advance our understanding of the potential contribution marketing might make to helping politics adapt to the ever-changing conditions of the twenty-first century.

Note

1 www.youtube.com/watch?v=MO_jvkgBdlM

References

Bai, M. (2008). *The argument: Inside the battle to remake democratic politics*. New York, NY: Penguin Books.

Barber, B.R. (2007). *Consumed: How markets corrupt children, infantilize adults and swallow citizens whole*. New York, NY: W.W. Norton & Company.

Berman, A. (2010). *Herding donkeys: The fight to rebuild the Democratic Party and reshape American politics*. New York, NY: Farrar, Straus and Giroux.

Boorstin, D.J. (1992). *The image: A guide to pseudo-events in America*. New York, NY: Vintage.

Boston Red Sox. (2007, May 22). Connector teams up with Red Sox to build enrollment in new health insurance plans. Press release from the Red Sox. http://boston.redsox.mlb.com/news/press_releases/press_release.jsp?ymd=20070522&content_id=1979252&vkey=pr_bos&fext=.jsp&c_id=bos

Coleman, S. (2007). Review of Lilleker and Lees-Marshment (2005) Political marketing: A comparative perspective. *Parliamentary Affairs, 60*(1), 180–186.

Ewen, S. (1996). *PR!—A social history of spin*. New York, NY: Basic Books.

Kingdon, J. (2002). *Agendas, alternatives and public policies*. Longman Classics Edition (2nd ed.). New York, NY: A. B. Longman.

Lees-Marshment, J., & Pettitt, R. (2014, forthcoming). Mobilising volunteer activists in political parties: The view from central office. *Contemporary Politics* (expected issue 2 or 3).

Lilleker, D.G. (2005). Political marketing: The cause of an emerging democratic deficit in Britain? In W. Wymer & J. Lees-Marshment (Eds.), *Current issues in political marketing* (pp. 5–26). Binghamton, NY: Best Business Books.

Lilleker, D.G., & Scullion, R. (Eds.). (2008). *Voters or consumers: Imagining the contemporary electorate*. Newcastle, UK: Cambridge Scholars Publishing.

Mills, C.W. (1956). *The power elite*. New York, NY: Oxford University Press.

New York Times Editorial Board. (2013, July 2). A chance for pro sports to help on healthcare. *New York Times*. www.nytimes.com/2013/07/03/opinion/a-chance-for-pro-sports-to-help-on-health-care.html

O'Cass, A., & Voola, R. (2010). Explications of political market orientation and political brand orientation using the resource-based view of the political party. *Journal of Marketing Management, 27*(5–6), 627–645.

Paleologos, D.A. (1997). A pollster on polling. *American Behavioral Scientist, 40*(8), 1183–1189.

Paré, D.J., & Berger, F. (2008). Political marketing Canadian style? The Conservative Party and the 2006 federal election. *Canadian Journal of Communication, 33*(1), 39–63.

Peters, R.S., & Rosenthal, C.S. (2010). *Speaker Nancy Pelosi and the new American politics*. New York, NY: Oxford University Press.

Postman, N. (1985). *Amusing ourselves to death: Public discourse in the age of show business.* New York, NY: Penguin Books.

Rowland, C. (2007, May 22). Ads for state health plan to target Red Sox Nation: $3m blitz aims to get viewers to buy policies before July 1 deadline. *The Boston Globe.* www.boston.com/business/globe/articles/2007/05/22/ads_for_state_health_plan_to_target_red_sox_nation/

Salisbury, R.H. (1969). An exchange theory of interest groups. *Midwest Journal of Political Science, 13*(1), 1–32.

Savigny, H. (2008a). *The problem of political marketing.* New York, NY: Continuum International Publishing Group Ltd.

Savigny, H. (2008b). The construction of the political consumer (or Politics: What not to consume). In D. Lilleker & R. Scullion (Eds.), *Voters or consumers: Imagining the contemporary electorate.* Newcastle, UK: Cambridge Scholars Publishing.

Savigny, H., & Temple, M. (2010). Political marketing models: The curious incident of the dog that doesn't bark. *Political Studies, 58*(5), 1049–1064.

Scammell, M. (2008). Brand Blair: marketing politics in the consumer age. In D. Lilleker & R. Scullion (Eds.), *Voters or consumers: Imagining the contemporary electorate.* Newcastle, UK: Cambridge Scholars Publishing.

Temple, M. (2010). Political marketing, party behaviour and political science. In J. Lees-Marshment, J. Stromback, & C. Rudd (Eds.), *Global political marketing* (pp. 263–277). London, UK: Routledge.

Temple, M. (2013). The media and the message. *Journal of Political Marketing, 12*(2/3), 147–165.

Turow, J. (1998). *Breaking up America: Advertisers and the new media world.* Chicago, IL: University of Chicago Press.

Turow, J. (2006). *Niche envy: Media discrimination in the digital age.* Cambridge, MA: MIT Press.

Tye, L.J. (2002). *The father of spin: Edward L. Bernays and the birth of public relations.* New York, NY: Henry Holt.

Williams, C.B. (2012). Trends and changes in journal of political marketing titles 2002–2011. *Journal of Political Marketing, 11*(1–2), 4–7.

LIST OF CONTRIBUTORS

Neil Bendle (Ivey Business School, Western University, Canada) is assistant professor of marketing. Prior to becoming an academic he was the director of finance for the British Labour Party. He researches decision making, political marketing, measuring marketing success, and competitive strategy and is the co-author of *Marketing Metrics and Behavioural Economics for Kids*. He blogs about his research interests at www.neilbendle.com.

Jeff Bergner (Christopher Newport University, United States) teaches American government and foreign policy. He has taught at the University of Pennsylvania, the University of Michigan, and Georgetown University. His most recent book (with Lisa Spiller) is *Branding the Candidate: Marketing Strategies to Win Your Vote* (Praeger, 2011). He has served as staff director of the U.S. Senate Foreign Relations Committee and as assistant secretary of state.

Michael John Burton (Ohio University, United States) is an associate professor of political science. With Daniel M. Shea, he has written *Campaign Craft: The Strategies, Tactics, and Art of Political Campaign Management* (Praeger, 2001, 2006, 2010), and *Campaign Mode: Strategic Vision in Congressional Elections* (Rowman & Littlefield, 2003). Dr. Burton spent several years as a political professional in Washington, including work in the office of Vice President Al Gore as special assistant to the chief of staff and assistant political director.

Robert Busby (Liverpool Hope University, United Kingdom) is a researcher in political marketing and American politics. His books include *Marketing the Populist Politician: The Demotic Democrat* (Palgrave, 2009), *Defending the American Presidency:*

Clinton and the Lewinsky Scandal (Palgrave, 2001), and *Reagan and the Iran-Contra Affair: The Politics of Presidential Recovery* (Macmillan, 1999).

Brian M. Conley (Suffolk University, United States) is an assistant professor of government at Suffolk University in Boston, Massachusetts. His principal research interests are in the areas of U.S. electoral politics, political parties, and political marketing. He received his PhD in political science from the New School for Social Research in New York City.

Kenneth Cosgrove (Suffolk University, United States) is associate professor of government at Suffolk University in Boston, Massachusetts. He is the author of *Branded Conservatives: How the Brand Brought the American Right from the Fringes to the Center of American Politics* (Peter Lang, 2007).

Edward Elder (University of Auckland, New Zealand) is a PhD candidate in political studies, with a focus on political marketing communication. Edward is also co-editor of the Political Marketing Group newsletter and is a tutor and research assistant at the University of Auckland.

R. Sam Garrett (Congressional Research Service and American University, United States) is specialist in American national government at the Congressional Research Service, Library of Congress, United States. He also serves as an adjunct faculty member at the American University School of Public Affairs, where he is also a research fellow at the Center for Congressional and Presidential Studies. He is the author of *Campaign Crises: Detours on the Road to Congress* (Lynne Rienner Publishers, 2010). See www.american.edu/spa/faculty/samg.cfm for additional details.

Girish J. "Jeff" Gulati (Bentley University, United States) is an associate professor of political science at Bentley University with areas of expertise in the U.S. Congress, campaigns and elections, e-government, and telecommunications policy. He also serves on the editorial board of the *Journal of Political Marketing* and the senior editorial board of the *Journal of Informational Technology & Politics*. See https://faculty.bentley.edu/details.asp?uname=jgulati for additional details.

Nigel Jackson (Plymouth University, United Kingdom) is reader in persuasion and communication. His work especially covers online political communication and his books include *Politics: The Basics* (Routledge, 2014), *Promoting and Marketing Events* (Routledge, 2013), *Political Campaigning, Elections and the Internet* (Routledge, 2011) and *The Marketing of Political Parties* (Manchester University Press, 2006).

Mireille Lalancette (Université du Québec à Trois-Rivières, Canada) researches political communication, gender, and media, with a particular emphasis on framing.

She is currently working on the transformations of political actors' representations in the context of spectacularization and personalization. She is also a researcher at the Political Communication Research Lab (GRCP).

Jennifer Lees-Marshment (University of Auckland, New Zealand) is a researcher in political marketing. Her books include *The Routledge Handbook of Political Marketing* (Routledge, 2012), *Political Marketing: Principles and Applications* (Routledge, 2009), *Global Political Marketing* (Routledge, 2010), *The Political Marketing Game* (Palgrave Macmillan, 2011) and *Political Marketing in Canada* (UBC, 2012). See www.lees-marshment.org for further details.

Darren G. Lilleker (Bournemouth University, United Kingdom) is associate professor of political communication. His work covers a range of topics in the field of political communication, political marketing, and citizen participation, with books including *Political Communication and Cognition* (Palgrave, 2014), *Political Campaigning, Elections and the Internet* (Routledge, 2011), and the best-selling textbook *Key Concepts in Political Communication* (Sage, 2006). See http://staffprofiles.bournemouth.ac.uk/display/dlilleker for further details.

Alex Marland (Memorial University of Newfoundland, Canada) researches political communication and electioneering. He was the lead editor of books about political marketing, political communication, and public policy, and has published in international journals on such topics as political talk radio, the management of political photography, and the merger of political parties.

William J. Miller (Flagler College, Florida, United States) is director of institutional research and effectiveness and an associate faculty in public administration and political science. His books include *Tea Party Effects on 2010 U.S. Senate Elections: Stuck in the Middle to Lose, Taking Sides: Clashing Views on Public Administration & Policy, The Political Battle over Congressional Redistricting, The 2012 Nomination and the Future of the Republican Party: The Internal Battle, Handbook on Teaching and Learning in Political Science*, and *Taking Sides: Clashing Views on Political Issues*.

Tasha Miracle (Ohio State University, United States) is a research student at the Moritz College of Law. She earned a master's in public administration from the George V. Voinovich School of Public Affairs at Ohio University (2011) and a bachelor of arts in political science (2009) at Ohio University with an emphasis in pre-law.

Mihaela-Alina Nastasoiu (Ivey Business School, Western University, Canada) is a PhD candidate in marketing. She has a master's in economics from the Central European University and worked for Proctor and Gamble. Her research interests include modeling decision making, behavioral economics, and customer analytics. Her website is www.ivey.uwo.ca/phd/people/marketing/alina-nastasoiu.htm.

Vincent Raynauld (Carleton University, Canada) is a researcher with an interest in political communication, social media, Web persuasion, and e-learning. He is currently serving as a research associate with the Research Group in Political Communication (RGPC) based in Laval University and as an academic adviser for Samara, a nonprofit organization researching political engagement in Canada.

Travis N. Ridout (Washington State University, United States) is Thomas S. Foley Distinguished Professor of Government and Public Policy. His books include *New Directions in Media and Politics* (Routledge, 2013), *The Persuasive Power of Campaign Advertising* (Temple, 2011), and *Campaign Advertising and American Democracy* (Temple, 2007).

Lisa Spiller (Christopher Newport University, United States) is Distinguished Professor of Marketing in Joseph W. Luter III School of Business and teaches direct and database marketing and integrated marketing communications, and has helped her university pioneer a major in direct and interactive marketing. She is coauthor (with Martin Baier) of the textbook *Contemporary Direct and Interactive Marketing*, 3rd edition (Racom, 2012), and is also coauthor (with Jeff Bergner) of *Branding the Candidate: Marketing Strategies to Win Your Vote* (Praeger, 2011).

André Turcotte (Carleton University, Canada) is an associate professor at Carleton University's School of Journalism and Communication and the graduate supervisor for the Clayton H. Riddell Graduate Program in Political Management. He holds a doctorate from the University of Toronto. He has also published articles in academic journals and chapters in several books. More recently, he has coauthored *Dynasties and Interludes*, which looks at the dynamics of electoral politics in Canada from 1867 to the present day.

Christine B. Williams (Bentley University, United States) is a professor of political science. She serves as managing editor, North America, for the *Journal of Political Marketing*, and on the editorial boards of the *Journal of Information Technology and Politics*, *Journal of Public Affairs*, and the *International Journal of e-Politics*. She edited and contributed to the book *Political Marketing in Retrospective and Prospective* (Routledge, 2012) and has published in a wide variety of academic journals. See https://faculty.bentley.edu/details.asp?uname=cwilliams for further details.

INDEX

2010 midterm election 68–9, 70, 123–4, 211–15, 284–5
2012 presidential election 61, 132–3, 139–43, 174–80, 228–33, 244–5, 285–6
2008 presidential election 48–52, 165, 174–80
2004 presidential election 224
2000 presidential election 226

Bush, George W. 15, 57, 100–3, 295

campaign crises 236–50
campaign finance 240–9
campaign technology 44–5, 66, 174–5, 180, 185–8, 197–8
campaigns 9–10, 14–15, 26–7, 86, 290–9; advertising in 220–33; advice/manuals for 32–9; candidate strategies towards markets in 100–3; celebrity endorsement during 139–43; crisis management, marketing, and money in 236–50; geo-targeting in 215, technology in 44–5, 50–2, 56–7, 165–6, 168–9, 173–80, 185–99
candidate strategy 100–8, 292
celebrity endorsement 130–44, 292–3
Clinton, Bill 8–9, 10–11, 14–15, 276
communication 6, 49, 51, 52, 56, 291, 293; of delivery 275, 276–7, 283–6; for interactivity 168–71; governing leader's 253–69, 295; modes of 172, 176, 180–1; populist type of 65, 67–8; for relationship marketing 195–6
crisis management 236–50, 294–5

database(s), database marketing 44–58, 290–1
delivery 11, 49, 57, 262–3, 267, 272–86, 295–6
Democrat(s), Democratic Party 10–11, 87, 178–80, 223, 245–7, 283, 301–2; nominees/candidates 91, 97–100, 165–6, 176, 279

electability 87, 89–91, 97–100, 105–8
elites 7–8, 64–5, 269, 290, 296
engagement 178, 196, 197, 298

Facebook 104, 106, 190, 191, 193, 196
feminism 203, 204, 206, 213, 215
fundraising 136–7, 140–1, 240, 245–6

gender politics 34–6, 202–17, 294, 303
governing 47, 53–6, 57–8, 253–5, 295–6
governors (governorship) 137, 149, 154–61, 162

health care 11, 54–5, 260–8, 272–86, 295

in touch, 255, 258, 261–2, 267, 295
interactivity 168–9, 172–3, 178
Internet 44–5, 165–6, 168–81, 214–15; *also see* Facebook, social media, Twitter

leadership 57, 210; signifiers of 204–5, 207, 216, 253–69, 294, 295
listening 57, 290; communicating quality of 253, 257, 258, 261–2, 269, 295

Mama Grizzly 202–17, 294
market intelligence 49, 114, 197
market segmentation 188, 192–5
marketing process model 48, 188
market-orientation 14–15, 47–50, 65; in government; 53–6, 58, 253–69, 273–4, 286, 295
microtargeting 31, 35, 37, 237
midterms 112, 214, 272, 284
mobilization 51, 64–5, 67, 81, 196, 210–11

niche marketing 126, 143, 207, 209–10

Obama, Barack 50–8, 97–100, 229–30, 232; branding and relationship building of 165–6, 173–81; communication by 11–12, 260–8; delivery by 278–85
ObamaCare 11, 261–8, 272–86
organizing 4, 53–4

Palin, Sarah 202, 203, 205, 209, 211–15
permanent campaign 28, 62
personal branding 148–62
political advertising 100–3, 220–33, 245, 249, 294; examples of 52, 91–2, 213–14, 246–8, 285–6, 295–6

political loyalty ladder 170, 178
primaries 83–108, 292; examples of 123, 157, 214, 215, 227, 279
product-orientation 114, 125
professionals 2, 30, 237–8, 241–2, 249–50, 298–9
publicity 133, 136

relationship marketing 45–7, 165–81, 185–99, 293
Republican(s), Republican Party 9, 81, 119–20, 154–62, 202–17, 224; nominees/candidates 91–2, 94–6, 100, 105–6, 123–4, 244–6
Romney, Mitt 95, 104–6, 140

sales-orientation 47, 114, 124–5
social media 63–5, 66, 69–81, 123, 174–6, 185–99, 293–4, 301
social movement 112–7, 292

targeting (target, targets) 26–41, 67, 169–70, 192–5, 208–10, 220–33, 237; examples of 9–10, 14–15, 173–4, 215, 290
Tea Party 61–82, 112–7, 281, 291–2
trust (trustworthy/trustworthiness or honest/honesty) 257, 258–9, 263–4, 303
Twitter 68–80, 123, 175–6, 190–3, 291

viability 86, 89, 90, 98–100, 107
volunteers (or members or supporters or activists) 6, 10, 51–2, 169–71, 193, 293; members 92, 122; supporters 165, 167, 179